Current Trends
and Legal Issues in
Special Education

David Bateman and Mitchell Yell thank their families for their understanding and love.
David: Lis, Lük, and Em. Mitch: Joy, Nick, Eric, and Alex.
We dedicate this textbook to Dr. Barbara Bateman, a giant in the field of special education and an inspiration to both of us.

CURRENT TRENDS AND LEGAL ISSUES IN SPECIAL EDUCATION

Edited by David F. Bateman
and Mitchell L. Yell

FOR INFORMATION:

Corwin

A SAGE Company

2455 Teller Road

Thousand Oaks, California 91320

(800) 233-9936

www.corwin.com

SAGE Publications Ltd.

1 Oliver's Yard

55 City Road

London, EC1Y 1SP

United Kingdom

SAGE Publications India Pvt. Ltd.

B 1/I 1 Mohan Cooperative Industrial Area

Mathura Road, New Delhi 110 044

India

SAGE Publications Asia-Pacific Pte. Ltd.

18 Cross Street #10-10/11/12

China Square Central

Singapore 048423

Program Director: Jessica Allan

Content Development Editor: Lucas Schleicher

Senior Editorial Assistant: Mia Rodriguez

Production Editor: Tori Mirsadjadi

Copy Editor: Meg Granger

Typesetter: Cenveo Publisher Services

Proofreader: Rae-Ann Goodwin

Indexer: Maria Sosnowski

Cover Designer: Candice Harman

Marketing Managers: Brian Grimm and
                                  Deena Meyer

Printed in the United States of America.

ISBN 978-1-5443-0200-3

This book is printed on acid-free paper.

21 22 23 10 9 8 7 6 5 4

Contents

Acknowledgments

Corwin gratefully acknowledges the contributions of the following reviewers:

Debi Gartland
Professor of Special Education
Towson University
Towson, MD

Lisa Graham
Director of Early Childhood Education (ECE)
Douglas County School District (DCSD)
ECE DC Opportunities Center
Lone Tree, CO

Nichole Kristensen
Statewide Special Education Instructional Coordinator
Boise State University
Boise, ID

Suzanne Kucharczyk
Assistant Professor
University of Arkansas
Fayetteville, AR

Pamela Nevills
Former Special Education Local Plan Area (SELPA) Program Director,
Current Developer of Adult Studies
Fallbrook, CA

Tanna Nicely
Principal
Knox County Schools/South Knoxville Elementary
Knoxville, TN
LaQuita Outlaw
Principal (Grades 6–8)
Bay Shore Middle School
Bay Shore, NY

Jay Posick
Principal
Merton Intermediate School
Merton, WI

Erin Schons
Assistant Education Director
Children's Home Society of Sioux Falls
Sioux Falls, SD

Marge Terhaar-Yonkers
Professor
Department of Education, Meredith College
Raleigh, NC

About the Editors

David F. Bateman, PhD, is a professor at Shippensburg University in the Department of Educational Leadership and Special Education, where he teaches courses on special education law, assessment, and facilitating inclusion. He is a former due process hearing officer for Pennsylvania, overseeing more than 580 hearings. He uses his knowledge of litigation relating to special education to assist school districts in providing appropriate supports for students with disabilities and in preventing and recovering from due process hearings. He has been a classroom teacher of students with learning disabilities, behavior disorders, intellectual disability, and hearing impairments, and a building administrator for summer programs. Dr. Bateman earned a PhD in special education from the University of Kansas. He has recently coauthored the following books: *A Principal's Guide to Special Education*, *A Teacher's Guide to Special Education*, *Charting the Course: Special Education in Charter Schools*, and the forthcoming *Special Education Leadership: Building Effective Programming in Schools*. In his spare time, he is a competitive duathlete.

Mitchell L. Yell, PhD, is the Fred and Francis Lester Palmetto Chair in Teacher Education and a professor in special education at the University of South Carolina. His professional interests include special education law, positive behavior support, IEP development, and parent involvement in special education. Dr. Yell has published 124 journal articles, four textbooks, and 26 book chapters, and has conducted numerous workshops on various aspects of special education law, classroom management, and progress monitoring. His textbook, *Special Education and the Law*, is in its fifth edition. He is coeditor (with Jim Shriner) of the *Journal of Disability Policy Studies*. He also serves as a state-level due process review officer in South Carolina. Prior to working in higher education, Dr. Yell was a special education teacher in Minnesota for 16 years. In his free time, Dr. Yell enjoys family time, reading, chess, poker, and martial arts.

About the Contributors

Kate Ascetta is an assistant professor of early childhood special education in the Department of Educational Studies. Her research interests include the development and assessment of effective instructional practices, specifically online, that promote professional growth in teachers and lead to increased language and communication skills in young children. In her spare time she's all about balance—staying active outdoors and cooking up homemade meals.

Seth B. Bernstein, PsyD, is the senior vice president of Community Investments at United Way of Palm Beach County, Florida. In various roles over the past 25 years, he has partnered with his local school district—the 10th largest in the nation. He's implemented multiple evidence-based programs in schools and the community, and worked with researchers on several of these efforts. He enjoys reading and any time outdoors, in addition to being with his wife and helping his two sons successfully navigate college.

Mary Lynn Boscardin, PhD, is a professor in the College of Education at the University of Massachusetts Amherst and president-elect of the International Council of Exceptional Children. Professor Boscardin has published extensively in journals such as *Journal of Educational Administration*, *Journal of School Leadership*, *Journal of Educational Finance*, *Journal of Special Education*, *Exceptionality*, *Journal of Special Education Leadership*, and *Remedial and Special Education*. She has been the recipient of several U.S. Department of Education, Office of Special Education grants. She edits the *Journal of Special Education Leadership* and coedited *Handbook of Leadership and Administration for Special Education* (2012, 2019). She is the former president of the International Council of Administrators of Special Education (CASE), a current member of the CASE Executive Committee and Board of Directors, and the president of the Council for Exceptional Children. She has given keynote addresses and presentations internationally and nationally. Her scholarly interests include special education policy and finance, program and systems evaluation, strategic leadership approaches, and professional network mapping.

Ameet N. Bosmia, EdS, NCSP, is the coordinator of psychological and evaluation services at Shelby County Schools in Columbiana, Alabama. His work focuses primarily on the identification of students with special education needs, youth suicide prevention, and developing a multitiered system of supports in schools. His research interests lie in the role of implementation of comprehensive school mental health support systems and the expanding role of school psychologists within it.

Mark Matthew Buckman is a doctoral student in the Department of Special Education at the University of Kansas. His work focuses on supporting schools in implementing comprehensive, integrated, three-tiered (Ci3T) models of prevention. His research interests include measuring treatment integrity of school-wide support models such as Ci3T, and supporting in-service teachers' implementation of evidence-based practices to support students' academic, social, and behavioral development.

Meghan M. Burke, PhD, BCBA-D, is an associate professor in special education at the University of Illinois at Urbana-Champaign. Her research interests include parent advocacy, caregiving roles, and family–school partnerships. Outside of work, she enjoys spending time with her son.

Kelly M. Carrero, PhD, BCBA, is an assistant professor in the Department of Psychology and Special Education at Texas A&M University-Commerce. Prior to entering academia, Dr. Carrero served children from culturally and linguistically diverse backgrounds identified with exceptionalities and behavioral health concerns in a variety of settings, including disciplinary alternative education placements, juvenile justice facilities, and self-contained classrooms for students with autism and severe challenging behaviors. She advocates for students with exceptionalities and behavioral health concerns through training stakeholders, disseminating research, and engaging in community service (nationally and locally).

Christine A. Christle, EdD, is an associate professor in Special Education Programs at the University of South Carolina. Her research interests include the prevention of youth delinquency and the school variables that promote or discourage student success. She coordinates the MAT and MEd Special Education Programs, and serves as student advisor, student teaching supervisor, and instructor. In her spare time, she enjoys gardening, cooking, and playing tennis.

Jenifer Cline, MA, works as the continuing education and technical assistance unit manager for the state of Montana and prior to that worked as a special education administrator for 10 years. She has been an active member of the Montana Council of Administrators of Special Education and remains active in the Council of Administrators of Special Education, currently serving in the role of secretary.

Lauren W. Collins, PhD, is an assistant professor of special education at San Diego State University. Lauren's research is focused on the identification and dissemination of evidence-based practices for students with EBD and other high-incidence disabilities; the relationship between behavioral and academic performance, specifically in the area of reading; and supporting special education teachers during induction through the translation of research into practice. When she isn't working, Lauren enjoys spending time outside or sharing a good meal with the people who make her laugh.

Bryan G. Cook, PhD, is a professor in the special education program at the Curry School of Education and Human Development at the University of Virginia. His research areas include evidence-based practices in special education, bridging the research-to-practice gap in education, and applying open-science principles to education research. Cook is coeditor of the journal *Behavioral Disorders* and the annual volume *Advances in Learning and Behavioral Disabilities*, is past president of the Council for Exceptional

Children's (CEC's) Division for Research, chaired the work group that generated CEC's Standards for Evidence-Based Practices in Special Education, and codirects the Consortium for the Advancement of Special Education Research (CASPER).

Michelle Dunn, EdS, is a doctoral candidate in the department of special education at Clemson University and a certified school psychologist. Her research interests include promoting social emotional learning and positive behavioral supports with students at risk for emotional/behavioral disorders. In her free time she enjoys spending time with her husband and four children and running destination marathons.

Cynthia Farley, MEd, is the coordinator for the Exceptional Students and Elementary Education dual licensing program at the University of Hawai'i at Mānoa on the gorgeous island of Oahu. She has 20+ years teaching experience in general education and special education classrooms. Her research interests include evidence-based practices, research-to-practice gap, and teacher preparation. When not teaching, mentoring, and supervising teacher candidates, she can be found surfing and chasing waterfalls.

Samantha E. Goldman, PhD, is an assistant professor of special education at Assumption College in Worcester, Massachusetts. Her research interests include family–school partnerships, alternative dispute resolution, and addressing challenging behavior of students with autism spectrum disorders and other disabilities. While a doctoral student at Vanderbilt University, she coordinated the Volunteer Advocacy Project, an advocacy training. She also has experience as an ABA therapist and elementary school special education teacher. In her free time she enjoys traveling, running, and curling up with a good book.

June E. Gothberg, PhD, is an assistant professor for education leadership, research, and technology at Western Michigan University. Dr. Gothberg serves as the director of the Career Connections Research Center and the WMU principal investigator for the National Technical Assistance Center on Transition (NTACT). Previously, she was the director of transition projects for the Michigan Department of Education, Office of Special Education. She spent 10 years working in the classroom teaching at-risk students, court-involved youth, and students with special needs. Her research activities focus on policy development, implementation of evidence-based practices, improving outcomes for persons with disabilities, school–community partnerships, family engagement, and prisoner reentry. Dr. Gothberg is often called upon as a keynote speaker, consultant, trainer, and strategic planner.

Samantha N. Hartley, MA, is a doctoral candidate in clinical-community psychology at the University of South Carolina. Her research focuses on frameworks for integrating efforts addressing student behavioral and mental health needs. Her passion lies in program evaluation, as well as understanding and promoting factors that help schools do school mental health well. When not working with teens or diving through data, she enjoys combing through used bookstores, baking blondies, and comparing East vs. West Coast hiking opportunities (as a native Californian, she remains biased).

Stephanie Hopkins, MEd, is a doctoral candidate at the University of Missouri. She is a member of a federal STEM grant focusing on mathematics education in special education. When she was a practitioner in the field, she was a special education teacher. Her research and expertise focus on preservice teacher education and content preparation. She loves to work out, go sailing, eat brussels sprouts, and go hiking with her husband and golden retriever.

Timothy J. Landrum, PhD, is a professor of special education at the University of Louisville. His research and writing focus on emotional and behavioral disorders (EBD) and evidence-based practice in special education. He has taught students with EBD in public schools, and began his career teaching young children with autism in a little red schoolhouse in rural Virginia.

Kathleen Lynne Lane is a professor in the Department of Special Education at the University of Kansas and interim associate vice chancellor for research. Dr. Lane's research interests focus on designing, implementing, and evaluating comprehensive, integrated, three-tiered (Ci3T) models of prevention to (a) prevent the development of learning and behavior challenges and (b) respond to existing instances, with an emphasis on systematic screening.

Courtney Lavadia, MEd, is a graduate student in the school psychology doctoral program at Texas A&M University. Her clinical interests include promoting resilience, strengths, and psychosocial well-being of children and adolescents within the context of pediatric psychology. Her current research involves understanding how these factors impact therapeutic alliance and overall therapy outcomes. She is an adrenaline junkie who loves being outdoors, and enjoys adventure sports like skiing, mountain biking, and canyoneering. When not on adventures, she can be found playing the piano, painting, or snuggling with her two cats.

Cameron S. Massey, MA, is a doctoral student at the University of South Carolina and the associate director of the Psychology Services Center. Prior to pursuing his doctorate, he was a master's level psychologist in the Appalachian region of North Carolina for several years, working with community members with a wide array of emotional and behavioral concerns. His main research interests are in implementation of school-based mental health programs that serve adolescents in rural communities.

Gloria McGillen, MA, is a doctoral student in counseling psychology at the University of Missouri–Columbia. She is a graduate clinician at the University of Missouri Counseling Center. Her research and clinical interests include mental health, vocational well-being, and sociocultural diversity among the U.S. working class and poor.

Dr. Holly Marie Menzies is chair and professor in the Division of Special Education & Counseling at California State University, Los Angeles. She earned her PhD at the University of California, Riverside. Before becoming a professor, Dr. Menzies was both a general education and special education teacher, and worked with elementary and middle school students.

Wendy Peia Oakes is an associate professor at the Mary Lou Fulton Teachers College at Arizona State University. Her work focuses on practices that improve educational access and outcomes for young children with and at risk for emotional and behavioral disorders. For example, her research addresses comprehensive, integrated, three-tiered (Ci3T) models of prevention; the implementation of evidence-based academic and behavioral interventions; and professional development for preservice and in-service educators in implementing practices with fidelity.

Anthony J. Plotner is an associate professor at the University of South Carolina. His work focuses on the community inclusion of individuals with intellectual disability, specifically transition to college, supported employment, and the collaboration across systems to promote positive student outcomes. When he is not busy working, he enjoys coaching his son's baseball team and daughter's volleyball team.

Angela M. T. Prince is an assistant professor of special education at Iowa State University, where she researches secondary transition for students with disabilities, postschool outcomes, and legal issues in special education. Angela enjoys crafting with her daughter, lounging on white sand beaches with her husband, and taking the family's two fur babies for walks. She claims her best ideas develop while riding her aqua moped.

Chad A. Rose, PhD, is an associate professor in the Department of Special Education at the University of Missouri, and the director of the Mizzou Ed Bully Prevention Lab. He earned his PhD from the Department of Special Education at the University of Illinois at Urbana-Champaign in 2010. Dr. Rose's research focuses on the intersection of disability labels and special education services within the bullying dynamic, unique predictive and protective factors associated with bullying involvement among students with disabilities, and bully prevention efforts within a multitiered educational framework. Since 2009, Rose has authored or coauthored several articles or book chapters that directly address bullying, challenging behaviors, or behavioral assessment.

Dr. Joseph B. Ryan is the Stanzione Distinguished Professor of special education at Clemson University. He is the founder and executive director of Clemson LIFE (Learning Is for Everyone), a nationally recognized postsecondary education program for young adults with intellectual disabilities. Dr. Ryan has more than 80 publications and serves as the editor of the journal *Beyond Behavior*.

James G. Shriner, PhD, is an associate professor in the Department of Special Education at the University of Illinois at Urbana-Champaign. His work includes research on the effects of federal and state education policies and priorities on educational services for students with disabilities, with a focus on decision-making supports for IEP teams. Shriner currently serves as a member of the stakeholder advisory group for the National Center on Educational Outcomes and of the Illinois State Board of Education Assessment Review Committee. He is coeditor (with Mitch Yell) of the *Journal of Disability Policy Studies*.

Jessica Simpson, MEd, is currently a doctoral student at the University of Missouri studying mental health and behavioral disorders. Prior to entering her doctoral program, she taught elementary and middle school resource in Jefferson City, Missouri, and Long Beach, California. Jessica is passionate about understanding and overcoming mental health issues affecting today's youth.

Chris A. Sweigart, PhD, is a special education consultant at the Ohio Valley Educational Cooperative. His interests include evidence-based practices for improving the lives of at-risk youth facing serious challenges, such as mental health and behavior disorders and academic failure, as well as methods to improve teachers' implementation of these practices. Chris spends as much time as possible playing and laughing with his wife and children, who are his best teachers.

Martha L. Thurlow is director of the National Center on Educational Outcomes and senior research associate at the University of Minnesota. During her career, Dr. Thurlow's work has emphasized the need to ensure accessible curricula and assessments for students with disabilities, English learners, and English learners with disabilities, with the ultimate goal being to enable these students to leave school ready for success in college or a career. She has worked toward this end by addressing the implications of U.S. education policy for these students, striving to improve inclusion and access to appropriate assessments for all students, and collaborating with others on standards-based educational systems and inclusion for these students.

Kimberly J. Vannest, PhD, is a professor in the Special Education Division in Educational Psychology at Texas A&M University. Author of numerous articles, books, software, and parent guides, she is interested in improving the short- and long-term outcomes of students with and at risk of emotional and behavioral disabilities.

Mark D. Weist is professor, clinical community and school psychology, and director of the School Behavioral Health Team at the University of South Carolina (USC). Prior to moving to USC in 2010, he was on the faculty of the University of Maryland, where he helped found and direct the Center for School Mental Health (http://csmh.umaryland.edu), providing leadership to the advancement of school mental health (SMH) policies and programs in the United States. He has edited 11 books and has published and presented widely in SMH and in the areas of trauma, violence and youth, evidence-based practice, cognitive behavioral therapy, positive behavioral interventions and supports (PBIS), and on an interconnected systems framework (ISF) for SMH and PBIS.

Lauryn Young, PhD, serves the school district of Palm Beach County, Florida, as a school psychologist. She earned her doctorate degree in school psychology from the University of South Carolina and has continued her professional relationship as an adjunct instructor in the Department of Psychology. Lauryn is keenly interested in assisting youth with emotional and behavioral disabilities reach their full potential in school and in their communities. In her spare time, she enjoys traveling with her husband, trying new culinary dishes, and playing video games on her Xbox.

Introduction

Teachers and administrators working in the field of special education encounter many difficult situations on a daily basis. Examples of these situations include incidences of bullying, student placement issues, teacher and service provider shortages, use of technology, transition programming, and concerns related to ensuring that special education programs provide students with a free appropriate public education—such as collaborating with parents, developing individualized education programs, and using appropriate disciplinary procedures. We believe that an up-to-date textbook focusing on the pertinent trends and legal issues facing special education is needed. The various authors in this volume examine and illustrate a range of issues that educators and parents frequently face. Thus, it is our intention in this textbook to provide a resource for administrators (both general and special education) as well as teachers (both general and special education) as they are confronted with these issues.

This textbook is devoted to exploring these trends and issues, and provides a resource to those facing the reality of school-based problems and the implementation of current federal and state mandates. The authors of the various chapters are leaders in their fields, and their work will help ensure that individuals who provide services to students with disabilities understand the issues affecting the provision of special education services. We believe that incorrect or inadequate information often leads to inappropriate decision making regarding students with disabilities and their special education programs. When empowered with correct information, however, individuals will be more likely to follow the legal mandates guaranteed by the federal laws, and the services they provide to students with disabilities will be more likely to enable their students to make progress in their educational programs.

Hot Topics

Special Education Law, Litigation, and Policy Guidance

David F. Bateman and Mitchell L. Yell

This Chapter Will Cover:

1. A discussion related to avoiding discriminating against students with disabilities.
2. Policy guidance on attention deficit hyperactivity disorder and addressing behavior problems in individualized education programs.
3. Summaries of current remedies in special education, methodological disputes, placing students with disabilities in the least restrictive environment, deliberate indifference, service animals, website accessibility, charter schools, and independent educational evaluation.

Federal laws have played an important role in the formation of special education since the passage of the Education for All Handicapped Children Act (EAHCA) in 1975. The EAHCA, which was renamed the Individuals with Disabilities Education Act (IDEA) in 1990, has remained a driving force in special education. There are two reasons for this. Reason one is that every 5 or 6 years certain parts of the IDEA are reauthorized, which means that Congress revisits the law to reauthorize various activities and programs that were established in the IDEA. For example, Part D of the IDEA authorizes the Office of Special Education and Rehabilitative Services (OSERS) in the U.S. Department of Education to spend federal funds on certain activities. When Congress reauthorizes Part D, it allows OSERS to continue to allocate federal funds to these activities. Often when the IDEA is being reauthorized, Congress also amends the law. It is important to keep abreast of any amendments to the IDEA. Reason two is that often disputes occur between a student's parents and school personnel when issues regarding a student's special education are not settled to the satisfaction of either party. In such situations the IDEA includes the dispute resolution procedures of mediation, the resolution session, and the impartial due process hearing, which either the parents or the school district personnel may use. The other major dispute resolution mechanism that is available to parents but not school district personnel is a state's complaint resolution system. Either of the two dispute resolution systems may lead to litigation in the courts to settle these disputes. The majority of special education litigation occurs in the federal courts at the level of the U.S. District Courts. Some litigation is even taken to the higher level of federal district courts, the U.S. Circuit Courts of Appeals. A few special education cases have even reached the highest court in the United States, the Supreme Court. The results of this litigation can have important implications for special education.

Our purpose in this chapter is to briefly examine some of this litigation and how it affects special education. Prior to examining this litigation, we look at three additional issues of importance to special education: avoiding discriminating against students with disabilities, policy guidance from the U.S. Department of Education, and remedies that courts may impose on school districts when parents prevail in litigation.

Avoiding Discriminating Against Students With Disabilities

Congressional efforts to address the educational needs of students with disabilities originally consisted of two different approaches. The first approach was to protect students with disabilities from discrimination as Congress had done in 1964, when a law was passed—Title VI of the Civil Rights Act—to protect persons who were discriminated against because of race, color, creed, or national origin, and in 1972, when Congress protected persons who were discriminated against because of sex in Title IX of the Education Amendments. To this end, in 1973 Congress passed Section 504 of the Rehabilitation Act (hereinafter Section 504), which protected persons with disabilities from discrimination based on their disability. The second approach was to pass a funding bill that combined an educational bill of rights for students with disabilities with the promise of federal financial incentives for states. This law was the EAHCA of 1975. In this section of the chapter, we will address the first approach taken by Congress: Section 504.

The key to understanding Section 504 is to recognize that it is a civil rights law, which prohibits discrimination against persons with disabilities in programs that receive federal financial assistance. The law, therefore, applies to public elementary and secondary schools. Section 504 requires that

> no otherwise qualified individual with a disability in the United States ... shall, solely by reason of her or his disability, be excluded from the participation in, be denied the benefits of, or be subjected to discrimination under any program or activity receiving Federal financial assistance. (Section 504, 29 U.S.C. § 794[a])

Discrimination is the unequal treatment of persons with disabilities solely because of their disability and typically involves exclusion or inferior treatment. According to the U.S. Supreme Court, discrimination that violates Section 504 often is not deliberate but is the result of thoughtlessness, neglect, and indifference. It is important, therefore, that school district administrators, teachers, and support staff understand their responsibilities under Section 504.

Additionally, Section 504 requires administrators, teachers, school psychologists, and other school personnel to identify students with disabilities and afford these students educational opportunities equivalent to those received by students without disabilities. Neither may school districts provide students with disabilities a program, aid, benefit, or service that is not as effective as those provided to students without disabilities. Thus, students with disabilities should be allowed to participate in the same academic and nonacademic activities as their nondisabled peers. To use a sports metaphor, Section 504 requires that students with disabilities be educated on a level playing field.

Policy Guidance on Attention Deficit Hyperactivity Disorder and Addressing Behavior Problems in Individualized Education Programs

The U.S. Department of Education includes a number of offices, such as OSERS and the Office for Civil Rights (OCR). Additionally, the Office of Special Education Programs (OSEP) is located within OSERS. OSERS, OCR, and OSEP are important to state and local special education officials, administrators, and teachers because these offices provide leadership, enforcement, and fiscal resources to assist states and local school districts to educate students with disabilities. One way that OSERS, OCR, and OSEP accomplish this is through developing, communicating, and disseminating federal policy interpretations on special education through policy letters, guidance documents, and memos. Although these decisions do not have the force of law, they may be cited in hearings or court cases because they do have some legal authority. Guidance from OSERS, OCR, and OSEP, which are sometimes in the form of a "Dear Colleague" letter (DCL) and "Questions and Answers," are open to the public and are very important to special education administrators and teachers because information from OSERS and OSEP provides official guidance and clarification on the implementation of the IDEA and, in the case of OCR, the implementation of Section 504 of the Rehabilitation Act of 1973.

Two particularly important policy guidance letters were issued by OCR and OSEP in 2016. Both were issued as letters addressed to Dear Colleague and discussed educators' responsibility toward students with attention deficit hyperactivity disorder (ADHD) and to include positive behavioral interventions and supports in the individualized education programs (IEPs) of students in special education who exhibit problem behavior.

On July 26, 2016, OCR issued the letter on students with ADHD. The purpose of the letter was to clarify and provide guidance to school district personnel on their responsibilities when educating students with ADHD. The authors of the OCR letter noted that (a) federal law prohibits discrimination on the basis of disability, (b) students with ADHD are entitled to protections under the law, and (c) schools need to provide equal opportunity to students with disabilities. Moreover, the letter writers asserted that students with ADHD could be denied a free appropriate public education (FAPE) under Section 504 when school district personnel make two types of errors in identifying students with ADHD and providing programming for these students.

The first error may occur when evaluating a student with ADHD. Denial of FAPE problems may occur in the evaluation process when school district personnel (a) fail to refer or identify students with ADHD, (b) fail to evaluate students in a timely manner after it is determined that a student needs an evaluation, and (c) conduct an inadequate evaluation.

The second error may occur when a student with ADHD is evaluated as qualifying under Section 504 but school personnel fail to provide appropriate educational programming for the student. This can occur when school district personnel (a) choose inappropriate services for a student, (b) educate a student in an inappropriate setting, (c) fail to inform relevant staff regarding their responsibilities to a student, and (d) select and provide services to a student based on inappropriate considerations such as administrative and financial factors.

When planning for the education of students with ADHD under Section 504, therefore, it is important that school personnel conduct individualized evaluations of students who, because of their disability, need or are believed to need special education or related services. Moreover, school personnel must ensure that qualified students with disabilities receive appropriate services that are based on their individualized and specific needs and not consider issues such as cost and administrative convenience. School personnel must also avoid making decisions based on stereotypes or a generalized misunderstanding of a disability.

The August 1, 2016, DCL from OSEP addressed the importance of school district personnel using positive behavioral interventions and supports when developing an IEP for a student with disabilities who exhibits problem behavior served under the IDEA. In the DCL, officials at OSEP noted that the U.S. Department of Education strongly supports student safety in the schools and that in certain circumstances this may include using disciplinary procedures with students when necessary to protect other students. The writers of the DCL also observed that researchers have shown that school-wide, small-group, and individual behavioral supports that address the function of behavior and reinforce positive student behaviors are associated with increases in academic engagement, academic achievement, and fewer dropouts and suspensions. Moreover, students are more likely to learn when they are taught predictable school and classroom expectations and routines, acknowledged for exhibiting positive academic and social behavior, prompted and corrected when their behavior does not meet expectations, and treated with respect.

School personnel are encouraged to educate students in environments that are safe, supportive, and conducive to teaching and learning by effectively supporting and responding to student behavior, which includes addressing problem behaviors in the IEPs of students in special education.

Writers of the DCL suggested that to meet the FAPE requirements of the IDEA for students in special education with problem behaviors, an IEP team must consider a student's need for positive behavioral interventions and supports within his or her IEP. Additionally, the officials at OSEP asserted that IEP teams may violate the FAPE requirement of the IDEA if they (a) fail to consider including positive behavioral interventions and supports in response to the problem behavior of a student with disabilities, (b) do not schedule an IEP team meeting to review the IEP to address behavioral concerns after a reasonable parental request, (c) neglect to discuss a parent's concerns about the student's behavior and its effects on the student's learning during an IEP meeting, or (d) fail to implement the behavior supports included in a student's IEP.

Officials at OSEP also indicated strong support for improving behavioral supports within a student's IEP through implementing a school-wide, multitiered behavioral framework. The writers of the DCL also observed that research supported the idea that implementing such multitiered systems of support could help improve school climate, school safety, and academic achievement for all students, including students with disabilities.

Remedies in Special Education

When parents and teachers cannot settle their differences at the IEP meeting, either party may request a due process hearing. Additionally, the losing party in a due process hearing may file a suit in state or federal court. In most instances, parents of students with disabilities cannot file a civil suit under IDEA in federal court until they have exhausted their administrative remedies (i.e., due process hearing). When a parent does file a civil suit and the court rules against a school district, a court may award remedies or reliefs, which are actions a court may take to impose a penalty on the school district for violating the law. In fact, under the IDEA, broad discretion is given to courts in determining remedies for violating the law: A "court is authorized to grant 'such relief as the court determines is appropriate,' including attorneys' fees, reimbursement for a private educational placement, and compensatory education" (20 U.S.C. § 1415[i][2][C][iii]).

Compensatory Education

The purpose of awards of compensatory education is "to place children with disabilities in the same position they would have occupied but for the school district's violations of IDEA," by providing the educational services children should have received in the first instance (*Reid v. District of Columbia*, 2005, p. 516). Essentially, this means the state education agency (SEA), hearing officers, or courts order the school district to compensate students for the wrong that the school district has caused them by violating the IDEA. Compensatory education is awarded when it is determined that a school district has failed to provide a FAPE and may include violations of the IDEA such as failing to properly conduct Child Find activities and failing to offer or implement an appropriate IEP.

Compensatory education can be awarded by an SEA in response to a state complaint by a student's parents or by hearing officers or courts. Although there are differences in how SEAs, hearing officers, and courts determine the amount of compensatory education, it is clear that they may grant any relief deemed necessary for violations of FAPE. In fashioning such awards, SEAs, hearing officers, or courts will often attempt to provide compensation for the educational benefits that would have accrued had the school district not violated the IDEA. Often such determinations include estimates of the duration and severity of the violation. Compensatory education awards have included supplementary tutoring, extended school-year services, and even educational services beyond the IDEA's statutory age limit of 21.

Tuition Reimbursement

The U.S. Supreme Court in the case of *Burlington School Committee v. Massachusetts Department of Education* (1985) ruled that a student's parents may be reimbursed for the costs accrued in unilaterally placing their child in a private school when a school district failed to make FAPE available to the child and the private placement was proper. Chief Justice William Rehnquist wrote in the opinion for a unanimous court that the purpose of tuition reimbursement was to essentially require a school district to belatedly pay for what it should have been providing all along. Thus, long-standing case law and the IDEA provide the potential for private school tuition reimbursement, including related out-of-pocket expenses absorbed by parents, if a school district has failed in its obligation to provide FAPE to a child with a disability.

In determining if reimbursement of tuition is warranted, a hearing officer or court will use what is referred to as the three-step Burlington–Carter analysis. In this three-step analysis, the first step is to examine the school district's proposed program, or actual program, at the time the family made the decision to seek a private placement and determine whether the school's program would have provided or did provide a FAPE to the student. If the school district programming is not appropriate at step one, the second step is an examination of the appropriateness of the private placement. This does not mean that the private placement has to follow all the procedural requirements of the IDEA but, rather, that the private school provides a good and beneficial educational program. Third, if the private placement is appropriate at step two, the third step is for a court to examine the equities, such as the reasonableness of the cost of the private placement in comparison with other private alternative placements, between the parties to see if those equities impact the claim for reimbursement.

Attorneys' Fees

When the IDEA first became law in 1975 (it was then titled the Education for All Handicapped Children Act), the law did not contain any provisions regarding reimbursement of attorneys' fees for parents who had to hire an attorney to sue a school district for violating the law. In a 1986 amendment to the EAHCA, the Handicapped Children's Protection Act, Congress added a provision allowing courts to award attorneys' fees to a parent or guardian who prevailed in an action or proceeding under the EAHCA. The purpose of the attorneys' fees provision was to allow parents access to the courts when they had a legitimate claim against a school district. Because parents have to prevail on a significant issue to receive attorneys' fees, although it does not need to be the central issue, parents do incur some amount of risk when they bring a special education claim against a school district.

Parents who bring a civil suit against a school district can collect attorneys' fees only when they have prevailed and no further appeals are pending. For example, if a student's parents prevail in court but on appeal the school district prevails, the parents will not be able to collect attorneys' fees. Additionally, courts determine the amount of attorneys' fees to be awarded to prevailing parents.

In the recent U.S. Supreme Court case *Endrew F. v. Douglas County School District* (2017), Endrew's parents filed for a due process hearing, alleging that the Douglas County School District failed to provide their son with a FAPE and that the school district should reimburse them for the tuition they incurred by placing Endrew in a private school. The hearing officer ruled in favor of the school district. The parents then sued in the U.S. District Court for Colorado, where they lost again. The parents then appealed to the U.S. Appeals Court for the Tenth Circuit. They also lost at this level, so they filed a petition for writ of certiorari with the U.S. Supreme Court. The High Court took the case, overturned the previous decision, and remanded the case to the Tenth Circuit Court to reconsider its ruling in light of the Supreme Court's new FAPE standard. The Tenth Circuit Court remanded the case back to the U.S. District Court for Colorado, the first federal court to hear the Endrew case, to reconsider the case in light of the Supreme Court's FAPE standard. The U.S. District Court judge reversed his decision, ruling that the Douglas County School District had failed to provide a FAPE; therefore, Endrew's parents prevailed. Thus, two important elements for the award of attorneys' fees were met: (a) The parents prevailed on a significant issue, and (b) no further appeals were pending. The judge in the case ordered that the Douglas County School District reimburse Endrew's parents for tuition at the private placement and pay attorneys' fees and litigation costs.

Methodological Disputes

Parents and school district personnel occasionally disagree on the type of methodology that will be used in providing special education services to a student. These disagreements have sometimes reached the courts. For example, courts have heard methodology disputes in teaching reading (e.g., Orton-Gillingham, Wilson Reading) and teaching students with autism (e.g., Lovaas discrete trial training, Floortime). The law is quite clear on this point: As long as special education programs provide a FAPE, IEP teams have broad discretion in what types of educational methodology will be used in providing special education to a student. The team does not even need to identify a particular methodology in a student's IEP. In fact, courts have held that the IDEA does not permit parents to challenge their child's IEP in a due process hearing on the grounds that it is not the best program to use with their child.

It is very important, however, that school personnel not have an official or unofficial policy of refusing to adopt a particular methodology. If parents request a methodology and an IEP team denies the parents' request, if it is proven that a school or district had such a policy, that may constitute predetermination and subject a school district to legal liability under the IDEA. Thus, it is very important that if a parent requests a particular methodology, requests be discussed in the meeting. The IEP team does not have to agree to the methodology, but they should discuss it. Indeed, in Chief Justice William Rehnquist's majority opinion in the U.S. Supreme Court case *Board of Education of the Hendrick Central Hudson School District v. Rowley* (1982), he wrote, "The primary responsibility for formulating the education to be accorded a handicapped child, and for choosing the educational method most suitable to the child's needs, was left by the Act to state and local educational agencies in cooperation with the parents or guardian of the child" (p. 181).

Methodological disputes have also involved the IDEA requirement that special education services be based on peer-reviewed research. The IDEA requires that students' IEPs contain "a statement of the special education and related services and supplementary aids and services, based on peer-reviewed research to the extent practicable—that will be provided to the child" (IDEA, 20 U.S.C. § 1414[d][1][A][i][IV]). Although neither the IDEA nor the regulations defined the term *peer-reviewed research*, in the commentary accompanying the 2006 regulations to the IDEA, officials at the U.S. Department of Education noted that peer-reviewed research generally refers "to research that is reviewed by qualified and independent reviewers to ensure that the quality of the information meets the standards of the field before the research is published" (Statement of Special Education and Related Services, 2006).

In 2006, the U.S. Department of Education clarified the relationship between peer-reviewed research and FAPE as follows:

> [Special education] services and supports should be based on peer-reviewed research to the extent that it is possible, given the availability of peer-reviewed research.... States, school districts, and school personnel must, therefore, select and use methods that research has shown to be effective, to the extent that methods based on peer-reviewed research are available. This does not mean that the service with the greatest body of research is the service necessarily required for a child to receive FAPE. Likewise, there is nothing in the Act to suggest that the failure of a public agency to provide services based on peer-reviewed research would automatically result in a denial of FAPE. The final decision about the special education and related services, and supplementary aids and services that are to be provided to a child must be made by the child's IEP Team based on the child's individual needs ... if no such research exists, the service may still be provided, if the IEP team determines that such

services are appropriate. (Statement of Special Education and Related Services, 2006)

This language indicates that using the peer-reviewed research requirement as a basis for methodological disputes may not be fruitful because hearing officers and judges will ultimately base their rulings on whether or not a school district conferred FAPE and not on whether parents requested a methodology with a perceived greater research base. This view was confirmed in a 2012 decision by the U.S. Court of Appeals for the Third Circuit in *Ridley School District v. M. R. and J. R.* (hereinafter *Ridley*, 2012). In this case, the Ridley School District proposed that a phonics-based reading curriculum, Project Read, be used to teach a student with a learning disability. The parents of the student, however, wanted the school district to use the Wilson reading curriculum. The case went all the way to the Third Circuit Court, which held the following:

> First, although schools should strive to base a student's specially designed instruction on peer-reviewed research to the maximum extent possible, the student's IEP team retains flexibility to devise an appropriate program, in light of available research. Second, under the IDEA, courts must accord significant deference to the choices made by school officials as to what constitutes an appropriate program for each student. (p. 33)

The court noted that hearing officers and judges should only "assess the appropriateness of an IEP on a case-by-case basis, taking into account the available research" (*Ridley*, 2012, p. 37). The court further asserted that if a school failed to implement a program based on peer-reviewed research, even though such research was available, that fact would "weigh heavily against finding that the school district provided FAPE" (p. 37). The court recognized "that there may be cases in which the specially designed instruction proposed by a school district is so at odds with current research that it constitutes a denial of a FAPE" (p. 13).

Placing Students With Disabilities in the Least Restrictive Environment

According to the IDEA, placement decisions for students in special education must be made by persons (a) knowledgeable of the provisions of the law, (b) familiar with a student's evaluation data, and (c) aware of the various placement options in the student's school district. The team that makes a student's placement decision, which is usually a student's IEP team, must determine his or her placement at least annually based on the student's IEP. A student's placement should be as close as possible to the child's home. Moreover, placement decisions must be made in conformity with the least restrictive environment (LRE) mandate of the IDEA, which requires that students with disabilities be educated alongside their nondisabled peers when possible. The IDEA requires that to the maximum extent appropriate, children with disabilities, including children in public or private institutions or other care facilities, are educated with children who are not disabled, and that special classes, separate schooling, or other removal of children with disabilities from the regular educational environment occurs only when the nature or severity of the disability is such that education in regular classes with the use of supplementary aids and services cannot be achieved satisfactorily. (IDEA, 20 U.S.C. § 1412)

To ensure that school districts have placement options from which to choose the LRE for a student that meets his or her educational needs, the IDEA requires that school districts have a range or continuum of alternative placement options available. The continuum represents an entire spectrum of placements where a student's special education program can be implemented and includes the following settings: (a) the general education classroom, which includes the general classroom with supplementary aids and services such as a resource room; (b) a self-contained setting; (c) special schools; (d) home instruction; and (e) instruction in hospitals and institutions. The IDEA does not require that all school districts have the entire continuum within the district; rather, it requires that the options be available if needed to meet the needs of a particular student. If a district does not have an appropriate placement, therefore, the district officials must provide the appropriate placement option through means such as contractual arrangements with other school districts.

The issue of LRE has been the subject of considerable litigation. Although the many LRE cases had different facts and situations, the courts' rulings regarding school districts' LRE obligations have been remarkably similar. These court rulings all include some general rules that school district personnel should follow when determining a student's LRE. First, the decision to place students must be based on their individual needs. Placements cannot be made solely on factors such as a student's disability, the availability of services, or administrative convenience. Second, a student's placement may not be predetermined. That is, a student's parents must be included when making placement decisions. Third, the IEP team must determine the contents of a student's appropriate special education before making a placement decision, because only after a student's program has been determined (e.g., special education services) and the IEP has been developed will a team have a basis for determining the LRE where the student's needs can best be met. Finally, the IDEA requires that whenever possible, students with disabilities should be educated alongside students without disabilities. In situations where a more restrictive setting is required to deliver an appropriate education, school district personnel should still attempt to educate students together whenever possible.

Deliberate Indifference

Most of the highlighted case law on deliberate indifference relates to student-on-student bullying. The most notable case is *Davis v. Monroe County Board of Education* (1999), where the Supreme Court asked whether the school had "deliberate indifference." Deliberate indifference is the conscious or reckless disregard of the consequences of one's acts or omissions. It entails something more than negligence but is satisfied by something less than acts or omissions for the very purpose of causing harm or with knowledge that harm will result. In the Davis case, the court held that a school is liable for damages if it failed to respond to known acts of severe student-on-student harassment, thereby creating an environment denying the victim equal access to education.

As applied to students with disabilities, the emphasis is on the school's duty to ensure safety, health, and an effective learning environment. Deliberate indifference requires both knowledge that harm to a federally protected right is substantially likely and failure to act on that likelihood (*Duvall v. County of Kitsap*, 2001). Similar to what is written in the remedies section about when a district knew or should have known, deliberate indifference is shown when a student (or parent) notifies a district of the need for an accommodation or where the need for an accommodation is obvious or required. An example would be when a student needs an aide for clean intermittent catheterization, the district is clearly aware of the need, and the district is deliberately indifferent to the student's need for accommodations and hence potentially responsible for discrimination, entitling the family to monetary damages.

Deliberate indifference can apply to monetary damages for students eligible under both the IDEA and Section 504. School officials should not be automatically shielded from liability just by resorting to solutions that have been shown to be ineffective. Finally, moreover, while deliberate indifference is certainly a factually driven issue, when the facts are largely undisputed, it can be determined as a matter of law. See *Davis*, which states, "[Deliberate indifference] is not a mere reasonableness standard" (p. 649).

Two cases highlight the deliberate indifference standard.

T. K. and S. K. v. New York City Department of Education (2016): A school district denied the parents of a third-grade girl with disabilities the right to "meaningful participation" in the development of their child's IEP. The district officials refused to discuss the parents' concerns about bullying in the child's IEP meeting and wound up paying for the costs of a full year of private schooling.

Krebs v. New Kensington-Arnold School District (2016): The parents of a ninth-grade girl who committed suicide after suffering 3 years of persistent bullying at school were entitled to pursue their claim for monetary damages against the school district. The parents alleged that their complaints and requests for help were ignored or dismissed by school administrators.

Service Animals

The U.S. Department of Justice's service animal regulation is a general provision, describing a general condition that could be discriminatory if not allowed (U.S. Department of Justice, 2015). "Generally, a public entity shall modify its policies, practices, or procedures to permit the use of a service animal by an individual with a disability." "Permitting" is not an absolute rule. It is subject to exceptions where the animal is not under control or not housebroken (28 C.F.R. § 35.136[b]), under a health and safety or "direct threat" exclusion

(28 C.F.R. § 35.139), and under the "fundamental alteration" rule (28 C.F.R. § 35.130[b][7]). Moreover, 28 C.F.R. § 35.103, in effect, requires the regulation to be interpreted consistently with other laws, including Section 504.

A service animal supplanting instruction is a fundamental alteration both to a school's unique mission of imparting necessary skills for lifelong independence and self-support and to a student's right to receive specially designed instruction and related services to acquire skills and otherwise be provided an educational opportunity equivalent to that of nondisabled peers. (See, e.g., 28 C.F.R. § 35.130 [b][1][iii].) For most students, a service animal will not supplant instructional opportunity. Physical work performed by service animals, such as picking up items, pulling a wheelchair, and opening doors, as well as other types of work, such as seizure alert, diabetes support, or allergen detecting, do not relate to curricula. Only a small number of service dogs are likely to alter educational instruction in a fundamental way by impairing acquisition of skills.

For students with disabilities, the IEP must allow the student "(i) To advance appropriately toward attaining the annual goals; (ii) To be involved in and make progress in the general education curriculum … ; and (iii) To be educated and participate with other children with disabilities and nondisabled children in the activities described in this section" (34 C.F.R. § 300.320[a][4]). The IEP team must additionally consider "related services," which are "such developmental, corrective, and other supportive services as are required to assist a child with a disability to benefit from special education" (34 C.F.R. § 300.34). Related services include, among others, teaching a student to use a service animal (34 C.F.R. § 300.34[c][7]). The IEP, and instruction, must be gauged in relation to the student's potential (*Polk v. Central Susquehanna I.U. 16*, 1989).

There are two recent cases that shed light on this topic.

United States v. Gates-Chili Central School District (2016): This case interprets the U.S. Department of Justice's regulations requiring a service animal to be "under the handler's control." The government (OCR) claimed the child in question needed assistance only with untethering and occasional prompting. The district argued an adult handler was required to command the dog. The issue in the case was whether the student could control the dog when tethered to it.

A. P. v. Pennsbury School District (2016): A federal court denied the parent's request for a preliminary injunction allowing her child with disabilities to attend school with her service dog. The school district had refused to permit the dog on campus after it had bitten a classmate and had exhibited frequent incidents of barking, growling, nipping, and chewing on classroom supplies. The court noted that the Department of Justice regulations expressly permit a school district to ban a dog that cannot be controlled by its handler and bites others.

Website Accessibility

This is not necessarily a special education topic; however, school districts need to ensure their websites are accessible to individuals with disabilities.

The Americans with Disabilities Act (ADA) Section 508 requires that people with disabilities should not be discriminated against. Specifically, communications to people with disabilities should be as effective as communications to those without disabilities. To be compliant, school districts must make reasonable modifications to technology tools and websites to ensure equal opportunities and access to content, software, and equipment for people with disabilities.

The U.S. Access Board set a deadline requiring websites at any federally funded organizations to comply with the Section 508 Standards by January 18, 2018. All public schools should start a compliance review of their websites sooner rather than later. Web accessibility means people with disabilities can perceive, understand, navigate, and interact with the Web and that they can contribute to the Web. Web accessibility also benefits others, including individuals with changing abilities due to aging. Web accessibility encompasses all disabilities that affect access to the Web, including visual, auditory, physical, speech, cognitive, and neurological disabilities.

There are five main tips for school districts to consider related to website accessibility.

1. Ensure an understanding of website compliance requirements. There are many summary documents clarifying website accessibility. One that is easy to access and understand is by the Web Accessibility Initiative (https://www.w3.org/WAI/WCAG20/quickref/). This has descriptions and modules for most areas that need to be covered.

2. Establish clear guidelines for your district for website accessibility. Provide training examples as to how to apply those guidelines to your website update process.

3. Develop or provide training. Make sure everyone who is updating your district websites understands the requirements.

4. Periodically check or audit your website. Look for problems. Look for errors. Then make sure these problems and errors are corrected in a timely fashion.

5. Ask for help. Put a link or comment button on your website seeking clarification or more information about accessing material.

Charter Schools

Charter schools operate as a separate, independent local educational agency and have the same requirements as traditional public schools. With the increasing number of states approving charter schools, it is important to focus on the guidance provided by OSEP related to the provision of both special education services and services for students eligible under Section 504.

Section 504 Charter Guidance

- Charter school students with disabilities (and those seeking to attend) have the same rights under Section 504 and Title II of the ADA as do other public school students with disabilities.

- Students with disabilities have a right to nondiscrimination in recruitment, application, and admission to charter schools.

- During the admission process, a charter school generally may not ask a prospective student if he or she has a disability.

- Charter school students with disabilities have the right to a FAPE under Section 504.

The IDEA Charter Guidance

- Children with disabilities who attend charter schools and their parents retain all rights and protections under Part B of the IDEA (such as FAPE), just as they would at other public schools.

- Under the IDEA, a charter school may not unilaterally limit the services that must be provided a particular student with a disability.

- The LRE provisions require that, to the maximum extent appropriate, students with disabilities attending public schools, including public charter schools, be educated with students who are nondisabled.

- Students with disabilities attending charter schools retain all the IDEA rights and protections included in the IDEA discipline procedures.

According to OCR representatives around the country, schools and districts should adopt a wide range of possible approaches to help facilitate this outcome. For example, via trainings, parent meetings, and in other informal settings, school and district administrators often encourage staff and parents to

1. promote early identification and evaluation of students by attending to and reporting signs and indicators of a possible disability;

2. secure detailed and comprehensive information from various sources (e.g., family members, doctors, school nurses, teachers, social workers) prior to making eligibility and service-related decisions on behalf of a student who may have a disability;

3. communicate with appropriate teachers and nonclassroom staff members (e.g., coaches, gym teachers, librarians, cafeteria workers) about the aids and services to which a student with a disability may be entitled;

4. consider the context within which different school staff interact with students (e.g., a gymnasium vs. a classroom) when making

decisions about the aids and services that will be most effective in meeting a student's needs;

5. monitor implementation of aids and services to assess effectiveness and ensure consistent provision of these aids and services by all school staff (e.g., by teachers in different classrooms);

6. encourage communication on a regular basis between home and school, and among relevant school staff, regarding all students but in particular students with disabilities;

7. observe interpersonal relationships among students and interactions between staff and students to identify and address signs of a hostile school environment and bullying; and

8. document, via e-mails, letters, notes, or other means, important information (e.g., key meetings and conversations, relevant dates, decisions, and actions taken) relating to parent and staff efforts to secure or provide aids and services to a student with a disability, address incidents of bullying and harassment, or raise and resolve disagreements and disputes.

Finally, as a part of a DCL (68 IDELR 108 [OSERS/OSEP 2016]), officials at OSERS opined that students with disabilities who attend virtual schools maintain the same IDEA rights as students attending "brick-and-mortar" schools (e.g., Child Find, FAPE, related services).

Independent Educational Evaluations

The IEP process begins with a full and individualized evaluation of a student's needs. A judge in a U.S. District Court pointed out the crucial importance of an evaluation when he noted that a faulty evaluation

> goes to the heart of the IEP; the child's level of academic achievement and functional performance is the foundation upon which the IEP will be developed. Without a clear identification of [the child's] present levels, the IEP team cannot set measurable goals, evaluate the child's progress, and determine which special education and related services are needed. (*Kirby v. Cabell County Board of Education*, 2006, p. 694)

Thus, a student's evaluation is fundamental to FAPE because his or her needs are thoroughly detailed in the IEP so that the IEP team can develop a special education program that confers a FAPE. Because an evaluation is so crucial to a student's program, Congress included a means by which a student's parents could request that an independent educational evaluation (IEE) be conducted by a qualified examiner not employed by the school district when the parents disagreed with the school district's evaluation. According to regulations implemented in the IDEA, "a parent has the right to an independent educational evaluation at public expense if the parent disagrees with an evaluation obtained by the public agency" (34 C.F.R. § 300.502[b][1]). School districts must respond to a parental request for an

IEE by either agreeing to pay for the IEE or by initiating a due process hearing to defend the appropriateness of the evaluation with which the parents disagree (34 C.F.R. 300.507-300.513).

A student's parents can always obtain an IEE at their own expense, and the IEP team must consider the results of the evaluation. If a student's parents believe that the school district's evaluation was not accurate or complete and the parents express disagreement with the district's reevaluation, they can request an IEE at public expense. Before parents may request an IEE, the district must have conducted an evaluation of their child. It would be premature for parents to request an IEE prior to the district conducting its evaluation (*G. J. v. Muscogee County School District*, 2012). A student's IEP team must always consider the results of the IEE no matter whether the parents or the school district paid for it.

In a recent decision, the New Jersey Superior Court held that parents had a right to an IEE at public expense when a student's IEP team reviewed existing data and determined that new assessments were unnecessary. Because the IEP team made the determination that no new testing or information was needed, the court held that the team's finding had constituted an evaluation under the IDEA and therefore permitted the parents to request an IEE at public expense (*Haddon TWP School District v. New Jersey Department of Education*, 2016).

A school district may have certain agency criteria for an IEE (e.g., location of the independent evaluator, qualifications of the evaluator, the same criteria the school district uses in conducting its own evaluations), but the district may not impose additional conditions or a timeline when parents request an IEE at public expense. Moreover, when parents request an IEE, school district officials must provide the parents with information about where an IEE may be obtained and agency criteria. This information must be provided in a timely manner.

There are two situations in which an IEE cannot be requested by a student's parents. One situation occurs if a child's parents have not given a school district permission to conduct an evaluation; in such a situation the parents do not have the right to request an IEE because the IEE is predicated on the parents disagreeing with the school district's evaluation (*G. J. v. Muscogee County School District*, 2012). The second situation occurs if a student's parents have waited too long to request an IEE in response to a school district's evaluation. For example, in a state-level due process hearing, parents' request for a publicly funded IEE was denied when they waited for 3 years after the school district's evaluation was conducted.

An important lesson for school districts is that parents have the right to request an IEE at public expense if they have expressed disagreement with a school district's evaluation of their child. Although parents must inform school district personnel that they disagree with the district's evaluation before they request the IEE, school district officials may not demand that a student's parents specify the basis of their disagreement before the district acts with respect to the IEE. When an IEE is requested, the school district must exercise one of its two options: pay for the IEE or request a due process hearing to prove the appropriateness of its evaluation as soon as possible. It is never permissible to ignore parents' request for an IEE or to delay action on parents' request for an IEE.

REFLECTING AND UNDERSTANDING

1. What are some steps districts can take to avoid discrimination against students with disabilities?

2. What are some steps districts can take to address behavior problems in IEPs?

3. What are the main remedies in special education?

4. What are some steps districts can take related to methodological disputes?

5. What guidance should be addressed related to LRE?

6. What is deliberate indifference, and why should educators be concerned?

7. What is the latest guidance on charter schools?

8. What is an IEE, and what actions should school officials take when an IEE is requested by a student's parents?

ONLINE RESOURCES

- ADA National Network on Service Animals in Schools: https://adata.org/publication/service-animals-booklet

- CEEDAR Center, Technical Assistance: https://ceedar.education.ufl.edu

- Center on Response to Intervention at American Institutes for Research: https://www.rti4success.org/

- Collaborative for Academic, Social, and Emotional Learning: https://www.casel.org/

- Comprehensive, Integrated, Three-Tiered Models of Prevention: http://www.ci3t.org/

- National Center on Intensive Interventions: https://intensiveintervention.org/

- Office of Special Education Programs Technical Assistance Center on Positive Behavioral Interventions and Supports: http://www.pbis.org/

- Substance Abuse and Mental Health Services Administration National Registry of Evidence-Based Programs and Practices: https://www.samhsa.gov/nrepp

- U.S. Department of Education's What Works Clearinghouse: https://ies.ed.gov/ncee/wwc/

- Web Accessibility Initiative: https://www.w3.org/WAI/fundamentals/accessibilityintro/

RECOMMENDED READINGS

Books

Angelov, A. D. S., & Bateman, D. F. (2016). *Charting the course: Special education in charter schools.* Arlington, VA: Council for Exceptional Children.

Brown-Chidsey, R., & Bickford, R. (2015). *Practical handbook of multi-tiered systems of support building academic and behavioral success in schools.* New York, NY: Guilford Press.

Yell, M. L. (2019). *The law and special education* (5th ed.). Upper Saddle River, NJ: Pearson.

Article

Yell, M. L., & Bateman, D. F. (2017). *Endrew F. v. Douglas County School District* (2017): Free appropriate public education and the U.S. Supreme Court. *Teaching Exceptional Children, 50*, 1–9.

Briefs, Practice Guides, and Reports

Simonsen, B., Freeman, J., Goodman, S., Mitchell, B., Swain-Bradway, J., Flannery, B., Sugai, G.... Putman, B. (2015). *Supporting and responding to behavior: Evidence-based classroom strategies for teachers.* Washington, DC: Office of Special Education Programs, U.S. Department of Education. Retrieved from https://www.osepideast-hatwork.org/evidencebasedclassroomstrategies

U.S. Department of Education. (2016). *Dear colleague letter on behavioral supports.* Washington, DC: Author. Retrieved from https://sites.ed.gov/idea/files/dcl-on-pbis-in-ieps-08-01-2016.pdf

U.S. Department of Education. (2016). *Dear colleague letter and resource guide on students with ADHD.* Washington, DC: Author. Retrieved from https://www2.ed.gov/about/offices/list/ocr/letters/colleague-201607-504-adhd.pdf

U.S. Department of Education. (2016). *Frequently asked questions about the rights of students with disabilities in public charter schools under Section 504 of the Rehabilitation Act of 1973.*

U.S. Department of Education, Office for Civil Rights. (2010). *Free appropriate public education for students with disabilities: Requirements under Section 504.* Retrieved from https://www2.ed.gov/about/offices/list/ocr/docs/edlite-FAPE504.html

U.S. Department of Education, Office for Civil Rights. (2016). *Disability discrimination: Frequently asked questions.* Retrieved from https://www2.ed.gov/about/offices/list/ocr/frontpage/faq/disability.html

U.S. Department of Education, Office of Special Education and Rehabilitative Services. (2016, December 28). *Frequently asked questions about the rights of students with disabilities in public charter schools under the Individuals with Disabilities Education Act.* Retrieved from https://sites.ed.gov/idea/files/policy_speced_guid_idea_memosdcltrs_faq-idea-charter-school.pdf

PROFESSIONAL ORGANIZATIONS

Association for Positive Behavior Support: http://www.apbs.org/

Center for Appropriate Dispute Resolution in Special Education: https://www.cadreworks.org

Council for Exceptional Children: https://www.cec.sped.org/

National Association of School Psychologists: https://www.nasponline.org

National Center for Special Education in Charter Schools: http://www.ncsecs.org

REFERENCES

A. P. v. Pennsbury Sch. Dist., 68 IDELR 132 (E.D. Pa. 2016).

Americans with Disabilities Act. 42 U.S.C. ch. 126 § 12101 *et seq.*

Americans with Disabilities Act Regulations, 28 C.F.R. § 35.136(a) (2012).

Board of Education of the Hendrick Hudson Central School District v. Rowley, 458 U.S. 176 (1982).

Burlington School Committee v. Massachusetts Department of Education, 471 U.S. 359 (1985).

Davis v. Monroe County Board of Education, 526 U.S. 629 (1999).

Duvall v. County of Kitsap (9th Cir. 2001) 260 F.3d 1124, 1139.

Endrew F. v. Douglas County School District RE-1, 580 U.S. ___, 137 S.Ct. 988 (2017).

G. J. v. Muscogee County School District, 668 F.3d 1258 (11th Cir, 2012).

Haddon TWP SD v. New Jersey Department of Education 67 IDELR 44 (2016).

Individuals with Disabilities Education Act, 20 U.S.C. §§ 1400 *et seq.* (2006 & Supp. V. 2011).

Individuals with Disabilities Education Act Regulations, 34 C.F.R. § 300 *et seq.* (2012).

Kirby v. Cabell County Board of Education, Civil Action No. 3:05-0322, (consolidated with 3:03-0320). (S.D.W. Va. Sep. 19, 2006).

Krebs v. New Kensington-Arnold School District, 69 IDELR 9 (W.D. Pa. 2016).

Polk v. Central Susquehanna I.U. 16, 853 F.2d 171, 180 (3rd Cir. 1988), *cert. denied*, 488 U.S. 1030 (1989).

Reid v. District of Columbia (2005). 401 F.3d 516, 518 (D.C. Cir. 2005).

Ridley School District v. M. R. and J. R., 680 F.3d 260 (3d Cir. 2012).

Statement of Special Education and Related Services, 71 Fed. Reg. 156 (August 14, 2006).

T. K. and S. K. v. New York City Dept. of Educ., 67 IDELR 1, 810 F.2d 869 (2d. Cir. 2016).

United States v. Gates-Chili Cent. Sch. Dist., 68 IDELR 70 (W.D.N.Y. 2016).

U.S. Department of Justice. (2015). *Frequently asked questions about service animals and the ADA.* Washington, DC: Author.

Researchers are increasingly advocating for the thoughtful integration of these tiered support systems into a single, coherent framework that is more efficient and provides optimal support to address the academic, social, emotional, and behavioral needs of all students, including those with or at risk for disabilities (e.g., Hawken, Vincent, & Schumann, 2008; McIntosh & Goodman, 2016; Stewart, Benner, Martella, & Marchand-Martella, 2007; Sugai & Horner, 2009; Utley & Obiakor, 2015).

—**Research for Application 84.324N,**
Institute of Education Sciences (2017, p. 15)

Comprehensive, Integrated, Three-Tiered (Ci3T) Models of Prevention

Considerations for the Field

*Kathleen Lynne Lane, Wendy Peia Oakes,
Mark Matthew Buckman, and Holly Mariah Menzies*

This Chapter Will Cover:

1. Guidance for school leaders and special educators on designing, implementing, evaluating, and sustaining comprehensive, integrated, three-tiered (Ci3T) models of prevention.

2. Ci3T models and how they are a broadening of multitiered systems of support to address the integration of academic, behavioral, and social–emotional domains for all learners—including students receiving special education services.

3. How Ci3T models are designed and implemented using data-informed decision making in multiple facets—including efforts to assist students as well as faculty and staff.

4. Potential benefits of Ci3T models.

5. Four considerations for reflection when examining the utility of these models for meeting students' multiple needs.

Educational leaders across the United States are charged with the task of meeting students' academic, behavioral, and social needs in the most efficient, effective manner possible. This is indeed a formidable task given PK–12 students vary widely in their individual skills in each domain. Fortunately, federal, state, and local leaders have moved beyond a within-child, reactive perspective for meeting this challenge and have recognized the importance of a systems-level response by designing, implementing, and evaluating integrated educational systems to meet students' multiple needs (Walker, Forness, & Lane, 2014).

A comprehensive, integrated, three-tiered (Ci3T) model of prevention is one framework for a unified system to address students' academic, behavioral, and social needs (Lane, Oakes, Cantwell, & Royer, 2016; McIntosh & Goodman, 2016; Yudin, 2014). Historically, there has been a progression of tiered systems: response to intervention (RTI), emphasizing academic domains (Fuchs, Fuchs, & Compton, 2012); positive behavioral interventions and supports (PBIS), emphasizing behavioral domains (Horner & Sugai, 2015); multitiered systems of support (MTSS), emphasizing academic and behavioral domains; interconnected system framework (ISF), emphasizing behavioral and mental health domains (Weist, Lever, Bradshaw, & Owens, 2014); and now Ci3T. Ci3T can be described as a broadening of MTSS, expanded to include principles of RTI and PBIS, coupled with the implementation of a validated program to address social–emotional learning (e.g., Positive Action; Flay, Allred, & Ordway, 2001). Ci3T provides one comprehensive, integrated, data-informed prevention model enabling general educators, special educators, administrators, families, and students to partner in using system- and student-level data to inform practices and attain educational goals.

> Researchers have suggested that an integrated MTSS framework may have several advantages over separate tiered support systems, including more efficient service delivery and use of resources. An integrated system also has the potential to more seamlessly address students' interrelated academic and behavior problems and ensure that academic and behavioral supports are aligned without counteracting one another (McIntosh & Goodman, 2016). An integrated MTSS model may be especially beneficial for students with or at risk for disabilities who often struggle in both the academic and behavioral realm and whose difficulties in one domain are often related to difficulties in the other (e.g., Nelson, Benner, Lane, & Smith, 2004). (Research for Application 84.324N, Institute of Education Sciences, 2017, p. 15)

This chapter provides guidance for school leaders and special educators in designing, implementing, evaluating, and sustaining Ci3T models of prevention. We illustrate how Ci3T models are designed and implemented using data-informed decision making in multiple facets—including how to best assist students as well as educators. Next, we explore potential benefits of Ci3T models. Finally, we suggest four considerations for reflection when examining the utility of these models for meeting students' multiple needs.

Designing and Implementing Ci3T Models of Prevention

As part of the design process, a school-site Ci3T leadership team is assembled. This team includes an administrator with decision-making authority, one to two general education teachers, a special education teacher, another one to two people of their choice (e.g., instructional coach, social worker, and/or school psychologist), a parent, and a student (the son or daughter of the parent team member). This Ci3T leadership team engages in a year-long, multisession, systematic professional learning series that involves feedback from the full faculty and staff as part of an iterative feedback process (Lane et al., 2016). The end result is the development of a Ci3T implementation manual that defines roles and responsibilities for key stakeholders (students, faculty and staff, parents, and administrators), procedures for teaching, procedures for reinforcing, procedures for monitoring, an assessment schedule, secondary (Tier 2) intervention grids, and tertiary (Tier 3) intervention grids. The Ci3T implementation manual essentially serves as a collaboratively designed and transparent agreement for how the school operates; it is inclusive of all district initiatives, programs, and practices.

During implementation, Ci3T leadership teams collaborate with Ci3T district leaders to collect and monitor system-level data, including (a) treatment integrity data collected in fall and spring to determine the extent to which primary (Tier 1) prevention efforts are implemented as designed (Gresham, 1989) and (b) social validity data (also collected in fall and spring) to examine faculty and staff's views regarding primary (Tier 1) prevention goals, procedures, and outcomes (Wolf, 1978). In addition, these same leaders examine multiple sources of student-level data to monitor students' performance—for all students, including those receiving special education services—across all three domains (e.g., academics screenings, behavior screening, state achievement tests, office disciplinary referrals [ODRs]), along with school progression data (e.g., attendance and credit accrual). More precisely, data-informed decision making within Ci3T models includes reviewing academic and behavioral screening data together to (a) understand trends in student performance over time for the school as a whole, (b) inform the use of teacher-delivered supports (e.g., increasing students' opportunities to respond; Common, Lane, Cantwell, Brunsting, & Oakes, 2017), and (c) determine which students may require Tier 2 and Tier 3 interventions in addition to primary prevention efforts (Oakes, Lane, Cox, & Messenger, 2014). Under optimal conditions, strategies, practices, and programs at each level of prevention (Tiers 1, 2, and 3) would involve use of evidence-based practices to maximize efficient responses to students' needs (Cook & Tankersley, 2013). In addition, treatment integrity and social validity data would also be interpreted when examining student-level data to ensure accurate conclusions are drawn regarding intervention effectiveness before connecting students with more intensive levels of prevention. It would be both ineffective and inefficient to recommend a student receive Tier 2 supports in academic, behavioral, or social domains if evidence was not available to indicate Tier 1 (primary prevention) efforts were implemented as planned (e.g., with integrity).

Data-Informed Professional Development for Faculty and Staff

In addition to using a data-informed decision-making process when choosing instructional practices to improve student outcomes, this same data-informed decision-making process is also used to make choices about professional development for faculty and staff. Specifically, information gleaned from social validity and treatment integrity data can determine areas of implementation success as well as targets for development. For example, in looking at social validity data collected at Tier 1 using the Primary Intervention Rating Scale (Lane et al., 2009), a school-site Ci3T leadership team or Ci3T district leaders might notice respondents are concerned about using behavior-specific praise to acknowledge students who meet expectations. Perhaps they are worried that reinforcing expected behaviors will impede students' intrinsic motivation. Treatment integrity data collected using the Ci3T Treatment Integrity: Teacher Self-Report (Lane, 2009b) might also indicate that faculty and staff self-report little use of behavior-specific praise, which is also confirmed by direct observations conducted in individual classrooms using the Ci3T Treatment Integrity: Direct Observation (Ci3T TI: DO; Lane, 2009a) tool. If this theme is evident in a single school or across several schools, then school administrators' or district leaders' response could be to offer a wide range of professional learning opportunities to address this misconception about behavior-specific praise (e.g., topical professional learning sessions, practice guides, research briefs, webinars, and on-demand narrated presentations). Through these various avenues, faculty and staff could access or be exposed to research-based information explaining that applied behavior analytic principles are widely—and successfully!—used to shape behaviors (Cooper, Heron, & Heward, 2007). By acknowledging prosocial and academic enabling, malleable behaviors students can control such as effort rather than intelligence or ability, we teach students they are capable of engaging in behaviors that support school and social success. Oftentimes students may feel school is "done *to* them" and that their behaviors are not actually part of the equation of their success. By teaching, giving students opportunities to practice, and providing reinforcement (often through the use of a ticket, paired with behavior-specific praise), we increase the likelihood of students engaging in these desirable behaviors until such time they receive naturally occurring reinforcement for engaging in the desired behaviors (e.g., enjoying more free time in the evenings when they use class time to complete work, rather than completing unfinished work at home, and perhaps being able to go to a friend's house during this free time). This is but one illustration of how to use implementation data to inform professional learning opportunities for faculty and staff.

Another example of data-informed professional learning is to examine student-level screening data along with treatment integrity and social validity data to determine if there are classes in which more than 20% of students are screening into moderate or high-risk categories for externalizing and/or internalizing behaviors. In these instances, teachers might access or refine their use of low-intensity strategies as noted previously. For example, a teacher might incorporate or refine the use of instructional choice (Royer, Lane, Cantwell, & Messenger, 2017) or use high-probability requests (Common et al., 2017) to increase engagement (and thereby also decrease off-task behavior). An instructional coach who conducted the Ci3T TI: DO might support these efforts by modeling and providing performance feedback on the use of these strategies

Finally, some states and school districts have also conducted a professional learning survey to learn more about additional professional learning needs (Lane, Carter, Jenkins, Dwiggins, & Germer, 2015). As part of these surveys, administrators as well as faculty and staff report the extent to which they are using the various concepts, strategies, and practices adopted as part of their Ci3T model (e.g., using screening data to inform decisions; teaching social–emotional skills lessons school-wide, using data to inform targeted supports; learning practical strategies to manage challenging behavior). In addition, these surveys also solicit feedback as to preferred avenues to access this information: district-wide professional learning days, book studies, practice guides, and so on. The intent here is to provide a wide range of feasible learning opportunities. Thus, the messaging is clear: (a) The expectation is that the school's Ci3T implementation plan will be fully installed to meet students' multiple needs in academic, behavioral, and social domains, and (b) leaders are committed to empowering faculty and staff with the full set of skills needed to achieve this goal.

At its core, Ci3T is a data-informed model that relies on data for decision making at a variety of levels. Close attention is paid to developing systems, structures, and tools to facilitate high-quality, sustained, practice-based professional learning and coaching to sustain and refine implementation. This is accomplished by developing structures to assist district and school-site Ci3T leadership teams to lead effectively and efficiently. The Ci3T model creates a collaborative, integrated context for general and special educators, administrators, and families to work together to better meet the academic, behavior, and social needs of all students with the use of evidenced-based strategies, practices, and programs at each level. The Ci3T model is premised on the most recent conceptualization of inclusive schooling (Sailor & McCart, 2014) that emphasizes changes in educational structures rather than perpetuating policies that focus on student characteristics as an explanation for school failure. The principle of equity is at the foreground of this model because the onus is on schools and school personnel to provide instructional experiences that support all learners at the Tier 1 level. For example, teachers prioritize the use of instructional strategies to increase equity in education, such as using explicit instruction, activating and building background knowledge, increasing students' opportunities to respond, and providing performance feedback (Chaparro, Nese, & McIntosh, 2015). In addition, Ci3T models facilitate equitable access to supports with the use of reliable, valid screening tools to detect and assist students who might require more than primary prevention efforts in academic, behavior, and/or social–emotional domains (Lane, Menzies, Ennis, & Bezdek, 2013).

Potential Benefits of Ci3T Models

As discussed at the onset of this chapter, educational leaders across the country are shifting away from reactive approaches to managing learning, behavioral, and social challenges and are moving toward a systemic approach to preventing and responding to these challenges in an inclusive context (Walker et al., 2014). While there are a number of well-established tiered structures developed to meet this charge, our work focuses on Ci3T models of prevention as the first tiered system dedicated to academic, behavior, and social–emotional domains in *one* integrated system. Too often schools have attempted to build MTSS systems in sequence, often beginning with reading, then math, then— time permitting—behavior, with no attention to social–emotional learning. Yet, given that the general education system is responsible for meeting the multiple needs of most students—including the 20% of school-age youth who struggle with emotional and behavioral disorders (e.g., internalizing and externalizing behaviors; Forness, Freeman, Paparella, Kauffman, & Walker, 2012), it is critical that schools develop and install integrated systems that create collaborative structures to facilitate the work between general and special educators. Additionally, a system is needed in which faculty and staff can continue their professional learning as in-service teachers so they can acquire or enhance the skill sets necessary for preventing and responding to challenging behaviors in a respectful manner so as to maintain a positive, productive learning environment. Teachers still report not feeling well prepared by their teacher education programs to address the behavioral challenges they face on a daily basis (Oliver & Reschly, 2010). Professional learning is needed to facilitate ongoing skill development to manage acting-out behavior (Colvin, 2004), with an emphasis on proactive, feasible positive behavior supports. The Ci3T model provides school systems with feasible, effective structures that facilitate transparency and efficiency between all stakeholders committed to student success, including faculty and staff, administrators, families, and the students themselves (Lane et al., 2016).

The Institute for Education Sciences (IES) acknowledged the benefit of integrated tiered systems as a framework that "provides academic, social, emotional, and behavioral support for all students, and provides resources and supports that teachers and other school personnel need to support" for students who have—or are at risk for—learning and behavioral challenges (RFA 84.324A, IES, 2017, p. 17). In fact, IES recently issued a call for inquiry to enhance the field's understanding of comprehensive, integrated frameworks and how they function to assist educators and students—including students with intensive intervention needs. These integrated frameworks prioritize not only academic success but also success in behavioral performance and strong mental health, with models including several keystone features: a continuum of evidence-based supports, reliable and valid screening tools to ensure early detection of challenges, data-informed decision making, high-quality professional learning, and clear communication structures for all stakeholder groups. No doubt it is a formidable task for administrators to design, implement, and evaluate these structures. Although challenging, it is indeed possible to address this lofty charge through respectful partnerships between the research and practice communities (Lane, 2017).

During the past 20 years, Lane, Menzies, Oakes, and colleagues have conducted a series of descriptive, experimental, and psychometric studies offering evidence of the utility of various features of Ci3T models (e.g., Lane & Menzies, 2005; Lane, Menzies, Ennis, & Oakes, 2015; Lane, Oakes, & Menzies, 2014; Lane et al., 2018). In brief, some of the lessons learned include the following:

1. Faculty and staff who rate the plan as more socially valid during the design process are more apt to implement Tier 1 practices with integrity than are faculty and staff who rate Tier 1 practices as less socially valid (Lane et al., 2009).

2. Descriptive studies suggest that schools implementing Ci3T as planned experience decreases in the overall level of behavioral risk for students as measured by systematic screening tools (Lane, Kalberg, Bruhn, Mahoney, & Driscoll, 2008; Lane, Menzies, Oakes, & Kalberg, 2012).

3. K–12 behavior screening scores for both externalizing and internalizing behaviors predict academic performance (e.g., reading

measures, GPA, course failures) as well as performance on social and behavioral indicators (e.g., ODRs, suspensions, self-control skills) (Ennis, Lane, & Oakes, 2012; Lane et al., 2008, 2013; Oakes et al., 2010).

4. Experimental studies at Tier 2 (IES-funded group and single-case designs) offer evidence as to how academic interventions (e.g., Self-Regulated Strategy Development for writing) have yielded improved academic skills (e.g., written expression) and increases in academic engagement (Lane et al., 2011).

5. Functional assessment-based interventions conducted as Tier 3 supports using single-case design methodology within Ci3T models have demonstrated a functional relation between the introduction of these interventions and improved performance for students with intensive intervention needs (Cox, Griffin, Hall, Oakes, & Lane, 2011).

6. Teachers working in Ci3T schools may experience lower levels of burnout relative to national norms (Oakes, Lane, Jenkins, & Booker, 2013).

Collectively, this evidence indicates that various components of the Ci3T model yielded promising outcomes for students and teachers. Nonetheless, there are additional areas of inquiry needed to refine the design, implementation, and evaluation of Ci3T models of prevention. As we shift toward examining issues of sustainability, it will be important to empower district leaders with the knowledge, confidence, and resources not only to install but to sustain and refine implementation. To this end, we offer the following considerations for reflecting on the utility of Ci3T models of prevention for meeting students' multiple needs.

Considerations: Reflecting on Structures for Sustainable Ci3T Models of Prevention

District commitment and leadership, infrastructures for data-informed decision making, data-informed professional learning, and data structures to support Tier 2 and Tier 3 implementation are all areas that pose challenges when scaling Ci3T models of prevention. We briefly describe each topic and offer a challenge to the field for moving each area of inquiry forward.

Establishing District Commitment and Leadership

District leaders such as superintendents, assistant superintendents, directors of student support services, and directors of curriculum and instruction are inundated with literally hundreds of decisions and tasks each day. As these leaders commit to designing, implementing, and evaluating Ci3T models of prevention, it is important to establish this framework as a district priority. Few would argue the importance of prioritizing students' academic, behavioral, and social–emotional skills development. However, successful implementation requires a clearly articulated rationale for the "why" behind Ci3T, dedicated and ongoing professional learning during the design and implementation phases, and well-defined communication structures. For example, in districts where Ci3T is fully installed, there is a Ci3T district leadership team, a Ci3T leadership team at each school, and dedicated time in each faculty and staff meeting for implementation and evaluation activities. Ci3T is not one more thing; it is a framework for organizing all initiatives and practices and for reflecting the values of a district.

An important consideration is how to best support district-level leaders in maintaining a strong commitment. Too often practices, strategies, programs, and/or frameworks are abandoned before they are fully installed. A lesson learned from the implementation sciences literature is that changes in student performance typically occur after 2 to 3 years of sustained, high-fidelity implementation. In our own work we have observed teachers working through their initial concerns or hesitancies in this same time frame. Yet, too often in education, we adopt early and then abandon efforts before desired outcomes have the opportunity to come to fruition. Sustainability requires district leaders to support the shift in practices through clear and supportive communication and professional learning.

Developing Infrastructures to Support Data-Informed Decision Making at Tier 1

As part of designing and implementing a Ci3T model, teams are taught to engage in data-informed decision-making efforts at every level of prevention—including Tier 1. This means there must be infrastructure in place to assess treatment integrity and social validity data as well as student performance data. To effectively and efficiently use these data, integrated systems are needed so appropriate stakeholders can access and interact with these data in a secure and timely manner to inform decision making.

Another common barrier is how to access or build systems for managing these multiple sources of data. Ideally, these systems need to be highly secure, financially feasible, user-friendly, and capable of managing multiple sources of data over multiple time points. For example, a superintendent needs to be able to examine faculty and staff performance within and across school sites in relation to student performance. Teachers need the ability not only to determine one student's performance over time but to examine performance patterns for various groups of students (e.g., their homeroom class or seventh period) relative to treatment integrity and social validity data. Attention to the protection of data and educators' ease of access to needed data should guide the selection of systems.

Empowering Teachers Using Data-Informed Professional Learning

High-quality, respectful, data-informed professional learning is another core feature of Ci3T models of prevention. As various data sources are explored, Ci3T district leaders and Ci3T leadership teams need to be prepared with a range of professional activities to support ongoing learning and refinements. In considering which content to feature, leaders will need to use reputable sources (e.g., U.S. Department of Education's What Works Clearinghouse, Substance Abuse and Mental Health Services Administration, and Collaborative for Academic, Social, and Emotional Learning) to determine the extent to which there is sufficient evidence to suggest that if implemented with fidelity, the strategy, practice, or program will yield the desired outcomes. When providing professional learning for procedures for monitoring, leaders will want to stay current on reliability and validity evidence for the tools selected (e.g., see National Center on Intensive Intervention). In addition to considering various content considerations, it is also important to seek feedback on the preferred and feasible avenues of professional learning. Not all faculty and staff will be able (or want) to attend after-school presentations. Some will need access to on-demand resources, whereas still others will need access to resources that do not require an Internet connection (research briefs or book studies; Lane, Carter, et al., 2015).

An area of attention is ensuring a detailed and transparent approach for using data to inform professional learning and then making the connection between the Ci3T model and the content of a particular professional learning activity. As described in this chapter, the content for professional learning is determined in part from faculty and staff input. Ideally, each professional activity (session, practice guide, webinar) would be designed with a clear connection to the Ci3T model. Think of a directional map in a mall with a label that reads "You are here." The same logic could apply to a professional learning activity: "You are here" within your Ci3T model. It is important for all professional learning activities to connect back to the mission and vision that guided the development of the Ci3T model, for the district to avoid the temptation to shift to the next "bright and shiny" initiative rather than fully addressing committed priorities.

Connecting Students to Tier 2 and Tier 3

We conclude with a consideration related to connecting students to Tier 2 and Tier 3 supports. As part of Ci3T models, each implementation manual features a Secondary (Tier 2) Intervention Grid and a Tertiary (Tier 3) Intervention Grid (available from Ci3T.org). These grids offer transparency and organization of available sources, with explicitly stated data-based inclusion criteria supporting equal access to these supports according to student need. The grids enable educators to quickly provide students with evidence-based supports at the first sign of concern—according to inclusion criteria. For districts with equity priorities, equal access to needed supports is paramount. It is important to note that special education is not a Tier 3 support. Students receiving special education services—like students receiving general education supports—are active participants in primary prevention (Tier 1) efforts, with access to Tier 2 and Tier 3 supports as appropriate.

A fourth challenge in need of attention with respect to using these intervention grids as intended is a data system that interfaces Tier 1 practices with Tier 2 and Tier 3 grids. Ideally, systems would be developed to provide (a) connections between Tier 1 performance patterns and target supports,

(b) a structure for monitoring Tier 2 and Tier 3 supports as accessed by students, and (c) progression data (e.g., treatment integrity, social validity, and progress monitoring [frequent, repeated measurement sensitive to change]) to illustrate students' experience with these targeted and intensive supports.

Of course there are numerous considerations when designing, implementing, and evaluating Ci3T models of prevention. We respectfully offer these four as a foundation to begin conversations among educational leaders.

Conclusion

We provided guidance for school leaders and special educators, who often play a vital role in system change efforts, on designing, implementing, evaluating, and sustaining Ci3T models of prevention. We described Ci3T models, noting how they offer a broadening of MTSS to address academic, behavioral, and social–emotional domains for all learners—including students receiving special education services. Then we provided a concise discussion of how Ci3T models are designed and implemented using data-informed decision making in multiple facets—including efforts to assist students as well as faculty and staff. Next, we explored potential benefits of Ci3T models. Finally, we addressed four sustainability considerations for the field to reflect on as we consider the utility of these models for meeting students' multiple needs. In the sections below, we offer Internet resources, recommended readings, and professional organizations to encourage continued inquiry and exploration of tiered systems of support as a structure for meeting students' academic, behavior, and social–emotional needs.

REFLECTING AND UNDERSTANDING

1. What is a comprehensive, integrated, three-tiered (Ci3T) model of prevention?

2. How are Ci3T models different from traditional multitiered systems of support (MTSS)?

3. How are the learning domains integrated in Ci3T models?

4. How are students receiving special education services supported in Ci3T models?

5. How are multiple sources of data examined by Ci3T leadership teams?

6. What are some of the potential benefits of Ci3T models for faculty and staff as well as students?

ONLINE RESOURCES

- Center of Response to Intervention at American Institutes for Research: https://www.rti4success.org/

- Center on the Developing Child, Harvard University: https://developingchild.harvard.edu/

- Collaborative for Academic, Social, and Emotional Learning: https://www.casel.org/

- Comprehensive, Integrated, Three-Tiered Models of Prevention: http://www.ci3t.org/

- MTSS for Mathematics: http://ceedar.education.ufl.edu/cems/math/

- National Association of School Psychologists: http://www.nasponline.org/research-and-policy/current-law-and-policy-priorities/policy-priorities/the-every-student-succeeds-act/essa-implementation-resources/essa-and-mtss-for-decision-makers

- National Center on Intensive Interventions: https://intensiveintervention.org/

- Office of Special Education Programs National Technical Assistance Center on Positive Behavioral Interventions and Supports: http://www.pbis.org/

- Substance Abuse and Mental Health Services Administration National Registry of Evidence-Based Programs and Practices: https://www.samhsa.gov/nrepp

- U.S. Department of Education's What Works Clearinghouse: https://ies.ed.gov/ncee/wwc/

- Zero to Three: https://www.zerotothree.org/

RECOMMENDED READINGS

Books

Brown-Chidsey, R., & Bickford, R. (2015). *Practical handbook of multi-tiered systems of support building academic and behavioral success in schools.* New York, NY: Guilford Press.

Kent McIntosh, K., & Goodman, S. (2016). *Integrated multi-tiered systems of support: Blending RTI and PBIS.* New York, NY: Guilford Press.

Lane, K. L., Oakes, W. P., Cantwell, E. D., & Royer, D. J. (2016). *Building and installing comprehensive, integrated, three-tiered (Ci3T) models of prevention: A practical guide to supporting school success.* Phoenix, AZ: KOI Education.

Article

Lane, K. L., Carter, E., Jenkins, A., Dwiggins, L., & Germer, K. (2015). Supporting comprehensive, integrated, three-tiered models of prevention in schools: Administrators perspectives. *Journal of Positive Behavior Interventions, 17*, 209–222. doi:10.1177/1098300715578916

Briefs, Practice Guides, and Reports

Barrett, S., Eber, L., & Weist, M. (Eds.). (2014). *Advancing education effectiveness: Interconnecting school mental health and school-wide positive behavior support.* Retrieved from http://www.pbis.org/common/cms/files/pbisresources/Final-Monograph.pdf

Epstein, M., Atkins, M., Cullinan, D., Kutash, K., & Weaver, R. (2008). *Reducing behavior problems in the elementary school classroom: A practice guide* (NCEE #2008-012). Washington, DC: National Center for Education Evaluation and Regional Assistance, Institute of Education Sciences, U.S. Department of Education. Retrieved from https://ies.ed.gov/ncee/wwc/PracticeGuide/4

Simonsen, B., Freeman, J., Goodman, S., Mitchell, B., Swain-Bradway, J., Flannery, B., Sugai, G.… Putman, B. (2015). *Supporting and responding to behavior: Evidence-based classroom strategies for teachers.* Washington, DC: Office of Special Education Programs, U.S. Department of Education. Retrieved from https://www.osepideasthatwork.org/evidencebasedclassroomstrategies

PROFESSIONAL ORGANIZATIONS

Association for Positive Behavior Supports: http://www.apbs.org/

Council for Children with Behavioral Disorders: http://www.ccbd.net/home

Council for Exceptional Children: https://www.cec.sped.org/

Division for Early Childhood: http://www.dec-sped.org/

REFERENCES

Chaparro, E. A., Nese, R. N. T., & McIntosh, K. (2015). *Examples of engaging instruction to increase equity in education.* Eugene: Center on Positive Behavioral Interventions and Supports, University of Oregon.

Colvin, G. (2004). *Managing the cycle of acting-out behavior in the classroom.* Eugene, OR: Behavior Associates.

Common, E. A., Lane, K. L., Cantwell, E. D., Brunsting, N., & Oakes, W. P. (2017). *Teacher-delivered strategies to increase students' opportunities to respond: A systematic methodological review.* Manuscript in preparation.

Cook, B., & Tankersley, M. (Eds.). (2013). *Effective practices in special education.* Boston, MA: Pearson.

Cooper, J. O., Heron, T. E., & Heward, W. L. (2007). *Applied behavior analysis* (2nd ed.). Upper Saddle River, NJ: Pearson.

Cox, M., Griffin, M. M., Hall, R., Oakes, W. P., & Lane, K. L. (2011). Using a functional assessment-based intervention to increase academic engaged time in an inclusive middle school setting. *Beyond Behavior, 20*, 44–54.

Ennis, R. P., Lane, K. L., & Oakes, W. P. (2012). Score reliability and validity of the Student Risk Screening Scale: A psychometrically sound, feasible tool for use in urban elementary schools. *Journal of Emotional and Behavioral Disorders, 20*, 241–259.

Flay, B. R., Allred, C. G., & Ordway, N. (2001). Effects of the Positive Action program on achievement and discipline: Two matched-control comparisons. *Prevention Science, 2*, 71–89.

Forness, S. R., Freeman, S. F. N., Paparella, T., Kauffman, J. M., & Walker, H. M. (2012). Special education implications of point and cumulative prevalence for children with emotional or behavioral disorders. *Journal of Emotional and Behavioral Disorders, 20*, 4–18.

Fuchs, D., Fuchs, L. S., & Compton, D. L. (2012). Smart RTI: A next-generation approach to multilevel prevention. *Exceptional Children*, 78, 263–279.

Gresham, F. M. (1989). Assessment of treatment integrity in school consultation and prereferral intervention. *School Psychology Review*, 18, 37–50.

Hawken, L. S., Vincent, C. G., & Schumann, J. (2008). Response to intervention for social behavior: Challenges and opportunities. *Journal of Emotional and Behavioral Disorders*, 16(4), 213–225.

Horner, R. H., & Sugai, G. (2015). School-wide PBIS: An example of applied behavior analysis implemented at a scale of social importance. *Behavior Analysis in Practice*, 8, 80–85. doi:10.1007/s40617-015-0045-4

Lane, K. L. (2009a). *CI3T treatment integrity: Direct observation tool*. Unpublished instrument.

Lane, K. L. (2009b). *Teacher self-report form*. Unpublished instrument.

Lane, K. L. (2017). Building strong partnerships: Responsible inquiry to learn and grow together TECBD-CCBD keynote address. *Education and Treatment of Children*, 40, 597–618.

Lane, K. L., Carter, E., Jenkins, A., Dwiggins, L., & Germer, K. (2015). Supporting comprehensive, integrated, three-tiered models of prevention in schools: Administrators perspectives. *Journal of Positive Behavior Interventions*, 17, 209–222. doi:10.1177/1098300715578916

Lane, K. L., Harris, K., Graham, S., Driscoll, S. A., Sandmel, K., Morphy, P., Hebert, M.… Schatschneider, C. (2011). Self-regulated strategy development at tier-2 for second-grade students with writing and behavioral difficulties: A randomized control trial. *Journal of Research on Educational Effectiveness*, 4, 322–353.

Lane, K. L., Kalberg, J. R., Bruhn, A. L., Driscoll, S. A., Wehby, J. H., & Elliott, S. (2009). Assessing social validity of school-wide positive behavior support plans: Evidence for the reliability and structure of the Primary Intervention Rating Scale. *School Psychology Review*, 38, 135–144.

Lane, K. L., Kalberg, J. R., Bruhn, A. L., Mahoney, M. E., & Driscoll, S. A. (2008). Primary prevention programs at the elementary level: Issues of treatment integrity, systematic screening, and reinforcement. *Education and Treatment of Children*, 31, 465–494.

Lane, K. L., & Menzies, H. (2005). Teacher-identified students with and without academic and behavioral concerns: Characteristics and responsiveness to a school-wide intervention. *Behavioral Disorders*, 31, 65–83.

Lane, K. L., Menzies, H. M., Ennis, R. P., & Bezdek, J. (2013). School-wide systems to promote positive behaviors and facilitate instruction. *Journal of Curriculum and Instruction*, 7, 6–31.

Lane, K. L., Menzies, H. M., Ennis, R. P., & Oakes, W. P. (2015). *Supporting behavior for school success: A step-by-step guide to key strategies*. New York, NY: Guilford Press.

Lane, K. L., Menzies, H. M., Oakes, W. P., & Kalberg, J. R. (2012). *Systematic screenings of behavior to support instruction*. New York, NY: Guilford Press.

Lane, K. L., Oakes, W. P., Cantwell, E. D., & Royer, D. J. (2016). *Building and installing comprehensive, integrated, three-tiered (Ci3T) models of prevention: A practical guide to supporting school success*. Phoenix, AZ: KOI Education. (Interactive eBook)

Lane, K. L., Oakes, W. P., Cantwell, E. D., Royer, D. J., Leko, M., Schatschneider, C., & Menzies, H. M. (2018). Predictive validity of Student Risk Screening Scale for Internalizing and Externalizing (SRSS-IE) scores in secondary schools. *Journal of Emotional and Behavioral Disorders*. https://doi.org/10.1177/1063426617744746

Lane, K. L., Oakes, W. P., & Menzies, H. M. (2014). Comprehensive, integrated, three-tiered (Ci3T) models of prevention: Why does my school—and district—need an integrated approach to meet students' academic, behavioral, and social needs? *Preventing School Failure*, 58, 121–128.

McIntosh, K., & Goodman, S. (2016). *Integrating multi-tiered systems of support: Blending RTI and PBIS*. New York, NY: Guilford Press.

Nelson, J. R., Benner, G. J., Lane, K., & Smith, B. W. (2004). An investigation of the academic achievement of K–12 students with emotional and behavioral disorders in public school settings. *Exceptional Children, 71,* 59–73.

Oakes, W. P., Lane, K. L., Cox, M., & Messenger, M. (2014). Logistics of behavior screenings: How and why do we conduct behavior screenings at our school? *Preventing School Failure, 58,* 159–170. doi:10.1080/1045988X.2014.895572

Oakes, W. P., Lane, K. L., Jenkins, A., & Booker, B. B. (2013). Three-tiered models of prevention: Teacher efficacy and burnout. *Education and Treatment of Children, 36,* 95–126. doi:10.1353/etc.2013.0037

Oakes, W. P., Wilder, K., Lane, K. L., Powers, L., Yokoyama, L., O'Hare, M. E., & Jenkins, A. B. (2010). Psychometric properties of the Student Risk Screening Scale: An effective tool for use in diverse urban elementary schools. *Assessment for Effective Intervention, 35,* 231–239.

Oliver, R. M., & Reschly, D. J. (2010). Special education teacher preparation in classroom management: Implications for students with emotional and behavioral disorders. *Behavioral Disorders, 35,* 188–199.

Royer, D. J., Lane, K. L., Cantwell, E. D., & Messenger, M. L. (2017). A systematic review of the evidence-base for instructional choice in K–12 settings. *Behavioral Disorders, 42,* 89–107. doi:http://dx.doi.org.www2.lib.ku.edu/10.1177/0198742916688655

Sailor, W. S., & McCart, A. B. (2014). Stars in alignment. *Research and Practice for Persons With Severe Disabilities, 39*(1), 55–64.

Stewart, R. M., Benner, G. J., Martella, R. C., & Marchand-Martella, N. E. (2007). Three-tier models of reading and behavior: A research review. *Journal of Positive Behavior Interventions, 9*(4), 239–253.

Sugai, G., & Horner, R. H. (2009). Responsiveness-to-intervention and school-wide positive behavior supports: Integration of multi-tiered system approaches. *Exceptionality, 17*(4), 223–237.

Utley, C. A., & Obiakor, F. E. (2015). Special issue: Research perspectives on multi-tiered system of support. *Learning Disabilities: A Contemporary Journal, 13*(1), 1–2.

Walker, H. M., Forness, S. R., & Lane, K. L. (2014). Design and management of scientific research in applied school settings. In B. Cook, M. Tankersley, & T. Landrum (Eds.), *Advances in learning and behavioral disabilities* (Vol. 27, pp. 141–169). Bingley, UK: Emerald.

Weist, M. D., Lever, N., Bradshaw, C., & Owens, J. S. (2014). Further advancing the field of school mental health. In M. Weist, N. Lever, C. Bradshaw, & J. Owens (Eds.), *Handbook of school mental health: Research, training, practice, and policy* (2nd ed., pp. 1–16). New York, NY: Springer.

Wolf, M. M. (1978). Social validity: The case for subjective measurement or how applied behavior analysis is finding its heart. *Journal of Applied Behavior Analysis, 11,* 203–214.

Yudin, M. (2014). *PBIS: Providing opportunity.* A keynote address presented at the National PBIS Leadership Forum: PBIS Building Capacity & Partnerships to Enhance Educational Reform, Rosemont, IL.

3

Free Appropriate Public Education

The Essence of Special Education

David F. Bateman and Mitchell L. Yell

This Chapter Will Cover:

1. The Education for All Handicapped Children Act (EAHCA) of 1975, a federal law whose primary purpose was to ensure that eligible students with disabilities received a free appropriate public education (FAPE).

2. The FAPE mandate of the EAHCA (the name of the law was changed to the Individuals with Disabilities Education Act, or the IDEA, in 1990), which has been controversial and engendered numerous due process hearings and court cases.

3. The U.S. Supreme Court ruling on the issue of FAPE in the first special education case heard by the High Court: *Board of Education of the Hendrick Hudson Central School District v. Rowley* (1982).

4. The Supreme Court's two-part test for hearing officers and judges to use in ruling on FAPE disputes (First, did the school district adhere to the procedures of the law? Second, was the student's individualized education program, or IEP, reasonably calculated to confer educational benefit?).

5. The second part of the test, the educational benefit standard, which led to disagreements among the circuit courts as to what degree of educational benefit was needed to confer a FAPE.

6. The IDEA's reauthorization and amendment a number of times after the original passage in 1975 (although the intent of the IDEA shifted from process and procedures to quality and student outcomes, the definition of FAPE did not change).

7. The U.S. Supreme Court's second case on the FAPE requirement of the IDEA, *Endrew F. v. Douglas County School District*, in 2017.

8. The Supreme Court's new educational benefit standard to be used in ruling on FAPE disputes (Was a student's IEP reasonably calculated to enable a student to make progress appropriate in light of the student's circumstances?).

9. The litigation and legislation on FAPE, which has had an important influence on how special education should develop and implement students' IEP.

When Congress passed the Education for All Handicapped Children Act (EAHCA) in 1975, about 20% of all students with disabilities were receiving a public education (Yell, 2019). Additionally, another 3 million children with disabilities who were in public schools were not receiving an education that met their needs (Yell & Bateman, 2017). To correct these problems and to ensure that all eligible students with disabilities received an appropriate public education, Congress passed the EAHCA (Yell, 2019).

The EAHCA provided federal financial assistance to states to aid school districts in educating students with disabilities who were eligible for special education services under the law. To qualify for this financial assistance, states had to submit state plans that ensured that all eligible students with disabilities would receive a *free appropriate public education* (FAPE). Students with disabilities under the law, therefore, were entitled to receive special education and related services that consisted of specially designed instruction and services to meet their unique educational needs. Thus, the primary responsibility of special educators was, and is, to provide special education and related services that conferred a FAPE to all eligible students with disabilities. For this reason, the FAPE requirement is critically important; it is our responsibility as special educators to ensure that the special education programs we develop and provide to each of our student confers a FAPE.

Although the EAHCA has undergone a number of changes since 1975, including changing the name of the law to the Individuals with Disabilities Education Act (IDEA) in 1990, the FAPE definition and requirement has remained unchanged. Court cases in the years since the passage of the EAHCA, however, have clarified the meaning of FAPE and are, therefore, extremely important to special education staff, teachers, and administrators. In this chapter we will (a) describe the original FAPE language of the law and later federal legislation concerning the provision of FAPE; (b) consider the first Supreme Court case on FAPE from 1982, *Board of Education of the Hendrick Hudson Central School District v. Rowley*; (c) highlight interpretations of the FAPE standard in court cases following the Supreme Court's 1982 ruling; (d) examine the most recent Supreme Court case on FAPE, *Endrew F. v. Douglas County School System* (2017); and (e) discuss the implications for the provision of FAPE following the two seminal Supreme Court rulings.

The Definition of FAPE in the EAHCA/IDEA

In 1975 Congress passed the EAHCA, later renamed the IDEA. The EAHCA provided federal grants to states "to assist them to provide special education and related services to children with disabilities" (IDEA, 20 U.S.C. § 1401 [a][9][A–D]). The statute's primary purpose was "to ensure that all children with disabilities had available to them a free appropriate public education that emphasizes special education and related services designed to meet their unique needs and prepare them for further education, employment, and independent living" (IDEA, 20 U.S.C. § 1401 [a][9][A–D]). Specifically, the law required that states receiving funds through the IDEA make a FAPE available to every eligible student with a disability residing in the state (IDEA, 20 U.S.C. § 1401 [a][9][A–D]). The FAPE requirement embodied Congress's ambitious objective of promoting educational opportunities for students with disabilities (*School Committee of the Town of Burlington v. Massachusetts Department of Education*, 1985).

The EAHCA, and now the IDEA, defined FAPE as special education and related services that

a. have been provided at public expense, under public supervision and direction, and without charge;

b. meet the standards of the state educational agency;

c. include an appropriate preschool, elementary school, or secondary school education in the state involved; and

d. are provided in conformity with the individualized education program, or IEP (IDEA, 20 U.S.C. § 1401 [a][18]).

When the EAHCA was first written, the authors of the statute realized that they could not define a FAPE for each student by detailing the specific substantive educational requirements for individual students in the law; so instead they defined a FAPE primarily in terms of the procedures that school district personnel had to follow to ensure that parents and school personnel would collaborate to develop an individual student's program of special education and related services. The assumption was that if parents and school district personnel collaborated in a meaningful way, that would ensure the development of an appropriate education for students with disabilities. The legal definition of a FAPE, therefore, was primarily procedural rather than substantive. These procedures included requirements such as the following: (a) providing notice to parents when their child's education program is discussed so the parents can participate in the discussions in a meaningful way; (b) inviting parents to participate in meetings to develop their child's educational program, including the meeting to develop their child's IEP; (c) securing parental consent prior to initiating evaluations of their child or placing their child in a special education program; (d) allowing parents the opportunity to examine their child's educational records; (e) permitting parents to obtain an independent educational evaluation at public expense if the parents disagree with the school's evaluation; and (f) including dispute resolution procedures that would allow a child's parents to file a state complaint, request mediation, receive an impartial due process hearing, and file a suit in federal or state court to resolve the issue.

In a ruling in *Board of Education of the Hendrick Hudson Central School District v. Rowley* (1982), the U.S. Supreme Court addressed the importance of the procedural aspects of the EAHCA as follows:

> It seems to us no exaggeration to say that Congress placed every bit as much emphasis upon compliance with procedures giving parents and guardians a large measure of participation at every stage of the administrative process … as it did upon the measurement of the resulting IEP against a substantive standard. We think that the congressional emphasis upon full participation of concerned parties throughout the development of the IEP … demonstrates the legislative conviction that adequate compliance with the procedures prescribed would in most cases assure much if not all of what Congress wished in the way of substantive content in an IEP. (p. 181)

Soon after the passage of the EAHCA, due process hearing officers and courts were called upon to settle controversies between school district personnel and a student's parents regarding his or her special education services and whether these services provided FAPE. In 1982, one of these cases made it all the way to the U.S. Supreme Court. In this case, *Board of Education of the Hendrick Hudson Central School District v. Rowley* (hereinafter *Rowley*), the High Court considered the meaning of FAPE.

Board of Education of the Hendrick Hudson Central School District v. Rowley (1982)

Amy Rowley, an elementary school student, was deaf, though she had "minimal residual hearing and [was] an excellent lipreader" (*Rowley*, 1982, p. 184). She received her education in the regular classroom along with her nondisabled classmates. The school provided Amy an FM hearing aid that amplified words spoken into a wireless receiver held by the teacher or fellow students during classroom activities. For 1 hour each day, Amy was pulled out of class to receive tutoring from an instructor for students who were deaf. She also received services from a speech therapist for 3 hours a week. Amy's parents requested that her school provide a sign language interpreter for the first-grade class. Following an unsuccessful trial period with a sign-language interpreter, however, Amy's IEP team decided not to include the services of the interpreter in her IEP.

Amy's parents disagreed with the school district's program, asserting that by not providing Amy with a sign-language interpreter, the school district had failed to provide her with a FAPE as required by the EAHCA. Amy's parents requested a hearing and the case eventually was heard by the U.S. District Court for the Southern District of New York (*Rowley v. Board of Education of the Hendrick Hudson Central School District*, 1980). The district court found that, even without a sign-language interpreter, Amy performed better than the average child in her class and was advancing easily from grade to grade. The court also found that Amy was a well-adjusted child who interacted and communicated well with her classmates and teachers. Nonetheless, the district court found that Amy understood considerably less than students without a hearing disability and was not learning as much, or performing as well academically, as she would if she were not deaf. The disparity between Amy's achievement and her potential led the court to decide that she was not receiving a FAPE, which the district court defined as "an opportunity to achieve [her] full potential commensurate with the opportunity provided to other children" (*Rowley*, 1980, p. 534). The district court held, therefore, that the Hendrick Hudson Central School District had failed to provide Amy with a FAPE. The school district appealed the district court's ruling to the U.S. Court of Appeals for the Second Circuit, which affirmed the district court's decision (*Board of Education of the Hendrick Hudson Central School District v. Rowley*, 1982). The school district then appealed the case to the U.S. Supreme Court. The primary question that the school district's attorneys asked the Court was what was meant by the EAHCA's requirement that students with disabilities be provided a FAPE.

Readers should note that the facts of *Rowley* were unique and certainly not typical of most students eligible for special education. Amy Rowley was a very bright and high-achieving student who was doing better than most of her nondisabled peers—even without the educational interventions her parents argued were appropriate.

The High Court sided with the school district, thus overturning the lower courts' rulings. The Supreme Court expressly declined to establish any one test for determining the adequacy of educational benefits conferred on all children covered by the EAHCA and "confine[d] [its] analysis" to the situation of "a handicapped child who is receiving substantial specialized instruction and related services, and who is performing above average in the regular classrooms of a public school system" (*Rowley*, 1982, p. 188). In a situation such as Amy's, the Court explained, a student's receipt of good marks and advancement from grade to grade is "an important factor" (p. 189) in determining whether the child has received a FAPE. The Court emphasized, however, even that factor was not conclusive: "We do not hold today that every handicapped child who is advancing from grade to grade in a regular public school system is automatically receiving a 'free appropriate public education'" (p. 197).

The Court in *Rowley* rejected various maximalist claims regarding the scope of a district's obligations, but it did not embrace any overarching standard for determining what constitutes an appropriate education. The Court observed that Congress had not provided a "comprehensive statutory definition of the phrase 'free appropriate public education'" (*Rowley*, 1982, p. 182). According to the Court, "whatever Congress meant by an 'appropriate' education, it is clear that it did not mean a potential-maximizing education" (p. 188).

Finally, the Court developed what has come to be known as the *Rowley* two-part test. In decided FAPE cases, courts were to answer the following two questions: "First, has the State complied with the procedures set forth in the Act? And second, is the individualized educational program developed through the Act's procedures reasonably calculated to enable the child to receive educational benefits?" (*Rowley*, 1982, p. 191).

FAPE and the 1990 Amendments to the IDEA

In the 1990 amendments to the IDEA, Congress did not change the definition of a FAPE, but it did clarify its intent. A House report on the 1990 reauthorization of the IDEA recognized that more support for students with disabilities was necessary to achieve Congress's goal of providing meaningful educational opportunities:

> Today the education of students with disabilities is at a crossroads. The focus over the past 14 years in educating students with disabilities has been on processes and procedures related to special education with access to public education as the goal. The time has come to shift the focus to quality and student outcomes. Simply assuring that services are present or placing students with disabilities into general classrooms is no longer good enough. (H.R. Rep. No. 101-544, at 30, 1990)

Whereas it may once have been considered sufficient to get these students through school with little consideration for whether they were making significant progress, this new emphasis rejected the passive approach to educating students with disabilities. Instead, Congress envisioned educational programs for students with disabilities that culminate, to the extent possible, in skills and knowledge that these students can put to use beyond the classroom (H.R. Rep. No. 101-544, at 9, 1990). The 1990 amendments changed the name of the act from the EAHCA to the IDEA, added the categories of autism and traumatic brain injury, and included language regarding assistive technology and transition services.

Transition to post-education life was seen as critical to the value of the educational opportunities provided to students. Congress examined the plight of students with disabilities who, having completed their education, "have no jobs, further training, or programs available to them," some of whom are "forced to linger at home, with literally nothing to do" (USCCAN report at 1760, 1990). "Years of valuable special education are wasted in such situations," and "most importantly, human potential and hope are needlessly destroyed" (USCCAN report at 1732, 1990). To remedy this situation Congress required that the IEPs of students with disabilities who reached age 14 had to include a plan to help those students transition to postschool life. Congress thus recognized the importance of providing students with disabilities with meaningful instruction to ready them for their later transition to post-education life.

FAPE and the 1997 Amendments to the IDEA

In 1997, Congress reauthorized and amended the IDEA in the IDEA Amendments. In support of these amendments to the IDEA, Senator Jim Jeffords testified before a hearing of the Senate Labor and Human Resources Committee:[1]

> The bottom line is that when it comes time to graduate from high school we must make sure that our students, all students, have the skills to either pursue post-secondary education or training or to get a good job and be contributing members of our community to the utmost of their ability.... IDEA was originally enacted in 1975.... After 22 years, I think it is appropriate to acknowledge that schools have changed. The range of disabilities seen in schools has changed. Our expectations for children with disabilities have changed. And the expectations we've placed on each other as educators and parents have changed.

The 1997 amendments were passed with overwhelming support after Congress found "educational achievement and post-school outcomes for children with disabilities remain less than satisfactory" (Senate Report

---

[1] Testimony of Sen. Jeffords, R-VT, Chairman, Hearing of Senate Labor and Human Resources Committee, Specialized Education Programs Reauthorization, Jan. 29, 1997.

No. 104-275, at 14, 1996). Although access to education had dramatically improved, children with disabilities were still failing courses at a disproportionately high rate and were twice as likely to drop out of school when compared with other students. "Too often we in education have limited our expectations for children with disabilities.... These low expectations result in low performance and dismal results" (Senate Report No. 104-275, at 17).

Congress thus determined "the promise of the law [had] not been fulfilled," and sought to revise the IDEA to ensure not merely access to education but also a "quality public education" for all children with disabilities (House of Representatives Rep. No. 105-95, at 84–85 [1997]).

As Congressman Frank Riggs, one of the amendment's cosponsors, explained,

> We are changing the focus of the bill by raising expectations for the educational achievement for all students, especially those with learning disabilities. States under the legislation must establish goals for the performance of children with disabilities and develop indicators to judge their progress. A child's individualized educational program, otherwise known as an IEP, will focus on meaningful and measurable annual goals. (143 Cong. Rec. 8012, statement of Rep. Riggs, 1997)

Thus, the goals of the amendments to IDEA in 1997 were to implement "high expectations for [special education] children" and to "ensur[e] their access in the general curriculum to the maximum extent possible" (IDEA, 1997). Finally, the purpose of the amendments was to strengthen implementation of the IDEA and shift the IDEA from a compliance-driven model to a performance-driven model, and generally improve the quality of education for children with disabilities. As Congress noted, the overriding goal was to replace low expectations with high expectations. Additionally, Congress also aligned the IDEA with the substantial reform and accountability measures adopted in the Elementary and Secondary Education Act of 1965.

FAPE and the 2004 Amendments to the IDEA

In 2004, Congress amended and reauthorized the IDEA in the Individuals with Disabilities Education Improvement Act. In the findings section preceding the 2004 amendments to the IDEA (IDEA, 1400[c][5][A-H] 2004), Congressional authors declared, after almost 30 years of research and experience, that "having high expectations for such children and ensuring their access to the general education curriculum in the regular classroom, to the maximum extent possible," would lead to more effective outcomes (IDEA[c][5][A]) and would prepare students "to lead productive and independent adult lives, to the maximum extent possible" (IDEA[c][5][A][ii]). Congress also found the education of children with disabilities would be more effective if implementation of the IDEA were coordinated with more general school improvement efforts. By including children with disabilities in those broader efforts, Congress found, states can "ensure that such children benefit from such efforts and that special education can become a service for such children rather than a place where such children are sent" (IDEA[c][5][3]). To advance this objective, Congressional authors noted that the IDEA's FAPE requirement should be designed to prepare students with disabilities for further education, employment, and independent living (IDEA[d][1][A]).

Clearly, there had been changes to the expectations of schools related to the provision of services for students with disabilities since 1982 when *Rowley* was decided. In the various amendments to the IDEA and the No Child Left Behind Act, Congress seemed to demand high educational expectations for students with disabilities and to require that special education programs in public schools prepare students with disabilities for meaningful participation in society.

Post-*Rowley* Interpretations of FAPE in the Courts

In the years following the *Rowley* decision, hearing officers and judges had to use the two-part *Rowley* test in deciding FAPE cases. In the first part of the *Rowley* FAPE test, hearing officers and judges were required to determine if a school had adhered to the procedural requirements of the IDEA. This part of the test proved relatively straightforward; however, the second part of the *Rowley* test—whether the school's IEP was reasonably calculated to confer educational benefits—was far less clear. During this period, the U.S. Circuit Court of Appeals for the various circuits began to apply different standards in deciding what amount of educational benefits was sufficient for a school district to have conferred FAPE. The U.S. solicitor general referred to this split among the courts as "an entrenched and acknowledged circuit conflict" (Brief for the United States as Amicus Curia, 2016, p. 8). Whereas at least six circuits had adopted a variation of the some or de minimis degree of educational benefit as being sufficient to confer a FAPE, two other circuits used a meaningful benefit standard to determine FAPE (Yell & Bateman, 2017).

According to the de minimis view of educational benefit, if a school offered an education that was more than trivial, the school district met the second part of the *Rowley* test. Thus, the circuits using this low standard would generally find that if a school's IEP was reasonably calculated to provide any degree of educational benefit, no matter how little, that would be sufficient to show that the school district had met the FAPE standard announced in *Rowley*. Circuit courts that adopted a higher educational benefit standard typically required that an IEP had to be reasonably calculated to confer meaningful benefit.

This split made it more likely that the U.S. Supreme Court would eventually hear another FAPE case to interpret the educational benefit standard set in *Rowley*. This opportunity presented itself in an appeal of the U.S. Court of Appeals for the Tenth Circuit decision in *Endrew F. v. Douglas County School District* (2015). In this case, the Tenth Circuit had used the educational benefit standard of "merely more than de minimis as sufficient to confer a FAPE" (*Endrew F.*, 2015, p. 17).

Endrew F. v. Douglas County School District (2017)

The Supreme Court agreed to hear a challenge to the FAPE standard in the *Endrew F. v Douglas County* case (hereinafter *Endrew F.*). The specifics of the case are important to help understand how the landscape of FAPE has changed since 1982. Endrew F. (Drew) was a child with attention deficit hyperactivity disorder and autism. Drew's autism affected his cognitive functioning, language and reading skills, and social and adaptive abilities. He also had problems with his ability to communicate his needs and emotions. He was eligible for special education and related services as a student with autism. He attended school in the Douglas County School District in Colorado from preschool through fourth grade. The district provided him an IEP for each school year from kindergarten through fourth grade.

Unfortunately, Drew's academics seemed to stall in third and fourth grade, and his problem behaviors worsened. After a disagreement with school personnel over Drew's academic and functional progress, his parents enrolled him in a local private school for students with autism, the Firefly Autism House. While at the private school, Drew made academic, social, and behavioral progress. After about 6 months in the Autism Firefly House, Drew's parents met with school officials about possibly enrolling him in the Douglas County School System. The parents and IEP team members then convened to develop an IEP for Drew. They requested that the public school develop an IEP that included similar programming to that of the private school. The public school officials, however, responded with an IEP that essentially mirrored Drew's fourth grade IEP. Drew's parents decided to continue his education at the Autism Firefly House and filed a due process hearing requesting tuition reimbursement by the Douglas County School District for the private school placement. The hearing officer sided with the district, finding that Drew had made some educational progress during his time at the public school. The parents appealed to federal district court, which upheld the hearing officer's decision based on evidence that Drew had made "at the least, minimal progress" in public school. The court concluded that Drew had received all that the IDEA requires.

The parents appealed to the U.S. Court of Appeals for the Tenth Circuit. The Tenth Circuit Court affirmed the hearing officer's and the lower court's decisions. It interpreted *Rowley* to hold that the IDEA requires states to provide "some educational benefit" that "must *merely be more than de minimis*" (*Endrew F.*, 2015, p. 17). The court stated that the district's IEP for Drew was adequate under that minimal standard. An important note: the court acknowledged that even under the "merely more than *de minimis*" test, "this is without question a close case" (p. 23). Nevertheless, because the Tenth Circuit had such a low standard for educational benefit and the court found indications of some minimal benefit, it ruled in favor of the Douglas County School District. Despite losing at every level, the parents decided to appeal to the U.S. Supreme Court. At this point, Drew's parents' primary concern was to have the High Court clarify exactly what constituted a FAPE under the IDEA. The specific question they asked the Supreme Court justices to rule on was the following: "What is the level of educational benefit that school districts must confer on children with disabilities to provide them with a free appropriate public education guaranteed by the Individuals with Disabilities

Education Act" (Petition for Writ of Certiorari, 2015). On September 29, 2016, the Supreme Court agreed to hear the case, and on January 22, 2017, the Court heard oral arguments in *Endrew F.*

During the oral arguments, the justices seemed to be wary of the de minimis or trivial educational benefit advocated for by the district. For example, Justice Breyer noted that even if the phrase "some benefit" in the *Rowley* decision were ambiguous, the combination of "some benefit" and "make progress" results in a more stringent standard than "more than merely de minimis." There were numerous questions asked about the development of the de minimis standard, and since the standard was not part of Congress's intention or specific language regarding the IDEA, what prevented the Court from coming up with a new standard? This was specifically addressed by Justices Ginsburg and Kagen, who wanted the educational benefit standard to be more than de minimis. Specifically, they talked about a "standard with a bite."

The Supreme Court handed down a unanimous ruling on March 22, 2017. The ruling noted that 35 years before, in *Rowley*, the Court had declined to endorse any one standard for determining when students with disabilities are receiving sufficient educational benefits to satisfy the requirements of the IDEA. In the opinion, Justice Roberts observed, "That more difficult problem is before us today" (*Endrew F.*, 2017, p. 1). The Court held that "to meet its substantive obligation under the IDEA, a school must offer an IEP reasonably calculated to enable a child to make progress appropriate in light of the child's circumstances" (p. 15).

The *Endrew F.* Decision on Remand to the Tenth Circuit and Colorado District Court

The Supreme Court ordered that the decision of the U.S. Court of Appeals for the Tenth Circuit be vacated and the case be remanded for further proceedings consistent with the High Court's FAPE standard. On August 2, 2017, the Tenth Circuit Court vacated its prior opinion and remanded the case back to the U.S. District Court for Colorado to hold further proceedings consistent with the Supreme Court's new standard.

On February 12, 2018, the judge for the district court issued his ruling. The judge reversed his previous decision, overturned the decision of the administrative law judge in the *Endrew F.* due process hearing, and ruled that the Douglas County School District had failed to provide Endrew with a FAPE (Education Week, 2018). The judge further ordered the school district to reimburse Endrew's parents for tuition at Firefly Autism House, transportation costs, and attorneys' fees and court costs.

Implications of *Rowley* and *Endrew F.* for Special Educators

The *Endrew F.* decision requires that school districts provide eligible students with an opportunity to make educational progress and does not impose a rigid, one-size-fits-all test that prevents educator discretion. The standard is flexible and individualized, and it promotes a common-sense educational decisions process that schools and teachers in some states have already been following.

The *Rowley* procedural provisions require school personnel to design an IEP in conjunction with the child's parents, consider the child's unique needs and capabilities, determine what special education and related services will help the child learn, develop appropriate goals, and measure progress. This is not a new process. The expectation of educational progress protects children with disabilities by ensuring that the IEP process is not merely a formality but instead produces a program advancing Congress's goal of meaningfully enhancing the lives and opportunities of these students.

Schools must ultimately ensure that each child's IEP is tailored to his or her needs and is reasonably calculated to provide an opportunity to make progress. The degree of progress required must reflect both (1) a relevant assessment of the child's capabilities and potential, and (2) the IDEA's over-arching goals of preparing children with disabilities for "further education, employment, and independent living" (IDEA, 2004). Notably, the *Rowley* and *Endrew F.* decisions do not require districts to "maximize each child's potential" or "achieve strict equality of opportunity or services" (*Endrew F.*, 2017). They do, however, promote "high expectations" for children with disabilities—and avoid "low expectations"—just as Congress intended (IDEA, 2004).

It is also important to note that a FAPE requires that a student's IEP address all his or her needs. This includes academic and functional needs. Functional needs refer to areas such as daily living skills, social skills, communication, and behavior (Yell, 2019). The judge in the U.S. District Court's remand of the *Endrew F.* case addressed the importance of including a student's problem behaviors in his or her IEP when the behaviors impede a student's learning or the learning of others.

> The District's inability to develop a formal plan or properly address (Endrew's) behaviors that had clearly disrupted his access to educational progress starting in his second grade year does, under the new standard articulated by the Supreme Court in this case, impact the assessment of whether the educational program it offered to (Endrew) was or was not reasonably calculated to enable him to make progress appropriate in light of his circumstances. The District's inability to properly address Petitioner's behaviors that, in turn, negatively impacted his ability to make progress on his educational and functional goals, also cuts against the reasonableness of the April 2010 IEP. (Education Week, 2018, p. 17)

Additionally, the *Rowley* and *Endrew F.* decisions describe a straight-forward approach for the development of IEPs. This will result in different IEPs for different children with different capabilities (see, e.g., *Rowley*, 1982, p. 202). For example, a child with learning disabilities may require special instruction in reading skills, along with appropriately modified classroom materials, to be educated in the general education classroom and partici-pate fully in the general education curriculum. For that child, educational progress might mean a different degree of learning and academic achievement than for nondisabled classmates.

A child with a significant intellectual disability may need to receive a majority of instruction outside the general education classroom. Progress for that student might encompass mastery of basic life skills—such as self-care, socialization, basic reading, and functional math (e.g., counting money and telling time)—that could eventually enable the child to work and live independently.

The Court made it clear: The IEP reflects a reasonable determination—made by the IEP team—of the degree of progress a particular child can make in light of his or her unique circumstances. In each case, that progress helps the child master knowledge and develop essential skills, which will continue to advance the underlying purposes of the IDEA (2004).

The Court also clarified school personnel's responsibility to collaborate with parents to determine the degree of progress appropriate for their child with a disability. In most cases, schools and parents will reach consensus on an IEP that is reasonably calculated to help the child learn and succeed. When schools and parents disagree, hearing officers can adjudicate disputes and ensure that the IEP in fact provides the child with the opportunity to make significant progress. A reminder to districts: The purpose of judicial review is not to have courts "imposing their view of preferable educational methods upon the States" (*Rowley*, 1982, p. 191). Rather, its purpose is to ensure that decision makers have exercised reasonable educational judgment in concluding that a particular IEP will enable educational progress for the particular child at issue. Both the substantive FAPE standard and the standard of review respect the expertise of district officials while also protecting the educational rights of children with disabilities.

Expecting that students eligible for special education will make progress is not new; however, the emphasis the U.S. Supreme Court put on progress certainly is. The decision in *Endrew F.* reflects Congress's goal of ensuring that students have the opportunity to make educational progress at school. Without such progress, those children would be unable to attain further education, employment, or economic self-sufficiency. Denying them the chance to make such progress would undermine the goal of equal opportunity and ratify the low expectations that Congress unambiguously rejected in the IDEA.

REFLECTING AND UNDERSTANDING

1. Examine the evolving standards of what constitutes a FAPE from the *Rowley* decision through IDEA 1997 and IDEA 2004 to *Endrew F.* How has the concept of FAPE changed since the EAHCA was passed in 1975? Is there a new FAPE standard?

2. What is peer-reviewed research? How can peer-reviewed research be used to help ensure a FAPE is delivered to students in special education? Describe the decision in *Ridley School District v. M. R.* (2012).

3. Explain the controversy over FAPE and educational methodology.

4. Describe how placement decisions are related to FAPE.

5. Describe the primary components of a FAPE.

ONLINE RESOURCES

- Board of Education of the Hendrick Hudson Central School District v. Rowley, 458 U.S. 291 (1982): https://www.law.cornell.edu/supremecourt/text/458/176

- Cedar Rapids Community School District v. Garrett F., 526 U.S. 66 (1999): https://supreme.justia.com/cases/federal/us/526/66/case.html

- Center on Response to Intervention at American Institutes for Research: https://www.rti4success.org/

- Cypress-Fairbanks Independent School District v. Michael F., 118 F.3d 245 (5th Cir. 1997): https://casetext.com/case/cypress-fairbanks-isd-v-michael-f

- Irving Independent School District v. Tatro, 468 U.S. 883 (1984): https://casetext.com/case/irving-independent-school-dist-v-tatro

- Oyez.com, recording of oral arguments in *Endrew F.*: https://www.oyez.org/cases/2016/15-827

- Polk v. Central Susquehanna Intermediate Unit 16, 853 F.2d 171 (3rd Cir. 1988): https://casetext.com/case/polk-v-ctl-susquehanna-intermediate-unit-16

- Ridley School District v. M. R. (2012), 680 F.3d 260 (3rd. Cir. 2012): https://casetext.com/case/ridley-sch-dist-v-mr-2

- SCOTUSblog entry on *Endrew F.*: http://www.scotusblog.com/case-files/cases/endrew-f-v-douglas-county-school-district/

- U.S. Department of Education's What Works Clearinghouse: https://ies.ed.gov/ncee/wwc/

- Winkleman v. Parma City School District, 550 U.S. 516 (2007): https://supreme.justia.com/cases/federal/us/550/516/

- Zero to Three: https://www.zerotothree.org/

RECOMMENDED READINGS

Articles

Crockett, T., Yell, M. L., Katsiyannis, A., & Collins, T. (2010). The U.S. Supreme Court and parental rights under the Individuals with Disabilities Act. *Focus on Exceptional Children, 43*, 1–16.

Rowley, A. J. (2008). Rowley revisited: A personal narrative. *Journal of Law and Education, 37*, 311–324.

Yell, M. L., & Bateman, D. F. (2017). *Endrew v. Douglas County* Supreme Court decision. *Teaching Exceptional Children, 50*(10), 7–15.

Yell, M. L., & Bateman, D. F. (2018). Free appropriate public education and *Endrew v. Douglas County School System* (2017): Implications for personnel preparation. *Journal of Teacher Education and Special Education, 41*, 1–12.

Yell, M. L., & Crockett, J. (2011). Free appropriate public education. In J. M. Kauffman & D. P. Hallahan (Eds.), *Handbook of special education* (pp. 70–90). Philadelphia, PA: Taylor & Francis/Routledge.

Yell, M. L., Katsiyannis, A., & Hazelkorn, M. (2007). Reflections on the 25th anniversary of the Supreme Court's decision in *Board of Education v. Rowley. Focus on Exceptional Children, 39*(9), 1–12.

Yell, M. L., & Rozalski, M. (2013). The peer-reviewed research requirement of the IDEA: An examination of law and policy. In B. G. Cook, M. Tankersley, & T. J. Landrum (Eds.), *Evidence-based strategies* (pp. 1–26). London, UK: Emerald.

Zirkel, P. A. (2013). Is it time for elevating the standard for FAPE under the IDEA? *Exceptional Children, 79*, 497–508.

Briefs, Practice Guides, and Reports

Simonsen, B., Freeman, J., Goodman, S., Mitchell, B., Swain-Bradway, J., Flannery, B., Sugai, G.... Putman, B. (2015). *Supporting and responding to behavior: Evidence-based classroom strategies for teachers.* Washington, DC: Office of Special Education Programs, U.S. Department of Education. Retrieved from https://www.osepideasthatwork .org/evidencebasedclassroomstrategies

U.S. Department of Education. (2016). *Dear colleague letter and resource guide on students with ADHD.* Washington, DC: Author. Retrieved from https://www2.ed.gov/about/offices/list/ocr/letters/ colleague-201607-504-adhd.pdf

U.S. Department of Education, Office of Special Education and Rehabilitative Services. (2016, December 28). *Frequently asked questions about the rights of students with disabilities in public charter schools under the Individuals with Disabilities Education Act.* Retrieved from https://sites.ed.gov/idea/files/ policy_speced_guid_idea_memosdcltrs_faq-idea -charter-school.pdf

PROFESSIONAL ORGANIZATIONS

Association for Positive Behavior Supports: http://www.apbs.org/

Center for Appropriate Dispute Resolution in Special Education: https://www.cadreworks.org

Council for Children With Behavioral Disorders: http://www.ccbd.net/home

Council for Exceptional Children: https://www.cec.sped.org/

Division for Early Childhood: http://www.dec-sped.org/

REFERENCES

Board of Education of the Hendrick Hudson Central School District v. Rowley, 458 U.S. 291 (1982).

Brief for the United States as amicus curia. (2016, August). Retrieved from http://www.scotusblog.com/wp-content/ uploads/2016/08/15-827-US-Amicus.pdf

Education Week. (2018). *Endrew F., by and through his parents and next friends, Joseph and Jennifer F. v. Douglas County School District RE-1.* Retrieved from http://blogs.edweek.org/edweek/speced/Endrew%20Order.pdf

Elementary and Secondary Education Act of 1965, 20 U.S.C. § 16301 *et seq.*

Endrew F. v. Douglas County School District RE-1, 798 F.3d. 1328 (2015).

Endrew F. v. Douglas County School District RE-1, 137 S.Ct. 988, 580 U.S. ___ (2017). Retrieved March 22, 2017, from http://www.supremecourt.gov/opinions/16pdf/15-827_0pm1.pdf

Individuals with Disabilities Education Act, 20 U.S.C. § 1400 *et seq.*

Petition for a Writ of Certiorari in Endrew F. v. Douglas County School District RE-1. (2015, December 22), Question presented by petitioner. Retrieved from http://www.scotusblog.com/wp-content/uploads/2016/05/15-827-Petition -for-Certiorari.pdf

Ridley School District v. M. R. (2012), 680 F.3d 260 (3rd. Cir. 2012).

Rowley v. Board of Education of the Hendrick Hudson Central School District, 632 F.2d 945 (2nd Cir. 1980).

School Committee of the Town of Burlington v. Massachusetts Department of Education, 471 U.S. 359 (1985).

Yell, M. L. (2019). *The law and special education* (5th ed.). Upper Saddle River, NJ: Pearson.

Yell, M. L., & Bateman, D. F. (2017). *Endrew F. v. Douglas County School District* (2017): Free appropriate public education and the U.S. Supreme Court. *Teaching Exceptional Children, 50,* 1–9.

Working With Parents

Meghan M. Burke and Samantha E. Goldman

This Chapter Will Cover:

1. Family–school partnerships, which are reciprocal relationships between families of children with disabilities and school professionals (strong family–school partnerships lead to positive outcomes for students and their families).

2. The principles of family–school partnerships: communication, commitment, equality, skills, trust, and respect.

3. Several barriers to family–school partnerships, including unequal power dynamics, poor professional skills, ineffective communication, an absence of respect, and a lack of trust.

4. Facilitated individualized education program (IEP) meetings, parent training, advocacy training, multitiered systems of support, and person–family interdependent planning, which may improve family–school partnerships.

5. The importance of including extended family members, being culturally responsive, looking beyond the IEP, and addressing teacher training in family–school partnerships.

As the foremost scholars in research about families of individuals with disabilities, Ann and Rud Turnbull ground their research in their personal experiences raising their son, Jay, who had a significant intellectual disability, autism, and an emotional–behavioral disorder. In his book *The Exceptional Life of Jay Turnbull* (2011), Rud Turnbull details the importance of family–professional partnerships per his own experience with Jay as well as through a research and policy lens. In summary, Rud Turnbull wrote, "We have concluded that the joy quotient is the ultimate measure of the work families and professionals do together for a person with a disability. The enviable life that Jay had, and that other families and individuals affected by disability should have, results from humane policy, its effective implementation, and partnerships among professionals, families, and community members" (p. 336). In this chapter, we use this quote to guide our discussion about family–school partnerships, recognizing that when strong family–school partnerships are present, individuals with disabilities are more likely to lead enviable lives.

Road Map for This Chapter

First, we introduce family–school partnership by describing its basic principles and the importance of building positive partnerships between families and schools. Then, we identify the barriers to fulfilling strong family–school partnerships. We next describe current practices to facilitate strong family–school partnerships. Finally, we conclude with directions for the future. At the end of the chapter, we recommend Internet resources, books, articles, and newsletters.

The Definition, Principles, and Importance of Family–School Partnerships

Definition

Family–school partnerships broadly refer to the reciprocal relationship between families of children with disabilities and school professionals. Specifically, families and school professionals should derive benefits from their partnership with each other. Ultimately, this partnership should lead to improved outcomes for children with disabilities (Turnbull, Turnbull, Erwin, Soodak, & Shogren, 2015). Further, especially given the increasing diversity in the United States, family–school partnerships must be culturally responsive.

Principles

The term *family–school partnership* may mean different things to various people. To operationalize family–professional partnerships, Blue-Banning, Summers, Frankland, Nelson, and Beegle (2004) conducted 33 focus groups and 33 interviews with parents of individuals with and without disabilities, service providers, and administrators. They identified six principles of family–professional partnerships: communication, commitment, equality, skills, trust, and respect. See Table 4.1 for more information about each principle.

Importance

Both policy and research demonstrate the importance of family–school partnerships. Regarding the former, the Individuals with Disabilities Education Act (IDEA, the federal special education law), along with other policies, strongly encourages family–school partnerships. Indeed, IDEA mandates parent involvement via rights and safeguards for parents, such as participating in meetings, reviewing school records, obtaining an independent evaluation, denying consent or disagreeing with decisions, and resolving disputes using mediation or due process (IDEA, 2004). Further, decades of research have demonstrated the positive impact of family–school partnerships on

Table 4.1   Definitions and Examples of the Indicators of Family–School Partnerships

Principle	Definition	Example
Communication	Parents and professionals should engage in positive, accessible, and respectful dialogue.	Having a daily log between the parent and the school; sharing information about the child between the parent and the school
Commitment	Parents and professionals should be devoted to the child, especially with respect to promoting the goals of the child.	Being flexible about meeting times with the parent and the professionals; being willing to go "above and beyond" for the child
Equality	Parents and professionals should have equitable roles wherein each person feels equally valued in the partnership.	Using first names of the parents and professionals when communicating; making sure each person is allowed a seat at the table
Skills	Parents and professionals should have competence to work with the child with a disability.	Being willing to take time to work with the child to achieve his or her goals; individualizing support for the child
Trust	Parents and professionals must be able to count on each other.	Being reliable (i.e., doing what you say you will do); keeping the child safe
Respect	Parents and professionals must regard each other with high esteem.	Being cautious about overstepping boundaries; being open-minded

Source: Adapted from Blue-Banning, Summers, Frankland, Nelson, and Beegle (2004).

outcomes for students with disabilities, their families, and schools (see Table 4.2 on the next page).

Barriers to Fulfilling the Principles of Family–School Partnerships

Despite the numerous benefits of strong family–school partnerships provided in Table 4.2, often these partnerships are not realized (Connor & Cavendish, 2018). Several barriers prevent schools and families from building strong partnerships. These barriers typically relate to the following categories: unequal power dynamics, poor professional skills, ineffective bidirectional communication, an absence of respect, and a lack of trust between families and schools.

Unequal Power Dynamic

One commonly cited barrier to developing strong partnerships is an unequal power dynamic between parents and professionals (Zeitlin & Curcic, 2014).

Table 4.2	Research-Based Benefits of Family–School Partnerships for Students With Disabilities
Type of Outcome	**Strong family–school partnerships lead to . . .**
Student outcomes	• Improved academic achievement, appropriate behaviors and attendance (Bryan & Henry, 2012) • More appropriate placements of students with disabilities (Wolery, 1989) • Decreased likelihood of unsound educational programming (Fish, 2008)
School outcomes	• Less conflict with families (Burke & Goldman, 2015; Mueller, Singer, & Draper, 2008) • Greater parent satisfaction with the IEP (Slade, Eisenhower, Carter, & Blacher, 2018) and with collaboration with the school (LaBarbera, 2017) • Reduced conflict resolution expenses (Mueller, 2009)
Family outcomes	• Reduced maternal stress (Burke & Hodapp, 2014) • Improved family quality of life (Wang et al., 2004) • Improved maternal parenting efficacy (Benson, 2015)

In the context of individualized education program (IEP) meetings specifically, there is a clear imbalance of power between parents and school personnel (Childre & Chambers, 2005; Williams, 2007). Parents report feeling excluded from decision making and experience many barriers to their participation as equal members of the IEP team (Mueller & Buckley, 2014). During IEP meetings, parents may be overwhelmed by the excessive amounts of paperwork as well as the legal jargon commonly used by educators (Zeitlin & Curcic, 2014). Even when parents attempt to overcome these barriers by learning about the special education process, they are further challenged by systemic barriers (Fish, 2008). For example, all parents must be provided with an explanation of their rights under IDEA, called procedural safeguards. However, documents that are given to parents of students with disabilities to describe these safeguards are written, on average, at a college graduate reading level (Mandic, Rudd, Hehir, & Acevedo-Garcia, 2010). Although intended to explain parents' rights in the special education process, inaccessible procedural safeguards create further barriers to equal family–school partnerships.

Lack of Professional Skills to Partner With Families

Unfortunately, many teachers are unprepared to overcome systemic barriers. Teachers may struggle to forge relationships with families due to a lack of teacher preparation relating to the skills (e.g., fostering bidirectional communication) required for effectively partnering with families (Lawson, Alameda-Lawson, Lawson, Briar-Lawson, & Wilcox, 2014; Martinez, Conroy, & Cerreto, 2012). Teachers report feeling unskilled at working with families; specifically, research has shown that teachers are not prepared with the skills, dispositions, and knowledge they need to promote partnerships with families (Ratcliff & Hunt, 2009).

Poor Communication

Parents frequently cite lack of communication with teachers as a barrier to partnerships. Parents report being the passive recipients of information rather than active participants in bidirectional communication. Further, communication from the school is often deficit-focused or provided in response to problem behavior (Osher & Osher, 2002), rather than the school finding opportunities to share positive information about student accomplishments. Such poor-quality, infrequent, deficit-focused communication may negatively impact family–school partnerships.

Lack of Respect

Parents also report a lack of respect between families and schools. A lack of respect may be demonstrated both from families toward school professionals (Burke et al., 2018) and from school professionals toward families (Simon, 2006; Soodak & Erwin, 2000). Regarding the former, school professionals report that they understand the need for parents to advocate on behalf of their children with disabilities (Burke et al., 2018). However, school professionals also report that parents should advocate in assertive (not aggressive) ways. Regarding the latter, families often report feeling disrespected by school professionals. Such disrespect can occur in nonintentional ways. For example, parents report that school professionals come late to IEP meetings and/or do not attend the entire IEP meeting; this is disrespectful to parents. Also, parents report that school professionals often refer to parents as "Mom" or "Dad" instead of using their names; this often makes parents feel relegated to nonprofessional roles (Burke, 2012).

Absence of Trust

A lack of trust between families and the school exists for several reasons. First, parents may bring with them a historical distrust of the school (Harry, 2002; Soodak & Erwin, 2000). Additionally, a lack of trust in professionals may generalize from distrust with other systems (e.g., the medical system, early intervention) to the school system (Summers et al., 2005). Past negative experiences with service delivery systems along with a historical distrust of schools may cause parents to generalize their distrust to the current school; such trust must be earned back by schools over time.

Parents may also lack trust in schools due to concerns about teachers' preparedness to meet the students' needs (Brownell, Sindelar, Kiely, & Danielson, 2010). Parents express concern about whether teachers have the information to understand their child's needs, strengths, likes, and dislikes (Friesen & Huff, 1990). Further, when school teams disagree with families and refuse to provide requested services, this leads to more distrust (Burke et al., 2018). Unfortunately, when such trust is lost, it is difficult to regain and is damaging to the family–school partnership.

Practices to Support Family–School Partnerships

Although there are many barriers to fulfilling strong family–school partnerships, several promising practices can help facilitate and sustain productive partnerships across school contexts. These include the use of facilitated IEP (FIEP) meetings, parent training, advocacy training, multitiered systems of support (MTSS), and person–family interdependent planning.

Facilitated IEPs

One practice that has promise for sustaining collaborative partnerships is the use of FIEP meetings. This involves the use of a trained, neutral facilitator who is requested by the family or school to assist during an IEP meeting. The facilitator creates an agenda, states ground rules, guides the discussion to promote communication and collaboration for all team members, clarifies issues to help with problem solving, keeps the team on task, and uses a "parking lot" to note any ideas for later discussion that do not match the focus of the meeting (Mueller, 2009). Typically, an FIEP meeting is used when the family or school is aware of a potential source of conflict and proactively requests a facilitator to avoid escalation of a disagreement (Mason & Goldman, 2017). Thus, the FIEP is an example of an alternative dispute resolution practice that may help avoid the need for more formal dispute resolution practices (i.e., due process complaint and hearing).

As of 2016, FIEP was available to schools and families in 36 states (Center for Appropriate Dispute Resolution in Special Education, 2016). Although state-to-state variations exist, data collected by states that use FIEP have shown it to be effective in reaching full or partial agreement on the IEP in the large majority of cases (Goldman & Mason, 2018; Mason & Goldman, 2017). Though additional research is needed to establish the long-term efficacy of this practice compared with other dispute resolution procedures, FIEP holds promise and is recommended for inclusion in the next reauthorization of IDEA (Pudelski, 2016).

Parent Training

When IDEA was passed in 1975, Congress acknowledged that parents would need training and support to become advocates for their offspring with disabilities. Accordingly, Congress began funding Parent Training and Information Centers (PTIs). With at least one PTI in every state in the country, PTIs are missioned with educating and empowering parents of children (aged 0–26) with disabilities about their special education rights. PTIs are also missioned with helping parents and schools build collaborative partnerships. To execute their mission, PTIs provide information and referral assistance, special education rights trainings, and individualized assistance. In 2012, PTIs served more than 665,529 parents of children with disabilities (National Parent Technical Assistance Center, 2012). Notably, PTIs are especially purposed with reaching out to traditionally underserved families (e.g., culturally and linguistically diverse [CLD] families). To this end, in

2012, 27% of the families served by PTIs were CLD families (National Parent Technical Assistance Center, 2012).

Little research has been conducted about the effectiveness of PTIs. Of the limited extant research, Barton (1999) conducted focus groups with parents who either worked at a PTI or received support from a PTI. Participants reported that the PTI helped them feel more empowered and educated to share their perspectives and advocate for services in IEP meetings. Similarly, in a pre/post survey study of 44 parents of children with disabilities who received assistance from a PTI, participants demonstrated significant increases in empowerment, special education knowledge, and satisfaction with services (Burke, 2016). Notably, minority and low-income families reported the greatest increases.

Advocacy Training

In addition to PTIs, parents may also seek special education advocates to assist them in accessing services and collaborating with the school. Within the past decade, advocacy trainings have become more common (Burke, 2013). The purpose of advocacy training is to develop individuals who are knowledgeable about special education and demonstrate advocacy skills to assist families of children with disabilities in accessing appropriate educational services. Advocacy trainings range with respect to duration, content, and format. For example, the Special Education Advocate Training (SEAT, conducted by the Council of Parent Attorneys and Advocates) comprises 115 hours of classroom instruction and at least 40 hours of a practicum or field experience with an advocate and/or attorney. The SEAT is offered via a web-based curriculum. In comparison, the Volunteer Advocacy Project (VAP) comprises 36 hours of instruction and is offered both in person and via simultaneous webcasting. Although both trainings develop special education advocates, there are dramatic differences in their length and format (Burke, 2013).

Given the recency of the emergence of advocacy trainings, there is little data demonstrating their effectiveness. For the VAP, extant research has shown that VAP advocates demonstrate significant increases in knowledge and advocacy skills after completing the training (Burke, Mello, & Goldman, 2016) and go on to advocate, pro bono, for families of children with disabilities (Goldman, Burke, Mason, & Hodapp, 2017). Further, the VAP is feasible given its low cost, high attendance and low attrition, and positive participant satisfaction (Burke, Mello, & Goldman, 2016). More research is needed to determine the effect of advocacy trainings on student outcomes and family–school partnerships.

Multitiered Systems of Support

Originating in the field of public health, MTSS uses preventive strategies with increasing levels of intensity across three tiers of supports. This framework has been adapted for education and special education and is commonly applied in school settings to promote academic outcomes (i.e., response to intervention [RTI]) and student behavior (i.e., positive behavior supports

[PBS]; Sugai & Horner, 2009). Within an MTSS framework, family–school partnership is considered to be an important factor for implementation (Garbacz, Witte, & Houck, 2017).

As shown in Figure 4.1, families can be included in many ways across the three tiers of support in systems such as PBS or RTI. However, an MTSS framework can also be used to conceptualize supports that may be provided by schools to promote family–school partnerships based on a family's level of need (Muscott et al., 2008). To do so, schools should create a school-wide plan for building partnership and delineate differentiated strategies for families in need of more intensive supports (Minch, Kincaid, Tremaine, & Thomas, 2017). A universal level of support for family–school partnerships may include common practices such as clear communication (e.g., newsletters that delineate school expectations), providing basic resources to parents, and informing parents about available community services (Lewis, Mitchell, Horner, & Sugai, 2017). However, some families will need more targeted forms of support in addition to this foundational, comprehensive system of supports for family–school partnership (see Figure 4.1). An even smaller proportion of families will require the most intensive, individualized

Figure 4.1   Practices to Promote Parent-School Partnerships Within Multitiered Systems of Support

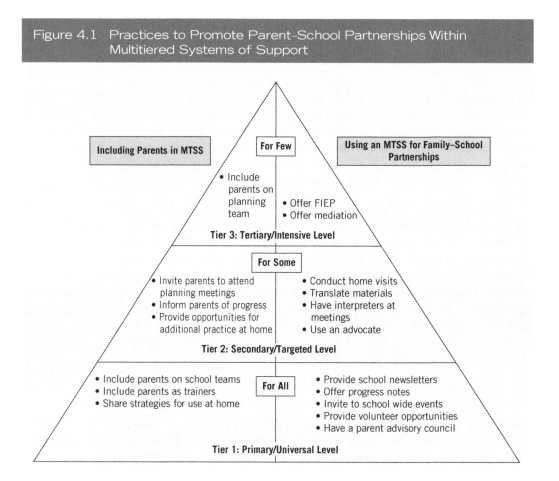

Sources: Modified from Engiles, Hebdon, Rauscher, and Wiley (2015) and Lewis, Mitchell, Horner, and Sugai (2017).

supports to build a strong partnership with the school. By including families and addressing their needs using MTSS, schools meet families at their respective levels of need to promote effective family–school partnerships for all.

Person–Family Interdependent Planning

As students with disabilities plan to transition from school services to adult services, there is a strong emphasis on person-centered planning. However, the family (and, correspondingly, family–school partnership) continues to be important. Indeed, for transition planning to be successful, it is crucial to have family input (Neece, Kraemer, & Blacher, 2009). One way to balance person-centered planning with family involvement is person–family interdependent planning, wherein the individual and the family jointly identify services and goals for the individual with a disability (Kim & Turnbull, 2004). Person–family interdependent planning acknowledges that the transition out of school impacts both the individual with a disability and the family. Also, it highlights that, for individuals with more significant disabilities, ongoing support from the family may be needed to facilitate self-determination (Jordan & Dunlap, 2001).

Unfortunately, few studies have used the person–family interdependent planning framework. In one of the few studies, Heller, Miller, and Factor (1997) created and tested a future planning intervention among adults with intellectual and developmental disabilities. Specifically, they included the individual with a disability and his or her family (i.e., parent and siblings) in the intervention, recognizing that future planning requires the involvement of the individual and relevant family members. Other transition interventions are increasingly recognizing the need to include both the individual and the family (e.g., Taylor, Hodapp, Burke, Waitz-Kudla, & Rabideau, 2017). However, more research is needed to determine how to best include all relevant stakeholders, including how to leverage family–school partnerships within this framework.

Directions for the Future

A recurring theme in this chapter is the need for additional research about families of individuals with disabilities and how professionals can best work with families. Specifically, we believe there are four next steps for research and practice: (1) expanding the definition of *family*, (2) being culturally responsive, (3) looking beyond the IEP, and (4) improving teacher training.

Expanding the Definition of *Family*

To date, most family research has focused only on mothers of children with disabilities (Burke, Patton, & Taylor, 2016). Yet researchers and professionals must recognize that there are family members other than mothers who are critical to include in partnerships. Every family constellation is different (e.g., stepparents, foster families), and families may have different primary or shared caregivers for the child with a disability (e.g., grandparents). Also, given that siblings often fulfill future caregiving roles for their brothers and sisters with intellectual and developmental disabilities (Burke, Taylor, Urbano, & Hodapp, 2012), they should also be included in research and practice. To these ends, we hope to see an increasing focus in research and practice about working with different family members. Moving forward, it is crucial to expand beyond our focus on traditional family structures and mothers as primary caregivers.

Being Culturally Responsive

Although most students with disabilities reflect CLD backgrounds (Office of Special Education Programs, 2013), there continues to be a need for more culturally responsive practices at schools. Most special education teachers do not represent CLD backgrounds (Clifford et al., 2005); relatedly, teachers struggle to collaborate with CLD families (Wolfe & Durán, 2013). Lack of knowledge may be another reason why schools engage in culturally insensitive practices (Jung, 2011) and perceive culturally diverse families as passive and uninvolved (Kalyanpur & Harry, 1997). For example, CLD parents are often relegated to listening roles when working with professionals. Put simply, barriers to family–school partnerships tend to be exacerbated among CLD families.

To these ends, we hope to see research and practice become more culturally responsive. Fortunately, we are not without some guidance here. For example, with respect to Latino families of individuals with intellectual disabilities, Magaña (2000) outlined several ways to make research more culturally responsive in relation to the development of a study, participant recruitment, measures, data collection, and analysis. School leaders and special education staff may also benefit from Magaña's suggestions especially when conducting program evaluation. Additionally, Bal and Trainor (2016) developed a rubric to help researchers conduct culturally responsive intervention studies, and other researchers have developed models for guiding culturally responsive instruction (e.g., Cartledge & Kourea, 2008). Thus, tools exist to help school leaders and staff conduct culturally responsive practices. Additionally, increasingly advocacy trainings are targeting CLD families. For example, Jamison and colleagues (2017) developed a family peer advocacy model for African American and Latino caregivers of children with autism spectrum disorder. Moving forward, we should use such tools, programs, and research guidance to ensure cultural responsiveness for families.

Going Beyond IEPs

When considering family involvement in special education, there is also a need to look beyond the IEP meeting and focus on other activities that relate to family–school partnerships (Burke, 2012). Although there is a vast body of research connecting parent involvement to positive student outcomes for students without disabilities (Jeynes, 2007; Nye, Turner, & Schwartz, 2006), research on parent involvement interventions for students with disabilities focuses primarily on increasing parent participation in IEP meetings

(Goldman & Burke, 2017). The activities that are important for parents of individuals without disabilities, such as strong communication, volunteering at school, and including parents in decision making (Epstein, 2001), should also be encouraged for parents of students with disabilities. See Table 4.3 for suggested practices to promote family–school partnerships.

Table 4.3   Suggested Practices for Addressing Barriers Across School Contexts

Barrier	In IEP Meetings	Beyond IEP Meetings
Unequal power dynamic	• Use a special education advocate, as needed. • Sit at a round table so all individuals can see one another. • Remind parents of their right to bring anyone who knows the student and his or her needs. • Write procedural safeguards notices at an accessible reading level. • Share draft IEPs and evaluations with families before the meeting. • Encourage parents to take the IEP home to review it before asking them to sign the IEP. • Ask parents for feedback about the format and structure of the IEP meeting.	• Ask parents to be on school teams. • Request parent feedback informally and in a variety of ways. • Hold parent trainings at the school. • Host a parent support group at the school.
Poor teacher training	• Conduct mock IEP meetings in teacher preparation programs. • Require teachers to attend IEP meetings during student teaching.	• Use family panels in classes. • Have parents co-teach classes. • Simulate parent–teacher conferences. • Offer a course on working with families. • Provide in-service trainings about working with families. • Encourage teachers to attend a special education rights training at a PTI.
Ineffective communication	• Use an experienced facilitator. • Share meeting notes/minutes. • Use a "parking lot" (i.e., an area to write down for later discussion issues that come up during a meeting). • Ask structured and individualized questions for parents to answer. • Be strength-based (versus deficit-focused). • Prompt parents with questions to consider before the meeting.	• Provide communication in the format that is preferred by the parent. • Use bidirectional communication journals. • Call/e-mail/text a parent to report a student accomplishment. • Call parents noncontingently to check in about their concerns every month. • When reporting negative information, always offer some positive information. • Provide frequent progress monitoring.

(Continued)

Table 4.3 (Continued)

Lack of respect	• Schedule meetings at times that are convenient for parents. • Arrive on time and attend the whole meeting. • Refer to parents by their names (not "Mom" or "Dad").	• Ask parents about their child. • Recognize that parents are experts about their children. • Include parents in all decision making.
Lack of trust	• Use a facilitator. • Document the receipt of services for the parent. • Demonstrate knowledge of the child's needs, strengths, likes, and dislikes. • Answer and justify the response to provide or decline to provide requested services.	• Invite parents to spend time in the classroom. • Connect parents with a school/community liaison or advocate. • Connect with parents at community events (e.g., after-school programs). • Build relationships with other caregivers and family members.

Teacher Training

To address some of the many barriers to effective family–school partnerships, teacher preparation programs must work to remedy this issue directly. Most teachers report that working with families is their greatest weakness and their teacher preparation programs did not teach them how to collaborate with families (Lawson et al., 2014; Martinez et al., 2012). Further, teachers' abilities to promote partnership and engage families directly predicts parents' actual levels of involvement (Walker & Dotger, 2012). Therefore, revising teacher preparation programs to explicitly teach and evaluate these skills could have a direct, positive impact on family–school partnerships (Gerich, Trittel, & Schmitz, 2017; Walker & Dotger, 2012).

In addition to teacher preparation programs, in-service programs can also help develop teachers' skills for collaborating with families. For example, such programs can include parents of individuals with disabilities as co-teachers along with course instructors. In this way, the principles of family–school partnership can be embedded throughout the program. Additionally, programs can use role-playing scenarios and conduct mock IEP meetings (Mueller, 2013). In these training situations, teacher participants can practice using family-centered strategies during IEP meetings and other interactions with families. Recent research suggests that mock IEP meetings and role-play scenarios may increase the use of family-friendly strategies in IEP meetings (e.g., Holdren et al., 2016).

Conclusion

In addition to the practices discussed in this chapter and the suggested future directions for research and practice related to family–school partnerships, there are several resources available to professionals in learning how to partner with families. Some of these resources relate to practices and organizations mentioned in this chapter (e.g., PTIs) while additional resources are also suggested. For example, along with a PTI, every state has a Protection and Advocacy (P&A) agency, which provides legal assistance about special education. In the concluding sections of this chapter, we suggest various types of resources.

REFLECTING AND UNDERSTANDING

1. What is the definition of family–school partnerships?

2. Describe one or two principles of family–school partnerships and related practices.

3. Name two or three barriers to family–school partnerships.

4. Identify two or three practices to improve family–school partnerships.

5. Name two or three resources about family–school partnerships.

ONLINE RESOURCES

- How to find your Parent Training and Information Center: http://www.parentcenterhub.org/find-your-center/

- How to find your Protection and Advocacy (P&A) agency: http://www.ndrn.org/about/paacap-network.html

- Iris Center module about collaborating with families: https://iris.peabody.vanderbilt.edu/module/fam/

- PACER Center for parent training and information resources: http://www.pacer.org/

- Positive Behavioral Interventions and Supports website on families: https://www.pbis.org/family

RECOMMENDED READINGS

Book

Turnbull, A. P., Turnbull, H. R., Erwin, E. J., Soodak, L. J., & Shogren, K. A. (2015). *Families, professionals, and exceptionality: Positive outcomes through partnerships and trust* (7th ed.). New York, NY: Pearson.

Articles

Bal, A., & Trainor, A. A. (2016). Culturally responsive experimental intervention studies: The development of a rubric for paradigm expansions. *Review of Educational Research, 86,* 319–359.

Blue-Banning, M., Summers, J. A., Frankland, H. C., Nelson, L.L., & Beegle, G. (2004). Dimensions of family and professional partnerships: Constructive guidelines for consideration. *Exceptional Children, 70,* 167–184.

Magaña, S. M. (2000). Mental retardation research methods in Latino communities. *Mental Retardation, 38*(4), 303.

NEWSLETTERS, ORGANIZATIONS, AND EVENTS

Join the newsletter of your state PTI.

Join the list-serve of your statewide P&A.

Join the Council for Exceptional Children organization.

Attend the Center for Appropriate Dispute Resolution in Special Education conference.

REFERENCES

Bal, A., & Trainor, A. A. (2016). Culturally responsive experimental intervention studies: The development of a rubric for paradigm expansions. *Review of Educational Research, 86*, 319–359.

Barton, E. L. (1999). Informational and interactional functions of slogans and sayings in the discourse of a support group. *Discourse & Society, 10*, 461–486.

Benson, P. R. (2015). Longitudinal effects of educational involvement on parent and family functioning among mothers of children with ASD. *Research in Autism Spectrum Disorders, 11*, 42–55.

Blue-Banning, M., Summers, J. A., Frankland, H. C., Nelson, L. L., & Beegle, G. (2004). Dimensions of family and professional partnerships: Constructive guidelines for collaboration. *Exceptional Children, 70*, 167–184.

Brownell, M. T., Sindelar, P. T., Kiely, M. T., & Danielson, L. C. (2010). Special education teacher quality and preparation: Exposing foundations, constructing a new model. *Exceptional Children, 76*, 357–377.

Bryan, J., & Henry, L. (2012). A model for building school–family–community partnerships: Principles and process. *Journal of Counseling and Development, 90*(4), 408–420.

Burke, M. M. (2012). Examining family involvement in regular and special education: Lessons to be learned from both sides. *International Review of Research in Developmental Disabilities, 43*, 187–218.

Burke, M. M. (2013). Improving parental involvement: Training special education advocates. *Journal of Disability Policy Studies, 23*, 225–234.

Burke, M. M. (2016). Effectiveness of parent training activities on parents of children with intellectual or developmental disabilities: Empowerment, knowledge, and satisfaction with services. *Research and Practice in Intellectual and Developmental Disabilities, 3*, 85–93.

Burke, M. M., & Goldman, S. E. (2015). Identifying the associated factors of mediation and due process in families of students with autism spectrum disorder. *Journal of Autism and Developmental Disorders, 45*, 1345–1353.

Burke, M. M., & Hodapp, R. M. (2014). Relating stress of mothers of children with developmental disabilities to family–school partnerships. *Intellectual and Developmental Disabilities, 52*, 13–23.

Burke, M. M., Meadan-Kaplansky, H., Patton, K. A., Pearson, J. N., Cummings, K. P., & Lee, C. (2018). Advocacy for children with social-communication needs: Perspectives from parents and school professionals. *Journal of Special Education, 51*, 191–200.

Burke, M. M., Mello, M. P., & Goldman, S. E. (2016). Examining the feasibility of a special education advocacy training. *Journal of Developmental and Physical Disabilities, 28*, 539–556.

Burke, M. M., Patton, K. A., & Taylor, J. L. (2016). Family support: A literature review of families of adolescents with disabilities. *Journal of Family Social Work, 19*, 252–285.

Burke, M. M., Taylor, J. L., Urbano, R. C., & Hodapp, R. M. (2012). Predictors of future caregiving by siblings of individuals with intellectual and developmental disabilities. *American Journal on Intellectual and Developmental Disabilities, 117*, 33–47.

Cartledge, G., & Kourea, L. (2008). Culturally responsive classrooms for culturally diverse students with and at risk for disabilities. *Exceptional Children, 74*, 351–371.

Center for Appropriate Dispute Resolution in Special Education. (2016). *Trends in dispute resolution under Individuals with Disabilities Education Act.* Retrieved from http://www.cadreworks.org/sites/default/files/resources/TrendsinDisputeResolutionundertheIDEAOCT16.pdf

Childre, A., & Chambers, C. R. (2005). Family perceptions of student centered planning and IEP meetings. *Education and Training in Developmental Disabilities, 5*, 217–233.

Clifford, R. M., Barbarin, O., Chang, F., Early, D. M., Bryant, D., Howes, C., Burchinal, M., & Pianta, R. (2005). What is prekindergarten? Characteristics of public prekindergarten program. *Applied Developmental Science, 9*, 126–143.

Connor, D. J., & Cavendish, W. (2018). Sharing power with parents: Improving educational decision making for students with learning disabilities. *Learning Disability Quarterly, 41*(2), 79–84.

Engiles, A., Hebdon, H., Rauscher, K., & Wiley, J. (2015, October). *Moving toward systemic, integrated, responsive, and sustainable family engagement approaches.* Symposium conducted at the meeting of the Consortium for Alternative Dispute Resolution, Eugene, Oregon.

Epstein, J. L. (2001). *School, family, and community partnerships: Preparing educators and improving schools.* Boulder, CO: Westview Press.

Fish, W. W. (2008). The IEP meeting: Perceptions of parents of students who receive special education services. *Preventing School Failure, 53,* 8–14.

Friesen, B. J., & Huff, B. (1990). Parents and professionals as advocacy partners. *Preventing School Failure, 34,* 31–39.

Garbacz, S. A., Witte, A. L., & Houck, S. N. (2017). Family engagement foundations: Supporting children and families. In M. Weist, S. Garbacz, K. Lane, & D. Kincaid (Eds.), *Aligning and integrating family engagement in positive behavioral interventions and supports* (pp. 9–30). Center for Positive Behavioral Interventions and Supports. Eugene: University of Oregon Press.

Gerich, M., Trittel, M., & Schmitz, B. (2017). Improving prospective teachers' counseling competence in parent–teacher talks: Effects of training and feedback. *Journal of Educational and Psychological Consultation, 27,* 203–238.

Goldman, S. E., & Burke, M. M. (2017). The effectiveness of interventions to increase parent involvement in special education: A systematic literature review and meta-analysis. *Exceptionality: A Special Education Journal, 25,* 97–115.

Goldman, S. E., Burke, M. M., Mason, C. Q., & Hodapp, R. M. (2017). Correlates of sustained volunteering: Advocacy for students with disabilities. *Exceptionality: A Special Education Journal, 25,* 40–53.

Goldman, S. E., & Mason, C. Q. (2018). Predictors of participant perceptions of facilitated individualized education program meeting success. *Journal of Disability Policy Studies, 29,* 43–53.

Harry, B. (2002). Trends and issues in serving culturally diverse families of children with disabilities. *Journal of Special Education, 36,* 132–140.

Heller, T., Miller, A. B., & Factor, A. (1997). Adults with mental retardation as supports to their parents: Effects on parental caregiving appraisal. *Mental Retardation, 35*(5), 338–346.

Holdren, N. O., Singer, G. H. S., McIntosh, S., Oliver, K., O'Neil, M., & Wood, L. (2016). *A teacher's role in facilitating meaningful parent participation in IEP meetings.* Presentation at TASH, St. Louis, Missouri.

Individuals with Disabilities Education Act, 20 U.S.C. 1400, *et seq.* (2004).

Jamison, J. M., Fourie, E., Siper, P. M., Trelles, M. P., George-Jones., J., Buxbaum Grice, A., Krata, J.... Kolevzon, A. (2017). Examining the efficacy of a family peer advocate model for Black and Hispanic caregivers of children with autism spectrum disorder. *Journal of Autism and Developmental Disorders, 47,* 1314–1322.

Jeynes, W. H. (2007). The relationship between parental involvement and urban secondary school student academic achievement. *Urban Education, 42,* 82–110.

Jordan, B., & Dunlap, G. (2001). Construction of adulthood and disability. *Mental Retardation, 39,* 286–296.

Jung, A. W. (2011). Individualized education programs (IEPs) and barriers for parents from culturally and linguistically diverse backgrounds. *Multicultural Education, 19*(3), 21–25.

Kalyanpur, M., & Harry, B. (1997). A posture of reciprocity: A practical approach to collaboration between professionals and parents of culturally diverse backgrounds. *Journal of Child and Family Studies, 6,* 487–509.

Kim, K., & Turnbull, A. P. (2004). Transition to adulthood for students with severe intellectual disabilities: Shifting toward person–family interdependent planning. *Research and Practice for Persons With Severe Disabilities, 29,* 53–57.

LaBarbera, R. (2017). A comparison of teacher and caregiver perspectives of collaboration in the education of students with autism spectrum disorders. *Teacher Education Quarterly, 44,* 35–56.

Lawson, H. A., Alameda-Lawson, T., Lawson, M. A., Briar-Lawson, K. H., & Wilcox, K. C. (2014). Three parent and family interventions for rural schools and communities. *Journal of Education and Human Development, 3*(3), 59–78.

Lewis, T. J., Mitchell, B. S., Horner, R., & Sugai, G. (2017). Engaging families through school-wide positive behavior support: Building partnerships across multi-tiered systems of support. In M. Weist, S. Garbacz, K. Lane, & D. Kincaid (Eds.), *Aligning and integrating family engagement in positive behavioral interventions and supports* (pp. 31–42). Center for Positive Behavioral Interventions and Supports. Eugene: University of Oregon Press.

Magaña, S. M. (2000). Mental retardation research methods in Latino communities. *Mental Retardation, 38*(4), 303.

Mandic, C. G., Rudd, R., Hehir, T., & Acevedo-Garcia, D. (2010). Readability of special education procedural safeguards. *Journal of Special Education, 30*, 1–9.

Martinez, D. C., Conroy, J. W., & Cerreto, M. C. (2012). Parent involvement in the transition process of children with intellectual disabilities: The influence of inclusion on parent desires and expectations for postsecondary education. *Journal of Policy and Practice in Intellectual Disabilities, 9*(4), 279–288.

Mason, C. Q., & Goldman, S. E. (2017). Facilitated individualized education planning: The state of implementation and evaluation. *Journal of Disability Policy Studies, 27*, 212–222.

Minch, D., Kincaid, D., Tremaine, V., & Thomas, R. (2017). Translating family engagement strategies to practice in local sites implementing PBIS. In M. Weist, S. Garbacz, K. Lane, & D. Kincaid (Eds.), *Aligning and integrating family engagement in positive behavioral interventions and supports* (pp. 43–70). Center for Positive Behavioral Interventions and Supports. Eugene: University of Oregon Press.

Mueller, T. G. (2009). IEP facilitation: A promising approach to resolving conflicts between families and schools. *Teaching Exceptional Children, 41*, 60–67.

Mueller, T. G. (2013). *Moving research to practice: Lessons learned regarding meaningful home–school collaboration.* Webinar for CADRE.

Mueller, T. G., & Buckley, P. C. (2014). The odd man out: How fathers navigate the special education system. *Remedial and Special Education, 35*(1), 40–49.

Mueller, T. M., Singer, G. H. S., & Draper, L. M. (2008). Reducing parental dissatisfaction with special education in two school districts: Implementing conflict prevention and alternative dispute resolution. *Journal of Educational and Psychological Consultation, 18*, 191–233.

Muscott, H. S., Szcesiul, S., Berk, B., Staub, K., Hoover, J., & Perry-Chisholm, P. (2008). Creating home–school partnerships by engaging families in schoolwide positive behavior supports. *Teaching Exceptional Children, 40*, 6–14.

National Parent Technical Assistance Center. (2012). *Parent centers helping families.* Newark, NJ: Author.

Neece, C. L., Kraemer, B. R., & Blacher, J. (2009). Transition satisfaction and family well-being among parents of young adults with severe intellectual disability. *Intellectual and Developmental Disabilities, 47*, 31–43.

Nye, C., Turner, H., & Schwartz, J. (2006). Approaches to parent involvement for improving the academic performance of elementary school age children. *Campbell Systematic Reviews, 4.*

Office of Special Education Programs. (2013). *37th annual report to Congress.* Washington, DC: Author.

Osher, T., & Osher, D. (2002). The paradigm shift to true collaboration with families. *Journal of Child and Family Studies, 11*, 47–60.

Pudelski, S. (2016). Rethinking special education due process: A proposal for the next reauthorization of the Individuals with Disabilities Education Act. *American Association of School Administrators.* Retrieved from http://www.aasa.org/uploadedFiles/Policy_and_Advocacy/Public_Policy_Resources/Special_Education/AASARethinkingSpecialEdDueProcess.pdf

Ratcliff, N., & Hunt, G. (2009). Building teacher–family partnerships: The role of teacher preparation programs. *Education, 129*, 495–506.

Simon, J. B. (2006). Perceptions of the IEP requirement. *Teacher Education and Special Education, 29*, 225–235.

Slade, N., Eisenhower, A., Carter, A. S., & Blacher, J. (2018). Satisfaction with individualized education programs among parents of young children with ASD. *Exceptional Children, 84,* 242–260.

Soodak, L. C., & Erwin, E. J. (2000). Valued member or tolerated participant: Parents' experiences in inclusive early childhood settings. *Journal of the Association for Persons With Severe Handicaps, 25,* 29–41.

Sugai, G., & Horner, R. (2009). Responsiveness-to-intervention and school-wide positive behavior supports: Integration of multi-tiered system approaches. *Exceptionality: A Special Education Journal, 17,* 223–237.

Summers, J. A., Hoffman, L., Marquis, J., Turnbull, A. P., Poston, D., & Nelson, L. L. (2005). Measuring the quality of family–professional partnerships in special education services. *Exceptional Children, 72,* 65–83.

Taylor, J. L., Hodapp, R. M., Burke, M. M., Waitz-Kudla, S. N., & Rabideau, C. (2017). Training parents of youth with autism spectrum disorder to advocate for adult disability services: Results from a pilot randomized controlled trial. *Journal of Autism and Developmental Disorders, 47,* 846–857.

Turnbull, A., Turnbull, H. R., Erwin, E. J., Soodak, L. C., & Shogren, K. A. (2015). *Families, professionals, and exceptionality* (7th ed.). Boston, MA: Pearson.

Turnbull, H. R. (2011). *The exceptional life of Jay Turnbull: Disability and dignity in America 1967–2009.* Amherst, MA: White Poppy Press.

Walker, J. M., & Dotger, B. H. (2012). Because wisdom can't be told: Using comparison of simulated parent–teacher conferences to assess teacher candidates' readiness for family–school partnership. *Journal of Teacher Education, 63,* 62–75.

Wang, M. P., Turnbull, A. P., Summers, J. A., Little, T. J., Poston, D., Mannan, H., & Turnbull, H. R. (2004). Severity of disability and income as predictors of parents' satisfaction with their family quality of life during early childhood years. *Research and Practice for Persons With Severe Disabilities, 29*(2), 82–94.

Williams, E. R. (2007). Unnecessary and unjustified: African-American parental perceptions of special education. *Educational Forum, 71,* 250–261.

Wolery, M. (1989). Transitions in early childhood special education: Issues and procedures. *Focus on Exceptional Children, 22*(2), 1–16.

Wolfe, K., & Durán, L. K. (2013). Culturally and linguistically diverse parents' perceptions of the IEP process: A review of current research. *Multiple Voices for Ethnically Diverse Exceptional Learners, 13,* 4–18.

Zeitlin, V. M., & Curcic, S. (2014). Parental voices on individualized education programs: 'Oh, IEP meeting tomorrow? Rum tonight!' *Disability & Society, 29*(3), 373–387.

Transition is not a linear process, for it must take into account the wide variation in the development of adolescents and their particular needs for long-range planning and services. Interpretation of laws in our federal system is subject to wide variation among the states, and therefore transition services look very different in communities across the nation.

—Kochhar-Bryant and Greene (2009)

Current Special Education Legal Trends for Transition-Age Youth

Angela M. T. Prince, Anthony J. Plotner, and June E. Gothberg

This Chapter Will Cover:

1. Details for children who qualify for special education services are entitled to postsecondary transition planning and services, when to begin them, and how long to continue them.

2. Clarity on what transition services are and whom the district should invite to the meetings if a purpose of the meeting will be the consideration of the postsecondary goals for the child, and the transition services needed to assist the child in reaching those goals (Sec. 300.321 [b][1]).

3. How an IEP team can develop proper, measurable postsecondary goals based on age-appropriate transition assessments related to training, education, employment, and, where applicable, independent living skills (Section 300.320[b][1]).

4. The importance of a public agency providing the child with a summary of the child's academic achievement and functional performance that includes recommendations on how to assist the child in meeting the child's postsecondary goals (300.305[e][3]) so he or she can secure assistance at the next level after exiting high school.

The primary purpose of the Individuals with Disabilities Education Act (IDEA) is to ensure that all children with disabilities have available to them a free appropriate public education that emphasizes special education and related services designed to meet their unique needs and prepare them for further education, employment, and independent living (300.1[a]). To this end, students with disabilities in public school are entitled to transition planning and services beginning no later than their 16th birthday. These coordinated services are intended to increase the successful postschool outcomes in postsecondary education or training, employment, and independent living. Recent litigation has been decided on cases that include both the rights of the student with the disability and rights of parents in participating in the transition planning process.

Transitioning from high school to adult life is one of the most challenging times for all youth; however, this step to adulthood presents additional demands for individuals with disabilities (Plotner, Oertle, Reed, Tissot, & Kumpiene, 2017). Most youth with disabilities have the same aspirations as their nondisabled peers—a chance to engage in

Key Terms

- individualized postsecondary goals
- rights of transition-age youth and their families
- postsecondary transition planning
- summary of performance
- transition assessment

employment, go to college, live in a safe and comfortable home, and have meaningful opportunities to participate and contribute to their community (Carter, 2012). The area of secondary transition education and services for youth with disabilities has received much attention in the past three decades (Gothberg, Greene, & Kohler, 2018). Unfortunately, findings from the National Longitudinal Transition Study-2 (NLTS2) found that youth with disabilities continue to lag behind their peers without disabilities in important postschool outcomes (Newman, Wagner, Cameto, & Knokey, 2009; Wagner, Newman, & Javitz, 2014). Research shows that effective transition planning for youth with disabilities is critical to achieving positive postschool outcomes for these individuals in the areas of postsecondary education and training, employment, and independent living (Test et al., 2009). The most recent reauthorization of IDEA (20 U.S.C. §1400 *et seq.*) addresses this through policy, with the focus shifted to a results-based orientation seeking to improve postsecondary results for students with disabilities (Gaumer Erickson, Noonan, Brussow, & Gilpin, 2014). This reauthorization clarified that the purpose of education for students with disabilities is to *prepare* students for life after high school (Gothberg, Peterson, Peak, & Sedeghat, 2015). Specifically,

> the purpose of IDEA is to ensure that all children with disabilities have available to them a free appropriate public education (FAPE) that emphasizes special education and related services designed to meet their unique needs and prepare them for further education, employment, and independent living. (20 USC 1400, § 601[d][1][A])

Prior to IDEA, many children with disabilities either were denied entry into public school, were placed in segregated settings, or were in regular classrooms without adequate support for their needs (Katsiyannis, Yell, & Bradley, 2001), thereby denying FAPE.

Under the current mandate, the individualized education program (IEP) for each child with a disability must address transition services requirements beginning no later than the first IEP, to go into effect when the child turns 16, or younger if determined appropriate by the IEP team, and must be updated annually thereafter. The IEP must include (a) appropriate measurable postsecondary goals based on age-appropriate transition assessments related to training, education, employment, and, where appropriate, independent living skills and (b) the transition services (including courses of study) needed to assist the student with a disability in reaching those goals. Federal funding for research and technical assistance has helped uncover the most effective practices for providing transition education and services. The National Technical Assistance Center on Transition (NTACT, 2018) has identified 20 predictors for postschool success and more than 100 classroom-based practices. NTACT uses the Taxonomy for Transition Programming 2.0 (the Taxonomy; Kohler, Gothberg, Fowler, & Coyle, 2016) as a framework, with the predictors and practices grouped under five main areas: (a) student-focused planning, (b) student development, (c) interagency collaboration, (d) family engagement, and (e) program structures. Recently, international experts in the areas of juvenile reentry representing Africa, Australia, Canada, Finland, Japan, New Zealand, Slovenia, the United Kingdom, and the United States upheld the *Taxonomy* as one of the most effective tools for implementing successful reentry of incarcerated youth back into their communities (O'Neill, 2018).

Providing FAPE for children with disabilities, however, remains a controversial issue (McLaughlin, 2010). The first statutory interpretation of FAPE for students with disabilities was handed down by the U.S. Supreme Court in *Hendrick Hudson Central School District Board of Education v. Rowley* (1982). In this landmark case, the Court held that the Act guaranteed a substantively adequate program that is "reasonably calculated to enable the child to receive educational benefits." Further, the Court issued a two-part test for courts to use in determining whether a school has met its FAPE obligations under IDEA.

When applying part one, a court must determine if a school district has adhered to the procedural requirements of the IDEA. When applying part two, a court must determine if a student's IEP was designed to confer educational benefit (Prince, Plotner, & Yell, 2014). *Rowley* is known as the case that established a "some benefit" or "floor of opportunity" standard for the services a school must provide to students with disabilities (Weber, 2012, p. 1). For 35 years, *Rowley* has stood as the defining case whenever considerations of FAPE for students with disabilities have come before various courts, as well as broadly impacting the field of education law in general (Mead & Paige, 2008).

On March 22, 2017, the U.S. Supreme Court issued the first statutory interpretation of FAPE for students with disabilities since *Rowley*, making it one of the most significant special education cases to reach the High Court in three decades. In a unanimous decision in *Endrew F. v. Douglas Country School District* (2017; hereafter *Endrew F.*), the Court ruled that IEPs must give student with disabilities more than a de minimis, or minimal, educational benefit. The decision by the Court sets precedence for a more uniform stand of services under IDEA. Chief Justice John G. Roberts, writing for a unanimous Court, stated,

> When all is said and done, a student offered an educational program providing "merely more than *de minimis*" progress from year to year can hardly be said to have been offered an education at all. For children with disabilities, receiving instruction that aims so low would be tantamount to "sitting idly … awaiting the time when they were old enough to 'drop out.'" (*Endrew F.*, 2017, p. 14)

This reinforces one of the primary purposes of IDEA: to *prepare* children with disabilities to lead productive lives as independent adults to the greatest extent possible (20 U.S.C. § 1400[c][5][A][ii]).

Provision of Transition Planning and Services

Based on the need to prepare youth with disabilities for successful post-school life, a transition component was included for the first time in the IEPs of eligible students with disabilities in 1990. With further reauthorizations of the act in 1997 and 2004, IDEA continued to improve transition services for eligible students with disabilities.

IDEA defines transition services as follows:

(a) Transition services means a coordinated set of activities for a child with a disability that—(1) Is designed to be within a results-oriented process, that is focused on improving the academic and functional achievement of the child with a disability to facilitate the child's movement from school to post-school activities, including postsecondary education, vocational education, integrated employment (including supported employment), continuing and adult education, adult services, independent living, or community participation; (2) Is based on the individual child's needs, taking into account the child's strengths, preferences, and interests; and includes— (i) Instruction; (ii) Related services; (iii) Community experiences; (iv) The development of employment and other post-school adult living objectives; and (v) If appropriate, acquisition of daily living skills and provision of a functional vocational evaluation. (IDEA Regulations 34 C.F.R. § 300.43[a])

Whereas legal requirements related to the student's age when transition planning must take place have changed over time, the last reauthorization of IDEA requires that transition services begin no later than when the student is 16 years old, or younger if determined by a student's IEP team (IDEA regulations 34 C.F.R. § 300.320[b]). Considering the benefits of earlier transition planning, many states (e.g., South Carolina) require that this process begin at a younger age (McConnell, Martin, & Hennessey, 2015; Yell, Delport, Plotner, Petcu, & Prince, 2015).

IEP Team

IDEA specifies that, at a minimum, the transition-age child's IEP team must include (a) parents of the child, (b) special education teacher, (c) general education teacher, (d) a qualified representative of the public agency, (e) an individual who is qualified to interpret evaluation results and their instructional implications (may be an existing member of the team), and (f) other individuals, at the discretion of the parents or the agency, who have knowledge or expertise related to the child (300.321[a]). In addition, a student must be invited to participate in the IEP meeting when transition services are being determined (U.S. Department of Education, 2017). The school district bears the responsibility to ensure that required participants attend the IEP meeting; however, it is obligated to ensure that representatives of outside agencies attend IEP meetings (Wright, Wright, & O'Connor, 2010) if the child's parent consents.

Transition Service Planning and Implementation

IDEA specifies three major requirements in transition service planning and implementation: (a) age-appropriate transition assessments related to training, education, employment, and, where appropriate, independent living skills; (b) appropriate measurable postsecondary goals updated annually based on the assessments; and (c) transition services that include courses of study designed to assist the student in reaching those goals (Burton, 2017). To ensure that the schools comply with these requirements, the U.S. Department of Education established the State Performance Plan, Annual Performance Reports special education performance indicators. Indicator 13 was established and became effective with the 2010 data collection in regard to quality IEPs, measuring certain requirements of compliance for transition planning (Gothberg, Kohler, & Coyle, 2016). Specifically, the indicator requires

> [p]ercent of youth aged 16 and above with an individualized education program (IEP) that includes appropriate measurable postsecondary goals that are annually updated and based on age appropriate transition assessment, transition services, including courses of study, that will reasonably enable the student to meet those postsecondary goals, and annual IEP goals related to the student's transition service needs. There must also be evidence that the student was invited to the IEP team meeting where transition services are to be discussed and evidence that, if appropriate, a representative of any participating agency was invited to the IEP Team meeting with the prior consent of the parent or student who has reached the age of majority. (20 U.S.C. 1416[a][3][B])

Age-Appropriate Transition Assessments

While IDEA requires age-appropriate transition assessment, it does not provide a definition for it. That being the case, federal policy guidance has indicated that the definition provided by the Division of Career Development and Transition (DCDT) of the Council for Exceptional Children serve as the official definition (Walker, Kortering, Fowler, Rowe, & Bethune, 2016). DCDT defines transition assessment as an "ongoing process of collecting data on the individual's needs, preferences, and interests as they relate to the demands of current and future working, educational, living, and personal and social environments" (Sitlington, Neubert, & LeConte, 1997, pp. 70–71). Transition assessments determine the present levels of student's academic achievement and functional performance and form the basis for defining goals and services in the IEP.

Appropriate Measurable Postsecondary Goals

While IDEA requires "appropriate measurable postsecondary goals based upon age-appropriate transition assessments related to training, education, employment, and, where appropriate, independent living skills"

(§ 300.320b), again, it does not provide a definition. Supporting guidance on determining if an IEP is compliant under Indicator 13 only questions where the goals occur after the student graduates from school and, based on the information available on the student's present levels of performance, whether the goals seem appropriate or misaligned. O'Leary (2008) suggests that postsecondary goals are outcome statements that specify what the student will do, when, and to what extent. Peterson et al. (2013) suggests that postsecondary goals serve as "the litmus test for evaluating the relevance of every other component of the plan" (p. 49). Thus, transition-age students' annual IEP goals must align with their postsecondary goals (Test, Aspel, & Everson, 2006). That is, each postsecondary goal should have at least one transition goal, indicating specific skills that the student needs to achieve the postsecondary goals (NTACT, 2018). After the student has graduated with a regular high school diploma or exceeded the mandatory age limit to receive services under IDEA, a school has no further obligations to measure the student's progress toward achieving his or her goals; however, it has to provide the student with a summary of performance statement (U.S. Department of Education, 2017).

Transition Activities and Services

IDEA defines transition services as a coordinated set of activities that help improve academic and functional achievement of a transition-age student with a disability and facilitate successful movement to postschool activities, including alignment of the student's course of study with the postsecondary and annual IEP goals (Kochhar-Bryant, 2008; Test et al., 2006). According to IDEA's definition of transition services, the educational program of a transition-age child should address the following transition activity areas: (a) instruction (e.g., reading, math); (b) related services (e.g., speech and language, occupational, and physical therapies); (c) community experiences (e.g., leisure skills, transportation); (d) employment (e.g., job search); (e) postschool adult living (i.e., choice making, goal setting, and advocacy); (f) daily living skills (e.g., cooking, dressing); and (g) functional vocational evaluation (e.g., work samples, situational assessments) (IDEA Regulation 34 C.F.R. § 43[a]). Other transition services can be included, if the transition team establishes that they are necessary to provide a FAPE for an eligible student. The student's transition IEP must also indicate the roles of people responsible for implementing transition services—which people and/or which transition statement that encompasses a coordinated set of activities (Test et al., 2006).

Summary of Performance

Upon transition-age students' graduation with a regular high school diploma or aging out and, therefore, termination of eligibility for the special education services, the IEP team should provide them with a Summary of Performance (SOP). The SOP must include (a) a summary of a student's academic achievement, (b) a summary of a student's functional performance, and (c) recommendations on how to assist a student in meeting his or her postsecondary goals (IDEA Regulations 34 C.F.R. §. 300.305[e][3]). When a student graduates with a general educational development (GED) diploma or alternate diploma but has not exceeded the mandatory age limit to receive services under IDEA, a SOP is not mandated because these documents do not terminate a student's eligibility under IDEA (IDEA Regulations, 34 C.F.R. § 300.102[a][3][iv]). A SOP does not automatically ensure qualification for services or accommodations after leaving high school; however, it may be helpful in determining eligibility for accommodations (U.S. Department of Education, 2017).

Although providing a FAPE is the cornerstone of IDEA, it has been a challenging and often litigious endeavor. According to IDEA, "as the graduation rates for children with disabilities continue to climb, providing effective transition services to promote successful post-school employment or education is an important measure of accountability for children with disabilities" (Section 601[14]). This emphasis on postschool outcomes as a measure of accountability was specifically addressed in the 1990 and subsequent amendments to IDEA.

Despite the emphasis on transition, many students with disabilities continue to experience unfavorable secondary and postsecondary outcomes. Often, students with disabilities experience academic and behavioral challenges while in high school that seem to negatively impact successful school completion. In 2014–2015, 45.2% of students with disabilities ages 14 through 21 who exited school graduated with a regular high school diploma and 11.8% aged out (U.S. Department of Education, 2017). Further, students with disabilities were twice as likely to be excluded from school for disciplinary reasons than were their same-age peers in 2013–2014 (U.S. Department of Education, 2016).

Successful postschool outcomes for students with disabilities are significantly lower than for their nondisabled peers in virtually every category (Kellems, Springer, Wilkins, & Anderson, 2016): Postsecondary education, employment, and independent living opportunities lag while incarceration rates rise (see McFarland, Cui, & Stark, 2018; Wagner et al., 2006). Becoming involved with the criminal justice system is more prevalent among young adults with disabilities than young adults in the general population (Sanford et al., 2011). Additionally, findings from the NLTS2 found that young adults with disabilities who had been out of high school for up to 8 years were less likely than their nondisabled peers to enroll in postsecondary education (60% vs. 67%), earned less than peers per hour ($10.40 vs. $11.40), and were less likely to live independently (45% vs. 59%).

Federal transition policy is distinguished by efforts to validate effective transition interventions and to ground transition policies and practices in rigorous research (Kohler et al., 2016; Morningstar, Bassett, Cashman, Kochhar-Bryant, & Wehmeyer, 2012; Test et al., 2009). A review of the literature has identified 20 in-school predictors of postschool outcomes in the areas of education, employment, and independent living (NTACT, 2016). The use of evidence-based and promising practices (EBPPs) has become a focus in education since the No Child Left Behind Act of 2001 and IDEA in 2004. The recent reauthorization of the Elementary and Secondary Education Act, now referred to as the Every Student Succeeds Act (ESSA), goes farther, replacing No Child Left Behind's requirement to use *scientifically based research* as the foundation for education programs and interventions with the ESSA requirement to implement *evidence-based interventions* that have proven effective at producing results and improving outcomes when implemented.

To assist students and youth with disabilities to achieve their postschool and career goals, Congress enacted two key statutes that address the provision of transition services: IDEA and the Rehabilitation Act of 1973, as amended by Title IV of the Workforce Innovation and Opportunity Act. IDEA is administered by the Office of Special Education Programs (OSEP), and Titles I, III, and VI, Section 509, and Chapter 2 of Title VII of the Rehabilitation Act are administered by the Rehabilitation Services Administration (RSA). OSEP and RSA provide oversight and guidance regarding the administration and provision of transition services by state education agencies (SEAs), local educational agencies, and state vocational rehabilitation (VR) agencies (U.S. Department of Education, 2017). The focus of this chapter is primarily on the transition planning and services related to IDEA and recent decisions based on these statutes; however, this chapter is not intended to be an exhaustive review of recent decisions.

Courts have often held that procedural violations do not deny FAPE unless they result in a substantial deprivation of a student's or parents' rights. Courts have applied that general principle in connection with the procedural requirements for transition planning. For instance, IDEA does not specify that the transition plan must be a separate document. Rather, two cases at the appellate court level found the opposite: The entire IEP was viewed as having provided adequate transition services and was agreed on during properly convened and conducted IEP meetings (*Chuhran v. Walled Lake Consolidated Schools*, 1993/1995; *Urban ex rel. Urban v. Jefferson County Sch. Dist. R-1*, 1996).

Regardless of a student's ability level, he or she is entitled to receive transition services no later than his or her 16th birthday (34 C.F.R. §300.320[b]). SEAs may elect to begin planning prior to this, whether by implementing services for all students with disabilities or by assessing individual student need. State law may also provide alternative provisions of education (e.g., virtual school, charter school). In these circumstances, the alternate program—rather than the student's home-zoned school—becomes responsible for ensuring that the student receives FAPE, including postsecondary transition services (*Dutkevitch v. Pennsylvania Cyber Charter School*, 2012).

Transition services must be reasonably calculated to meet the student's needs, whether that includes graduating with a regular high school diploma or reaching the maximum age of services (34 CFR 300.102[a][3][ii]). Students who need a higher level of supports may require transition plans that emphasize the development of functional or independent living skills (*Dracut School Committee v. Bureau of Special Education Appeals*, 2010). Transition services, like other services included in the IEP, must be provided as written. If a district creates a transition plan as part of the student's IEP but fails to implement it, a denial of FAPE may occur.

Schools should review IDEA's procedural and substantive requirements with all relevant staff members to ensure they are providing FAPE. In *Department of Education, State of Hawaii, v. Patrick P., Gordean L.-W., and Thomas W.* (2012), the IEP team relied on postsecondary transition requirements found in the IDEA 1997 version of the law, depriving the student of educational opportunities. Similarly, in *Northwest Colorado Board of Cooperative Educational Services* (2014), the SEA denied FAPE when the general education teachers were not adequately prepared to support a student in reaching her postsecondary transition goals related to communication, self-advocacy, and peer interactions.

Rights of the Transition-Age Youth

IDEA requires that the IEP in effect when a student turns 16 include appropriate postsecondary transition goals and services (20 U.S.C. § 1414[I][B] [614][d][1][A][i][VIII], 2006) that are "based upon age appropriate transition assessments related to training, education, employment, and, where appropriate, independent living skills" (34 CFR 300.320[b][1]). Postsecondary goals should be based on transition assessments and reflect the youth's strengths, preferences, and interests. Failure to conduct transition assessments, lack of individualized vocational and career-based training, and postsecondary transition goals that do not match the student's course of study (e.g., participation in postsecondary education while placed on an occupational diploma track) may result in a denial of FAPE (*Jefferson County Board of Education v. Lolita S.*, 2014).

Transition Assessment

School districts are not relieved of their duty to provide meaningful transition assessment based on a student's ability level. Rather, the obligation remains to collect meaningful transition assessment data that reflect the student's skills and interests (*K. C. v. Mansfield Indp. Sch. Dist.*, 2009). *Gibson v. Forest Hills Local School District Board of Education* (2016; hereafter *Gibson*) was a monumental case at the appellate level. The U.S. Court of Appeals for the Sixth Circuit found that the school district disregarded their obligation to evaluate the student's postsecondary transition needs both in not providing transition-appropriate assessments and not inviting the student to attend an IEP meeting that included postsecondary transition planning and services (34 CFR 300.321[b][1]). Because the student did not attend the IEP team meeting, the district should have taken other steps to ensure that the child's preferences and interests were considered (34 CFR 300.321[b] [2]). In this case, the court ruled that a series of procedural errors amount to a substantive denial of FAPE, which entitled parents to an independent evaluation (transition assessments), compensatory transition services, and attorneys' fees.

Yet judicial rulings and administrative decisions vary widely as to what level of detail is required for postsecondary transition planning. At the appellate court level, recent decisions show variance in the rule of procedural and substantive errors in postsecondary transition planning. Eleven days after the *Gibson* ruling, the U.S. Court of Appeals for the Second Circuit acknowledged that the district's failure to document certain details about the student's postsecondary transition plan was problematic but did not amount to a denial of FAPE (*Douglas Public School*, 2010). The fact that the IEP did not specify the amount of time the student would spend on academic and vocational instruction and the mother's objection to the amount of time spent on vocational instruction did not warrant the district's having to pay for the student's unilateral private placement. The IEP team's discussion of annual goals and services did not negate the adequacy of the IEP, the student's progress on the IEP, or the parent's involvement in the process. Therefore, the district provided the student with a FAPE.

Individual Transition Plan

While it may help a district document its transition planning efforts, there is no requirement that the IEP contain a stand-alone transition plan (*M. Z. v. N.Y.C. Dep't of Educ.*, 2013). While some states have elected to make the transition plan an independent component within the IEP, the legal emphasis is progress toward postsecondary transition goals over time (*K. C. v. Mansfield Indp. Sch. Dist.*, 2009; *K. C. ex rel. Her Parents v. Nazareth Area School District*, 2011; *Rosinsky v. Green Bay Area School Dist.*, 2009). In the case of *Sebastian M. v. King Philip Regional School District and Massachusetts Department of Elementary and Secondary Education* (2011), the parents argued that a district denied their son FAPE because his IEP lacked a transition plan. However, the court held that the district complied, because Sebastian received transition services as outlined in the IEP.

While IDEA does not prohibit a district from including some uniform guidance on postsecondary transition planning for all students with a disability, a transition plan must also address a student's individual transition needs and offer services addressing those needs. In the unpublished opinion of *Rodrigues v. Fort Lee Board of Education* (2011), the student's IEP included a checklist for what seniors needed to accomplish to successfully transition. The IEP also provided the needed individualization, as the student's transition plan also included goals and services related to her personal college goals and social skills needs.

Summary of Performance

Finally, a student with a disability has a right to a completed SOP upon graduating with a regular high school diploma or aging out of eligibility (34 CFR 300.305[e][3]). The SOP is designed to help students identify their strengths, needs, and goals so they can secure assistance at the next level, whether in postsecondary education or employment. Each SOP must include information about the student's academic achievement and functional performance and recommendations on how to assist the child in meeting his or her postsecondary goals (71 Fed. Reg. 46,645, 2006).

Rights of the Family

Under IDEA 2004, parents and legal guardians have the right to examine education records, participate in IEP meetings, and be involved in placement decisions (34 CFR § 300.501) if their child has not reached the age of majority (34 CFR § 300.320[c]). However, parent involvement in the IEP does not mean that parent preferences rule in the process. Based on *J.D.G. v. Colonial School District* (2010), a district must consider parental input when developing an IEP but is not required to design the program based solely on a parent's view of his or her child's abilities. Similar decisions have been made at the state level (*Council Rock School District*, 2015; *Pocatello School District #25*, 2009; *Simi Valley Unified School District*, 2008).

Parent Participation

If transition services proposed by the IEP team included the areas of employment, education, and independent living, decisions more often supported the placement proposed by the IEP team, rather than the parent's preference. Conversely, if parents were impeded from participating in IEP meetings where transition planning was discussed, decisions sided in favor of the parents (*Carrie I. v. Department of Education, State of Hawaii*, 2012). School districts can ensure parental participation by inviting parents to IEP meetings, communicating with them formally and informally on a frequent basis, and allowing them to invite participants to the meetings (*Virgin Islands Department of Education, State Office of Special Education*, 2010). To the extent appropriate, with the consent of the parents or student who has reached the age of majority, the district must invite a representative of any participating agency that is likely to be responsible for providing or funding transition services (34 CFR 300.321[b][3]).

Recommendations for Transition Practices

IDEA requires that the IEP in effect when a student turns 16 include appropriate measurable postsecondary transition goals and services (20 U.S.C. § 1414[l][B][614][d], 2006), though states can elect to begin earlier. A transition plan must reflect the individual needs and interests of the student. While it may also include generic information, the more it focuses on the student's goals and service needs, the more likely it is to benefit the student and uphold the legal obligation. Regardless of the student's abilities, the student must be included in the transition planning process to the greatest extent possible. IEP teams may have to adapt the format of their meetings to accommodate student participation. At the very least, the legal standard of inviting the student to the meeting must be upheld (34 CFR 300.321[b]).

Endrew F. and Transition Planning

With the most recent Supreme Court decision in *Endrew F.*, supporting that de minimus is not enough, transition litigation regarding FAPE has the potential to grow exponentially. It is more important now than ever that schools not only focus on compliance with federal law but also on the spirit of IDEA of preparing youth for their future. Recent guidance from the U.S. Department of Education (2017) states,

There are a number of opportunities and programs available for students preparing to exit secondary school. Many of these education and training opportunities involve formal or informal connections between educational, VR, employment, training, social services, and health services agencies. Specifically, high schools, career centers, community colleges, four-year colleges and universities, and State technical colleges are key partners. These partners offer Federal, State, and local funds to assist a student preparing for postsecondary education. (p. 2)

With that in mind, it would be advantageous for schools to ensure IEPs are not only compliant but also individualized, of high quality, and legally defensible (Peterson et al., 2013). Further, school personnel and members of the transition planning team need to implement transition plans with integrity. As can be seen with the detailed reports in the cited litigation, too often students with disabilities and their families become frustrated with the lack of credible planning and follow-through. From the transition assessment phase to the implementation of the course of study, school personnel have a responsibility to each student. While the Court made it clear in *Rowley* that students with disabilities are not entitled to the "best" education has to offer, they do require more than the minimum. Through the reauthorizations of various acts, Congress has set the expectation that educational decisions need to be founded in EBPPs. It is a school's responsibility to ensure that transition education and services are based on effective practices backed by research and not on the status quo or anecdotal evidence. As more research is conducted to identify EBPPs associated with increased successful outcomes, these need to be reflected in every student's IEP.

IDEA is overdue for reauthorization. Since 2004, researchers have identified education practices that have increased the in-school and postschool success of students with disabilities (see Institute of Education Sciences, 2018; Kohler et al., 2016; Test et al., 2009). To date, NTACT has identified 20 predictors and more than 100 practices that met the rigor to be included as evidence-based or promising practices, which are included in the *Taxonomy for Transition Programming 2.0* (Kohler et al., 2016) and the *Transition Program Tool for State Capacity Building and Local Improvement Planning* (Kohler, Gothberg, & Coyle, 2017). NTACT holds annual national and state capacity-building institutes to assist interdisciplinary teams to conduct transition needs assessment at the program level and create comprehensive state capacity building and local improvement plans to increase the implementation of evidence-based transition practices. This innovative planning process has been shown to increase interagency collaboration and improve outcomes for youth with disabilities in the areas of dropout prevention, graduation, and postschool outcomes (Gothberg, Bukaty, & Kohler, 2018). This new knowledge needs to inform updates to federal policy. In addition, much has been learned through targeted, individualized instruction and services provided through multitiered systems of support (MTSS) that schools across the country implement with all students. MTSS combined with universal design for learning delivered in whole-school reform efforts has shown promise for creating increased equity in inclusive settings (Sailor, 2016). These advancements in education for students with disabilities lay a foundation for Congress as they move to reauthorize IDEA once again.

Conclusion

Despite the Supreme Court's unanimous decision in *Endrew F.* interpreting the scope of the FAPE requirements in IDEA as more than de minimis, emphasizing that every child be offered the chance to meet challenging objectives, little has changed in the year since the decision (Zirkel, 2018). The U.S. Department of Education (2017) recommended that SEAs "review policies, procedures, and practices to provide support and appropriate guidance to school districts and IEP Teams to ensure that IEP goals are appropriately ambitious and that all children have the opportunity to meet challenging objectives" (p. 8). Further, the department advised that a school, to meet its substantive obligation under IDEA, must "offer an IEP reasonably calculated to enable a child to make progress appropriate in light of the child's circumstances and expressly rejected the merely more than *de minimis*, or trivial progress standard" (p. 9). It identified that IEP teams must

> implement policies, procedures, and practices relating to (1) identifying present levels of academic achievement and functional performance; (2) the setting of measurable annual goals, including academic and functional goals; and (3) how a child's progress toward meeting annual goals will be measured and reported, so that the Endrew F. standard is met for each individual child with a disability. Separately, IEP Teams and other school personnel should be able to demonstrate that, consistent with the provisions in the child's IEP, they are providing special education and related services and supplementary aids and services; making program modifications; providing supports for school personnel; and allowing for appropriate accommodations that are reasonably calculated to enable a child to make progress appropriate in light of the child's circumstances and enable the child to have the chance to meet challenging objectives. (p. 9)

Thus, it is our recommendation that Congress act, uphold the decision, and provide further clarity to the reauthorization. In accordance, state and local education agencies need to ensure that youth with IEPs are supported and reasonably challenged throughout the transition process with the provision of EBPPs. Finally, an *appropriate* education is one that supports youth with disabilities so they receive substantive educational benefits as determined by measures applicable to all students and have the support needed to successfully transition into adult life.

REFLECTING AND UNDERSTANDING

1. Why is postsecondary transition planning important?

2. What are the three major requirements in transition service planning and implementation specified in IDEA?

3. What are the federal requirements for transition assessment?

4. When should outside agencies be invited to an IEP meeting?

5. List and describe the three components that must be included in the summary of performance.

6. Describe parents' rights in the secondary transition and planning process for their child with a disability.

ONLINE RESOURCES

- Center for Parent Information and Resources: http://www.parentcenterhub.org/transitionadult/

- National Council on Disability: https://ncd.gov/publications

- National Parent Center on Transition and Employment (PACER): http://www.pacer.org/transition/learning-center/laws/

- National Technical Assistance Center on Transition (NTACT): https://www.transitionta.org/sites/default/files/dataanalysis/Transition_Indicators_101_Final.pdf

- Topic brief, Secondary Transition: https://sites.ed.gov/idea/files/postsecondary-transition-guide-may-2017.pdf

- Transition Coalition: https://transitioncoalition.org/blog/tc-materials/workforce-innovation-and-opportunity-act-brief-tips-for-transition/

- U.S. Department of Education: https://www2.ed.gov/policy/landing.jhtml?src=pn

- U.S. Department of Labor: https://www.dol.gov/general/topic/disability/laws

- Wrights Law: http://www.wrightslaw.com/info/trans.index.htm

RECOMMENDED READINGS

Books

Johnson, D. R., Thurlow, M. L., & Schuelka, M. J. (2012). *Diploma options, graduation requirements, and exit exams for youth with disabilities: 2011 national study* (Technical Report 62). Minneapolis: University of Minnesota, National Center on Educational Outcomes.

Kohler, P. D., Gothberg, J. E., Fowler, C., Coyle, J. (2016). *Taxonomy for transition programming 2.0: A model for planning, organizing, and evaluating transition education, services, and programs.* Kalamazoo: Western Michigan University.

Articles

Petcu, S. D., Yell, M. L., Cholewicki, J. M., & Plotner, A. J. (2014). Issues of policy and law in transition services: Implications for special education leaders. *Journal of Special Education Leadership, 27*, 66–75.

Prince, A. M. T., Katsiyannis, A., & Farmer, J. (2013). Postsecondary transition under IDEA 2004: A legal update. *Intervention of School and Clinic, 48*, 286–293. doi:10.1177/1053451212472233

Prince, A. M. T., Plotner, A. J., & Yell, M. L. (2014). Postsecondary transition and the courts: An update. *Journal of Disability Policy Studies, 25*(1), 41–47. doi:10.1177/1044207314530469

Yell, M. L., Delport, J., Plotner, A., Petcu, S., & Prince, A. M. T. (2015). Providing transition services: An analysis of law and policy. In B. G. Cook, M. Tankersley, & T. J. Landrum (Eds.), *Transition of youth and young adults* (pp. 63–87). Bingley, UK: Emerald Group.

Zirkel, P. A. (2018). An analysis of the judicial rulings for transition services under the IDEA. *Career Development and Transition for Exceptional Individuals, 41*(3), 136–145.

PROFESSIONAL ORGANIZATIONS

CEC Division on Career Development and Transition: http://www.dcdt.org/

National Center on Secondary Education and Transition: http://www.ncset.org

National Technical Assistance Center on Transition (NTACT): https://transitionta.org

PACER's National Parent Center on Transition and Employment: http://www.pacer.org/transition

Think College: https://thinkcollege.net

Transition Coalition: https://transitioncoalition.org

REFERENCES

Burton, N. (2017). *Creating effective IEPs: A guide to development, writing, and implementing plans for teachers.* Thousand Oaks, CA: Sage.

Carrie I. v. Department of Education, State of Hawaii, 869 F.Supp.2d 1225, 1244-45 (D. Haw. 2012).

Carter, E. (2012). *Transition matters: Supporting the rigor, relevance, and reach of transition research* [Congressional Briefing]. Washington, DC.

Chuhran v. Walled Lake Consolidated Schools, 839 F. Supp. 465 (E.D. Mich. 1993), aff'd, 51 F.3d 271 (6th Cir. 1995).

Council Rock School District, 115 LRP 26443 (SEA PA, 2015).

Department of Education, State of Hawaii, v. Patrick P., Gordean L.-W., and Thomas W., 60 IDELR 6 (U.S. District Court, Hawaii, Nov. 5, 2012).

Douglas Public School, 110 LRP 68668 (SEA MA, 2010).

Dracut School Committee v. Bureau of Special Education Appeals, No. 09-10966 (1d Cir. Sept. 3, 2010).

Dutkevitch v. Pennsylvania Cyber Charter School, No. 12-1472 (3d Cir. Aug. 17, 2012).

Endrew F., a Minor, by and Through His Parents and Next Friends, Joseph F. et al. v. Douglas County School District RE–1, 64 IDELR 38, (D., Co. 2014), 580 U.S. ____ (2017).

Every Student Succeeds Act, Pub. L. No. 114-95 (2015).

Gaumer Erickson, A. S., Noonan, P. M., Brussow, J. A., & Gilpin, B. J. (2014). The impact of IDEA Indicator 13 compliance on postsecondary outcomes. *Career Development and Transition for Exceptional Individuals, 37,* 161–167.

Gibson v. Forest Hills Local School District Board of Education, No. 14-3834 (6th Cir. Jul. 15, 2016).

Gothberg, J. E., Bukaty, C., & Kohler, P. D. (2018, April). *School improvement: The correlation between strategic planning, technical soundness, and results.* Paper presented at the American Educational Research Association Conference, New York, NY.

Gothberg, J. E., Greene, G., & Kohler, P. D. (2018). District implementation of research-based practices for transition planning with culturally and linguistically diverse youth with disabilities and their families. *Career Development and Transition for Exceptional Individuals.* doi:10.1177/2165143418762794

Gothberg, J. E., Kohler, P. D., & Coyle, J. L. (2016). *The evaluation toolkit* (4th ed.). Kalamazoo, MI: NTACT.

Gothberg, J. E., Peterson, L., Peak, M., & Sedaghat, J. (2015). Successful transition of students with disabilities to 21st-century college and careers: Using triangulation and gap analysis to address nonacademic skills. *TEACHING Exceptional Children, 47,* 344–351. doi:10.1177/0040059915587890.

Hendrick Hudson Central School District Board of Education v. Rowley, 458 U.S. 176 (1982).

Individuals with Disabilities Education Improvement Act, P. L. 114-38, 20 U.S.C. § 1414 *et seq.* (2006).

Individuals with Disabilities Education Improvement Act Regulations, 34 C.F.R. §300 *et seq.* (2012).

Institute of Education Sciences. (2018). *What Works Clearinghouse.* Retrieved from https://ies.ed.gov/ncee/wwc/

J.D.G. v. Colonial School District, Civ. No. 09-502-SLR.

Jefferson County Board of Education v. Lolita S., No. 13-15170 (11th Cir. Sept. 11, 2014).

K. C. v. Mansfield Indp. Sch. Dist., 52 IDELR 103 (N.D. Tex. 2009).

K. C. ex rel. Her Parents v. Nazareth Area School District, 806 F. Supp. 2d 806, 822 (E.D. Pa. 2011).

Katsiyannis, A., Yell, M. L., & Bradley, R. (2001). Reflections on the 25th anniversary of the Individuals With Disabilities Education Act. *Remedial and Special Education, 22,* 324–334.

Kellems, R. O., Springer, B., Wilkins, M. K., & Anderson, C. (2016). Collaboration in transition assessment: School psychologists and special educations working together to improve outcomes for students with disabilities. *Preventing School Failure: Alternative Education for Children and Youth, 60,* 215–221.

Kochhar-Bryant, C. (2008). *Collaboration and system coordination for students with disabilities: From early years to postsecondary.* Columbus, OH: Merrill/Prentice Hall.

Kochhar-Bryant, C. A., & Greene, G. (2009). *Pathways to successful transition for youth with disabilities: A developmental process* (2nd ed.). Upper Saddle River, NJ: Pearson.

Kohler, P. D., Gothberg, J. E., & Coyle, J. (2017). *Transition program tool for state capacity building and local improvement planning.* Kalamazoo: Western Michigan University.

Kohler, P. D., Gothberg, J. E., Fowler, C., & Coyle, J. (2016). *Taxonomy for transition programming 2.0: A model for planning, organizing, and evaluating transition education, services, and programs.* Kalamazoo: Western Michigan University.

M. Z. v. N.Y.C. Dep't of Educ., 12-cv-4111, 2013 WL 1314992 (S.D.N.Y. Mar. 21, 2013).

McConnell, A., Martin, J., & Hennessey, M. (2015). Indicators of postsecondary employment and education for youth with disabilities in relation to GPA and general education. *Remedial and Special Education, 36,* 327–336.

McFarland, J., Cui, J., & Stark, P. (2018). *Trends in high school dropout and completion rates in the United States: 1972–2014* (NCES 2018-117). Washington, DC: National Center for Education Statistics.

McLaughlin, M. J. (2010). Evolving interpretations of educational equity and students with disabilities. *Exceptional Children, 76,* 265–278.

Mead, J. F., & Paige, M. A. (2008). Parents as advocates: Examining the history and evolution of parents' rights to advocate for children with disabilities under the IDEA. *Journal of Legislation, 34*(2), 123–167.

Morningstar, M. E., Bassett, D. S., Cashman, J., Kochhar-Bryant, C., & Wehmeyer, M. L. (2012). Aligning transition services with secondary education reform: A position statement of the Division on Career Development and Transition. *Career Development and Transition for Exceptional Individuals, 35*, 132–142.

National Technical Assistance Center on Transition. (2016). Predictors by outcome area. Retrieved from http://transitionta.org/sites/default/files/Pred_Outcomes_0.pdf

National Technical Assistance Center on Transition. (2018). *Effective practices and predictors matrix.* Retrieved from https://transitionta.org/epmatrix

Newman, L., Wagner, M., Cameto, R., & Knokey, A. M. (2009). *The post-high school outcomes of youth with disabilities up to 4 years after high school: A report of findings from the National Longitudinal Transition Study-2* (NCSER Report No. 2009-3017). Menlo Park, CA: SRI International. Retrieved from www.nlts2.org/reports/200904/nlts2report200904complete.pdf

No Child Left Behind Act of 2001, P.L. 107-110, 20 U.S.C. § 6319 (2002).

Northwest Colorado Board of Cooperative Educational Services, 114 LRP 28795 (SEA CO 2014).

O'Leary, E. (2008, April). *Developing and writing measurable postsecondary goals.* Presentation at the 28th Annual Texas Educational Diagnosticians' Association Conference, Waco, TX.

O'Neill, S. C. (Ed.). (2018). *Incarcerated youth transitioning back to the community.* Singapore: Springer Nature Singapore.

Peterson, L. Y., Burden, J. P., Sedaghat, J. M., Gothberg, J. E., Kohler, P. D., & Coyle, J. L. (2013). Triangulated IEP transition goals: Developing relevant and genuine annual goals. *Teaching Exceptional Children, 45*(6), 46–57.

Plotner, A. J., Oertle, K. M., Reed, G. J., Tissot, K., & Kumpiene, G. (2017). Centers for Independent Living and their involvement with transition-age youth with disabilities. *Journal of Vocational Rehabilitation, 46*, 39–48. doi:10.3233/JVR-160841

Pocatello School District #25, 109 LRP 75169 (Idaho State Educational Agency, 2009).

Prince, A. M. T., Plotner, A. J., & Yell, M. L. (2014). Postsecondary transition and the courts: An update. *Journal of Disability Policy Studies, 25*(1), 41–47. doi:10.1177/1044207314530469

Rodrigues v. Fort Lee Board of Education, No. 11-1467 (3d Cir. Sept. 9, 2011).

Rosinsky v. Green Bay Area School Dist., 667 F.Supp.2d 964, 991 (E.D. Wis. 2009).

Sailor, W. (2016). Equity as a basis for inclusive educational systems change. *Australasian Journal of Special Education,* 1–17. doi:10.1017/jse.2016.12

Sanford, C., Newman, L., Wagner, M., Cameto, R., Knokey, A. M., & Shaver, D. (2011). *The post-high school outcomes of young adults with disabilities up to 6 years after high school: Key findings from the National Longitudinal Transition Study-2 (NLTS2)* (NCSER 2011-3004). National Center for Special Education Research.

Sebastian M. v. King Philip Regional School District and Massachusetts Department of Elementary and Secondary Education, 774 F. Supp. 2d 393 (U.S. District Court, Massachusetts, 2011).

Simi Valley Unified School District, 50 IDELR 267 (California State Educational Agency, 2008).

Sitlington, P. L., Neubert, D. A., & Leconte, P. J. (1997). Transition assessment: The position of the Division on Career Development and Transition. *Career Development for Exceptional Individuals, 20*, 69–79.

Test, D. W., Aspel, N. P., & Everson, J. M. (2006). *Transition methods for youth with disabilities.* Upper Saddle River, NJ: Pearson.

Test, D. W., Mazzotti, V. L., Mustian, A. L., Fowler, C. H., Kortering, L., & Kohler, P. (2009). Evidence-based secondary transition predictors for improving postschool outcomes for students with disabilities. *Career Development for Exceptional Individuals, 32*(3), 160–181. doi:10.1177/0885728809346960

Urban ex rel. Urban v. Jefferson County Sch. Dist. R-1, 89 F.3d 720, 727 (10th Cir. 1996).

U.S. Department of Education. (2016). *38th annual report to Congress on the implementation of the Individuals with Disabilities Education Act, 2008.* Washington, DC: Office of Special Education and Rehabilitative Services, Office of Special Education Programs. Retrieved from https://www2.ed.gov/about/reports/annual/osep/2016/parts-b-c/38th-arc-for-idea.pdf

U.S. Department of Education, Office of Special Education and Rehabilitative Services. (2017). *A transition guide to postsecondary education and employment for students and youth with disabilities,* Washington, DC. Retrieved from https://sites.ed.gov/idea/idea-files/significant-policy-guidance-a-transition-guide-to-postsecondary-education-and-employment-for-students-and-youth-with-disabilities/

Virgin Islands Department of Education, State Office of Special Education, 110 LRP 49154 (Virgin Islands State Educational Agency, 2010).

Wagner, M., Friend, M., Bursuck, W. D., Kutash, K., Duchnowski, A. J., Sumi, W. C., & Epstein, M. (2006). Educating students with emotional disturbances: A national perspective on school programs and services. *Journal of Emotional and Behavior Disorders, 14,* 12–30.

Wagner, M. M., Newman, L. A., & Javitz, H. S. (2014). The influence of family socioeconomic status on the post–high school outcomes of youth with disabilities. *Career Development and Transition for Exceptional Individuals, 37,* 5–17.

Walker, A. R., Kortering, L. J., Fowler, C. H., Rowe, D., & Bethune, L. (2016). *Age appropriate transition assessment toolkit* (4th ed.). Charlotte, NC: NTACT.

Weber, M. C. (2012). Common-law interpretation of appropriate education: The road not taken in Rowley. *Journal of Law and Education, 41,* 95–128.

Wright, P. W. D., Wright, P. D., & O'Connor, S. W. (2010). *Wrightslaw: All about IEPs.* Deltaville, VA: Harbor House Law Press.

Yell, M. L., Delport, J., Plotner, A., Petcu, S., & Prince, A. M. T. (2015). Providing transition services: An analysis of law and policy. In B. G. Cook, M. Tankersley, & T. J. Landrum (Eds.), *Transition of youth and young adults* (pp. 63–87). Bingley, UK: Emerald Group.

Zirkel, P. A. (2018). An analysis of the judicial rulings for transition services under the IDEA. *Career Development and Transition for Exceptional Individuals, 41*(3), 136–145.

A right delayed is a right denied.

—Martin Luther King, Jr.

6

Discipline and Students With Disabilities

Kelly M. Carrero, Kimberly J. Vannest, and Courtney Lavadia

This Chapter Will Cover:

1. The protections students with disabilities have under federal law.
2. Why students with disabilities, particularly those from racially diverse backgrounds, are disproportionately subjected to exclusionary discipline.
3. The best practices for decreasing exclusionary discipline—such as aversive consequences (e.g., seclusion, restraint, corporal punishment), which are punitive practices often used as disciplinary responses to students with disabilities who commit behavioral infractions—and how to move toward restorative practices and positive behavioral interventions and supports.
4. Why functional behavior assessment and a behavioral intervention plan are the best ways to prevent and respond to challenging behaviors for students with disabilities.

Public education in America is predicated on the belief that it prepares the next generation of the nation's citizens to be active and innovative participants in our democracy and our workforce. American educators create microcosms for students to safely learn and explore social, moral, and intellectual principles determined valuable and necessary for participation in society. When students violate social norms or threaten safety in and around the school, discipline is administered by the teacher and, in more severe circumstances, the principal. When the appropriate response is not predetermined (i.e., discretion is needed), teachers and administrators identify and administer disciplinary sanctions that align with their personal values and best judgment (Kennedy, Murphy, & Jordan, 2017). However, when a student with a disability violates the student code of conduct and, more important, threatens the safety of the learning environment, many variables must be considered before delivering disciplinary sanctions. This chapter will present (a) legal foundations and legislative protections for disciplining students with disabilities, (b) controversial issues in discipline for students with disabilities, and (c) trends and best practices for making disciplinary decisions and proactively addressing challenging behaviors of students with disabilities.

Foundational Principles Within the Legal Framework Related to Discipline

Despite the vision and fortitude of Horace Mann's "common school agenda," access to public education has only recently become available to all children in America. Civil rights activists mobilized and paved the way for American children of color and/or with (dis)abilities to be guaranteed equal access to the "great equalizer"—an education—and learn skills necessary to participate in our democracy and have equal access to the American dream (see *Brown v. Board of Education*, 1954, and *Education for All Handicapped Children Act*, 1975). A review of our country's educational policies provides a chronological and paralleled reflection of the evolution of our country's democracy, values, and civil rights (Noguera, Pierce, & Ahram, 2015). So what is a teacher or administrator to do when a student violates the student code of conduct? Educators and administrators often have clear protocols in place for how to respond when students violate the district, school, or classroom codes of conduct. However, these prescribed disciplinary protocols are not necessarily the most relevant, ethical, or legally acceptable responses to discipline when a student with a disability misbehaves and violates the rules. Similar to the spirit of special education policy, appropriate disciplinary sanctions for a student with a disability should be based on individual data and myriad other factors related specifically to the student.

Protections for Students With Disabilities, No Matter How Terribly Behaved

Federal law mandates that as soon as a student meets criteria for special education and related services and chooses to access these services, he or she is granted certain rights, protections, and assurances (Individuals with Disabilities Education Act, 2004). In addition, public schools are required to provide him or her with a free and appropriate public education (FAPE) in the least restrictive environment (LRE). Interpretation and implementation of FAPE in the LRE are subjective; therefore, implementation practices are often challenging and controversial (Rozalski, Stewart, & Miller, 2010; Yell, 1995). Determining the most *appropriate* educational placement for a student is based on the individual student and his or her ability to access learning and make progress (see *Endrew F. v. Douglas County School District*, 2017). Moreover, ethical posture dictates that the individualized education program (IEP) team identify the least intrusive interventions possible and provide students with therapeutic and educational environments (Behavioral Analyst Certification Board, 2017; Council for Exceptional Children, 2015). These assurances, coupled with the popular belief that general education is the idealized placement for a student with disabilities, often result in students with disabilities being educated and included in general education settings that require unassisted adherence with the student code of conduct, unless otherwise specified in a student's IEP or Section 504 plan. It is important to note that behavioral infractions resulting in disciplinary actions can happen anywhere on school grounds, whether school is in session or not (e.g., Dallas

Independent School District, 2017; New York City Department of Education, 2017). Therefore, when a student with a disability violates the published and hidden student codes of conduct in a manner that would typically warrant suspension or expulsion, the IEP team may have to meet and discuss a change in placement (Yell, Rozalski, & Glasgow, 2001).

Suspension, Expulsion, and Change in Placement

District handbooks prescribe a protocol for district administrators to follow per federal, state, and board policies when responding to student violations of the student code of conduct. Similar to most legal documents regarding consequences for violations (e.g., criminal law), most districts delineate a hierarchy of offenses and apply sanctions according to the severity of the infraction. Consistent violations or a particularly heinous infraction will likely result with student (a) suspension (i.e., removal from the instructional environment, either within the school or outside of the school), (b) placement in an interim alternative educational setting (instruction is delivered off district property or in a secluded school for students with disciplinary concerns), or (c) expulsion (i.e., removal from the school permanently). When considering removing a student with a disability from school, administrators must be incredibly cautious that they do not violate federal law. IDEA (2004) permits district administrators to remove a student with a disability from his or her current placement for up to 10 days per school year without having to make a formal change of placement. During those 10 days of suspension (either successive days or isolated days), the district is *not* responsible for providing special education services or any educational services to the student. The IEP team will have to meet to discuss a formal change of placement because of disciplinary removals if a student is (a) removed from his or her current placement for 10 consecutive days or (b) removed frequently and a pattern has emerged (i.e., removals total more than 10 days in the school year; behavioral incidents that result in removals are similar in nature; and there are factors such as duration, proximity, and cumulative time of disciplinary removals; IDEA Regulations, 2013; 20 U.S.C. 1415[k]; §34 CFR 300.536). Beginning on the 11th day of suspension, either consecutive or isolated, a student with a disability is entitled to all the educational services, specially designed instruction, and related services prescribed in his or her current IEP. The district may consider making a formal change of placement before the 10 days of removal have been reached but cannot act on this placement without meeting with the IEP team to conduct a manifestation determination review.

Manifestation Determination

Manifestation determination review (MDR) is a process that the IEP team engages in—within 10 days of a change in placement because of the student's behavior—to determine if the problematic behaviors resulting in disciplinary actions were because of (a) impairments inherent in or related to the student's disability or (b) failure to implement the IEP (IDEA, 2013, §1415[k] [1][E][i]). At the MDR, the IEP team reviews all available data about the behavioral infraction(s) and implementation of the student's IEP. Determining whether a behavioral infraction is the result of a student's disability can be particularly challenging when reviewing for students with high-incidence disabilities (i.e., emotional disturbance, learning disabilities, mild intellectual disability, and/or "other," such as high-functioning autism, attention deficit hyperactivity disorder, and/or speech impairment; Gage, Lierheimer, & Goran, 2012). With the exception of emotional disturbance, students in most high-incidence disability categories present as able to make correct behavioral choices with little to no assistance and/or their IEP may not make specific mention of challenging behaviors that warrant intervention. For example, if a student with an identified learning disability has several incidents recorded of leaving school grounds without permission, the IEP team will have to determine if this behavior has any pattern to it that may be related to his learning disability. Is there evidence to suggest that the student leaves school when he knows he will have to perform an academic task or demand that he is not confident he can perform? If so, are his accommodations and modifications being implemented per his IEP? If so, does the IEP team need to revise the IEP? Does the IEP team need to conduct a functional behavior assessment and behavior intervention plan? All these are questions that would be examined at the MDR. If it is determined that there is a pattern to the behavior, but it does not appear to be related to the student's disability or failure to implement the IEP, the school is able to administer disciplinary sanctions in the same manner as it would for a student who does not have a disability (20 U.S.C. 1415[k][1][C], [k][2]; 34 C.F.R. 300.530[c]).

MDR and all protections for students with disabilities are designed to avoid discriminatory treatment on the basis of a student's disability. Zirkel (2015) presented an analysis of MDR rulings that have been brought to due process hearings and through the courts since the passage of IDEA 2004 and compares these findings with data from post IDEA 1997. Findings indicate that the number of MDR cases brought before hearing officers remains static despite policy efforts to refine criteria. Additionally, due process hearing officers and courts find in favor of parents for procedural claims (e.g., failure to consider additional diagnosis, lack of sufficient parental participation) and school districts for substantive issues (i.e., criteria justifying MDR decisions were met and accurate). If a change in placement is determined appropriate by the IEP team as a result of the MDR, the student could be placed in a disciplinary setting or simply a more restrictive setting. Youth with disabilities are disproportionately represented in juvenile correctional facilities and other court-involved programs (c.f., Gagnon, Barber, Van Loan, & Leone, 2009, and U.S. Department of Education, Office of Special Education and Rehabilitative Services, 2014).

Contextual and Controversial Issues Related to Discipline

Racial Disparities

Racial disparities in school discipline strategies have become a prominent point of interest for educational researchers over the past several decades.

In a groundbreaking study, the Council of State Governments Justice Center and Public Policy Research Institute tracked 928,940 sixth- to twelfth-grade students in the Texas public school system from 1999 to 2009, as well as juvenile records from statewide county juvenile probation departments (Fabelo et al., 2011). Conclusions made concerning formal punishment in schools (e.g., suspensions and expulsions) were astonishing. Particularly, African American students (specifically males) were at least 30% more likely, and Latinx students 20% more likely, to receive one or more disciplinary actions in comparison with their White counterparts. The study also showed that nearly 3 out of 4 students who received special education services were suspended or expelled at least once throughout their middle and high school years. As a result, all students who experienced a disciplinary action were more likely to be held back a grade or drop out of school; they also had a greater likelihood of coming into contact with the juvenile justice system. These striking disparities are evident beginning in preschool (U.S. Department of Education, Office for Civil Rights, 2014).

As shocking as these findings are, they are unfortunately not without precedent. Previous studies also suggest that racial, gender, and disability disparities often impact students' varying levels of involvement in the school disciplinary system (Achilles, Mclaughlin, & Croninger, 2007; Skiba, Michael, Nardo, & Peterson, 2002). Such work has further emphasized the extent and impact of the school-to-prison pipeline, which suggests that minority youth are not only more likely to undergo disciplinary action in school but their school behavioral records correlate to eventual involvement in the juvenile justice system. To target these difficult issues, policymakers began the Supportive School Discipline Initiative that coordinates federal action with promoting positive discipline strategies, such as restorative justice programs, in schools. The U.S. Department of Education released a resource package in 2014 containing guiding principles and best practices on how to improve school climate and discipline. Those resources can be found here: https://www2.ed.gov/policy/gen/guid/school-discipline/index.html.

Zero-Tolerance Policies and School Safety

Zero-tolerance policies originated in the 1980s era of "immediate and severe" punishment concerning both federal and state drug charges (Skiba, 2014). As the movement gained momentum, educators and administrators began to apply these methods, claiming to curb youth violence and promote safety in their schools. Unfortunately, fear continued to permeate school systems across the nation with ever-growing concerns of school violence. Responding to this concern, Congress passed the Gun-Free Schools Act in 1994, requiring the adoption of zero-tolerance policies to fight against weapon use in U.S. schools. National reports indicated subsequent decreases in youth crime rates (U.S. Department of Justice, Office of Juvenile Justice and Delinquency Prevention, 2014).

In 1999, the Columbine High School shooting became the largest case of school violence in recorded U.S. news. Consequently, there was an increase in harsher policies and greater zero-tolerance policies in schools. Suspension and expulsion rates for students are reported to be at an all-time high, with as many as 2 million students receiving suspensions or expulsions in the 2013 school year (Losen & Martinez, 2013). Although criticism of zero-tolerance policies has been present since its rise in the early 1990s, a second wave of criticism emerged when researchers began to study the effects of harsh disciplinary action on student outcomes (Fabelo et al., 2011; Skiba & Peterson, 1999).

The American Psychological Association (2008) developed a task force to review the effectiveness of zero-tolerance practices. Findings were clear that zero-tolerance policies were not only ineffective, but they resulted in collateral consequences for students, families, and communities, particularly for students from racial minority backgrounds. As a result, there was a nationwide call to develop best practices for school discipline strategies. Early identification of emotional and behavioral concerns, social–emotional learning programs, school-based mental health services, and positive behavioral interventions and supports are approaches resulting in decreased school suspensions, office referrals, and bullying while increasing positive student outcomes (e.g., academic achievement, academic engagement, social–emotional functioning; National Association of School Psychologists, 2013).

Physical Abuse of Students With Disabilities

In 2014, a Dallas news team (NBC-5) investigated the suspected abuse of children with disabilities across several North Texas schools. Released footage shows one teacher forcing a student with autism into a small, closet-like space and blocking the door so he was unable to leave. Many schools across Texas use similar spaces—called "calm rooms"—that are small padded rooms. These rooms were originally designed to provide a safe place for students to self-regulate when needed but have been grossly misused by some educators. Texas State Senator Eddie Lucio Jr. sponsored a bill that would require cameras in special education classrooms at the request of the parents. The bill passed in 2015, and Texas became the first state to require such equipment. Parents are praising the bill's passing, while Texas school districts are having a harder time accepting the change (Hope, 2016). There are claims that districts may potentially be required to pay millions of dollars on the new equipment, and districts are calling on federal agencies to cover the costs (Messer, 2013). Other critics suggest that this is a "Band-Aid fix" for an otherwise gaping wound; an alternative strategy could include better training regarding issues such as using restraint and seclusion in the school setting (Schuette, 2015).

Although disturbing in nature, physical abuse of children with disabilities while they are receiving educational services has been a major concern of federal agencies, local government, and advocacy rights groups for quite some time. In 2009, the National Disability Rights Network released a report documenting severe cases of abuse against students with disabilities and advocating for federal policy change concerning the treatment of those children in the U.S. public school system. The Government Accountability Office (2009) published a similar report later that year indicating students with disabilities were more likely to experience abuse and, in some cases, even death. The use of physical and mechanical restraints to modify the behavior of students with disabilities may sound like an unthinkable atrocity,

Unfortunately, since the admittance and education of students with disabilities in the public schools was mandated, even students with the most abhorrent behaviors have come to the schools, and educators are frequently at a loss as to how to manage or even contain their behaviors. At the conclusion of 2016, the U.S. Department of Education, Office for Civil Rights published a "Dear Colleague" letter to provide guidance to districts on the use and misuse of restraints and seclusions when imposed on students with disabilities (Lhamon, 2016). This letter was particularly important because it explicitly stated the disproportionate and discriminatory rates of restraints and seclusions for students with disabilities. Self-reported data from school districts for the 2013–2014 school year indicated that students receiving services under IDEA represented about 12% of the school population and 67% of the students who had been restrained and/or secluded that year.

In a review of almost 20 years of legal cases ruling on the use of aversive consequences for youth with disabilities who exhibited problematic behavior, Katsiyannis and colleagues found that cases of general abuse—corporal punishment, mechanical restraint, physical restraint, and seclusion—were the most commonly heard cases (Katsiyannis, Losiniski, Whitford, & Counts, 2017). Each of the aversive consequences described by the authors as "general abuse" were also widely legally acceptable for schools to administer to students, even students with disabilities. That said, courts have provided guidance stating that principals are ultimately responsible for deciding whether these often legal aversive consequences were delivered without excessive force and to "maintain or restore discipline" (Katsiyannis et al., 2017, p. 3). This legal guidance and tolerance for the use of aversive consequences for youth with disabilities positions students with disabilities, teachers, and administrators in vulnerable situations that could ultimately cause severe physical and emotional harm to all involved parties. To avoid the use of aversive consequences, teachers and administrators must be trained on current best practices for preventing and intervening in problematic behaviors.

Current Best Practices

The term *best practice* implies an outcome, and in this context our desired outcome is a fully functional contributory citizen in our society. With this end in mind, our best practices must be those that help us reach this goal. The use of evidence-based practices for behavior and discipline for individuals, classrooms, and schools is required in IDEA (2004), and positive school-wide approaches to discipline are an evidence-based best practice for reforming school climate, decreasing discipline problems, and enhancing learning environments. Effects are demonstrated for individuals, classrooms, and school-level improvements (Sugai & Horner, 2009).

School Climate

The environmental quality of a system, like a school, is made up of ecology, milieu, social system, and culture. Student–teacher interactions both verbal and nonverbal are indicative of or make up an observable and measurable aspect of climate. The level of warmth, the frequency of positive or negative interaction, and the ratio of one to another provide quantifiable data for understanding and measuring the construct of school climate. Climate demonstrates a relationship to other social and academic features on a campus, including achievement, discipline, teacher burnout, teacher effectiveness, and organizational health (Bevans, Bradshaw, Miech, & Leaf, 2007; Pas, Bradshaw, Hershfeldt, & Leaf, 2010; Thapa, Cohen, Guffey, & Higgins-D'Alessandro, 2013).

School climate is malleable and important enough to be noted in the most recent federal education policy: the Every Student Succeeds Act (2015). Creating or maintaining a positive school climate involves stakeholder buy-in and an understanding of the importance of the work and the relationship between climate and student outcomes. Climate change includes classroom-level behaviors of teachers related to instruction, redirection, behavioral feedback, and correction. Also important are the expectations for how teachers treat one another, as well as the student–teacher interactions. If school-wide behaviors are stated as "respect" and "responsibility," teachers who yell at students, do not return work in a timely way, use sarcasm, tear up assignments, mismanage a classroom, or treat equipment with little care or concern are failing to model the behavioral expectations, and denigrate the campus and classroom climate. Practices and responses to problematic behaviors can cultivate a culture that values all individuals, despite behavioral infractions, and provides opportunities for learning and growth when behavioral infractions occur.

Restorative Practice

Like many multicomponent systemic programs, a clear delimiting consensus about what is and is not a restorative practice is hard to find. Primary features include a philosophical orientation that moves away from punishment for punishment's sake, toward a focus on repairing harm and reintegrating into a social group (i.e., classroom). The practice originates in South Pacific culture, where accountability for harm and resolving conflict are primary considerations (Fronius, Persson, Guckenburg, Hurley, & Petrosino, 2016). School and classroom features may include techniques that structure a shared-community perspective where students have power in the decision making or are more empowered than in a control-oriented approach. The restorative practice processes may be seen as "more fair" to students and less likely to produce escalations of conflict (Braithwaite, 2004; Morrison & Vaandering, 2012). Restorative practices may also promote better school climate by enhancing connectedness.

Restorative practices appear to function most effectively when they are consistent with an overall approach, and consideration needs to be given to funding and sustainability, including professional development for existing and future staff. Key features include practices such as "circles" or dialogues, victim–offender mediation, and/or restorative conferences. Studies report improved climate (Mirsky, 2007; Mirsky & Wachtel, 2007), and descriptive studies report decreases in maladaptive and inappropriate behavior (Armour, 2013). All studies examining restorative practices' effect on student or school-based outcomes report decreases in exclusionary discipline and violent behavior (Fronius et al., 2016).

Multitiered Systems of Support and Positive Behavioral Interventions and Supports

Multitiered systems of support (MTSS) and positive behavioral interventions and supports (PBIS) provide preventive programming and instruction for all students at the school or classroom level to avoid the need for punitive disciplinary practices or restrictive practices. Some students will need more instruction and support, greater opportunities to practice, more feedback on skills, and additional structures for generalization and maintenance to engage in socially normed behavioral expectations. This practice is effective for students who are at risk for emotional and or behavioral disabilities (Lane, 2007; Lane, Oakes, & Menzies, 2014). A small number of students—about 1% to 5%—will require chronic management (Office of Special Education Programs [OSEP] Technical Assistance Center on PBIS, 2017). A hallmark feature of MTSS and PBIS is using data to make decisions. Therefore, practices selected for student interventions are based on the use of targeted individual assessment about within-child and environmental conditions that support problem behavior (e.g., functional behavior assessment).

As stated in the section about MDR, if a student with a disability is removed from the instructional setting for 10 or more days, he or she must have a change in placement and/or a new functional behavior assessment (FBA) needs to be conducted and/or a revised behavior intervention plan (BIP) must be designed and implemented. There are seven steps included in an FBA: (a) Gather descriptive data about the student and problematic behavior(s) using indirect assessments (e.g., interviews, records review, questionnaires); (b) operationally define the target behavior; (c) directly observe the behavior to collect data about antecedent events and consequent events, as well as some measure of the rate of occurrence; (d) analyze the data; (e) develop a hypothesis that includes information about the context, antecedent events, target behavior, and function of the target behavior; (f) share the hypothesis with the IEP team; and (g) test and confirm the hypothesis and share results with the IEP team. It is important to note that it is understood and accepted that all behavior is learned, is a form of communication, and serves a function. The term *function* means why someone uses a particular behavior. All behaviors serve one of two general functions: to gain something or to avoid something (Cooper, Heron, & Heward, 2007). Moreover, it is assumed that students use the most effective behaviors that will assist them in getting what they want and/or need or assist them in avoiding what they desire to avoid. It should be further assumed that if they were taught and competent in a more socially acceptable behavior that could serve the same function, they would use this more desirable behavior. Once the hypothesis has been confirmed and the function of the behavior has been identified, the BIP can be designed.

When developing the BIP, it is critical to use data gathered from the FBA to inform the plan. Teams can use process forms, such as the Competing Behavior Pathways form, to guide the development of the BIP. Elements to be considered with drafting the BIP are (a) setting events, antecedent events, and accommodations to mitigate these events; (b) desired function-based replacement behaviors to be taught; and (c) arrangement of consequences that will maintain desirable behaviors and extinguish problematic behaviors (see Table 6.1).

Table 6.1   Positive Behavioral Interventions and Supports Guidance Chart

Below is a description of interventions and supports to prevent and intervene in serious problem behaviors in students of all ages. Using these strategies is likely to decrease overall suspension/expulsion rates as well as overall problem behaviors. Evidence supports that the use of suspensions/expulsions is not an effective discipline strategy and leads to poor student outcomes (Council of State Governments, 2011). For these reasons, this chart includes several PBIS suggestions for an MTSS.

	Tier Description	Students Served	Implementation	Strategies
Universal Screener	Measure(s) used to identify students that are at risk or high risk	All students • General education • 504 eligible • Special education	**Who:** All school faculty and staff **Where:** At the school **When:** Three times in a school year (Fuchs, Fuchs, & Compton, 2012)	Behavior-related assessments: • Student Risk Screening Scale (Drummond, 1994) • BASC-3 Behavioral and Emotional Screening System (Reynolds & Kamphaus, 2015)

Tier 1 Universal Intervention	Prevention of problem behavior development through simple techniques that target all students both school-wide and in the classroom	All students
		• General education
		• 504 eligible
		• Special education
			Who: All school faculty and staff
			Where: In all settings
			When: All year
				Some examples from Kern and Clemens (2007) and Lane, Menzies, Ennis, and Oakes (2015):
				• Provide clear rules and expectations.
				  ○ Short, simple, and positive
				• Increase predictability.
				  ○ Create routines
				  ○ Give transition cues
				• Use behavior-specific praise (e.g., "You are doing a great job sitting quietly, Jane!").
				• Give effective instructions and commands.
				• Increase opportunities to respond.
				• Use active supervision.
				Additional supports: https://www.pbis.org/school/tier1supports

Tier 2 Targeted Intervention	Reducing the number of existing cases of students with at-risk behavior concerns (e.g., disruptive, tardy, refusal to complete tasks; U.S. Department of Education, OSEP, 2015)	Students with at-risk behaviors • 504 eligible • Special education **Who:** Staff who have experience in at-risk populations **Where:** In supplemental, small-group settings **When:** All year	Continue Tier 1 supports in addition to • Check-In/Check-Out (Todd, Campbell, Meyer, & Horner, 2008) • Behavior Contract (Anderson, 2002) • Daily Progress Reports (Volpe & Fabiano, 2013) • Self-monitoring (Menzies, Lane, & Lee, 2009) **Additional supports:** http://www.pbisworld.com/tier-2/; http://www.ci3t.org/pl

Tier 3 Intensive Intervention	Reducing the intensity and/or complexity of existing cases of students with high-risk behaviors through tailored, individual intervention (e.g., possession or use of controlled substances, chronic academic failure and truancy, possession and use of firearms and weapons; U.S. Department of Education, OSEP, 2015)	Students with high-risk behaviors
		• Special education
		• Students in alternative schools
		• Students in the juvenile justice system
		
		Who: Specially trained staff
		Where: One-on-one instructional time
		When: All year
			Identify and implement functional assessment-based interventions (Umbreit, Ferro, Liaupsin, & Lane, 2007):
			• Individualized support of previous interventions so they are tailor-made for each student
			  ○ Increased intensity
			  ○ Increased explicitness
			• Using wraparound services to involve family and community supports
			Additional information: http://www.pbis.org/school/tier-3-supports/what-is-tier-3-pbis;
			http://www.ci3t.org/fabi

Alternatives to out-of-school suspension for chronic and persistent severe problem behaviors (Peterson, 2005):

1. Problem-solving/contracting
2. Restitution
3. Mini-courses or skill modules
4. Parent involvement/supervision
5. Counseling
6. Community service
7. Behavior monitoring
8. Coordinated behavior plans
9. Alternative programming
10. In-school suspension

When determining teaching strategies to be used to teach the function-based replacement behaviors, it is important to identify whether the student has a skill deficit or a performance deficit that impedes his or her use of the function-based replacement behaviors. A *skill deficit* is when the student is unaware or unable to accomplish, achieve, or emit a specific behavior (e.g., student does not know how to ask peers to play a game of chase on the playground). A *performance deficit* is when a student knows the correct behavior but does not perform it in the necessary circumstances (e.g., student knows how to ask peers to play a game of chase on the playground but pushes them to get them to chase him or her instead). Once the team has determined whether the student has a skill deficit or performance deficit, specific teaching strategies can be identified. All educators working with the student in settings where the BIP is implemented (e.g., cafeteria, art class, bus) must be trained on the BIP. Teams should have evaluation measures in place to make sure each component of the BIP is being implemented, the student is making adequate progress, and the skills are being generalized. Failure to implement the BIP can lead to exclusionary discipline and due process.

Conclusion

Students with disabilities and/or students from racially diverse backgrounds are subjected to disproportionate rates of harsh and exclusionary discipline (Skiba et al., 2014; Vincent, Sprague, & Tobin, 2012). This perpetual trend implies the need to enhance educators' understanding and approach to working with students who exist outside of the "norm" or dominant group. To promote a positive school climate and equitable learning opportunities for students with disabilities, it is recommended that *all* educators—not just special education professionals—learn how to (a) establish and teach clear and consistent behavioral expectations, (b) deliver behavioral feedback—in the way of reinforcement or punishment—and safe opportunities for practice and/or reteaching of behavioral expectations, and (c) evaluate equitable school-wide disciplinary practices and culturally responsive behavioral approaches (Bal, 2018).

The next generation of our nation's citizens must be trained to be critical thinkers and responsible civic contributors; this training should include making the right behavioral choices within challenging contexts, such as high-demand work environments. Determining restitution or consequence for students with disabilities when they violate the student code of conduct can be a challenge for even the savviest educators. Thorough knowledge of federal law, district policies, and individual-specific nuances can position educators to make more informed decisions about how to best respond to student infractions. Educators are also encouraged to learn and practice employing the basic principles of behavior (Skinner, 1953) to better prevent and respond to problematic behaviors that students with disabilities may exhibit. Furthermore, the most current research indicates that installing proactive approaches, such as systematic screening and tiered behavioral supports, decreases student misbehavior. Schools using proactive approaches to student behavior can provide the perfect and most equitable soil for growing strong, empathic citizens.

REFLECTING AND UNDERSTANDING

1. List and describe the protections for students with disabilities under federal law when they have an alleged behavioral infraction.

2. In addition to sanctioned disciplinary actions, what additional consequences do many students—particularly students with disabilities from racially diverse backgrounds—experience as a result of multiple disciplinary actions?

3. Why were zero-tolerance policies enacted? Are they effective? Why or why not?

4. What are the current best practices in preventing and addressing student behavioral infractions? Describe the features of each practice.

5. What are the steps in functional behavior assessment? What elements must be considered in behavioral intervention plans?

ONLINE RESOURCES

- Behavior Doctor: http://behaviordoctor.org/material-download/

- Behavioral Institute for Children and Adolescents: https://www.behavioralinstitute.org/sheldon-braaten.html

- Comprehensive, Integrated, Three-Tiered (Ci3T) Models of Prevention: http://www.ci3t.org/pl

- Conscious Discipline: https://consciousdiscipline.com/

- Intervention Central: http://www.interventioncentral.org/behavioral-intervention-modification

- National Center on Intensive Intervention: https://intensiveintervention.org/

- Smiling Mind: https://www.smilingmind.com.au/mindfulness-in-education

- University of Kansas: http://www.specialconnections.ku.edu/~kucrl/cgi-bin/drupal/?q=behavior_plans

RECOMMENDED READINGS

Books

Cooper, J. O., Heron, T. E., & Heward, W. L. (2007). *Applied behavior analysis* (2nd ed.). Upper Saddle, NJ: Pearson.

Lane, K. L., Menzies, H. M., Ennis, R. P., & Oakes, W. P. (2015). *Supporting behavior for school success: A step-by-step guide to key strategies.* New York, NY: Guilford Press.

Articles

American Psychological Association. (2008). Are zero tolerance policies effective in the schools? An evidentiary review and recommendations. *American Psychologist, 63,* 852–862.

Bal, A. (2018). Culturally responsive positive behavior interventions and supports: A process oriented framework for systematic transformation. *Review of Education, Pedagogy, and Cultural Studies, 40*(2), 144–174. doi: 10.1080/10714413.2017.1417579

Council for Exceptional Children. (2015). *Ethical principles and professional practice standards for special educators.* Retrieved from https://www.cec.sped.org/Standards/Ethical-Principles-and-Practice-Standards

Government Accountability Office. (2009). *Seclusions and restraints: Selected cases of death and abuse at public and private schools and treatment centers.* Retrieved from http://www.gao.gov/assets/130/122526.pdf

Morrison, B. E., & Vaandering, D. (2012). Restorative justice: Pedagogy, praxis, and discipline. *Journal of School Violence, 11*(2), 138–155.

Pas, E. T., Bradshaw, C. P., Hershfeldt, P. A., & Leaf, P. J. (2010). A multilevel exploration of the influence of teacher efficacy and burnout on response to student problem behavior and school-based service use. *School Psychology Quarterly, 25*(1), 13–27. doi:10.1037/a0018576

REFERENCES

Achilles, G. M., McLaughlin, M. J., & Croninger, R. G. (2007). Sociocultural correlates of disciplinary exclusion among students with emotional, behavioral, and learning disabilities in the SEELS national dataset. *Journal of Emotional and Behavioral Disorders, 15*(1), 33–45.

American Psychological Association. (2008). Are zero tolerance policies effective in the schools? An evidentiary review and recommendations. *American Psychologist, 63,* 852–862.

Anderson, J. (2002). Individualized behavior contracts. *Intervention in School and Clinic, 37*(3), 168–172.

Armour, M. (2013). Real-world assignments for restorative justice education. *Contemporary Justice Review: Issues in Criminal, Social, and Restorative Justice, 16*(1), 115–136. doi:10.1080/10282580.2013.769300

Bal, A. (2018). Culturally responsive positive behavior interventions and supports: A process oriented framework for systematic transformation. *Review of Education, Pedagogy, and Cultural Studies, 40*(2), 144–174. doi:10.1080/10714413.2017.1417579

Behavioral Analyst Certification Board. (2017, July 6). *Professional and ethical compliance code for behavior analysts.* Retrieved from https://www.bacb.com/wp-content/uploads/2017/09/170706-compliance-code-english.pdf

Bevans, K., Bradshaw, C., Miech, R., & Leaf, P. (2007). Staff- and school-level predictors of school organizational health: A multilevel analysis. *Journal of School Health, 77,* 294–302. doi:10.1111/j.1746-1561.2007.00210.x

Braithwaite, J. (2004). Restorative justice and de-professionalization. *The Good Society, 13*(1), 28–31.

Brown v. Board of Education, 347 U.S. 483 (1954).

Cooper, J. O., Heron, T. E., & Heward, W. L. (2007). *Applied behavior analysis* (2nd ed.). Upper Saddle, NJ: Pearson.

Council for Exceptional Children. (2015). *Ethical principles and professional practice standards for special educators.* Retrieved from https://www.cec.sped.org/Standards/Ethical-Principles-and-Practice-Standards

Dallas Independent School District. (2017). *2017–2018 student code of conduct.* Retrieved from https://www.dallasisd.org/cms/lib/TX01001475/Centricity/Domain/11/code_of_conduct.pdf

Drummond, T. (1994). *The student risk screening scale (SRSS).* Grants Pass, OR: Josephine County Mental Health Program.

Education for All Handicapped Children Act [EHA] Pub. L. No. 93-380. 20 U.S.C. § 1401 *et seq.* (1975).

Endrew F. v. Douglas County School District. 580 U.S. 15-827. (2017). Retrieved from https://www.supremecourt.gov/opinions/16pdf/15-827_0pm1.pdf

Every Student Succeeds Act Pub. L. No. 114-95. 20 U.S.C. § 6301 *et seq.* (2015).

Fabelo, T., Thompson, M. D., Plotkin, M., Carmichael, D., Marchbanks, M. P., III, & Booth, E. A. (2011). *Breaking school rules: A statewide study of how school discipline relates to students' success and juvenile justice involvement.* New York, NY: Council of State Governments Justice Center and Public Policy Research Institute.

Fronius, T., Persson, H., Guckenberg, S., Hurley, N., & Petrosino, A. (2016, February). *Restorative justice in U.S. schools: A research review* (Rep.). Retrieved from https://jprc.wested.org/wp-content/uploads/2016/02/RJ_Literature-Review_20160217.pdf

Fuchs, D., Fuchs, L., & Compton, D. (2012). Smart RTI: A next-generation approach to multilevel prevention. *Exceptional Children, 78*(3), 263–279.

Gage, N. A., Lierheimer, K. S., & Goran, L. G. (2012). Characteristics of students with high-incidence disabilities broadly defined. *Journal of Disability Policy Studies, 23*(3), 168–178. doi:10.1177/1044207311425385

Gagnon, J. C., Barber, B. R., Van Loan, C., & Leone, P. E. (2009). Juvenile correctional schools: Characteristics and approaches to curriculum. *Education and Treatment of Children, 32*(4), 673–696.

Government Accountability Office. (2009). *Seclusions and restraints: Selected cases of death and abuse at public and private schools and treatment centers.* Retrieved from http://www.gao.gov/assets/130/122526.pdf

Gun-Free Schools Act. Pub. L. No. 103-382. 20 U.S.C. § 8921 *et seq.* (1994).

Hope, M. (2016). Cameras to protect special needs students coming to Texas classrooms. Breitbart. Retrieved from http://www.breitbart.com/texas/2016/09/06/cameras-protect-special-needs-students-coming-texas-classrooms/

Individuals with Disabilities Education Act. Pub. L. No. 101-476. 20 U.S.C. § 1400 *et seq.* (2004).

Individuals with Disabilities Education Act Regulations, § 34. C.F.R. 300.1 *et seq.* (2013).

Katsiyannis, A., Losinski, M., Whitford, D. K., & Counts, J. (2017). The use of aversives in special education: Legal and practice considerations for school principals. *NASSP Bulletin,* 1–16. doi:10.1177/0192636517741189

Kennedy, B. L., Murphy, A. S., & Jordan, A. (2017). Title 1 middle school administrators' beliefs and choices about using corporal punishment and exclusionary discipline. *American Journal of Education, 123*(2), 243–280. doi:10.1086/689929

Kern, L., & Clemens, N. H. (2007). Antecedent strategies to promote appropriate classroom behavior. *Psychology in the Schools, 44*(1), 65–75.

Lane, K. L. (2007). Identifying and supporting students at risk for emotional and behavioral disorders within multi-level models: Data driven approaches to conducting secondary interventions with an academic emphasis. *Education & Treatment of Children, 30*(4), 135–164.

Lane, K. L., Menzies, H. M., Ennis, R. P., & Oakes, W. P. (2015). *Supporting behavior for school success: A step-by-step guide to key strategies.* New York, NY: Guilford Press.

Lane, K. L., Oakes, W. P., & Menzies, H. M. (2014). Comprehensive, integrated, three-tiered models of prevention: Why does my school—and district—need an integrated approach to meet students' academic, behavioral, and social needs? *Preventing School Failure, 58*(3), 121–128.

Lhamon, C. E. (2016, December 28). *Dear colleague letter: Restraint and seclusion of students with disabilities.* Washington, DC: U.S. Department of Education, Office for Civil Rights.

Losen, D. J., & Martinez, T. E. (2013). *Out of school and off track: The overuse of suspensions in American middle and high schools.* Los Angeles: University of California, Los Angeles, Center for Civil Rights Remedies at the Civil Rights Project.

Menzies, H. M., Lane, K. L., & Lee, J. M. (2009). Self-monitoring strategies for use in the classroom: A promising practice to support productive behavior for students with emotional or behavioral disorders. *Beyond Behavior, 18,* 27–35.

Messer, O. (2013, March 28). Parents of abused children plead for cameras in special ed classrooms. *Texas Observer.* Retrieved from https://www.texasobserver.org/abused-special-ed-students-parents-cameras-classrooms/

Mirsky, L. (2007). Safersanerschools: Transforming school cultures with restorative practices. *Reclaiming Children and Youth, 16*(2), 5–12.

Mirsky, L., & Wachtel, T. (2007). "The worst school I've ever been to": Empirical evaluations of a restorative school and treatment milieu. *Reclaiming Children and Youth, 16*(2), 13–16.

Morrison, B. E., & Vaandering, D. (2012). Restorative justice: Pedagogy, praxis, and discipline. *Journal of School Violence, 11*(2), 138–155.

National Association of School Psychologists. (2013). *Effective school discipline policy and practice: Supporting student learning (Congressional brief 04-18)*. Retrieved from http://www.nasponline.org/research-and-policy/current-law-and-policy-priorities/briefings/effective-school-discipline-policy-and-practice-supporting-student-learning

National Disability Rights Network. (2009). *School is not supposed to hurt: Investigative report on abusive restraint and seclusion in schools*. Retrieved from http://www.ndrn.org/images/Documents/Resources/Publications/Reports/SR-Report2009.pdf

New York City Department of Education. (2017, April). *Citywide behavioral expectations to support student learning grades K–5*. Retrieved from https://www.schools.nyc.gov/docs/default-source/default-document-library/discipline-code-kindergarten-grade-5-english

Noguera, P. A., Pierce, J. C., & Ahram, R. (2015). Race, education, and the pursuit of equality in the twenty-first century. *Race and Social Problems*, 7(1), 1–4. doi:http://dx.doi.org/10.1007/s12552-014-9139-9

Office of Special Education Programs Technical Assistance Center on Positive Behavioral Interventions and Supports. (2017). *Positive behavioral interventions and supports* [Website]. Retrieved from http://www.pbis.org

Pas, E. T., Bradshaw, C. P., Hershfeldt, P. A., & Leaf, P. J. (2010). A multilevel exploration of the influence of teacher efficacy and burnout on response to student problem behavior and school-based service use. *School Psychology Quarterly*, 25(1), 13–27. doi:10.1037/a0018576

Peterson, R. L. (February, 2005). Ten alternatives to suspension. *Impact, Quarterly Publication of the Institute on Community Integration, University of Minnesota*, 18(2), 10–11. Retrieved from https://ici.umn.edu/products/impact/182/182.pdf

Reynolds, C. R., & Kamphaus, R. W. (2015). *BASC-3 behavioral and emotional screening systems*. Retrieved from http://www.pearsonclinical.com/education/products/100001402/behavior-assessment-system-for-children-third-edition-basc-3.html

Rozalski, M., Stewart, A., & Miller, J. (2010). How to determine the least restrictive environment for students with disabilities. *Exceptionality*, 18(3), 151–163. doi:10.1080/09362835.2010.491991

Schuette, R. (2015, December 15). Coming to Texas: Special-ed cams to protect students from their own teachers. *National Public Radio*. Retrieved from http://www.npr.org/sections/ed/2015/12/15/459405542/coming-next-year-to-texas-special-ed-classrooms-video-cameras

Skiba, R. J. (2014). The failure of zero tolerance. *Reclaiming Children and Youth*, 22(4), 27–33.

Skiba, R. J., Chung, C. G., Trachok, M., Baker, T. L., Sheya, A., & Hughes, R. L. (2014). Parsing disciplinary disproportionality contributions of infraction, student, and school characteristics to out-of-school suspension and expulsion. *American Educational Research Journal*, 51, 640–670.

Skiba, R. J., Michael, R. S., Nardo, A. C., & Peterson, R. L. (2002). The color of discipline: Sources of racial and gender disproportionality in school punishment. *The Urban Review*, 34(4), 317–342.

Skiba, R., & Peterson, R. (1999, January). The dark side of zero tolerance: Can punishment lead to safe schools? *Kappan*, 1–11.

Skinner, B. F. (1953). *Science and human behavior*. New York, NY: Macmillan.

Sugai, G., & Horner, R. H. (2009). Responsiveness-to-intervention and school-wide positive behavior supports: Integration of multi-tiered system approaches. *Exceptionality*, 17(4), 223–237.

Thapa, A., Cohen, J., Guffey, S., & Higgins-D'Alessandro, A. (2013). A review of school climate research. *Review of Educational Research*, 83(3), 357–385.

Todd, A. W., Campbell, A. L., Meyer, G. G., & Horner, R. H. (2008). The effects of a targeted intervention to reduce problem behaviors: Elementary school implementation of check in–check out. *Journal of Positive Behavior Interventions*, 10(1), 46–55.

Umbreit, J., Ferro, J., Liaupsin, C., & Lane, K. (2007). *Functional behavioral assessment and function based intervention: An effective, practical approach*. Upper Saddle River, NJ: Prentice Hall.

U.S. Department of Education, Office for Civil Rights. (2014). *Civil rights data collection data snapshot: School discipline* (US DOE, OCR Issue Brief Number 1). Retrieved from https://ocrdata.ed.gov/Downloads/CRDC-School-Discipline-Snapshot.pdf

U.S. Department of Education, Office of Special Education and Rehabilitative Services (2014). *36th annual report to Congress on the implementation of the Individuals with Disabilities Act.* Washington, DC: Author.

U.S. Department of Education, Office of Special Education Programs. (2015). *Supporting and responding to behavior: Evidence-based classroom strategies for teachers.* Washington, DC: Author.

U.S. Department of Justice, Office of Juvenile Justice and Delinquency Prevention (OJJDP). (2014). *Juvenile offenders and victims: Juvenile arrests 2012.* OJJDP National Report Series Bulletin (NCJ 248513). Retrieved from https://www.ojjdp.gov/pubs/248513.pdf

Vincent, C. G., Sprague, J. R., & Tobin, T. J. (2012). Exclusionary discipline practices across students' racial/ethnic backgrounds and disability status: Findings from the Pacific Northwest. *Education and Treatment of Children, 35*(4), 585–601.

Volpe, R. J., & Fabiano, G. A. (2013). *Daily behavior report cards: An evidence-based system of assessment and intervention.* New York, NY: Guilford Press.

Yell, M. L. (1995). Least restrictive environment, inclusion, and students with disabilities: A legal analysis. *Journal of Special Education, 28*(4), 389–404. doi:10.1177/002246699502800401

Yell, M. L., Rozalski, M. E., & Drasgow, E. (2001). Disciplining students with disabilities. *Focus on Exceptional Children, 33*(9), 1–20.

Zirkel, P. A. (2015). Manifestation determinations under IDEA 2004: An updated legal analysis. *Journal of Special Education Leadership, 29*(1), 32–45.

In the United States even today, research findings do not compete well against such established, persuasive information sources as one's personal experience or knowledge of what other schools are doing.... The prospective adopter is not likely to select the research-based solution solely because it stands on a base of scientific knowledge, especially if something else is less expensive, easier to install, preferred by the faculty, or otherwise attractive.

—Brickell (1967, p. 65)

The Research-to-Practice Gap in Special Education

Bryan G. Cook and Cynthia Farley

This Chapter Will Cover:

1. The existence of the research-to-practice gap in special education and its implications for student learning.
2. Why research-based practices are important for improving learner outcomes.
3. Causes of the research-to-practice gap, including obstacles to practitioners effectively consuming research and obstacles to researchers effectively disseminating their findings.
4. Resources for accessing trustworthy syntheses of research.
5. Using coaching, practice-based evidence, progress monitoring, and data-based decision making to support bridging the research-to-practice gap.
6. Balancing fidelity and adaptation when implementing research-based practices.

Logically, identifying and implementing instructional practices shown to be effective by scientific research, in lieu of less effective approaches, will improve educational outcomes. As such, it is a professional responsibility for educators to consider findings from high-quality, experimental research when making educational decisions. Nonetheless, the gap between research findings and typical classroom practice described by Brickell in 1967 continues to persist more than 50 years later. The *research-to-practice gap* refers to the discrepancy between (a) findings of high-quality research regarding which practices are and are not effective and (b) the actual practices implemented in schools and classrooms. Although the research-to-practice gap exists in many fields, it is particularly consequential in special education, as learners with and at risk for disabilities require highly effective instruction to achieve their goals and attain success in and out of school (Vaughn & Dammann, 2001). As summarized in Figure 7.1, in this chapter we explore the research-to-practice gap in special education by (a) examining the evidence for its existence, (b) considering its potential causes, and (c) suggesting ways to address it. Note that educators use different terms to refer to instructional practices supported as effective by scientific research, such as evidence-based practices, research-based practices, and empirically validated practices (Cook & Cook, 2013). In this chapter we use the term *research-based practices*.

Key Terms

- adaptation
- coaching
- data-based decision making
- fidelity
- practice-based evidence
- progress monitoring
- research synthesis
- research-based practice
- research-to-practice gap

Figure 7.1 Advance Organizer

- **Evidence of a Research-to-Practice Gap in Special Education**
  - Teacher Surveys
  - Observational Research
- **Possible Causes of the Research-to-Practice Gap**
  - Obstacles to Effectively Consuming Research
  - Obstacles to Effectively Disseminating Research
- **Recommendations for Bridging the Research-to-Practice Gap**
  - Access Trustworthy Research Syntheses to Identify Research-Based Practices
  - Support the Implementation of Research-Based Practices
  - Balance Fidelity and Adaptation
  - Engage in Progress Monitoring and Data-Based Decision Making
- **Conclusion**

Evidence of a Research-to-Practice Gap in Special Education

In this section, we review findings from two types of studies that provide evidence of a research-to-practice gap in special education: (a) surveys of teachers' use of research-based practices and (b) observational studies of teachers' actual implementation of instructional practices.

Teacher Surveys

In spite of growing emphasis on research-based practices, teachers' self-reports suggest they sometimes use generally ineffective practices as much as or more often than some generally effective practices. Burns and Ysseldyke (2009) randomly sampled members of the Council for Exceptional Children regarding their use of eight interventions—three of which were shown by research to have large effects on student learning, one moderate effects, and four small effects. Encouragingly, the 174 participating special educators reported engaging in some of the practices with large effects regularly (e.g., 83.3% of participants reported that they used applied behavior analysis almost daily) and some of the practices with small effects infrequently (only 16.7% reported using perceptual motor training almost daily). However, only 29.3% of participants reported using the practice with the largest effect, mnemonic instruction, almost daily; whereas 55.7% reported using modality instruction, which research has shown to have small effects, almost daily.

Gable, Tonelson, Sheth, Wilson, and Park (2012) surveyed more than 1,500 general educators and 1,400 special educators who taught students with emotional and behavioral disorders (EBD). Although teachers reported using some of the 20 research-based practices frequently (90.1% and 86.1% of special education teachers reported usually or always using [a] clear rules and expectations and [b] curricular and instructional modifications, respectively), they reported using some other research-based practices infrequently (e.g., only 27.3% and 26.1% of special educators reported usually or always using group-oriented contingency management and peer-mediated interventions, respectively).

Mazzotti and Plotner (2016) surveyed 592 transition-service providers in the Southeastern and Midwestern United States on their training in and use of research-based practices in the area of secondary transition. Participants reported low to moderate support and training for implementing research-based practices (e.g., 56% of respondents disagreed or strongly disagreed that their professional development opportunities fully prepared them to implement research-based practices). Results for implementing research-based practices were mixed. Respondents indicated moderate use of some targeted practices (e.g., 64% and 62% reported using self-management strategies and visual displays for academic instruction always or often, respectively) but seldom implemented other research-based practices (62% reported never using Whose Future Is It *Anyway?* in transition planning, and 51% reported never using training modules to facilitate parental involvement). Data were not collected on use of ineffective practices.

Finally, Cooper et al. (2018) surveyed 248 educators regarding training, use, and perceived effectiveness of 37 research-based classroom management practices. The majority of participants indicated they used most of the practices with effective results. However, a large group of educators reported not using some of the research-based practices. For example, 64.6%, 49.8%, and 31.8% of respondents indicated that they did not recruit reinforcement, use self-reinforcement, or use function-based interventions, respectively. In sum, educators' self-reports indicate a gap between research and practice. However, self-reports are not always valid (e.g., educators might under- or overestimate their use of certain practices) and should be corroborated through reliable observational research.

Observational Research

Consistent with educators' self-reports, findings from observational research point to a gap between research and practice in the instruction of students with and at risk for disabilities. Swanson (2008) reviewed 21 observational studies of reading instruction for students with learning disabilities (LD). Little phonics instruction was observed, with some studies reporting that no phonics instruction occurred. The most beneficial grouping structure (small groups) was rarely observed. Very little instruction involved reading comprehension, and when it did occur questioning seldom went beyond literal questions. Finally, students with LD were not engaged in the actual act of reading enough to impact their oral reading fluency ability. Overall, Swanson concluded "that there is a disconnect between what occurs during reading instruction for students with LD and research-supported components of effective reading instruction" (p. 130).

McKenna, Shin, and Ciullo (2015) extended Swanson's (2008) review, synthesizing 11 observational studies since 2000 in reading and math instruction for students with LD. In reading, although findings related to instruction in vocabulary and reading fluency were encouraging, few or no instances of application of skills to connected text, purposeful reading practice, comprehension strategy instruction, or individualized instruction were observed. In math, the studies reviewed reported little or no instruction using many research-based practices such as checking for understanding, explicit instruction, student verbalization and discussion of reasoning, visual representation, cognitive strategy instruction, and using a range and sequence of examples.

Related to classroom management, we focus on studies examining rates of teacher praise. Teacher praise, especially behavior-specific praise, has been shown by research to cause improvement in student outcomes such as on-task behavior (e.g., Sutherland, Wehby, & Copeland, 2000). Moreover, it is a simple and straightforward practice to implement. Nonetheless, based on their review of the research, Wehby, Symons, Canale, and Go (1998) concluded that teacher praise "is almost nonexistent in classrooms for children with E/BD" (p. 51). Reinke, Herman, and Stormont (2013) observed 33 elementary general education classrooms and found that teachers provided about 34 instances of praise per hour but provided behavioral-specific praise at a rate of less than eight times per hour. Additionally, only one of 33 teachers met the recommended 4:1 praise-to-reprimand ratio. Most recently, Floress, Jenkins, Reinke, and McKown (2018) conducted 140 observations of 28 elementary general education classrooms. They found similarly low rates of praise (35 praise statements per hour on average) that declined in upper elementary grades. Again, general praise was more common than behavior-specific praise, which occurred less than six times per hour on average.

Although few observational studies have been conducted regarding instruction for students with low-incidence disabilities, Pennington and Courtade (2015) observed 35 self-contained classrooms for students with moderate and severe disabilities. The authors reported an average rate of opportunities to respond of once per every 1.6 minutes, which is insufficient to meet recommended rates of student responding. Although teachers exceeded recommendations for the ratio of positive to negative feedback (a greater than 8:1 ratio was observed), low rates of error correction were observed. This instruction resulted in most observed students with moderate and severe disabilities being passively rather than actively engaged. Overall, both survey and observational research consistently indicate a gap between research and practice in special education.

Possible Causes of the Research-to-Practice Gap

Myriad factors likely underlie the research-to-practice gap, which interact with one another in complex and varied ways. In this section, we describe selected causes of the gap from both sides of the research-to-practice coin: consuming and disseminating research.

Obstacles to Effectively Consuming Research

When making instructional decisions, teachers appear not to value research evidence to the same degree as their own experience and the experiences of other teachers. For example, Landrum, Cook, Tankersley, and Fitzgerald (2002) found that teachers rated information from other teachers as significantly more trustworthy, usable, and accessible than information from professional journals. And when presented with information on an instructional practice written (a) in the style of a research report or (b) from the perspective of another teacher, teachers rated the information from another teacher as significantly more usable (Landrum, Cook, Tankersley, & Fitzgerald, 2007). More recently, Shipman (2014) reported that when seeking information for professional practice, 56% and 38% of teachers reported using websites and colleagues, respectively, on a daily basis; yet only 5% indicated they consulted professional journals daily.

Why don't teachers rely more on research evidence? Most teachers simply do not have the time or the advanced training in research and statistics to read and critically evaluate research reports. Additionally, many teachers do not feel that research is relevant for informing their instruction. Tightly controlled experiments, which are used to identify research-based practices, are often implemented by researchers rather than teachers, with relatively small groups of learners. Teachers often feel that these studies do not apply or generalize to their situations because (a) the controlled environments do not reflect the real "hurly-burly world of schools" (Crockett, 2004, p. 189) and (b) study participants do not represent their students (see Simons, Kushner, Jones, & James, 2003). Thus, even if a practice has been shown to be generally effective in multiple, high-quality experiments, teachers may nonetheless feel that it will not be effective in their specific classrooms and for their specific students. As one special educator commented, "I mean the research stuff looks good down on paper, but whenever you actually use it in a classroom, it doesn't really … I mean it may not fit with each student" (Jones, 2009, p. 110).

Although teachers and researchers can and should work together to enhance both practice and research, teaching and research oftentimes have different goals, values, and processes (Smith, Schmidt, Edelen-Smith, & Cook, 2013). Moreover, teachers sometimes feel that evidence-based reforms are being instituted in a top-down fashion in which research findings are being forced on them. Accordingly, many teachers have reacted with a distrust of research and researchers. As one special educator opined about research: "Yeah, I don't know if even when I hear research, I would really not pay that much attention to it because it's coming out of whoever's selling the program" (Boardman, Arguelles, Vaughn, Hughes, & Klingner, 2005,

p. 177). Perhaps it is not surprising that teachers fail to implement practices supported by research evidence that they may not fully understand, perceive as relevant, or trust.

Obstacles to Effectively Disseminating Research

How researchers disseminate research findings also bears significant responsibility for the research-to-practice gap. For educators to understand and apply research findings, researchers must disseminate them in ways that are trustworthy, usable, and accessible to practitioners (Carnine, 1997). However, as Cook, Cook, and Landrum (2013) noted, researchers typically report studies in scholarly journals and academic conference presentations using technical language and statistical analyses. This approach may be effective for communicating with other researchers, but it renders research inaccessible to practitioners without advanced training in research and statistics. Perhaps because "university faculty seldom have the skill sets (e.g., social marketing strategies) needed for them to be successful in disseminating programs" (McKenzie, Sallis, & Rosengard, 2009, p. 114), reports of research rarely influence practitioners. Researchers often engage in the empty-vessel fallacy when disseminating research findings: They assume that practitioners are empty vessels that, when filled with research findings, will act accordingly (Green, 2008). Researchers, therefore, tend to think that disseminating more research is the key to bridging the research-to-practice gap. To the contrary, there is plenty of educational research available (Miech, Nave, & Mosteller, 2005), but it is seldom reported in ways that are meaningful for teachers.

Teachers typically rely on professional development as their primary source of information and support for research-based practices. In-service training that is intensive and ongoing provides expert support and coaching, and incorporates active learning, which has been shown to be effective in changing teachers' instructional behaviors and improving student performance (Darling-Hammond, Hyler, & Gardner, 2017; Gulamhussein, 2013). However, "in areas like reading instruction, uses of computers, teaching of English language learners and *special education* students, U.S. investments in teacher learning appear to be increasingly focused on the least effective models of professional development—the short-term workshops" (Wei, Darling-Hammond, & Adamson, 2010, pp. v–vi; italics added). Indeed, didactic "one-shot" workshops are still commonplace, despite general knowledge of their ineffectiveness. Accordingly, 41% of teachers reported content-area professional development less than useful, and fewer than half of teachers felt professional development outside of their content area was useful (Darling-Hammond, Wei, Andree, Richardson, & Orphanos, 2009). All things considered, it is not surprising that special educators inconsistently implement research-based practices given the generally inadequate training and supports provided.

Recommendations for Bridging the Research-to-Practice Gap

Just as multiple causes underlie the research-to-practice gap, many approaches can be used to bridge it. In this section, we provide selected recommendations to minimize the research-to-practice gap: access trustworthy research syntheses to identify research-based practices, support the implementation of research-based practices, balance fidelity and adaptation, and engage in progress monitoring and data-based decision making.

Access Trustworthy Research Syntheses to Identify Research-Based Practices

Special educators are often encouraged to read research articles in peer-reviewed journals to identify what works (i.e., research-based practices). Although well intended, we believe this advice can be counterproductive. For one, special educators are trained to be experts in teaching students with disabilities, not in critically interpreting research. Most teachers have not undergone the years of specialized training needed to recognize the questionable research and pseudoscience frequently disseminated on the Internet and sometimes published in peer-reviewed journals. Second, because research studies can be misleading and even high-quality studies contain some error (Cook, 2014), it is important not to base instructional decisions on the findings of any single study. Rather, research findings warrant trust when multiple studies report similar, corroborating results. Thus, it is important to examine research findings across all relevant studies conducted. However, teachers typically do not have the time or training to systematically search for, analyze, and synthesize all the research on a given practice.

Fortunately, researchers have already synthesized findings across studies for many practices. Research syntheses can take different forms, including evidence-based reviews, meta-analyses, and narrative literature reviews (see Santangelo, Novosel, Cook, & Gapsis, 2015). In evidence-based reviews, researchers classify a practice (e.g., as an evidence-based practice) based on whether the number of high-quality, experimental studies that do and do not support the practice as effective meet predetermined standards. For example, Horner et al. (2005) proposed that a practice can be considered evidence based in special education if it is supported as effective by at least five high-quality single-case design studies that were conducted by a minimum of three independent groups of researchers and involve no fewer than 20 total participants.

Multiple organizations classify the evidence bases of practices in special education using predetermined standards. The What Works Clearinghouse (http://ies.ed.gov/ncee/wwc/) classifies instructional practices and programs for students with LD, for students with and at risk for EBD, and for early childhood special education on the basis of studies that meet rigorous quality criteria. Evidence for ESSA (https://www.evidenceforessa.org/) identifies programs in reading and math that meet the evidence standards proposed by the Every Student Succeeds Act for struggling learners. The National Autism Center (http://www.nationalautismcenter.org/national-standards-project/) and the National Professional Development Center on Autism Spectrum Disorders (http://autismpdc.fpg.unc.edu/evidence-based-practices) identify evidence-based practices for learners with autism spectrum disorders. And the National Technical Assistance Center on Transition (https://transitionta.org/effectivepractices) identifies instructional practices with different levels of research support in the area of transition.

To provide an estimate of the general effectiveness of a practice, meta-analyses calculate the average effect of that practice across multiple studies (see Banda & Therrien, 2008). Meta-analyses are commonly published in special education research journals, and the Campbell Collaboration (https://www.campbellcollaboration.org/library.html) publishes high-quality meta-analyses in the social sciences, including some related to special education. The Campbell Collaboration provides plain language summaries for each published meta-analysis.

Narrative literature reviews identify research-based practices without meta-analyzing findings or applying predetermined criteria. For example, the Council for Exceptional Children's Division for Learning Disabilities and Division for Research jointly publish Current Practice Alerts (http://teachingld.org/alerts), in which authors identify practices as research based (or not) for students with LD. The What Works Clearinghouse also publishes Practice Guides (https://ies.ed.gov/ncee/wwc/PracticeGuides), in which experts make research-based recommendations in specific instructional areas (e.g., teaching math to young students, reducing behavior problems).

We note two caveats to consider when accessing research syntheses. First, although we feel the resources noted here are trustworthy, the Internet (and professional development and peer-reviewed journals as well) is replete with less-than-trustworthy information (Test, Kemp-Inman, Diegelmann, Hitt, & Bethune, 2015). As such, we recommend that educators interpret and apply research findings in collaboration with someone with advanced research training. Second, research evidence is only one consideration in determining what and how to teach. Teachers must consider a host of other factors—such as student needs, family values, their own expertise, and available resources—when selecting instructional practices (Spencer, Detrich, & Slocum, 2012; Torres, Farley, & Cook, 2012). A practice should not be implemented just because it is research based if it is not a good match for the learner and the teacher.

Support the Implementation of Research-Based Practices

As Fixsen, Blase, Horner, and Sugai (2009) suggested, "choosing an evidence-based practice is one thing, implementation of that practice is another thing altogether" (p. 5). As described previously, training in how to implement research-based practices is often inadequate, resources for supplies and supports scarce, and typical school cultures unsupportive of new practices. Accordingly, teachers require supports to overcome these and other obstacles to implementing selected research-based practices—two of which we describe in this section: coaching and practice-based evidence.

In typical professional development, an administrator or researcher tells teachers what to do for a couple of hours, and then teachers are left to their own devices to sort out the challenges that inevitably arise when implementing the new practice. Coaching provides a stark and effective contrast to these one-shot in-services. Although coaching can take many forms, Knight (2009) summarized that effective coaching is job-embedded (i.e., occurs in and is focused on one's own classroom and instruction), intensive and ongoing (i.e., regular, frequent, and sustained), non-evaluative and confidential, and grounded in partnership and respectful communication. Whereas one-shot in-services are effective in transferring skills to practice about 10% of the time, coaching can result in a 95% transfer rate (Knight, 2009). Although administrators and external experts can provide coaching, teachers who are experts in a targeted practice can be effective coaches as well.

Teachers often question the relevance of research evidence derived from controlled studies involving participants and classrooms that differ from their own. Practice-based evidence, derived from real classrooms with learners similar to their own, tends to be more convincing to teachers (Cook & Cook, 2016). As one teacher noted, "You know, when I see a program, I don't go, 'Let me see your research'; I say, 'Let me talk to your teachers'" (Boardman et al., 2005, p. 176). Practice-based evidence is usually derived from qualitative research, classroom data, and teachers' stories. Given that practice-based evidence does not come from internally valid, experimental research, it should not be used to establish practices as research based. However, practice-based evidence can complement experimental evidence and facilitate the adoption of research-based practices by (a) demonstrating that the practice can work with typical students in typical classrooms; (b) showing the practice is feasible to implement; and (c) providing critical insights on how the practice works, for what groups of learners the practice might be more or less effective, and how the practice might be adapted effectively. We recommend that (a) teachers who have experience using a research-based practice generate practice-based evidence by collecting and sharing data on how the practice works in their class and (b) teachers adopting a new research-based practice seek out practice-based evidence from their colleagues.

Balance Fidelity and Adaptation

We have heard from many teachers that they tried a research-based practice but it did not work for them. Not always, but a common reason for such ineffectiveness is that the practice was not implemented with fidelity, or as designed. For example, a practice might be designed to be implemented

45 minutes a day, 4 days a week. Yet the teacher implemented it for only half an hour, 3 days a week. Or perhaps the teacher did not have access to all the materials, or decided to change a critical aspect of the practice. In these cases, it is not the practice that was ineffective but the implementation of the practice that was faulty. Simply put, if one does not implement a research-based practice as designed, one cannot expect the same positive outcomes achieved in the research. As such, teachers should carefully examine and adhere to the critical elements of research-based practices when implementing them.

Despite the importance of implementation fidelity, some level of adaptation is likely inevitable and may even be desirable (Harn, Parisi, & Stoolmiller, 2013; Leko, 2015). Just as one cannot become a master chef simply by following recipes, the most effective teachers do not rigidly adhere to implementation checklists. Instead, they know their students, rely on their expertise, and adjust on the fly when needed—sometimes changing aspects of a lesson to heighten their impact for students, sometimes reteaching content when students do not understand it. Indeed, the highest levels of fidelity are associated with diminished learning outcomes (Durlak & DuPre, 2008); some level of adaptation appears important and beneficial.

To appropriately balance fidelity and adaptation, we recommend that teachers

- adapt peripheral components of a research-based practice, rather than the vital core elements;

- give the practice time to work when implemented with fidelity, rather than adapt a practice too soon;

- have data-based reasons for making an adaptation (e.g., formative assessment data showing the practice was not effective for a student when implemented with fidelity); and

- use progress-monitoring data to determine the effectiveness of the adaptation (Leko, 2015; Torres et al., 2012).

In this way, adaptations can maximize the positive effects of a research-based practice for individual learners, but teachers still implement the essential elements of the practice as designed.

Engage in Progress Monitoring and Data-Based Decision Making

One important but frequently overlooked aspect of bridging the research-to-practice gap is conducting frequent and ongoing progress monitoring for the purpose of data-based decision making. No instructional practice, regardless of its research support, works for everyone—especially when teaching students with and at risk for disabilities. Research-based practices have been shown to work for most learners in a population, and therefore should be prioritized, but there will always be learners for whom a research-based practice is ineffective (i.e., nonresponders or treatment resistors)—even when implemented with fidelity. As such, educators should not assume that a student will be successful just because they have implemented a research-based practice.

Regardless of what instructional practices they are using, special educators should frequently and regularly monitor the progress of their individual students using a reliable approach such as curriculum-based measurement (see Hosp, Hosp, & Howell, 2016). Ultimately, the effectiveness of a practice depends not on its research base but on its actual impact on individual learners. Thus, the final step in bridging the gap between research and practice is reliably gauging the impact of research-based practices on individual learners and making appropriate instructional decisions based on those data. For example, if progress-monitoring data show a student is making adequate progress using a research-based practice when implemented with fidelity, the teacher should continue to implement the practice as such. If adequate progress is not being made, the teacher should (a) ensure the core elements of the practice are being implemented with fidelity and (b) consider ways to adapt peripheral aspects of the practice to make it more effective. If, after ensuring that the core elements are being implemented with fidelity and peripheral aspects of the practice have been adapted appropriately, the student continues not to make appropriate gains, then the student is likely a nonresponder to that research-based practice; in which case, the practice should be discontinued and another research-based practice selected.

Conclusion

Logically, students' performance will increase if they are taught using generally effective instructional practices rather than generally ineffective practices. Unfortunately, the research-to-practice gap that Brickell described in 1967 still exists in special education. That is, teachers sometimes use generally ineffective practices and do not consistently use generally effective practices. In this chapter, in addition to discussing (a) research documenting the research-to-practice gap in special education and (b) causes underlying the gap, we described selected approaches for bridging the research-to-practice gap—including using trustworthy research syntheses to identify research-based practices, supporting the implementation of research-based practices, balancing implementation fidelity with adaptation, and engaging in progress monitoring and data-based decision making. We conclude by listing selected resources, from the Internet as well as articles in professional journals, readers can use to find out more and stay up-to-date on these topics.

REFLECTING AND UNDERSTANDING

1. What is the research-to-practice gap in special education, why is it important, and does it exist in special education?

2. What are primary causes of the research-to-practice gap?

3. How can one access trustworthy syntheses of research to identify research-based practices?

4. How can coaching and practice-based evidence help bridge the research-to-practice gap?

5. How can teachers use progress monitoring and data-based decision making to help bridge the research-to-practice gap?

6. How can teachers balance implementing research-based practices with fidelity while also adapting instruction to meet unique learner needs?

ONLINE RESOURCES

- Current Practice Alerts: http://teachingld.org/alerts

- Evidence for ESSA: https://www.evidenceforessa.org/

- National Professional Development Center on Autism Spectrum Disorders: http://autismpdc.fpg.unc.edu/evidence-based-practices

- What Works Clearinghouse: http://ies.ed.gov/ncee/wwc/

- The online module from the IRIS Center: https://iris.peabody.vanderbilt.edu/module/ebp_02/

- Resources for progress monitoring: https://easycbm.com/ and https://dibels.uoregon.edu/

- Quality of progress monitoring tools: https://intensiveintervention.org/about-charts-resources

- Teacher-friendly modules on progress monitoring and data-based decision making: https://iris.peabody.vanderbilt.edu/module/gpm/ and https://iris.peabody.vanderbilt.edu/module/dbi2/

RECOMMENDED READINGS

Book Chapter

Cook, S. C., Rao, K., & Cook, B. G. (2016). Using Universal Design for Learning to personalize an evidence-based practice for students with disabilities. In M. Murphy, S. Redding, & J. Twyman (Eds.), *Handbook on personalized learning for states, districts, and schools* (pp. 239–247). Philadelphia, PA: Temple University, Center on Innovations in Learning.

Retrieved from http://www.centeril.org/2016handbook/resources/Cover_Cook_web.pdf

Articles

Collier-Meek, M. A., Fallon, L. M., Sanetti, L. M., & Maggin, D. M. (2013). Focus on implementation: Assessing and promoting treatment fidelity. *Teaching Exceptional Children, 45*(5), 52–59. doi:10.1177/004005991304500506

Leko, M. M. (2015). To adapt or not to adapt: Navigating an implementation conundrum. *Teaching Exceptional Children, 48*(2), 80–85. doi:10.1177/0040059915605641

Santangelo, T., Novosel, L., Cook, B. G., & Gapsis, M. (2015). Using the 6S Pyramid to identify research-based instructional practices for students with learning disabilities. *Learning Disabilities Research and Practice, 30*, 91–101. doi:10.1111/ldrp.12055

REFERENCES

Banda, D. R., & Therrien, W. J. (2008). A teacher's guide to meta-analysis. *Teaching Exceptional Children, 41*, 66–71. doi:10.1177/004005990804100208

Boardman, A. G., Arguelles, M. E., Vaughn, S., Hughes, M. T., & Klingner, J. (2005). Special education teachers' views of research-based practices. *Journal of Special Education, 39*, 168–180. doi:10.1177/00224669050390030401

Brickell, H. M. (1967). The role of research in the innovation process. In E. G. Guba (Ed.), *The role of educational research in educational change in the United States* (pp. 58–72). Bloomington, IN: National Institute for the Study of Educational Change. Retrieved from http://files.eric.ed.gov/fulltext/ED012505.pdf

Burns, M. K., & Ysseldyke, J. E. (2009). Reported prevalence of evidence-based instructional practices in special education. *Journal of Special Education, 43*, 3–11. doi:10.1177/0022466908315563

Carnine, D. (1997). Bridging the research-to-practice gap. *Exceptional Children, 63*, 513–521. doi:10.1177/001440299706300406

Cook, B. G. (2014). A call for examining replication and bias in special education research. *Remedial and Special Education, 35*, 233–246. doi:10.1177/0741932514528995

Cook, B. G., & Cook, L. (2016). Leveraging evidence-based practice through partnerships based on practice-based evidence. *Learning Disabilities: A Contemporary Journal, 14*, 143–157.

Cook, B. G., Cook, L. H., & Landrum, T. J. (2013). Moving research into practice: Can we make dissemination stick? *Exceptional Children, 79*, 163–180. doi:10.1177/001440291307900203

Cook, B. G., & Cook, S. C. (2013). Unraveling evidence-based practices in special education. *Journal of Special Education, 47*, 71–82. doi:10.1177/0022466911420877

Cooper, J. T., Gage, N. A., Alter, P. J., LaPolla, S., MacSuga-Gage, A. S., & Scott, T. M. (2018). Educators' self-reported training, use, and perceived effectiveness of evidence-based classroom management practices. *Preventing School Failure, 62*, 13–24. doi:http://dx.doi.org/10.1080/1045988X.2017.1298562

Crockett, J. B. (2004). Taking stock of science in the schoolhouse: Four ideas to foster effective instruction. *Journal of Learning Disabilities, 37*, 189–199. doi:10.1177/00222194040370030201

Darling-Hammond, L., Hyler, M. E., & Gardner, M. (2017). *Effective teacher professional development.* Palo Alto, CA: Learning Policy Institute. Retrieved from https://learningpolicyinstitute.org/sites/default/files/product-files/Effective_Teacher_Professional_Development_REPORT.pdf

Darling-Hammond, L., Wei, R. C., Andree, A., Richardson, N., & Orphanos, S. (2009). *Professional learning in the learning profession: A status report on teacher development in the United States and abroad.* Palo Alto, CA: National Staff Development Council.

Durlak, J. A., & DuPre, E. P. (2008). Implementation matters: A review of research on the influence of implementation on program outcomes and the factors affecting implementation. *American Journal of Community Psychology, 41*, 327–350. doi:10.1007/s10464-008-9165-0

Fixsen, D., Blase, K., Horner, R., & Sugai, G. (2009). *Concept paper: Developing the capacity for scaling up the effective use of evidence-based programs in state departments of education.* Retrieved from http://ea.niusileadscape.org/docs/FINAL_PRODUCTS/LearningCarousel/DevelopingCapacity.pdf

Floress, M. T., Jenkins, L. N., Reinke, W. M., & McKown, L. (2018). General education teachers' natural rates of praise: A preliminary investigation. *Behavioral Disorders, 43*(4), 411–422.

Gable, R. A., Tonelson, S. W., Sheth, M., Wilson, C., & Park, K. L. (2012). Importance, usage, and preparedness to implement evidence-based practices for students with emotional disabilities: A comparison of knowledge and skills of special education and general education teachers. *Education and Treatment of Children, 35*, 499–520.

Green, L. W. (2008). Making research relevant: If it is an evidence-based practice, where's the practice-based evidence? *Family Practice, 25*, i20–i24.

Gulamhussein, A. (2013). *Teaching the teachers: Effective professional development in an era of high stakes accountability.* Center for Public Education. Retrieved from http://www.centerforpubliceducation.org/Main-Menu/Staffingstudents/Teaching-the-Teachers-Effective-Professional-Development-in-an-Era-of-High-Stakes-Accountability/Teaching-the-Teachers-Full-Report.pdf

Harn, B., Parisi, D., & Stoolmiller, M. (2013). Balancing fidelity with flexibility and fit: What do we really know about fidelity of implementation in schools? *Exceptional Children, 79*, 181–193. doi:10.1177/001440291307900204

Horner, R. H., Carr, E. G., Halle, J., McGee, G., Odom, S., & Wolery, M. (2005). The use of single-subject research to identify evidence-based practice in special education. *Exceptional Children, 71*, 165–179. doi:10.1177/001440290507100203

Hosp, M. K., Hosp, J. L., & Howell, K. W. (2016). *The ABCs of CBM: A practical guide to curriculum-based measurement* (2nd ed.). New York, NY: Guilford Press.

Jones, M. L. (2009). A study of novice special educators' views of evidence-based practices. *Teacher Education and Special Education, 32*, 101–120. doi:10.1177/0888406409333777

Knight, J. (2009). Coaching. *Journal of Staff Development, 30*(1), 18–22.

Landrum, T. J., Cook, B. G., Tankersley, M., & Fitzgerald, S. F. (2002). Teachers' perceptions of the trustworthiness, useability, and accessibility of information from different sources. *Remedial and Special Education, 23*, 42–48. doi:10.1177/074193250202300106

Landrum, T. J., Cook, B. G., Tankersley, M., & Fitzgerald, S. F. (2007). Teacher perceptions of the useability of intervention information from personal versus data-based sources. *Education and Treatment of Children, 30*(4), 27–42. doi:10.1353/etc.2007.0025

Leko, M. M. (2015). To adapt or not to adapt: Navigating an implementation conundrum. *Teaching Exceptional Children, 48*(2), 80–85. doi:10.1177/0040059915605641

Mazzotti, V. L., & Plotner, A. J. (2016). Implementing secondary transition evidence-based practices: A multistate survey of transition service providers. *Career Development and Transition for Exceptional Individuals, 39*, 12–22. doi:10.1177/2165143414544360

McKenna, J. W., Shin, M., & Ciullo, S. (2015). Evaluating reading and mathematics instruction for students with learning disabilities: A synthesis of observation research. *Learning Disability Quarterly, 38*, 195–207. doi:10.1177/0731948714564576

McKenzie, T. L., Sallis, J. F., & Rosengard, P. (2009). Beyond the stucco tower: Design, development, and dissemination of the SPARK physical education programs. *Quest, 61*, 114–127.

Miech, E. J., Nave, B., & Mosteller, F. (2005). The 20,000 article problem: How a structured abstract can help practitioners sort out educational research. *Phi Delta Kappan, 86*, 396–400.

Pennington, R. C., & Courtade, G. R. (2015). An examination of teacher and student behaviors in classrooms for students with moderate and severe intellectual disability. *Preventing School Failure, 59*, 40–47. doi:http://dx.doi.org/10.1080/1045988X.2014.919141

Reinke, W. M., Herman, K. C., & Stormont, M. (2013). Classroom-level positive behavior supports in schools implementing SW-PBIS: Identifying areas for enhancement. *Journal of Positive Behavior Interventions, 15*, 39–50. doi:10.1177/1098300712459079

Santangelo, T., Novosel, L., Cook, B. G., & Gapsis, M. (2015). Using the 6S Pyramid to identify research-based instructional practices for students with learning disabilities. *Learning Disabilities Research and Practice, 30*, 91–101. doi:10.1111/ldrp.12055

Shipman, T. (2014). In-service teachers and their information-seeking habits: Does library instruction show a relationship to information-seeking habits for professional use? *National Teacher Education Journal, 7*(3), 53–64.

Simons, H., Kushner, S., Jones, K., & James, D. (2003). From evidence-based practice to practice-based evidence: The idea of situated generalization. *Research Papers in Education, 18*, 347–364. doi:10.1080/0267152032000176855

Smith, G. J., Schmidt, M. M., Edelen-Smith, P., & Cook, B. G. (2013). Pasteur's quadrant as the bridge linking rigor and relevance. *Exceptional Children, 79*, 147–161. doi:10.1177/001440291307900202

Spencer, T. D., Detrich, R., & Slocum, T. A. (2012). Evidence-based practice: A framework for making effective decisions. *Education and Treatment of Children, 35*, 127–151.

Sutherland, K. S., Wehby, J. H., & Copeland, S. R. (2000). Effect of varying rates of behavior-specific praise on the on-task behavior of students with EBD. *Journal of Emotional and Behavioral Disorders, 8*, 2–8. doi:10.1177/106342660000800101

Swanson, E. A. (2008). Observing reading instruction for students with learning disabilities: A synthesis. *Learning Disability Quarterly, 31*, 115–133. doi:10.2307/25474643

Test, D. W., Kemp-Inman, A., Diegelmann, K., Hitt, S. B., & Bethune, L. (2015). Are online sources for identifying evidence-based practices trustworthy? An evaluation. *Exceptional Children, 82*, 58–80. doi:10.1177/0014402915585477

Torres, C., Farley, C. A., & Cook, B. G. (2012). A special educator's guide to successfully implementing evidence-based practices. *Teaching Exceptional Children, 45*(1), 64–73. doi:10.1177/004005991204500109

Vaughn, S., & Dammann, J. E. (2001). Science and sanity in special education. *Behavioral Disorders, 27*, 21–29. doi:10.1177/019874290102700107

Wehby, J. H., Symons, F. J., Canale, J. A., & Go, F. J. (1998). Teaching practices in classrooms for students with emotional and behavioral disorders: Discrepancies between recommendations and observations. *Behavioral Disorders, 24*, 51–56. doi:10.1177/019874299802400109

Wei, R. C., Darling-Hammond, L., & Adamson, F. (2010). *Professional development in the United States: Trends and challenges* (Vol. 28). Dallas, TX: National Staff Development Council.

Accountability breeds response-ability.

—Steven Covey

What Educators Need to Know About Accountability

James G. Shriner and Martha L. Thurlow

This Chapter Will Cover:

1. How the term *accountability* can be applied in many ways in education—to students, to educators, and to districts and schools.

2. The specific criteria of the Elementary and Secondary Education Act's accountability indicators that state schools must now meet.

3. The shift of the Individuals with Disabilities Education Act accountability criteria from compliance-only to compliance *and* results.

4. Why assessments are a key part of accountability, and how numerous changes (including the use of technology) have been made to them to increase their appropriateness for students with disabilities.

5. The importance of educators using other measures of student performance, such as formative assessment procedures, due to the limitations of accountability assessments.

Accountability is an integral part of education and special education today. This chapter identifies the targets of accountability in the U.S. educational system. It highlights the accountability systems that arise from both the Elementary and Secondary Education Act (ESEA) and the Individuals with Disabilities Education Act (IDEA). The chapter explores the role of assessment in accountability systems and concludes with some lessons in accountability learned from students with disabilities.

Accountability refers to holding a person or organization responsible for an action or event. This term is applied in many ways in schools, depending on the party being held responsible. Further, the indicators used in the different accountability applications may or may not be connected to each other.

States and districts may implement accountability at the *student level*. A common example is requiring students to meet specific requirements (including testing requirements) to graduate from high school with a regular diploma. Another example is requiring students to perform at a certain level on a Grade 3 reading assessment to be promoted to Grade 4 without being required to undergo remediation. States and districts also may implement accountability at the *educator level*. Teacher evaluation systems may be based on observational systems such as that of Charlotte Danielson (2013) but, more recently, have attempted to include student performance in rating teachers and principals (Holdheide, Browder, Warren, Buzick, & Jones, 2012).

Key Terms

Elementary and Secondary Education Act (ESEA) Accountability

Accountability systems at the *school level* focus on the performance of students and are, perhaps, more familiar to educators and the public. School accountability was most evident in the No Child Left Behind (NCLB) reauthorization of ESEA enacted in 2001. Under NCLB, schools had to meet predetermined accountability standards with the ultimate universal goal that every student in every school be proficient in reading and math. Failing to meet performance targets could result in federally prescribed penalties, including the removal and/or replacement of staff. In the most recent reauthorization of ESEA in 2015, the Every Student Succeeds Act (ESSA), states were given more control over the indicators included in their accountability systems and how the state would act on the results of the accountability indicators (National Council on Disability, 2018).

Martin, Sargrad, and Batel (2016) described seven main categories of indicators that states are including in their statewide accountability systems: (a) achievement indicators, (b) growth indicators in multiple academic subjects, (c) English language acquisition indicators, (d) early warning indicators (e.g., chronic absenteeism), (e) persistence indicators (e.g., graduation rates), (f) college and career indicators (e.g., participation in college entrance exams), and (g) other indicators (e.g., access to arts). They noted that states vary tremendously in the accountability systems they are creating for their schools.

Accountability also exists at the *state level*. The U.S. Department of Education holds states responsible for many things, including developing accountability systems that meet the requirements in ESSA. The revised statute maintains the positive aspects of NCLB for meaningful data collection and public reporting of school results but eliminates mostly punitive Adequate Yearly Progress (AYP) proficiency goals that seemingly dominated NCLB. Rather, ESSA instead focuses on states' internal processes to establish their own goals and milestones.

Each state's accountability system must be based on multiple indicators and measure annual performance on those indicators (including status and/or growth as determined by the state). ESSA (§6311[c][4][B]) requires that the five indicators include (a) academic achievement as measured by state assessments in math and reading/language arts (Grades 3–8 and once in high school); (b) one other academic indicator for elementary and middle schools that can differentiate student performance; (c) 4-year graduation rates for high schools; (d) English language proficiency; and (e) at least one other indicator that is valid, reliable, comparable, and statewide (such as measures of student engagement, educator engagement, advanced coursework, postsecondary readiness, or school climate and safety). Specific requirements make it mandatory to assign "substantial weight" to indicators (a) through

(d) and to include at least 95% of all students (including students with disabilities as a subgroup) (see ESSA §6311[c][4][C][E]).

The fifth indicator is the new aspect of the accountability system under control of the state. Most of the 50 states and the District of Columbia (n = 35) have opted to use chronic absenteeism as this fifth indicator; six states are using school climate, five are using school discipline, and another five are using some other measure of health/wellness (Child Trends, 2017). Eight of these states are combining several measures, such as chronic absenteeism and school discipline. The prevalence of chronic absenteeism as the fifth indicator may create unique challenges for students with disabilities (Cortiella & Boundy, 2018).

Using these indicators, states are to set both short-term and long-term goals for accountability for students as a whole and for each subgroup of students. In turn, states will make and report accountability determinations for each school based on the data collected, and these data-based determinations will be reported publicly. There are two basic "levels" of improvement determinations under the law: comprehensive support and targeted support. On a periodic basis (3 years), states are to identify districts and schools needing improvement based on the lowest-performing 5% of Title I schools in the state, schools where one or more subgroups are underperforming, and high schools with graduation rates of less than 67%. Schools that are determined to be in need of comprehensive support will be required to develop and implement evidence-based strategies to help with identified areas of service in need of improvement (e.g., curriculum, data literacy) and to examine resource allocations and distributions for possible inequities. Finally, under ESSA, districts and schools may be identified for targeted support when one or more groups of students are "consistently underperforming" as determined by the state. Targeted support is under state control and further extends "professional learning opportunities for educator knowledge, skills and understanding" (Illinois State Board of Education, 2017, p. 147) and might include organizational, leadership, and capacity-building strategies specifically addressing the needs of the identified groups.

Individuals with Disabilities Education Act (IDEA) Accountability

Another lens for accountability emanates from IDEA. In the past, states' monitoring and compliance systems emphasized *procedural* indicators (e.g., timely eligibility determinations and individualized education program [IEP] meetings) as proxies for the provision of a free appropriate public education (FAPE) for students with disabilities. A lesser focus was placed on *substantive* indicators such as program quality and evaluations of student performance and outcomes. However, there has been an increased emphasis on the examination of child outcomes at the school, district, and state levels. In federal statutes and policies (e.g., NCLB), views of accountability that included the learning outcomes of students with disabilities also gained increased attention.

Following the changes to accountability enacted under NCLB but prior to the passage of ESSA, the Office of Special Education Programs (OSEP) in the U.S. Department of Education gradually refocused its mission of improving results for infants, toddlers, and youth with disabilities, placing increased emphasis on holding states accountable for providing a FAPE to students receiving special education services through a results-driven accountability (RDA) system (U.S. Department of Education, 2014). The implementation of RDA has changed the emphasis of compliance from the traditional *procedural* focus to a more *substantive* focus that increases the importance of student performance and measurable results.

Starting in 2015, OSEP used both procedural (compliance-oriented) data and substantive (results-oriented) data to make a determination of each state's "status" under IDEA (U.S. Department of Education, 2014). In 2016, four substantive indicators were used to determine whether the state *met requirements*, *needed assistance*, *needed intervention*, or *needed substantial intervention*. The four indicators were (a) participation of children with disabilities on regular statewide assessments, (b) participation and performance of children with disabilities on the most recent National Assessment of Educational Progress, (c) percentage of children with disabilities who graduated with a regular high school diploma, and (d) percentage of children with disabilities who dropped out.

Along with IDEA's focus on improving outcomes, all states now develop their own State Systemic Improvement Plans (SSIPs) and measure their own improvement through State-Identified Measurable Results (SIMRs). These plans describe the state's primary goals for infants and toddlers with, or at risk for, disabilities (Part C) and for K–12 students (Part B) served under the law. States are required to submit their SIMRs to the federal government and report the obtained data on a yearly basis. Working together with each state, OSEP and other agencies are using the SIMR data to evaluate the state's efforts and capacity to improve results and provide opportunities and resources to better implement the SSIP (U.S. Department of Education, 2014).

Because each state was to develop an SIMR that was meaningful to stakeholders within the state and that addressed a prioritized area of need, there is much variability among those submitted. For Part C results (infants/toddlers), the SIMRs can be grouped into four main categories: *social/emotional*, *knowledge and skills*, *behavioral skills to meet needs*, and *family-oriented outcomes*. Part B results (K–12) identified include SIMRs grouped as *graduation rates*, *reading/English-language arts performance*, *mathematics performance*, and *postschool outcomes*. It is important to note that some states selected SIMRs that are classified as "other" results. In these cases, they chose to combine areas of student outcomes or, in the case of Part C, student and family outcomes. Interestingly, the majority of states (n = 31) developed an SIMR for *social*/emotional skills for Part C and a *reading/English-language arts performance* for Part B (n = 35). Table 8.1 is a sampling of four states' SIMRs for Parts B and C. For interested readers, as of 2017, each state's SIMRs are published at https://osep.grads360. org/#report/apr/publicView.

State	IDEA Part	Focus Area	SIMR
Table 8.1 State-Identified Measurable Results (SIMRs) Part B and Part C Examples			
IL	B	Reading/English-language arts	The percentage of third-grade students with disabilities who are proficient or above the grade-level standard on the state English-language arts assessment will increase.
	C	Knowledge and skills	To increase the percentage of infants and toddlers with disabilities who demonstrate greater than expected progress in the acquisition and use of knowledge and skills in pilot (geographical) areas by 0.9 percentage points by the end of 2018.
MN	B	Graduation	The percentage of Black and American Indian students with disabilities, combined, who graduated from the 6-year cohort will increase.
	C	Knowledge and skills	Infants, toddlers, and preschool children with disabilities will substantially increase their rate of growth in the acquisition and use of knowledge and skills by the time they exit Part C or transition to kindergarten.
WI	B	Reading/English-language arts	State will increase the performance of students with IEPs on the statewide literacy assessment, Grades 3–8.
	C	Social/emotional	Infants and toddlers will demonstrate improved social and emotional functioning to enhance their learning and participation in activities within the community.
KY	B	Math	The percentage of students with disabilities performing at or above proficient in middle school math, specifically at the eighth-grade level, with emphasis on reducing novice performance through professional learning, technical assistance, and support to elementary/middle school teachers around implementing, scaling, and sustaining evidence-based practices in math will increase.
	C	Other: parental support for children's development	Early intervention providers will change their ability to coach parents on interventions and strategies to help their child develop and learn. Parents will change their self-perception of their ability to help their child develop and learn.

Source: Created using data and information from https://osep.grads360.org/#report/apr/publicView

Accountability for students with disabilities relies to a significant extent on the inclusion of students with disabilities in assessments. To be confident that assessment results for students with disabilities are valid and reliable, the assessments must be accessible so students with disabilities can show their knowledge and skills on the same challenging content as other students are expected to know and be able to do (Thurlow, Lazarus, Christensen, & Shyyan, 2016). Accessibility includes designing assessments from the beginning with a focus on accessibility for all students; developing accessibility and accommodations policies informed by the construct being measured, available research findings, and the purposes of the assessment; and providing an alternate assessment measuring the knowledge and skills of students with the most significant cognitive disabilities.

A paradigm shift in approaches to accessibility for students with disabilities has taken place in recent years. Rather than identifying only accommodations for students with disabilities (and sometimes English-language learners), the concept of accessibility was expanded to include the provision of universal design (UD) features and accessibility features for all students, including students who neither have a disability nor are identified as English-language learners (Shyyan, Thurlow, Larson, Christensen, & Lazarus, 2016). This expansion of the concept of accessibility means all educators need to be aware of the concept of accessibility and be able to identify students' needs and then make solid decisions about their needs for various accessibility features, both in instructional (learning) and assessment environments. From an instructional perspective, UD offers a framework for reducing barriers by allowing for multiple means of representation, expression, and engagement (Center for Applied Special Technology, 2008; Smith & Lowrey, 2017) and is a way to build flexibility and differentiation into instruction from the outset (Karvonen, 2009). From an assessment perspective, UD offers increased flexibility for individualization to reduce the need for accommodations as retrofitted options, thereby supporting better validity inferences from results.

Lessons Learned: Accessibility and Progress for Students With Disabilities as Part of Accountability

Several lessons were learned after the initial implementation of accountability assessments with expanded accessibility options (Lazarus & Heritage, 2016). Among these were the following:

- Student needs must be identified so barriers interfering with their ability to demonstrate what they know can be removed.

- Educators need to know how to confidently make appropriate accessibility and accommodation decisions.

The concept of accessibility also applies to alternate assessments based on alternate academic achievement standards (AA-AAAS). Many states' AA-AAAS now have levels of accessibility in addition to accommodations. Thus, the needs of students with significant cognitive disabilities for accessibility and/or accommodation provisions likely will require renewed attention and refinement.

In the same way the concept of accessibility was expanded, the recognition of the importance of a comprehensive assessment system also has changed. Year-end or summative accountability assessments have a limited purpose. Other assessments are needed to support educators in instructing their students to improve their performance on state assessments. Specifically, classroom assessments provide a way to measure progress toward achievement of the state standards. These classroom assessments can take a variety of forms, including a variety of formative assessments, such as curriculum-based measures for progress monitoring (see Shriner & Thurlow, 2012).

Brookhart and Lazarus (2017) offered a broad description of formative assessment as a process rather than any particular test or assessment. It is one activity within the learning process and involves the students themselves so they can answer these questions: "What am I trying to learn? What progress have I made toward my learning goal? What next steps will take me closer to my learning goal?" Brookhart and Lazarus delineate several formative assessment strategies that are used by effective teachers:

> First, they share the learning target with the students and make sure they understand it. Second, they have students do, make, say, or write things that produce evidence about their status on the learning target as they work. Third, they share success criteria with students, things to look for in their work that become the yardstick by which they will assess their own evidence to decide where they are and what they need to do, study, or understand next. (p. 16)

Brookhart and Lazarus note that educators may need to provide additional scaffolding for these strategies for students with disabilities and struggling learners.

Going Forward With Accountability: Implications for Educators

The key provisions regarding the inclusion of students with disabilities in accountability systems are preserved by new statutes in ESSA. However, ESSA allows states to have more control over what their accountability systems will look like—including assessment provisions for students. Because of these changes and the longstanding expectation of IDEA that all students with disabilities have access to and make progress in the general education curriculum, administrators and IEP team members have the responsibility to be informed about the implications for accountability under the law and about the best practices to support opportunities for improving student outcomes.

As a starting point, it is important that administrators and teachers know how their state and district are responding to the ESSA accountability requirements, including the specific limit on the number of students with significant cognitive disabilities who can participate in alternate assessment. The fact that the 1% cap applies to total participation may mean that updated decision rules for who should (and should not) take the AA-AAAS will be needed. Finding out about such decision changes and being informed about their application is a district, school, and teacher responsibility.

Participation decisions in either the general assessment or AA-AAAS for all students with disabilities will continue to have an impact on IEP team functioning and communication. The IEP—including annual goals and assessment decisions—is to reflect meaningful access to the general curriculum and is to be "based on a State's academic content standards for the grade in which a child is enrolled" (U.S. Department of Education, 2015, p. 3). Parents should be informed and participate in decisions about the extent to which their child's IEP addresses the challenging academic standards from which the general curriculum is derived (National Down Syndrome Congress, 2016). Also, should the decision be made for a student to participate in alternate assessment, parents must be clearly informed that (a) their child's academic achievement will be measured based on alternate achievement standards and (b) participation in AA-AAAS may delay or otherwise affect the student in completing the requirements for a regular high school diploma (20 U.S.C. §1111[b][2][D][II][aa], [bb]).

Of course, the changing "accessibility/accommodation" decision environment discussed earlier implies that administrators and teachers need to understand the levels of accessibility in their states' alternate assessments, the needs of students with significant cognitive disabilities, and how to make good decisions about accessibility for them. IEP teams must make careful efforts to document accessibility features and accommodations used in teaching situations and to evaluate the impact of their use on students' ability to engage with curriculum and the content of instruction and assessments (Albus, Thurlow, Liu, Lazarus, & Larson, 2018).

Finally, because of the student focus of ESSA, under Title II of the statute, states are expected to support educators in their development of capacities to best serve all students to meet core content areas and to develop as learners. In Illinois, for example, the state has proposed to provide access to "professional learning opportunities that enhance learning environments ... throughout the continuum of early childhood through college and career" (Illinois State Board of Education, 2017, p. 97). Educators should make themselves aware of professional development opportunities being offered by their districts and the state, as well as the establishment of virtual and in-person professional learning communities. The overarching goal of educator responsibility within an accountability-oriented system remains that of helping all students achieve to the highest levels they can by making progress relative to challenging academic content standards and in light of their individual circumstances.

REFLECTING AND UNDERSTANDING

1. What are the three main "levels" of accountability, and what is an example of each one?

2. How are students with significant cognitive disabilities included in accountability systems under the Every Student Succeeds Act?

3. How has the focus of accountability provision under the Individuals with Disabilities Education Act changed over time?

4. What are State-Identified Measurable Results, and how are they used in accountability systems?

5. Briefly describe the "paradigm shift" in approaches that has occurred with respect to including students with disabilities in meaningful instruction and assessment related to the general curriculum.

ONLINE RESOURCES

- Achieve: https://www.achieve.org

- Center for Applied Special Technology: http://www.cast.org

- Collaboration for Effective Educator, Development, Accountability and Reform: http://ceedar.education.ufl.edu/wp -content/uploads/2014/08/IC-7_ FINAL_08-27-14.pdf

- Council for Exceptional Children: Professional Development:

https://www.cec.sped.org/Professional -Development

- Early Childhood Technical Assistance Center: http://ectacenter.org/

- National Center for Systemic Improvement: https://ncsi.wested.org/

- Office of Special Education Programs, U.S. Department of Education: Results-Driven Accountability: https://www2.ed.gov/ about/offices/list/osers/osep/rda/index.html

RECOMMENDED READINGS

Articles

Holdheide, L., Browder, D., Warren, S., Buzick, H., & Jones, N. (2012). *Using student growth to evaluate educators of students with disabilities: Issues, challenges, and next steps.* Washington, DC: National Comprehensive Center for Teacher Quality (ERIC Document Reproduction Service No. ED543814).

Karvonen, M. (2009). Developing standards-based IEPs that promote effective instruction. In M. Perie (Ed.), *Considerations for the alternate assessment based on modified achievement standards (AA-MAS): Understanding the eligible population and applying that knowledge to their instruction and assessment* (pp. 51–89). New York:

New York Comprehensive Center & New York State Education Department. Retrieved from https://nceo .umn.edu/docs/AAMAS/AAMASwhitePaper.pdf

National Down Syndrome Congress. (2016). *Every Student Succeeds Act: Frequently asked questions about IEPs.* Roswell, GA: Author. Retrieved from https://www. ndsccenter.org/wp-content/uploads/ESSA-FAQs-and-IEP-Tips.pdf

Smith, S. J., & Lowrey, K. A. (2017). Applying the universal design for learning framework for individuals with intellectual disability: The future must be now. *Intellectual and Developmental Disabilities, 55*(1), 48–51.

REFERENCES

Albus, D., Thurlow, M. L., Liu, K. K., Lazarus, S. S., & Larson, E. D. (2018). *Educator perspectives on classroom implementation of accessibility features and accommodations.* Minneapolis: University of Minnesota, Data Informed Accessibility-Making Optimal Needs-Based Decisions (DIAMOND).

Brookhart, S., & Lazarus, S. (2017). *Formative assessment for students with disabilities.* Washington, DC: Council of Chief State School Officers, State Collaborative on Assessing Special Education Students.

Center for Applied Special Technology. (2008). *Universal design for learning (UDL) guidelines—Version 1.0.* Wakefield, MA: Author. Retrieved from http://udlguidelines.cast.org/binaries/content/assets/udlguidelines/udlg-v1-0/udlg_graphicorganizer_v1-0.pdf

Child Trends. (2017). *Analysis of ESSA state plans "School Quality or Student Success Indicator" 9/20/17.* Retrieved December 22, 2017, from https://www.childtrends.org/wp-content/uploads/2017/09/ESSA-Fifth-Indicator-Coding-Child-Trends-9-20-2017.pdf

Cortiella, C., & Boundy, K. (2018). *Students with disabilities and chronic absenteeism* (NCEO Brief Number 14). Minneapolis: University of Minnesota, National Center on Educational Outcomes.

Danielson, C. (2013). *The framework for teaching evaluation instrument* (Version 1.2). Retrieved November 21, 2017, from http://www.danielsongroup.org

Elementary and Secondary Education Act of 1965, 20 U.S.C. § 6301 *et seq.*

Every Student Succeeds Act of 2015, § 6301 *et seq.*

Holdheide, L., Browder, D., Warren, S., Buzick, H., & Jones, N. (2012). *Using student growth to evaluate educators of students with disabilities: Issues, challenges, and next steps.* Washington, DC: National Comprehensive Center for Teacher Quality (ERIC Document Reproduction Service No. ED543814).

Illinois State Board of Education. (2017). *Consolidated state plan under the Every Student Succeeds Act.* Springfield, IL: Author. Retrieved from https://www.isbe.net/Documents/ESSAStatePlanforIllinois.pdf

Individuals with Disabilities Education Act, 20 U.S.C. § 1401 *et seq.*

Individuals with Disabilities Education Act Regulations, 34 C.F.R. § 300 *et seq.*

Karvonen, M. (2009). Developing standards-based IEPs that promote effective instruction. In M. Perie, *Considerations for the alternate assessment based on modified achievement standards (AA-MAS): Understanding the eligible population and applying that knowledge to their instruction and assessment* (pp. 51–89). New York: New York Comprehensive Center & New York State Education Department. Retrieved from https://nceo.umn.edu/docs/AAMAS/AAMASwhitePaper.pdf

Lazarus, S. S., & Heritage, M. (2016). *Lessons learned about assessment from inclusion of students with disabilities in college and career ready assessments.* Minneapolis: University of Minnesota, National Center on Educational Outcomes.

Martin, C., Sargrad, S., & Batel, S. (2016). *Making the grade: A 50-state analysis of school accountability systems.* Washington, DC: Center for American Progress.

National Council on Disability. (2018). *Every Student Succeeds Act and students with disabilities.* Washington, DC: Author. Retrieved from https://ncd.gov/publications/2018/individuals-disabilities-education-act-report-series-5-report-briefs

National Down Syndrome Congress. (2016). *Every Student Succeeds Act: Frequently asked questions about IEPs.* Roswell, GA: Author. Retrieved from https://www.ndsccenter.org/wp-content/uploads/ESSA-FAQs-and-IEP-Tips.pdf

No Child Left Behind Act of 2001, 20 U.S.C. § 6301 *et seq.*

Shriner, J. G., & Thurlow, M. L. (2012). Curriculum-based measurement, progress monitoring and state assessments. In C. A. Espin, K. L. McMaster, S. Rose, & M. M. Wayman (Eds.), *A measure of success: The influence of curriculum-based measurement on education* (pp. 247–258). Minneapolis: University of Minnesota Press.

Shyyan, V. V., Thurlow, M. L., Larson, E. D., Christensen, L. L., & Lazarus, S. S. (2016). *White paper on common accessibility language for states and assessment vendors.* Minneapolis: University of Minnesota, Data Informed Accessibility—Making Optimal Needs-Based Decisions (DIAMOND).

Smith, S. J., & Lowrey, K. A. (2017). Applying the universal design for learning framework for individuals with intellectual disability: The future must be now. *Intellectual and Developmental Disabilities, 55*(1), 48–51.

Thurlow, M. L., Lazarus, S. S., Christensen, L. L., & Shyyan, V. (2016). *Principles and characteristics of inclusive assessment systems in a changing assessment landscape* (NCEO Report 400). Minneapolis: University of Minnesota, National Center on Educational Outcomes.

U.S. Department of Education. (2014). *Dear colleague letter on results driven accountability (RDA).* Washington, DC: Office of Special Education and Rehabilitative Services. Retrieved from https://www2.ed.gov/about/offices/list/osers/osep/rda/050914rda-lette-to-chiefs-final.pdf

U.S. Department of Education. (2015). *Dear colleague letter on free and appropriate public education (FAPE).* Washington, DC: U.S. Department of Education, Office of Special Education and Rehabilitation Services. Retrieved from http://www2.ed.gov/policy/speced/guid/idea/memosdcltrs/guidance-on-fape-11-17-2015.pdf

CHAPTER

9

Taking Aim at Current Trends in Early Childhood Special Education

Kate Ascetta

This Chapter Will Cover:

1. How to close the research-to-practice gap using an implementation science framework.
2. Ways to reduce high rates of expulsion and suspension in schools among students with disabilities.
3. How to raise awareness and support for mental health needs of young children and families.
4. Suggestions for how to increase cultural and linguistic diversity among the student population.

"We were struck by the absence of discussion of culture, poverty, and the changing demographics of families and children in the articles describing progress in our field" (Dunlap, Hemmeter, Kaiser, & Wolery, 2011, p. 242). Dunlap and colleagues were reflecting on the 25th anniversary of Public Law 99-457—a policy requiring special education services to include children under age 5—and the lack of diversity. Many educators and administrators find themselves grappling with how to best support children who have experienced risk factors that impact their engagement with the learning environment. Young children come to receive special education services through the provisions of the Individuals with Disabilities Education Act (2004) Part C (birth to 2 years) or Part B (3–21 years). Typically, families, medical professionals, or childcare providers will identify a need; this could happen as early as birth. The referral process to determine eligibility can vary from state to state (Dunst & Bruder, 2002). A child's assessment process likely uses developmental screeners such as the Ages and Stages Questionnaire (Bricker et al., 1999) or the Battelle Developmental Inventory Screening Test (Elbaum, Gattamorta, & Penfield, 2010). If the referral process leads to eligibility, we then begin the challenging task of planning and providing support services for children with, or at risk for, developmental delays as they enter our classrooms.

In recent decades, our classrooms have become increasingly more linguistically and culturally diverse (e.g., Zepeda, Castro, & Cronin, 2011). Teachers often feel unprepared to support their students in culturally responsive ways and report a lack of understanding of the most effective ways to engage families from cultures that differ from their own (Cheatham & Jimenez-Silva, 2012). Additionally, high rates of expulsion and suspensions are prevalent in early childhood classrooms across the United States

- cultural and linguistic diversity
- evidence-based practices
- implementation science
- trauma

(e.g., Gilliam, 2005; Splett & Hawks, 2011)—a trend that has lasting effects (such as decreased graduation rates and increased involvement in the juvenile justice system). Recent research has demonstrated that our young children and their families need easier access to mental health supports (National Scientific Council on the Developing Child, 2008/2012), and yet these needs often go unmet. The field of early childhood special education (ECSE) has a responsibility to address the needs of all children.

A strong research foundation provides an evidence base for practices that address causes of suspensions (Dunlap et al., 2011; Odom, 2009), mental health supports, and culturally diverse populations in our classrooms, and yet these practices are inconsistently implemented, resulting in a research-to-practice gap (e.g., Odom, 2009; Reichow, Boyd, Barton, & Odom, 2016). If we have tools that work, why don't we consistently use them in our classrooms? "I propose a focus on implementation as the tie that binds EI/ECSE practices that have emerged from the literature as evidence based to outcomes for children in classrooms, communities, and homes." (Odom, 2009, p. 53). Perhaps that is why Odom (2009) argued that focusing on implementation—the systematic practice of engaging communities in the sustained use of evidence-based interventions—is how ECSE can effectively reach children and families from diverse backgrounds.

This chapter will outline three trending topics facing the field of ECSE: (a) expulsion and suspension, (b) mental health supports, and (c) cultural and linguistic diversity. It will then conclude with an overview of current evidence-based professional development practices related to supporting teachers' implementation of evidence-based practices targeted at these three topics. The guiding framework of this chapter follows a model adopted from the implementation sciences literature—specifically, the RE:AIM (reach, effectiveness, adoption, implementation, and maintenance) model (Glasgow, Vogt, & Boles, 1999). Each of the three topics will first discuss the **reach**—who are the populations involved?—and the **effectiveness**—what are the current recommended practices? Then the final section, implications for practice, will review how to reach teachers and other specialists using professional development to address the research-to-practice gap and take **AIM**—the **adoption**, **implementation**, and **maintenance** of evidence-based practices. The remainder of the chapter will be laid out as such:

- Part 1: Reducing Expulsion and Suspensions in the Early Childhood Classrooms

  - Brief overview of expulsion rates

  - Brief overview of implicit bias and early childhood education

  - **R**—Who is disproportionally affected by high expulsion rates, and how do we reach teachers and administrators?

  - **E**—What are we currently doing that is effective?

- Part 2: Renewed Focus on Mental Health Supports for Young Children and Their Families

  o Brief overview of trauma and toxic stress

  o Connections to challenging behaviors

  o *R*—Who are we trying to reach?

  o *E*—What are we currently doing that is effective?

- Part 3: Meeting the Cultural and Linguistic Diversity of ECSE

  o Brief overview of changing demographics in U.S. schools

  o *R*—Who is impacted? Who are the increased populations?

  o *E*—What are we currently doing that is effective?

- Part 4: Using Professional Development for the Adoption and Implementation of Effective Practices—Implications for Practice

  o Overview of technology-enhanced professional development

  o *AIM*—Which strategies should we adopt, implement, and maintain to strengthen the workforce of educators?

  o Implications for practice

Part 1: Reducing Expulsion and Suspensions in the Early Childhood Classrooms

In 2005, Gilliam published work shedding light on a crisis in our early childhood classrooms—preschool children were 3 times more likely to be expelled or suspended than were their K–12 counterparts; the preschools reported expelling students at a rate 13 times higher than that of K–12 schools. Who does this primarily affect? What is the **reach** for young children? First, male students were expelled at a rate 4.5 times higher than were female students (Gilliam, 2005). African American students were expelled or suspended at 2 times the rate of their non–African American peers (Gilliam, 2005). A more recent study conducted by the U.S. Department of Education Office for Civil Rights in 2014 found that Black children represented 19% of the preschool population but made up 47% of all students expelled. The exclusionary practices happening in early childhood are troubling and need to be addressed.

Let's first examine what has contributed to so many young children being asked to leave the classroom in such disproportionate numbers. Recent studies have pointed to features of the classroom (i.e., student–teacher ratio, availability of behavioral supports and consultants) and of teachers (i.e., implicit bias, stress) that may be related to this pattern of suspension and expulsion (Dunlap et al., 2006). Student–teacher ratios can be challenging to address and maintain in certain programs despite the national recommendations and standards (Gilliam & Shahar, 2006). Many early childhood centers do not have access to mental health consultants, which would aid teachers in supporting young children and decrease expulsion and suspension (Gilliam, 2005; Gilliam & Shahar, 2006). ECSE program staff need training to create learning environments that build children's emotional competence and confidence (Dunlap et al., 2006). However, even once those foundational social–emotional skills (e.g., emotional literacy, developmental milestones) are being provided and taught, classroom staff may still need access to behavioral specialists. For example, about 21% of children ages 4 to 5 years who exhibit symptomatology of attention deficit hyperactivity disorder never receive access to behavioral therapy—the suggested first intervention for such disorders (Centers for Disease Control and Prevention, 2018). Children's needs are not being addressed, and teachers often are unprepared to support them.

Recent studies have attempted deeper examinations of why young Black males are being expelled and suspended at disproportionate rates, and have investigated the role that implicit bias plays in exclusionary practices in early childhood (Gilliam, Maupin, & Reyes, 2016). In one such study, researchers asked teachers to watch videos of young children and report any challenging behaviors exhibited by the students. These teachers reported that Black male students engaged in challenging behaviors at higher rates than did non-Black students, when in actuality no child in the video presented challenging behaviors (Gilliam et al., 2016). This has led researchers to explore the possibility that bias may unfairly shape the implementation of disciplinary polices in programs. Implicit bias is defined as "the automatic and unconscious stereotypes that drive people to behave and make decisions in certain ways" (Gilliam et al., 2016, p. 3). Gilliam and colleagues (2016) also found that teachers were more likely to express less empathy for children whose race differed from their own when learning about difficulties at home or other environmental factors. It may be that these unconscious associations between race and challenging behaviors have led to the disproportional rates of exclusionary actions taken with young Black male students. As early interventionists, we need to be particularly cognizant of implicit bias because it may lead to inappropriate rates of referrals for special education and inequitable educational experiences (Gregory, Skiba, & Noguera, 2010; Harry & Klingner, 2014). It is critical that we understand the possible impact our perceived expectations may have on interactions with students and the families we work with (Gilliam et al., 2016). We want to make sure that as we make referrals, conduct assessments, and implement intervention plans, we are acknowledging and addressing the possible role that implicit bias plays in the process.

We need to *reach* our teachers who work with young children of color and focus our efforts on practices that demonstrate positive outcomes for decreasing expulsion and increasing social–emotional development. We want to promote the social and emotional competence of young children in our classrooms to address the high rates of expulsion and suspensions. Teachers and the children they serve benefit from trainings and support related to social–emotional development (Dunlap et al., 2006). Currently, there are numerous evidence-based strategies that support teachers and promote the development of young children. Please see Table 9.1 for examples of practices currently being used in classrooms and programs to address the issue of suspension and expulsion—the *effectiveness*. In addition to the selected practices, it should be noted that providing mental health supports to early childhood teachers and giving them access to this content reduced the negative behaviors in children associated with challenging behavior (Gilliam et al., 2016). The mental health supports are addressed in the next section.

Table 9.1 Current Effective Practices to Address Suspension and Expulsion

Practice	Brief Description	Resource Links
Pyramid Model	Evidence-based practice uses a classroom-wide set of strategies to support the emotional development and competence of young children. Tiered approach to building classrooms that are emotionally responsive and teach skills that will support school readiness.	• http://challengingbehavior.cbcs.usf.edu/ • http://www.pyramidmodel.org/ • http://csefel.vanderbilt.edu/
Incredible Years:Teacher Training Program	Program targeted at more intensive needs; can be used for specific behavioral skills, whole class, and then small-group work as well. Focus on building social skills. Includes a parent training component.	• https://ies.ed.gov/ncee/wwc/Intervention/766 • http://www.incredibleyears.com/
Second Step	Program focused on social skills building and decreased aggression. Designed to be implemented with the whole classroom. Use of developmentally appropriate visuals and puppets to engage young learners.	• http://www.secondstep.org/early-learning-curriculum • https://ies.ed.gov/ncee/wwc/Intervention/792
Promoting Alternative Thinking Strategies (PATHS) Curriculum	Program focused on promoting social competence and fostering a learning environment that is responsive to students' emotional needs to prevent later challenges.	• http://www.pathstraining.com/main/curriculum/ • https://www.channing-bete.com/prevention-programs/paths/paths.html

Part 2: Renewed Focus on Mental Health Supports for Young Children and Their Families

Exposure to trauma and adverse early life experiences can lead to mental health needs for young children and their families (Shonkoff et al., 2012). As educators, it is critical that we understand the role trauma can play in affecting the behavioral and educational outcome of young children. Trauma can be caused by exposure to drugs, domestic violence, disruption of care, and untreated family mental health concerns (Shonkoff et al., 2012). While no racial or socioeconomic group is fully protected from adverse early life experiences, children from minority groups and/or experiencing poverty are at increased risk of lifetime exposure to violence, abuse, and drugs when compared with their peers (Lieberman, Chu, Van Horn, & Harris, 2011). These sustained exposures to toxic stress (i.e., high levels of chronic stress over a sustained period of time) can negatively impact a child's development and usually require intensive early intervention services (Shonkoff, Boyce, & McEwen, 2009). For example, children under the age of 5 represent 36% of all children who enter the foster care system (U.S. Department of Health and Human Services, 2017). This early disruption of care can lead to difficulties with attachment, negatively impact their engagement with others, and increase the likelihood of presenting challenging behaviors (Lieberman et al., 2011).

Trauma and unaddressed mental health issues can lead to challenging behaviors that impact a child's development (e.g., Perry, Dunne, McFadden, & Campbell, 2008). Close to 33% of preschool-age children demonstrate challenging behaviors that impact educational experiences in a negative way (Rescorla et al., 2011). We need to **reach** the mental health needs of our young children and address the underlying causes of these maladaptive behaviors. It is critical that we address the needs of children age birth to 5 years in our communities who are exposed to risk factors that can adversely affect their academic and social futures. Failing to address these challenges can result in long-lasting consequences (Dunlap et al., 2006). The mental health of young children impacts their behavior in classrooms (Lieberman et al., 2011), and the implementation of evidence-based practices has demonstrated positive **effects** for addressing these concerns in classrooms.

Table 9.2 Current Effective Practices to Address Mental Health Supports for Young Children and Families

Practice	Description	Resource Links
Positive Parenting Program (Triple P)	Designed to treat child behavior problems and promote positive parent–child relationships. Focuses on providing parents with information and skills to increase confidence and self-sufficiency related to supporting their child's behavior.	• https://www.triplep.net/glo-en/home/
Trauma-Focused Cognitive Behavioral Therapy	More intensive in nature, used when known exposure to trauma has occurred, and is dyadic in nature, working on the relationship between the child and their caregiver.	• https://tfcbt.musc.edu/ • https://tfcbt.org/
Child–Parent Interaction Therapy	More intensive one-on-one supports with real-time coaching, providing parents support with interactions with their child.	• http://www.pcit.org/

Please see Table 9.2 for a selection of current evidence-based practices implemented with young children. Many researchers and policymakers advocate for mental health consultations in response to increased challenging behavior observed in classrooms and high expulsion rates. A major area of concern in early childhood programs is access to trained staff (Green, Everhart, Gordon, & Garcia Gettman, 2006; Wesley & Buysse, 2004). In their review of the implementation of mental health consultations among Head Start programs, Green and colleagues (2006) found that the frequency with which the consultants met with teachers and/or families impacted the relationships and thus the outcomes of services provided. Finding ways to *reach* young children and *effectively* address their mental health needs must remain a priority for the field of ECSE.

Part 3: Meeting the Cultural and Linguistic Diversity of ECSE

The demographics (e.g., race/ethnicity, languages spoken, socioeconomic status) of children and families accessing early childhood services in the United States have shifted over the past decades. Based on the 2010 U.S. Census, cultural and linguistic minorities make up 46% of the children under 18 in the United States (O'Hare, 2011). In many communities in the United States, 50% of preschool-age children come from non-English-speaking homes (Espinosa, 2005). Over the past decade, Latino students represent the fastest growing school-age population—40% of the student population (Garcia & Jensen, 2009; Lugo-Neris, Jackson, & Goldstein, 2010). The demographics have also shifted regarding economic diversity: 25% of children attending an early childhood setting are experiencing severe poverty (Jiang, Ekono, & Skinner, 2015). As previously mentioned, severe poverty increases the risk of exposure to adverse experiences and impacts a child's development (e.g., Shonkoff et al., 2009). Importantly, while the cultural and linguistic diversity of our students has changed, this change has not been reflected in our staff and policies. Teachers regularly report that they feel unprepared to support the increasing number of students that come from linguistically diverse backgrounds (Zepeda et al., 2011). For example, most early childhood special educators are monolingual English speakers (Zepeda et al., 2011), which can make teachers feel less prepared to teach dual-language learners. Additionally, practitioners often struggle to build meaningful relationships with families from different cultural and linguistic backgrounds than their own—and that connection to family is foundational to ECSE (e.g., Cheatham & Jimenez-Silva, 2012; Cheatham & Santos, 2011).

The disconnect between early childhood special educators and the populations they work with can lead to inequitable educational experiences. While there is a great desire to support culturally and linguistically diverse early childhood populations, we continue to miss the mark—the achievement gap is not closing (e.g., Gutiérrez, Zepeda, & Castro, 2010). For example, Black children are more likely to be referred for behavioral issues and underreported for gifted and talented programs (Harry & Klingner, 2014). Dual-language learners are often vastly underrepresented in early intervention services (Morgan, Farkas, Hillemeier, & Maczuga, 2012) and then by school age are overrepresented in special education (Artiles, Kozleski, Trent, Osher, & Ortiz, 2010; Farnsworth, 2016). Another common concern in ECSE is the lack of accessibility to services in the students' native languages (Paradis, 2011; Zepeda et al., 2011). This creates challenges in maintaining the native language and addressing the underlying disability. Dual-language learners are often misdiagnosed with learning disabilities because the assessments were not conducted in their native language or reflective of their home culture (Durán, Cheatham, & Santos, 2011; Zepeda et al., 2011). It is critical that teachers have the support and training to understand that differences in language development do not represent a disability or need for services (Zepeda et al., 2011).

Many professionals are striving to bridge the gap and ensure the delivery of high-quality ECSE services to a diverse group of families—the *effectiveness*. Please see Table 9.3 for a sample of recommended practices currently being used to engage culturally and linguistically diverse populations. For example, Beneke and Cheatham (2016) proposed this idea of cross-cultural partnerships for early intervention/ECSE providers working with families. They build on the notion that this is a dynamic system that evolves over time and is based on democratic principles—wanting an exchange of ideas and equal participation from both parties (families and professionals).

Table 9.3 Current Effective Practices to Meet Cultural and Linguistic Diversity Populations

Practice	Description	Resource Links
Assessment Tool: Individual Growth and Development Indicators (IGDIs-Español)	Early literacy screening tool	• https://www.myigdis.com/preschool-assessments/early-literacy-assessments/ • http://www.schoolreadinessblog.com/understanding-dll-development-in-early-childhood/
Anti-Bias Curriculum	Provides guidance to teachers in establishing learning environments that support a diverse set of students	• https://www.naeyc.org/resources/topics/anti-bias-education/overview
Culturally Responsive Instruction	Instruction that focuses on building on students' assets and strengthening teachers' cultural competence	• https://eclkc.ohs.acf.hhs.gov/culture-language • https://iris.peabody.vanderbilt.edu/module/dll/#content • http://www.nectac.org/~pdfs/pubs/qualityindicatorsinclusion.pdf

They continue to argue that we need to understand the harm done when we remain rigid or assume features of culture to be true—that there is always a play between power and privilege. As mentioned earlier, implicit bias can also play a role here when we conceptualize working with culturally and linguistically diverse families (Gilliam, 2005; Harry & Klingner, 2014). For example, a power dynamic can occur when the emphasis is placed on English as the dominant language over a child's native or home language—thus privileging English over other languages (Delpit, 2006). We need to be aware of those biases and how they may impact or shape our interactions with children and families.

Part 4: Using Professional Development for the Adoption and Implementation of Effective Practices—Implications for Practice

"Professional development is facilitated teaching and learning experiences that are transactional and designed to support the acquisition of professional knowledge, skills, and dispositions as well as the application of this knowledge in practice" (National Professional Development Center on Inclusion, 2008, p. 3). The final section will focus specifically on how current professional development practices (*reach* and *effectiveness*) can lead to the *adoption*, *implementation*, and *maintenance* of evidence-based interventions to address the challenges that face early childhood special educators and programs. Recently, professional development research has focused on designing effective and efficient methods that are specifically related to reducing barriers to access through the use of technology. We seek, as Snyder, Hemmeter, and McLaughlin (2011) argued for on the 25th anniversary of PL 99-75, to move away from one-time workshops and instead use technology not simply as a delivery mechanism but as a mechanism for increased engagement between practitioners and the people they serve.

Currently, technology-enhanced professional development is reaching practitioners and supporting the *adoption*, *implementation*, and *maintenance* of evidence-based practices related to each of the three previous topics (i.e., suspension rates, mental health supports, and diverse populations). The integration of technology into professional development practices can increase the likelihood that evidence-based practices will get adopted and implemented, because more people can access them (e.g., Baumel, Pawar, Kane, & Correll, 2016; McGoron & Ondersma, 2015; Odom, 2009; Zaslow et al., 2010). Teachers and programs need access to supports, and technology can often reduce the barriers to engagement (Hall & Bierman, 2015; Odom, 2009). See Table 9.4 for examples of professional development that has integrated technology used in the *adoption* and **implementation** of evidence-based practices to **reach** children and families involved with ECSE.

Next we will provide examples of how technology-enhanced professional development (e.g., e-mail, videoconferencing, bug in ear) can be applied by teachers and programs to directly address the three previously discussed trends. Table 9.4 provides several evidence-based practical implications to address the reduction of challenging behavior, increasing mental health supports, and culturally and linguistically diverse student populations.

Table 9.4   Current Technology-Enhanced Professional Development Practices

Practice	Description	Resource Links
Applications	Websites or online learning modules accessed through a browsers/app	• https://ies.ed.gov/ncee/wwc/Intervention/1301 • https://curry.virginia.edu/myteachingpartner • https://infantnet.ori.org/infantnet/index.html
Mobile devices and equipment	Use of phones, tablets, or bug-in-ear devices to deliver and share content	• http://journals.sagepub.com/doi/full/10.1177/1053815117748692 • http://psycnet.apa.org/record/2010-08635-003 • https://developingchild.harvard.edu/innovation-application/innovation-in-action/find/

For example, as previously mentioned, programs often have limited access to behavior specialists or mental health consultants, and one way we can address this is through the use of technology (e.g., Antonini et al., 2014; Taylor et al., 2008). Telehealth shows promise as a way to increase the **adoption**, **implementation**, and **maintenance** of evidence-based practices in ECSE. For example, something as simple as sending electronic feedback on teachers' implementation of strategies from the Pyramid Model (Hemmeter, Snyder, Kinder, & Artman, 2011) as a way to decrease suspension and expulsion by supporting teachers' knowledge and skill development. Or perhaps the delivery of coaching via bug-in technology to provide real-time coaching without interrupting the natural environment of the classroom (e.g., Ottley, Grygas Coogle, Rahn, & Spear, 2017). Additionally, when technology is used to reduce barriers (e.g., finding childcare, transportation), parent participation and engagement increase (e.g., Carta, Lefever, Bigelow, Borkowski, & Warren, 2013). Technology-enhanced professional development shows great promise for strengthening teachers' instructional practices.

Conclusion

The field of special education faces significant challenges, including increasing equitable education for all children. As a field we will continue to work to *reach* children from linguistically and culturally diverse backgrounds, those who've experienced trauma or exposure to risk factors, and those developing their social and emotional competence. In conclusion, it is about understanding the **reach** of current trends and evidence-based practices shown to address those trends, the **effectiveness**, and examining what likely leads to sustained changes—the **adoption**, **implementation**, and **maintenance**. Below are lists of resources and ways to stay connected and informed as it relates to ECSE topics such as the ones discussed in this chapter, as well as future topics. As we look to the future of ECSE and what that means for the children and families we serve, let us remember to RE:AIM and focus on what matters: providing high-quality early childhood educational experiences to all children.

REFLECTING AND UNDERSTANDING

1. What are three major trends currently faced by the field of ECSE?

2. What is a guiding framework we, as a field, can use to address these trends? How might this framework guide your practice?

3. What are some contributing factors to high rates of suspension and expulsion in ECSE?

4. What role might trauma play in challenging behavior? How can we address these mental health concerns?

5. What does the research suggest are evidence-based practices for supporting a linguistically and culturally diverse student population?

6. How might you get connected with the larger ECSE community and stay informed in the use of evidence-based practices?

ONLINE RESOURCES

- Behavior Analyst Certification Board: https://www.bacb.com/find-a-certificant/

- Center on Enhancing Early Learning Outcomes: http://ceelo.org

- Center on the Social and Emotional Foundations for Early Learning: http://csefel.vanderbilt.edu/index.html

- Child Trends: https://www.childtrends.org/

- Division for Early Childhood: http://www.dec-sped.org/journals

- The Frank Porter Graham Child Development Institute: http://fpg.unc.edu/

- Juniper Gardens Children's Project: https://jgcp.ku.edu/

- National Institute for Early Education Research: http://nieer.org/

RECOMMENDED READING

Article

Zero to Three. (2018). *Preventing expulsion from preschool and child care*. Retrieved from https://www.zerotothree.org/resources/series/preventing-expulsion-from-preschool-and-child-care

PROFESSIONAL ORGANIZATIONS

Join Division for Early Childhood: http://www.dec-sped.org/

Find your state chapter—or start one today!

Join National Association for the Education of Young Children: https://www.naeyc.org/

Find your state chapter—or start one today!

REFERENCES

Antonini, T. N., Raj, S. P., Oberjohn, K. S., Cassedy, A., Makoroff, K. L., Fouladi, M., & Wade, S. L. (2014). A pilot randomized trial of an online parenting skills program for pediatric traumatic brain injury: Improvements in parenting and child behavior. *Behavior Therapy, 45*(4), 455–468.

Artiles A. J., Kozleski E. B., Trent S. C., Osher D., & Ortiz, A. (2010). Justifying and explaining disproportionality, 1968–2008: A critique of underlying views and culture. *Exceptional Children, 76,* 279–299.

Baumel, A., Pawar, A., Kane, J. M., & Correll, C. U. (2016). Digital parent training for children with disruptive behaviors: Systematic review and meta-analysis of randomized trials. *Journal of Child and Adolescent Psychopharmacology, 26*(8), 740–749.

Beneke, M. R., & Cheatham, G. A. (2016). Inclusive, democratic family–professional partnerships: (Re)conceptualizing culture and language in teacher preparation. *Topics in Early Childhood Special Education, 35*(4), 234–244.

Bricker, D., Squires, J., Mounts, L., Potter, L., Nickel, R., & Twombly, E. (1999). *Ages and stages questionnaires: A parent-completed, child-monitoring systems* (2nd ed.). Baltimore, MD: Paul H. Brookes.

Carta, J., Lefever, J., Bigelow, K., Borkowski, J., & Warren, S. (2013). Randomized trial of a cellular phone-enhanced home visitation parenting intervention. *Pediatrics, 132*(Suppl. 2), 167–173.

Centers for Disease Control and Prevention. (2018, June). *Key findings: Treatment of attention-deficit/hyperactivity disorder (ADHD) among children with special health care needs.* Atlanta, GA: U.S. Department of Health and Human Services, Centers for Disease Control and Prevention.

Cheatham, G. A., & Jimenez-Silva, M. (2012). Partnering with Latino families during kindergarten transition: Lessons learned from a parent-teacher conference. *Childhood Education, 88*(3), 177–184.

Cheatham, G. A., & Santos, R. M. (2011). Collaborating with families from diverse cultural and linguistic backgrounds. *Young Children, 66*(5), 76–82.

Delpit, L. (2006). *Other people's children: Cultural conflict in the classroom.* New York, NY: New Press.

Dunlap, G., Hemmeter, M. L., Kaiser, A. P., & Wolery, M. (2011). Introduction to PL 99-457 anniversary issues. *Journal of Early Intervention, 33,* 239–242.

Dunlap, G., Strain, P. S., Fox, L., Carta, J. J., Conroy, M., Smith, B. J., Kern, L.... Sowell, C. (2006). Prevention and intervention with young children's challenging behavior: Perspectives regarding current knowledge. *Behavioral Disorders, 32*(1), 29–45. https://doi.org/10.1177/019874290603200103

Dunst, C. J., & Bruder, M. B. (2002). Valued outcomes of service coordination, early intervention, and natural environments. *Exceptional Children, 68*(3), 361–375.

Durán, L. K., Cheatham, G. A., & Santos, R. M. (2011). Evaluating young children who are dual language learners: Gathering and interpreting multiple sources of data to make informed decisions. *Young Exceptional Children Monograph Series, 13,* 133–156.

Elbaum, B., Gattamorta, K. A., & Penfield, R. D. (2010). Evaluation of the Battelle Developmental Inventory, 2nd Edition, screening test for use in states' child outcomes measurement systems under the Individuals with Disabilities Education Act. *Journal of Early Intervention, 32*(4), 255–273.

Espinosa, L. M. (2005). Curriculum and assessment considerations for young children from culturally, linguistically, and economically diverse backgrounds. *Psychology in the Schools, 42*(8), 837–853.

Farnsworth, M. (2016). Differentiating second language acquisition from specific learning disability: An observational tool assessing dual language learners' pragmatic competence. *Young Exceptional Children, 21,* 92–110.

Garcia, E., & Jensen, B. (2009). *Early educational opportunities for children of Hispanic origins* (Social Policy Report, Vol. XXIII, No. II). Ann Arbor, MI: Society for Research in Child Development.

Gilliam, W. S. (2005). *Prekindergarteners left behind: Expulsion rates in state prekindergarten systems.* New Haven, CT:

Edward Zigler Center in Child Development and Social Policy. Retrieved from https://medicine.yale.edu/childstudy/zigler/publications/National%20Prek%20Study_expulsion%20brief_34775_5379_v1.pdf

Gilliam, W. S., Maupin, A. N., & Reyes, C. R. (2016). Early childhood mental health consultation: Results of a statewide random-controlled evaluation. *Journal of the American Academy of Child & Adolescent Psychiatry, 55*(9), 754–761.

Gilliam, W. S., & Shahar, G. (2006). Preschool and child care expulsion and suspension: Rates and predictors in one state. *Infants & Young Children, 19*(3), 228–245.

Glasgow, R. E., Vogt, T. M., & Boles, S. M. (1999). Evaluating the public health impact of health promotion interventions: The RE-AIM framework. *American Journal of Public Health, 89*(9), 1322–1327.

Green, B. L., Everhart, M., Gordon, L., & Garcia Gettman, M. (2006). Characteristics of effective mental health consultation in early childhood settings: Multilevel analysis of a national survey. *Topics in Early Childhood Special Education, 26*(3), 142–152.

Gregory, A., Skiba, R. J., & Noguera, P. A. (2010). The achievement gap and the discipline gap: Two sides of the same coin? *Educational Researcher, 39*(1), 59–68.

Gutiérrez, K. D., Zepeda, M., & Castro, D. C. (2010). Advancing early literacy learning for all children: Implications of the NELP report for dual-language learners. *Educational Researcher, 39*(4), 334–339.

Hall, C. M., & Bierman, K. L. (2015). Technology-assisted interventions for parents of young children: Emerging practices, current research, and future directions. *Early Childhood Research Quarterly, 33*, 21–32.

Harry, B., & Klingner, J. (2014). *Why are so many minority students in special education?* New York, NY: Teachers College Press.

Hemmeter, M. L., Snyder, P., Kinder, K., & Artman, K. (2011). Impact of performance feedback delivered via electronic mail on preschool teachers' use of descriptive praise. *Early Childhood Research Quarterly, 26*(1), 96–109.

Individuals with Disabilities Education Act, 20 U.S.C. § 1400 (2004).

Jiang, Y., Ekono, M., & Skinner, C. (2015). *Basic facts about low-income children: Children under 18 years, 2013.* New York, NY: National Center for Children in Poverty.

Lieberman, A. F., Chu, A., Van Horn, P., & Harris, W. W. (2011). Trauma in early childhood: Empirical evidence and clinical implications. *Development and Psychopathology, 23*(2), 397–410.

Lugo-Neris, M. J., Jackson, C. W., & Goldstein, H. (2010). Facilitating vocabulary acquisition of young English language learners. *Language, Speech, and Hearing Services in Schools, 41*(3), 314–327.

McGoron, L., & Ondersma, S. J. (2015). Reviewing the need for technological and other expansions of evidence-based parent training for young children. *Children and Youth Services Review, 59*, 71–83.

Morgan, P. L., Farkas, G., Hillemeier, M. M., & Maczuga, S. (2012). Are minority children disproportionately represented in early intervention and early childhood special education? *Educational Researcher, 41*(9), 339–351.

National Professional Development Center on Inclusion. (2008). *What do we mean by professional development in the early childhood field?* Chapel Hill: The University of North Carolina, FPG Child Development Institute, Author.

National Scientific Council on the Developing Child. (2008/2012). *Establishing a level foundation for life: Mental health begins in early childhood* (Working Paper No. 6, updated ed.). Retrieved from https://www.developingchild.harvard.edu

Odom, S. L. (2009). The tie that binds: Evidence-based practice, implementation science, and outcomes for children. *Topics in Early Childhood Special Education, 29*(1), 53–61.

O'Hare, W. P. (2011). *The changing child population of the United States: Analysis of data from the 2010 Census.* Baltimore, MD: Annie E. Casey Foundation.

Ottley, J. R., Grygas Coogle, C., Rahn, N. L., & Spear, C. F. (2017). Impact of bug-in-ear professional development on early childhood co-teachers' use of communication strategies. *Topics in Early Childhood Special Education, 36*(4), 218–229.

Paradis, J. (2011). Individual differences in child English second language acquisition: Comparing child-internal and child-external factors. *Linguistic Approaches to Bilingualism, 1*(3), 213–237.

Perry, D. F., Dunne, M. C., McFadden, L., & Campbell, D. (2008). Reducing the risk for preschool expulsion: Mental health consultation for young children with challenging behaviors. *Journal of Child and Family Studies, 17*(1), 44–54.

Reichow, B., Boyd, B. A., Barton, E. E., & Odom, S. L. (Eds.). (2016). *Handbook of early childhood special education.* Switzerland: Springer International.

Rescorla, L. A., Achenbach, T. M., Ivanova, M. Y., Harder, V. S., Otten, L., Bilenberg, N., Bjarnadottir, G.…. Verhulst, F. C. (2011). International comparisons of behavioral and emotional problems in preschool children: Parents' reports from 24 societies. *Journal of Clinical Child & Adolescent Psychology, 40*(3), 456–467.

Shonkoff, J. P., Boyce, W. T., & McEwen, B. S. (2009). Neuroscience, molecular biology, and the childhood roots of health disparities: Building a new framework for health promotion and disease prevention. *Jama, 301*(21), 2252–2259.

Shonkoff, J. P., Garner, A. S., Committee on Early Childhood, Adoption, and Dependent Care, Siegel, B. S., Dobbins, M. I., Earls, M. F., McGuinn, L.… Wood, D. L. (2012). The lifelong effects of early childhood adversity and toxic stress. *Pediatrics, 129*(1), e232–e246.

Snyder, P., Hemmeter, M. L., & McLaughlin, T. (2011). Professional development in early childhood intervention: Where we stand on the silver anniversary of PL 99-457. *Journal of Early Intervention, 33*(4), 357–370.

Splett, J., & Hawks, J. S. (2011). *The call to end preschool expulsion.* Columbia: Center for Family Policy and Research, University of Missouri.

Taylor, T. K., Webster-Stratton, C., Feil, E. G., Broadbent, B., Widdop, C. S., & Severson, H. H. (2008). Computer-based intervention with coaching: An example using the incredible years program. *Cognitive Behavior Therapy, 37*(4), 233–246.

U.S. Department of Education Office for Civil Rights. (2014). *Civil rights data collection: Data snapshot (early childhood).* Washington, DC: Author. Retrieved from http://www2.ed.gov/about/offices/list/ocr/docs/crdc-early-learning -snapshot.pdf

U.S. Department of Health and Human Services, Administration for Children and Families, Administration on Children, Youth and Families, Children's Bureau. (2017). *Adoption and foster care analysis and reporting (AFCARS) FY 2017.* Retrieved from https://www.acf.hhs.gov/cb

Wesley, P. W., & Buysse, V. (2004). Consultation as a framework for productive collaboration in early intervention. *Journal of Educational and Psychological Consultation, 15*(2), 127–150.

Zaslow, M., Tout, K., Halle, T., Whittaker, J. V., Lavelle, B., & Child Trends. (2010). *Toward the identification of features of effective professional development for early childhood educators* (literature review). Washington, DC: Office of Planning, Evaluation and Policy Development, U.S. Department of Education.

Zepeda, M., Castro, D. C., & Cronin, S. (2011). Preparing early childhood teachers to work with young dual language learners. *Child Development Perspectives, 5*(1), 10–14.

10

Current Trends in Bully Prevention

Maintaining a Positive School Climate and Culture

Chad A. Rose, Stephanie Hopkins, Gloria McGillen, and Jessica Simpson

---

This Chapter Will Cover:

1. Why bullying has become a pervasive and persistent issue for America's school-age youth, particularly for students with disabilities.

2. Recommendations for bullying interventions, including tips for how to best situate them within a multitiered framework that could include school-wide, classroom-wide, targeted groups, and selective strategies designed to meet the needs of a diverse student population.

3. The increased awareness and focus on implementing social and emotional learning and social and communication skill acquisition to reduce bullying among school-age youth.

One hundred eighty days a year, students fill the hallways and class-rooms of schools across the United States. Over the course of 13 years, these 180 days are designed to prepare students to acquire the academic, functional, and behavioral knowledge and skills necessary for postsecondary success. While many factors contribute to, or impede, the success of American youth, one factor has emerged as a persistent issue that transcends all school types and grade levels. This issue is bullying, which is a unique subset of peer aggression (Rodkin, Espelage, & Hanish, 2015) that includes three defining characteristics: (1) imbalance of physical or social power, (2) intent to cause physical or emotional harm, and (3) behaviors that are repeated or likely to be repeated across time or across multiple victims (Gladden, Vivolo-Kantor, Hamburger, & Lumpkin, 2014). Bullying can present as pervasive physical, verbal, indirect or relational (e.g., social exclusion, rumor spreading), or electronic (i.e., cyberbullying) aggression.

- bullying
- communication skills
- disabilities
- prevention
- social and emotional learning (SEL)
- social skills
- victimization

Ecological Systems Theory

Recent data from the U.S. Department of Education suggest that about 1 in 5 students experience school-based bullying over the course of one academic year (Musu-Gillette et al., 2018). The pervasiveness of bullying is grounded in the complex interactions between an individual and the social and environmental systems within which that individual is situated (Hong & Espelage, 2012). Specifically, bully prevention scholars have applied and adapted Bronfenbrenner's (1977, 1986) ecological systems theory (see Figure 10.1), which includes *microsystems* (i.e., interaction between an individual and the immediate setting), *mesosystems* (i.e., interactions between microsystems), *exosystems* (i.e., social structures that impinge on and influence the immediate settings in which the individual resides), *macrosystems* (i.e., overarching institutional patterns of the culture or subculture), and *chronosystems* (i.e., development and change over time). Consequently, Hong and Espelage (2012) argued that bullying develops as a function of an individual's ability, or inability, to navigate

Figure 10.1   Intersection of the Ecological Systems Theory and the Social–Ecological Framework of Bullying/Victimization

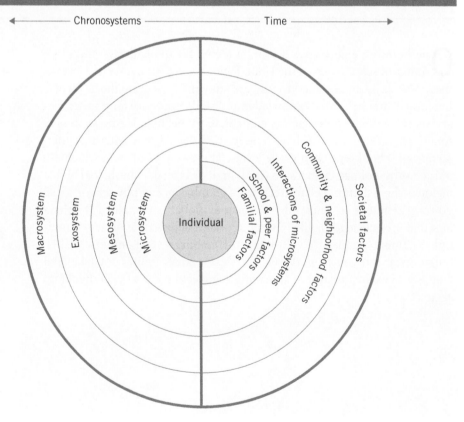

familial, peer-group, school, community, and societal structures and systems over time.

The strength of the ecological systems theory as it applies to bullying involvement is the systematic accounting for intersectionality (Hong & Espelage, 2012). Specifically, several factors place school-age youth at escalated risk for bullying involvement, including individual attributes and identities (e.g., gender, race, ethnicity, sexual orientation, gender identity, religious affiliation); family structure, discord, and connectedness; peer-group affiliation; school belongingness and success; neighborhood influences and violence; societal influences; and development over time (e.g., age, grade; Hong & Espelage, 2012; National Academies of Sciences, Engineering, and Medicine [NASEM], 2016). Therefore, as risk factors compound across the various social and environmental systems, the likelihood of becoming involved within the bullying dynamic, either as a perpetrator or victim, exponentially increases.

Disability as a Risk Factor

One subgroup of students who are especially vulnerable to bullying involvement is students with disabilities. Luckasson and Schalock (2012) argued that disability may, at least in part, result from "ineffective interactions between a person's capabilities and the demands of his or her environments" (p. 3). Rose and Gage (2017) found that students with disabilities are victimized more and engage in higher rates of bullying than their peers without disabilities over time. Evidence suggests that these discrepancies exist at, or before, school entry (Son, Parish, & Peterson, 2012) and continue through school exit (Blake, Lund, Zhou, Kwok, & Benz, 2012; Rose & Gage, 2017). While the dichotomization of disability status routinely identifies the disproportionate representation of youth with disabilities within the bullying dynamic (Rose, Monda-Amaya, & Espelage, 2011), some argue there is variability between subgroups of youth with disabilities (Rose et al., 2015). For example, students with behavior disorders have been identified as bully perpetrators more often than their peers with other disabilities (Rose & Espelage, 2012; Swearer, Wang, Maag, Siebecker, & Frerichs, 2012), where youth with autism spectrum disorders have been identified as frequent victims of bullying (Zablotsky, Bradshaw, Anderson, & Law, 2012, 2013). Rose (2017) argued that the disproportionality in bullying involvement among youth with disabilities is complex and is grounded in intersectionality, where factors such as disability status, label, severity, and characteristics; academic, functional, and behavioral skill deficits; special education services and location; and disability comorbidity serve as independent and interconnected risk factors.

The disproportionate representation of youth with disabilities within the bullying dynamic also has direct legal implications. At the present time, all 50 states have adopted antibullying legislation (Yell, Katsiyannis, Rose, & Houchins, 2016), and several directly or indirectly address bullying among youth with disabilities (Rose, 2017). While this is an important step in preventing bullying among all school-age youth, federal legislation directly prohibits disability-based bullying and harassment. Specifically, the U.S. Department of Education Office for Civil Rights and the Office of Special Education and Rehabilitative Services (2000, 2010, 2013, 2014) issued a series of "Dear Colleague" letters that outline potential civil rights violations associated with the bullying of individuals with disabilities. For example, disability-based harassment may violate Section 504 of the Rehabilitation Act of 1973 (29 U.S.C. § 794) and Title II of the Americans with Disabilities Act of 1990 (42 U.S.C. § 12131 *et seq.*), which supersedes a state, district, or school's bully prevention policy (Rose, 2017; Yell et al., 2016).

Intervention Efforts and Recommendations

Given the increasing evidence that youth with disabilities are disproportionately involved within the bullying dynamic (Rose & Gage, 2017), and state and federal laws prohibiting disability-based harassment and bullying (Yell et al., 2016), schools must begin to implement programming and interventions designed to reduce and prevent bullying among this subpopulation of youth. While Ttofi and Farrington (2011) found that existing bully prevention efforts, especially in the United States, produced underwhelming results, NASEM (2016) argued that the most effective and promising interventions are multicomponent programs. Espelage, Low, Van Ryzin, and Polanin (2015) suggested that bully prevention programs should be grounded in skill development. Therefore, bully prevention programs designed to reduce and prevent bullying among youth with disabilities should be designed to increase critical social and communication skills through routine assessment, universal systems, targeted lessons, and individual intervention (Rose & Monda-Amaya, 2012). Figure 10.2 outlines the layout and structure of a tiered approach to bully prevention.

School-Wide Assessment and Behavioral Screeners

To reduce and prevent bullying in schools, especially among youth who are at escalated risk, school stakeholders must first be aware of the prevalence and risk factors that are unique to their individual buildings and districts (Rose & Monda-Amaya, 2012). Systematic data collection within the context of individual schools or districts is especially germane to bully prevention due to the complexity of bullying; complications associated with accurately defining, measuring, and contextualizing bullying; and variations between student populations (Casper, Meter, & Card, 2015). Therefore, it is recommended that schools conduct a needs inventory and implement a systematic and frequent school-wide climate assessment

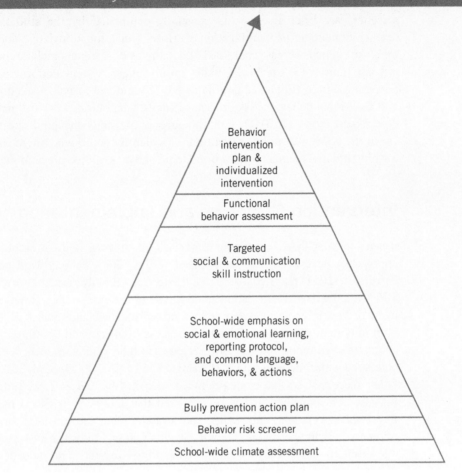

Behavior
intervention
plan &
individualized
intervention

Functional
behavior assessment

Targeted
social & communication
skill instruction

School-wide emphasis on
social & emotional learning,
reporting protocol,
and common language,
behaviors, & actions

Bully prevention action plan

Behavior risk screener

School-wide climate assessment

(Swearer, Espelage, & Napolitano, 2009). In addition to bullying measures, the climate assessment should, based on the school or district's identified need, evaluate school-related constructs such as perceptions of school climate, school belongingness, teacher social support, peer involvement and social supports, empathy, and supportive attitudes toward bullying. Ultimately, these data are important to establish present levels of bullying, assess risk and environmental factors, make data-based decisions regarding intervention implementation, and evaluate progress of existing, or newly implemented, intervention efforts (Swearer et al., 2009).

While a school-wide climate assessment is necessary for understanding the nature of bullying within a school or district, this level of assessment will not directly identify risk factors and skill deficits for specific individuals. For example, social and communication skill deficits are two of the most notable predictors of bullying involvement for youth with disabilities (Rose et al., 2011). To assess these skill deficits, and other underlying risk factors, schools should consider conducting a brief screener to identify youth, including those with disabilities, who would be candidates for receiving selective prevention (Preast, Bowman, & Rose, 2017). Behavioral screeners are brief assessments, generally completed by the students' teacher, that aid in the identification of critical social, functional, or behavioral skill deficits (Preast et al., 2017). Examples of screeners include, but are not limited to, the Social Skills Improvement System Performance Screening Guide (Elliott & Gresham, 2007b) and the Social, Academic, and Emotional Behavior Risk Screener (Kilgus, Chafouleas, Riley-Tillman, & von der Embse, 2013). Overall, the purpose of using behavioral screeners in the context of bully prevention is to identify youth who are at risk for bullying involvement and to provide proactive, selective prevention.

Intervention Structure and Implementation

Recent meta-analyses evaluating the effect of current bully prevention approaches have been met with mixed results. For example, Ttofi and Farrington (2011) reported a 20% to 23% decrease in bully perpetration and a 17% to 20% decrease in victimization across 44 separate studies. However, many of these interventions were conducted outside the United States, which is an important point of consideration, because European and Scandinavian countries often report more drastic decreases in bullying involvement when compared with American studies (Farrington & Ttofi, 2009; NASEM, 2016). Other meta-analyses have not produced such notable decreases in bullying involvement, where it has been argued that intervention efforts have improved perceptions, knowledge, and awareness but did not necessarily influence bullying behaviors (Merrell, Gueldner, Ross, & Isava, 2008).

While the meta-analyses have produced mixed results, and reductions of bullying behaviors in the United States have been underwhelming, recommendations for bully prevention programming remain relatively consistent. Specifically, NASEM (2016) found "the most likely effective bullying prevention programs are whole school, multicomponent programs that combine elements of universal and targeted strategies" (p. 235). One intervention framework that has considerable promise is positive behavioral interventions and supports (PBIS) (Bradshaw, 2013, 2015). In short, PBIS is *not* a bully prevention intervention; it is a multitiered problem-solving framework designed to systematically implement interventions to address social and emotional behavioral challenges (Lewis, Jones, Horner, & Sugai, 2010). Within the PBIS framework, interventions are implemented at the universal (i.e., school-wide), group (i.e., selective prevention), and individual levels, where interventions are based on school and student need (Lewis et al., 2010). While PBIS is not a bully prevention intervention, it is a promising framework for implementing bully prevention programming that is grounded in skill development while addressing the unique and individual needs of youth (Lewis & Rose, 2013).

Universal Prevention

The most immediate and necessary bully prevention strategy is school-wide prevention. While universal prevention begins with a school-wide assessment (NASEM, 2016; Rose & Monda-Amaya, 2012), using these data to build institutional capacity to establish a sustainable bully prevention approach, as well as acquire buy-in from teachers, administrators, students, parents, and community members, is paramount to long-term success (Bradshaw, 2015; Preast et al., 2017). At the present time, the majority of bullying prevention curricula implemented in American schools employ a universal intervention approach (i.e., school-wide) (NASEM, 2016; Ttofi & Farrington, 2011). The strength of a universal bully prevention approach is that all students and staff are immersed in the curriculum or prevention intervention, with the goal of both improving the school climate and reducing the prevalence of bullying among the entire student body.

In addition to establishing a baseline of school climate and bullying prevalence through the school-wide climate assessment, school leaders must establish a plan for school-wide prevention. For example, Lewis (2011) and Lewis and Rose (2013) outlined an action plan for bully prevention within a PBIS framework. This plan includes establishing a school-based bully prevention team, data collection, and six sequential intervention steps. First, the extent to which bullying is a problem within the school is assessed (e.g., Is bullying a problem? What types of bulling are occurring? Where is the bullying occurring? What strategies do staff feel are most successful to date?). Second, the school-based bully prevention team identifies prosocial behaviors that will serve as replacement behaviors for bullying. Third, the school-based prevention team outlines lesson plans and teaching strategies for teaching and reinforcing the replacement skills. Fourth, the school-based prevention team establishes a plan for increasing supervision in high-risk locations within and around the school. Fifth, the school-based prevention team establishes strategies and lesson plans for supporting students who are identified as victims of bullying. Finally, the school-based prevention team establishes a protocol for responding to bullying reports and training teachers and educational stakeholders in the building. Overall, this action plan was designed as a guide to help educators think more systematically about bully prevention.

School-Wide Interventions

School-wide bully prevention interventions have demonstrated positive outcomes related to social competence, self-esteem, and peer acceptance (Merrell et al., 2008). Although there are many school-wide intervention approaches being implemented in American schools, Second Step Social and Emotional Learning Program (Committee for Children, 2011), Steps to Respect (Committee for Children, 2009), and bully prevention in positive behavior support (BP-PBS) (Ross & Horner, 2009) are among the most promising, especially for youth with disabilities. This promise is conceivably connected to the fact that each of these programs directly or indirectly employs social and emotional learning (SEL) as the approach to skill acquisition. Specifically, SEL is grounded in self-awareness, social awareness, self-management, relationship skills, and responsible decision making (Collaborative for Academic, Social, and Emotional Learning [CASEL], 2012). These skills are critically important to the reduction of bullying within a school context (Preast et al., 2017), especially for students with disabilities, as social and communication skill deficits have been identified as two of the most notable predictors for bullying involvement among this subpopulation of youth (Rose et al., 2011). The focus on social and emotional skill development is especially important in the current educational landscape, where increasing numbers of youth with disabilities are served in the general education environment but continue to experience higher rates of victimization and engage in higher levels of bully perpetration over time (Rose & Gage, 2017).

The Second Step Social and Emotional Learning Program (Committee for Children, 2011) is a school-wide SEL curriculum designed to help school-age youth excel in social settings, both in and out of school. The primary impetus of the program is to help students gain social confidence and a skill set for emotion management, situational awareness, and academic achievement (Espelage, Low, Polanin, & Brown, 2013, 2015). Second Step includes a scaffolded curriculum from pre-K through eighth grade, where social and emotional skills are explicitly taught by teachers to all students through weekly lessons. Recent studies have demonstrated the success of Second Step in reducing bullying involvement, aggressive behaviors, and delinquency among school-age youth over time (Espelage, Low, Polanin, & Brown, 2013, 2015). Additionally, over a 3-year period, students with disabilities who received SEL programming through Second Step reported less bullying (Espelage, Rose, & Polanin, 2015), increased prosocial behaviors, and improved academic outcomes (Espelage, Rose, & Polanin, 2016).

Steps to Respect (Committee for Children, 2009) is a universal SEL intervention that is designed to reduce bullying and improve SEL outcomes for school-age youth. Steps to Respect is a scaffolded, 12-to-14-week curriculum that is primarily implemented in Grades K–5. Consistent with Second Step, Steps to Respect gets teachers involved in school-wide bullying prevention efforts, promotes the building of social and communication skills, and fosters positive interpersonal relationships between students. Steps to Respect has resulted in an improved school climate, decreased reports of bullying, increased willingness to intervene in bullying situations, and an overall decrease in aggressive behaviors (Brown, Low, Smith, & Haggerty, 2011; Frey, Nolen, Edstrom, & Hirschstein, 2005). While studies have not directly addressed bullying involvement among youth with disabilities, it is conceivable that the social and emotional skills taught through Steps to Respect would improve the outcomes of this subgroup of youth.

BP-PBS (Ross & Horner, 2009) is a bully prevention curriculum designed to be implemented as a universal intervention to reduce bullying among elementary and middle school youth. The curriculum includes teaching all students the concept of "being respectful" and employing a three-step response when confronted with perceived bullying behaviors. The three steps consist of gestures and words of saying stop with a hand signal to stop, walking away from the problem if the problem doesn't stop, and talking to an adult if needed (Ross & Horner, 2009, 2014). Additionally, the intervention uses precorrects prior to environmental or activity transition, teaching students to appropriately respond when the strategy is implemented, and training teachers on responding when they receive a report from a student (Ross & Horner, 2009, 2014). BP-PBS has demonstrated decreases in out-of-school suspensions, reductions in bullying behaviors, improved response skills, increased awareness of bullying, and increased willingness to intervene in bullying situations for youth with and without disabilities (Nese, Horner, Dickey, Stiller, & Tomlanovich, 2014; Ross & Horner, 2009, 2014). Additionally, BP-PBS demonstrates the utility of implementing a bully-specific intervention within the PBIS framework (Good, McIntosh, & Carmen, 2011).

While the aforementioned school-wide interventions are not exhaustive of all universal bully prevention approaches, they demonstrate the promise for reducing bullying involvement among youth with disabilities. Specifically, these approaches employ SEL, where students learn social awareness, self-awareness, self-management, responsible decision making, and relationship skills (CASEL, 2012) that are necessary for short- and long-term success. Most important, these approaches are grounded in skill development, which is paramount for prevention, especially for youth with disabilities, who often have social and communication skill deficits that increase their likelihood for bullying involvement (Rose et al., 2011).

Selective Prevention

The term *selective prevention* encompasses the process of identifying students who are nonresponders to universal prevention efforts and providing targeted interventions within the PBIS framework (Lane, Oakes, & Menzies, 2010). Within the context of bully prevention, the goal of selective prevention is to identify students who are at risk of escalated bullying involvement due to skill deficits (NASEM, 2016; Preast et al., 2017). Typically, bullying prevention programs at this level deliver specific skill instruction, such as social and communication skill training and coping skill instruction, with a more intensive dosage in small groups when compared with universal prevention (Rose & Monda-Amaya, 2012). About 15% of students do not respond to universal prevention efforts and require selective prevention at the Tier 2 level (Lane et al., 2010; Lewis et al., 2010). Selective prevention is disseminated flexibly and systematically, and interventions at this level establish a more concentrated plan for behavior supports for students who do not require a more rigorous and individualized plan (Lane et al., 2010; Lewis et al., 2010).

Identification of nonresponse to universal prevention and assessment of risk factors are critical for pinpointing students who are eligible for selective prevention. Therefore, in addition to school-wide assessments, it is recommended that schools employ a behavioral screening process that assesses critical risk factors (Preast et al., 2017). The justification for this approach is that teachers may not accurately identify youth who are chronically involved in bullying (Bradshaw, Sawyer, & O'Brennan, 2007), but are proficient at identifying skill deficits (Preast et al., 2017). In addition to behavioral screeners, schools could analyze and evaluate office disciplinary referrals (Irvin, Tobin, Sprague, Sugai, & Vincent, 2004), and conduct a record review, observations, and interviews (Rose & Monda-Amaya, 2012) to identify students who could benefit from selective prevention. Once students are identified, they should be placed in small groups, based on the identified deficit, and provided with targeted interventions.

Targeted Interventions

Targeted interventions are often delivered by school counselors or special education teachers in a small-group setting (McElearney et al., 2007). Generally, targeted interventions specific to bully prevention consist of intensive social–emotional skills training, coping skills, and deescalation. For example, the Social Skills Improvement System: Classwide Intervention Program (SSIS-CIP; Elliott & Gresham, 2007a) is a targeted social skills curriculum that includes 10 units, with three 20-minute lessons per unit, for students in Grades K–8. Each unit represents a different social skill, where Elliott and Gresham (2007a) argued that the 10 units are based on decades of research, of which these skills represent the most critical for school-age youth. The units cover (1) listening to others, (2) following steps, (3) following rules, (4) paying attention to work, (5) asking for help, (6) taking turns, (7) getting along with others, (8) staying calm, (9) doing the right thing, and (10) doing nice things for others. While few studies have evaluated SSIS-CIP as a bully prevention intervention, DiPerna, Lei, Bellinger, and Cheng (2015) demonstrated that the SSIS-CIP resulted in positive effects on social skills, including teacher ratings and internalizing behaviors, especially for students who demonstrated the lowest initial social skill proficiency. Therefore, by implementing the SSIS-CIP in combination with universal prevention, it is conceivable that reductions in bullying involvement and increases in academic outcomes may be expedited for youth with disabilities due to direct skill instruction and support at the universal and secondary tiers.

One new and promising targeted intervention for bully prevention and social and communication skill acquisition is Cool School (Language Express, Inc., 2016). Cool School is a comprehensive, targeted bully prevention program for students in Grades 3–5 that includes a total of 20 interactive, web-based lessons that cover topics such as interactions on the playground, riding the bus, cyberbullying and Internet safety, social exclusion, and bullying because of differences (e.g., adopted, disability, family structure). The lesson structure includes online webisodes that present a common compromising or challenging social situation and provide students with four response options. After the student selects a response option, the webisode completes the scenario and provides directions and recommendations regarding the specific choice. In each webisode, there is a response option that represents the best possible way to respond to the scenario. The curriculum and webisodes are accompanied by lesson plans for teachers to hold productive discussions regarding the situation, and recommendations for implementing the strategies in applied settings. Since Cool School is newly developed, empirical evaluations are still being conducted. However, several bully prevention scholars contributed to the development and refinement of the curriculum, which provides social validity. Additionally, the lessons are grounded in SEL and social and communication skill development, which establishes Cool School as a promising intervention for bully prevention, especially among youth with disabilities.

In addition to commercially developed targeted interventions, many schools make the decision to implement homegrown social and communication skill programs. When bully prevention is the immediate focus, these homegrown programs should focus on critical response skills, including what to do, what to say, and who to tell (Yasuda, Ievers-Landis, & Rose, 2016). In doing so, Preast and colleagues (2017) made recommendations for lesson plan structure, which includes six distinct steps (see Table 10.1). This type of structure, coupled with routine assessment, could assist in the development of critical social skills and support executive functioning while teaching students appropriate response skills when confronted with situations that could be construed as bullying.

Table 10.1 Social Skill Lesson Plan Development

Lesson Plan Step	Description
Selection of skills	Instructors should select a set of social and communication skills, based on results from the behavioral screener, that would most benefit the students identified for targeted intervention.
Skill introduction	Each lesson should include a mechanism by which the instructor introduces the skill. It is important to have an understanding of what executive functioning skills students will need to participate in the lesson.
Skill demonstration	The skill must be demonstrated, with consideration for skill variation based on environmental and social context. To support executive functioning skills, students could repeat the steps together through unison responding, then use silent self-talk to repeat the steps individually.

(Continued)

Table 10.1 (Continued)	
Lesson Plan Step	**Description**
Role play	The students must have an opportunity to role-play the skill in a controlled environment. To continue to support executive functioning skills, have the steps of the skill listed so all students can access, brainstorm situations that are applicable to the students, and give students time to practice role-playing.
Reinforce the skill	The instruction must establish opportunities for the students to engage in the skill in an applied environment while providing positive specific feedback.
Generalize the skill	The instructors should establish a protocol for skill generalization, which could include collaborating with the students' teachers and parents regarding strategies for increased opportunities to engage in the skill, as well as techniques for providing positive or behavior-specific praise.

Source: Adapted from Preast, Bowman, and Rose (2017).

Individualized Intervention

The most intensive level of support within a PBIS framework is individualized intervention (NASEM, 2016). Individualized interventions are appropriate for youth engaged in chronic or intensive bullying for whom prior levels of support have been insufficient and for students who experience chronic levels of victimization as a function of critical skill deficits (Rose & Monda-Amaya, 2012), which generally includes between 1% and 5% of the student population (Lane et al., 2010; Lewis et al., 2010). Through a three-stage process of screening, assessment, and intervention, it is possible to deliver highly targeted, individualized supports in school and community settings (Preast et al., 2017). Individualized interventions may address issues such as social or communication skill gaps or problems in socioemotional functioning that underlie the problem behaviors. Selecting an appropriate individualized intervention is contingent on the outcomes of assessment and the setting in which the intervention is delivered. Teachers, behavior specialists, mental health providers, and social workers are all commonly involved at this level of support (Bruns et al., 2016). In some cases, they may also collaborate with family and community members, or multidisciplinary teams, to deliver comprehensive or wraparound services (McCurdy et al., 2016).

A functional behavior assessment (FBA) is a particularly valuable tool for developing appropriate individualized interventions for bully reduction and prevention, and Rose and Monda-Amaya (2012) and McCurdy and colleagues (2016) urge its widespread adoption. An FBA is a common practice when establishing supports for youth with behavior disorders and provides insight into the functional and communicative aspects of behavior that maintain challenging behaviors within particular contexts (Scott & Cooper, 2017). From information gleaned through the FBA process, it is possible for a multidisciplinary team, which includes teachers, counselors, parents, and other professionals, to formulate a tailored and individualized behavior intervention plan (BIP) that is designed to reduce bullying and challenging behaviors, and/or provide students with critical response skills (Rose & Monda-Amaya, 2012). Additionally, the FBA and BIP should be integrated into the student's individualized education program (IEP), where the special education multidisciplinary team can establish annual measurable goals related to behaviors associated with bullying involvement (Rose & Monda-Amaya, 2012). Because IEPs are legally mandated under the Individuals with Disabilities Education Improvement Act (IDEA, 2004; Yell et al., 2016) and bullying involvement poses a threat to a meaningful and equitable education for youth with disabilities (Cornell, Gregory, Huang, & Fan, 2013; Espelage, Rose, & Polanin, 2015), systematic incorporation of the FBA and BIP into the IEP can be an effective and efficient approach for sustained individualized interventions and ongoing evaluation for reducing bullying involvement among youth with disabilities.

While the FBA and BIP have empirical support for addressing challenging behaviors among youth with disabilities (Scott & Cooper, 2017), research evidence on the effectiveness of individualized interventions for bullying involvement remains limited (Bradshaw, 2015; NASEM, 2016; Swearer, Wang, Collins, Strawhun, & Fluke, 2014). For example, Rose and Monda-Amaya (2012) recommended using interventions such as social narratives, teaching help-seeking strategies, and supporting self-determination to increase social competence, independence, and understanding of personal values, but admittedly recognized that these interventions have not been directly applied to bully involvement reductions. Additionally, NASEM (2016) identified 11 individualized interventions, a majority of which employ cognitive-behavioral therapy (CBT) techniques in individual or group formats, including the integration of trauma-informed treatment techniques, conflict resolution or interpersonal skills training, or family therapy. Targeted interventions that are grounded in CBT, such as the Healthy Environments and Response to Trauma in Schools (HEARTS) program (Dorado, Martinez, McArthur, & Leibovitz, 2016) and the School Mental Health Assessment, Research, and Training (SMART) Center (Bruns et al., 2016), suggest that increasing investment in the evaluations of school-based individualized interventions relevant to bullying could directly support students who are most in need of intervention and those most at risk for detrimental outcomes associated with prolonged bullying involvement. Furthering the development and implementation of bullying-specific individualized interventions, and rigorously evaluating these interventions using randomized control trial designs, is an important and pressing area of growth for the field of bully prevention, especially for youth with disabilities (Bradshaw, 2015; Rose, 2017).

Conclusion

Bullying is a pressing issue in American schools and a notable public health concern. Evidence suggests that students with disabilities are at escalated risk for bullying involvement due, in part, to social and communication skill deficits. Current state and federal laws prohibit school-based bullying and disability-based harassment. Specifically, Section 504 of the Rehabilitation Act of 1973 (29 U.S.C. § 794) and Title II of the Americans with Disabilities Act of 1990 (42 U.S.C. § 12131 *et seq.*) prohibit disability-based bullying and/or harassment (Yell et al., 2016). Therefore, it is critical for schools to implement programming that directly addresses bullying among school-age youth, including those with disabilities. It is recommended that bully prevention interventions be situated within a multitiered framework, including assessment, universal prevention, selective prevention, and individualized interventions that are anchored by SEL components. By infusing SEL within a multitiered framework, schools can provide support based on individualized need, while increasing critical skill acquisition, and capitalize on the 180 days of skill instruction.

REFLECTING AND UNDERSTANDING

1. What are some of the interventions that educators can use when it comes to intervening in or preventing bullying among school-age youth?

2. How can bully prevention efforts be situated within a multitiered educational framework?

3. What subpopulation of students is at escalated risk for bullying involvement?

What are some interventions that can benefit this population?

4. As a classroom teacher or school staff member, what are some interventions that can be used with all students in the building or classroom?

5. What are the steps of implementing an effective social skills lesson?

ONLINE RESOURCES

- Bully Police USA: http://bullypolice.org/

- Cartoon Network—Stop Bullying: https://www.cartoonnetwork.com/stop-bullying/

- College of Education and Human Sciences Bullying Research Network: https://cehs.unl.edu/BRNET/

- Mizzou Ed Bullying Prevention Lab: https://www.mizzoubullypreventionlab.com/

- The National Academies of Sciences Engineering Medicine: http://www.nationalacademies.org/

- PACER's National Bullying Prevention Center: https://www.pacer.org/bullying/resources/info-facts.asp

- Say NO Bullying: http://www.saynobullying.org

- Stomp Out Bullying—Change the Culture: https://www.stompoutbullying.org

- Stopbullying.gov: http://www.stopbullying.gov

- University at Buffalo Alberti Center for Bullying Abuse Prevention: https://ed.buffalo.edu/alberti.html

RECOMMENDED READINGS

Books

Bradshaw, C. (Ed.). (2017). *The handbook on bullying prevention: A lifecourse perspective.* Washington, DC: National Association of Social Workers Press.

Coloroso, B. (2010). *The bully, the bullied, and the bystander: From preschool to high school: How parents and teachers can help break the cycle of violence* (Updated ed.). New York, NY: HarperCollins.

Espelage, D. L., & Swearer, S. M. (Eds.). (2011). *Bullying in North American schools: A socio-ecological perspective on prevention and intervention.* New York, NY: Routledge.

Goldman, C., & Postel, D. (2012). *Bullied: What every parent, teacher, and kid needs to know about ending the cycle of fear.* San Francisco, CA: HarperOne.

Swearer, S. M., Espelage, D. L., & Napolitano, S. A. (2009). *Bullying prevention and intervention: Realistic strategies for schools.* New York, NY: Guilford Press.

Yasuda, P. M., Ievers-Landis, C. E., & Rose, C. A. (2016). *Say NO Bullying: A resource book for children and teens with disorders of short stature.* Glen Head, NY: Human Growth Foundation.

Articles

Espelage, D. L., Rose, C. A., & Polanin, J. R. (2015). Social-emotional learning program to reduce bullying, fighting, and victimization among middle school students with disabilities. *Remedial and Special Education, 36*, 299–311.

Espelage, D. L., Rose, C. A., & Polanin, J. (2016). Social-emotional learning program to promote prosocial and academic skills among middle school students with disabilities. *Remedial and Special Education, 37*(6), 323–332.

Rose, C. A., & Gage, N. A. (2017). Exploring the involvement in bullying among individuals with and without disabilities over time. *Exceptional Children, 83*, 298–314.

Rose, C. A., Monda-Amaya, L. E., & Espelage, D. L. (2011). Bullying perpetration and victimization in special education: A review of the literature. *Remedial and Special Education, 32*, 114–130.

Briefs, Practice Guides, and Reports

National Academies of Sciences, Engineering, and Medicine. (2016). *Preventing bullying through science, policy, and practice.* Washington, DC: National Academies Press.

PROFESSIONAL ORGANIZATIONS

American Psychological Association:
https://www.apa.org/

Council for Children With Behavioral Disorders:
http://www.ccbd.net/home

Council for Exceptional Children:
https://www.cec.sped.org/

National Association of School Psychologists:
https://www.nasponline.org/

National Center for Learning Disabilities:
https://www.ncld.org/

REFERENCES

Americans with Disabilities Act of 1990, 42 U.S.C. 12131 *et seq.*

Blake, J. J., Lund, E. M., Zhou, Q., Kwok, O., & Benz, M. R. (2012). National prevalence rates of bully victimization among students with disabilities in the United States. *School Psychology Quarterly, 27*(4), 210–222.

Bradshaw, C. P. (2013). Preventing bullying through positive behavioral interventions and supports (PBIS): A multitiered approach to prevention and integration. *Theory Into Practice, 52*, 288–295.

Bradshaw, C. P. (2015). Translating research to practice in bullying prevention. *American Psychologist, 70*(4), 322–332.

Bradshaw, C. P., Sawyer, A. L., & O'Brennan, L. M. (2007). Bullying and peer victimization at school: Perceptual differences between students and school staff. *School Psychology Review, 36*, 361–382.

Bronfenbrenner, U. (1977). Toward an experimental ecology of human development. *American Psychologist, 32*, 513–531.

Bronfenbrenner, U. (1986). Ecology of the family as a context for human development: Research perspectives. *Developmental Psychology, 22*, 723–742.

Brown, E. C., Low, S., Smith, B. H., & Haggerty, K. P. (2011). Outcomes from a school randomized controlled trial of Steps to Respect: A bullying prevention program. *School Psychology Review, 40*, 423–443.

Bruns, E. J., Duong, M. T., Lyon, A. R., Pullmann, M. D., Cook, C. R., Cheney, D., & McCauley, E. (2016). Fostering SMART partnerships to develop an effective continuum of behavioral health services and supports in schools. *American Journal of Orthopsychiatry, 86*(2), 156–170.

Casper, D. M., Meter, D. J., & Card, N. A. (2015). Addressing measurement issues related to bullying involvement. *School Psychology Review, 44*(4), 353–371.

Collaborative for Academic, Social, and Emotional Learning. (2012). *2013 CASEL guide: Effective social and emotional learning programs, preschool and elementary school edition.* Chicago, IL: Author.

Committee for Children. (2009). *Steps to respect.* Seattle, WA: Author.

Committee for Children. (2011). *Second Step social and emotional learning program.* Seattle, WA: Author.

Cornell, D., Gregory, A., Huang, F., & Fan, X. (2013). Perceived prevalence of bullying and teasing predicts high school dropout rates. *Journal of Educational Psychology, 105*, 138–149.

DiPerna, J. C., Lei, P., Bellinger, J., & Cheng, W. (2015). Efficacy of the Social Skills Improvement System Classwide Intervention Program (SSIS-CIP) primary version. *School Psychology Quarterly, 30*, 121–141.

Dorado, J. S., Martinez, M., McArthur, L. E., & Leibovitz, T. (2016). Healthy Environments and Response to Trauma in Schools (HEARTS): A whole-school, multi-level, prevention and intervention program for creating trauma-informed, safe and supportive schools. *School Mental Health, 8*, 163–176.

Elliott, S. N., & Gresham, F. M. (2007a). *Social skills improvement system: Classwide intervention program.* Minneapolis, MN: Pearson.

Elliott, S. N., & Gresham, F. M. (2007b). *Social skills improvement system: Performance screening guide.* Minneapolis, MN: Pearson.

Espelage, D. L., Low, S., Polanin, J. R., & Brown, E. C. (2013). The impact of a middle school program to reduce aggression, victimization, and sexual violence. *Journal of Adolescent Health, 53*(2), 180–186.

Espelage, D. L., Low, S., Polanin, J. R., & Brown, E. C. (2015). Clinical trial of Second Step middle-school program: Impact on aggression and victimization. *Journal of Applied Developmental Psychology, 37*(1), 52–63.

Espelage, D. L., Low, S., Van Ryzin, M. J., & Polanin, J. R. (2015). Clinical trial of Second Step middle school program: Impact on bullying, cyberbullying, homophobic teasing, and sexual harassment perpetration. *School Psychology Review, 44*, 464–479.

Espelage, D. L., Rose, C. A., & Polanin, J. R. (2015). Social-emotional learning program to reduce bullying, fighting, and victimization among middle school students with disabilities. *Remedial and Special Education, 36*, 299–311.

Espelage, D. L., Rose, C. A., & Polanin, J. (2016). Social-emotional learning program to promote prosocial and academic skills among middle school students with disabilities. *Remedial and Special Education. 37*(6), 323–332. doi: 10.1177/0741932515627475

Farrington, D. P., & Ttofi, M. M. (2009). School-based programs to reduce bullying and victimization. *Campbell Collaboration, 6*, 1–149.

Frey, K. S., Nolen, S. B., Edstrom, L. V. S., & Hirschstein, M. K. (2005). Effects of a school based social–emotional competence program: Linking children's goals, attributions, and behavior. *Journal of Applied Developmental Psychology, 26*, 171–200.

Gladden, R. M., Vivolo-Kantor, A. M., Hamburger, M. E., & Lumpkin, C. D. (2014). *Bullying surveillance among youths: Uniform definitions for public health and recommended data elements, Version 1.0.* Atlanta, GA: National Center for Injury Prevention and Control, Centers for Disease Control and Prevention, and U.S. Department of Education.

Good, C. P., McIntosh, K., & Carmen, G. (2011). Integrating bullying prevention into schoolwide positive behavior support. *Teaching Exceptional Children, 44*, 48–56.

Hong, J. S., & Espelage, D. L. (2012). A review of research on bullying and peer victimization in school: An ecological system analysis. *Aggressive and Violent Behavior, 17*, 311–322.

Individuals with Disabilities Education Improvement Act, Pub. L. No.108-446, 118 Stat. 2647 (2004).

Irvin, L. K., Tobin, T. J., Sprague, J. R., Sugai, G., & Vincent, C. G. (2004). Validity of office discipline referral measures as indices of school-wide behavioral status and effects of school-wide behavioral interventions. *Journal of Positive Behavior Interventions, 6,* 131–147. doi:10.1177/10983007040060030201

Kilgus, S. P., Chafouleas, S. M., Riley-Tillman, T. C., & von der Embse, N. P. (2013). *Social, academic, and emotional behavior risk screener.* Columbia, MO: Author.

Lane, K. L., Oakes, W., & Menzies, H. (2010). Systematic screenings to prevent the development of learning and behavior problems: Considerations for practitioners, researchers, and policy makers. *Journal of Disability Policy Studies, 21*(3), 160–172.

Language Express, Inc. (2016). *Cool School.* Encinitas, CA: Author.

Lewis, T. J. (2011). *SW-PBS bullying action plan.* Columbia: University of Missouri Center on School-Wide Positive Behavior Support.

Lewis, T. J., Jones, S. E. L., Horner, R. H., & Sugai, G. (2010). School-wide positive behavior support and students with emotional/behavioral disorders: Implications for prevention, identification and intervention. *Exceptionality, 18*(2), 82–93.

Lewis, T. J., & Rose, C. A. (2013, July). Addressing bullying behavior through school-wide positive behavior supports. *Education Week.* Arlington, VA: Council for Exceptional Children.

Luckasson, R., & Schalock, R. L. (2012). Human functioning, supports, assistive technology, and evidence-based practices in the field of intellectual disability. *Journal of Special Education Technology, 27*(2), 3–10.

McCurdy, B. L., Thomas, L., Truckenmiller, A., Rich, S. H., Hillis-Clark, P., & Lopez, J. C. (2016). School-wide positive behavioral interventions and supports for students with emotional and behavioral disorders. *Psychology in the Schools, 53,* 375–389.

McElearney, A., Adamson, G., Shevlin, M., Tracey, A., Muldoon, B., & Roosmale-Cocq, S. (2007). Independent schools counselling: Profiling the NSPCC service experience. *Child Care in Practice, 13*(2), 95–115. doi:10.1080/13575270701214121

Merrell, K. W., Gueldner, B. A., Ross, S. W., & Isava, D. M. (2008). How effective are school bullying intervention programs? A meta-analysis of intervention research. *School Psychology Quarterly, 23*(1), 26.

Musu-Gillette, L., Zhang, A., Wang, K., Zhang, J., Kemp, J., Diliberti, M., & Oudekerk, B. A. (2018). *Indicators of school crime and safety: 2017* (NCES 2018-036/NCJ 251413). Washington, DC: National Center for Education Statistics, U.S. Department of Education, and Bureau of Justice Statistics, Office of Justice Programs, U.S. Department of Justice.

National Academies of Sciences, Engineering, and Medicine. (2016). *Preventing bullying through science, policy, and practice.* Washington, DC: National Academies Press.

Nese, R. N. T., Horner, R. H., Dickey, C. R., Stiller, B., & Tomlanovich, A. (2014). Decreasing bullying behaviors in middle school: Expect respect. *School Psychology Quarterly, 29,* 272–286. http://dx.doi.org/10.1037/spq0000070

Preast, J., Bowman, N., & Rose, C. A. (2017). Creating inclusive classroom communities through social and emotional learning to reduce social marginalization among students with or at-risk for disability identification. In C. M. Curran & A. J. Peterson (Eds.), *Handbook of research on classroom diversity and inclusive education practice* (pp. 183–200). Hershey, PA: IGI Global.

Rehabilitation Act of 1973, 19 USC § 794.

Rodkin, P. C., Espelage, D. L., & Hanish, L. D. (2015). A relational framework for understanding bullying: Developmental antecedents and outcomes. *American Psychologist, 70,* 311–321.

Rose, C. A. (2017). Bullying among youth with disabilities: Predictive and protective factors. In C. Bradshaw (Ed.), *The handbook on bullying prevention: A lifecourse perspective* (pp. 113–123). Washington, DC: National Association of Social Workers Press.

Rose, C. A., & Espelage, D. L. (2012). Risk and protective factors associated with the bullying involvement of students with emotional and behavioral disorders. *Behavioral Disorders, 37*(3), 133–148.

Rose, C. A., & Gage, N. A. (2017). Exploring the involvement in bullying among individuals with and without disabilities over time. *Exceptional Children, 83*, 298–314.

Rose, C. A., & Monda-Amaya, L. E. (2012). Bullying and victimization among students with disabilities: Effective strategies for classroom teachers. *Intervention in School and Clinic, 48*, 99–107. doi: 10.1177/1053451211430119.

Rose, C. A., Monda-Amaya, L. E., & Espelage, D. L. (2011). Bullying perpetration and victimization in special education: A review of the literature. *Remedial and Special Education, 32*(2), 114–130.

Rose, C. A., Stormont, M., Wang, Z., Simpson, C. G., Preast, J. L., & Green, A. L. (2015). Bullying and students with disabilities: Examination of disability status and educational placement. *School Psychology Review, 44*(4), 425–444.

Ross, S. W., & Horner, R. H. (2009). Bully prevention in positive behavior support. *Journal of Applied Behavior Analysis, 42*, 747–759.

Ross, S. W., & Horner, R. H. (2014). Bully prevention in positive behavior support: Preliminary evaluation of third-, fourth-, and fifth grade attitudes toward bullying. *Journal of Emotional and Behavioral Disorders, 22*, 225–236. doi: 10.1177/1063426613491429

Scott, T. M., & Cooper, J. T. (2017). Functional behavior assessment and function-based intervention planning: Considering the simple logic of the process. *Beyond Behavior, 26*(3), 101–104.

Son, E., Parish, S. L., & Peterson, N. A. (2012). National prevalence of peer victimization among young children with disabilities in the United States. *Children and Youth Services Review, 34*(8), 1540–1545.

Swearer, S. M., Espelage, D. L., & Napolitano, S. A. (2009). *Bullying prevention and intervention: Realistic strategies for schools.* New York, NY: Guilford Press.

Swearer, S. M., Wang, C., Collins, A., Strawhun, J., & Fluke, S. (2014). Bullying: A school mental health perspective. In M. D. Weist, N. A. Lever, C. P. Bradshaw, & J. S. Owens (Eds.), *Handbook of school mental health: Research, training, practice and policy* (pp. 341–354). New York, NY: Springer.

Swearer, S. M., Wang, C., Maag, J. W., Siebecker, A. B., & Frerichs, L. J. (2012). Understanding the bullying dynamic among students in special and general education. *Journal of School Psychology, 50*(4), 503–520.

Ttofi, M. M., & Farrington, D. P. (2011). Effectiveness of school-based programs to reduce bullying: A systematic and meta-analytic review. *Journal of Experimental Criminology, 7*, 27–56.

U.S. Department of Education Office for Civil Rights. (2010). *Dear colleague letter.* Washington, DC: Author.

U.S. Department of Education Office for Civil Rights. (2014). *Dear colleague letter.* Washington, DC: Author.

U.S. Department of Education Office of Special Education and Rehabilitative Services. (2013). *Dear colleague letter.* Washington, DC. Author.

U.S. Department of Education Office of Special Education and Rehabilitative Services and Office for Civil Rights. (2000). *Dear colleague letter.* Washington, DC: Author.

Yasuda, P. M., Ievers-Landis, C. E., & Rose, C. A. (2016). *Say NO bullying: A resource book for children and teens with disorders of short stature.* Glen Head, NY: Human Growth Foundation.

Yell, M. L., Katsiyannis, A., Rose, C. A., & Houchins, D. E. (2016). Bullying and harassment of students with disabilities in schools: Legal considerations and policy formation. *Remedial and Special Education, 37*(5), 274–284.

Zablotsky, B., Bradshaw, C. P., Anderson, C. M., & Law, P. (2012). Involvement in bullying among children with autism spectrum disorders: Parents' perspectives on the influence of school factors. *Behavioral Disorders, JAMA Pediatrics, 37*, 179–191.

Zablotsky, B., Bradshaw, C. P., Anderson, C. M., & Law, P. (2013). Risk factors for bullying among children with autism spectrum disorders. *Autism, 18*, 419–427.

In providing school based mental health services, it is not enough to focus on the technical skills required to select and implement evidence-based practices. Successful innovators must also address the adaptive skills required to help educators and service providers become allies.

—Joanne Cashman, EdD, National Association of State Directors of Special Education, and co-convener, National Community of Practice on School Behavioral Health

Innovation in Schools

Expanded School Mental Health

Seth B. Bernstein, Lauryn Young, Ameet N. Bosmia,
Samantha N. Hartley, Cameron S. Massey, and Mark D. Weist

This Chapter Will Cover:

1. How the mental health needs of children and youth can be successfully addressed in schools with expanded school mental health (SMH) services.

2. The various SMH programs that have been developed, such as Cognitive Behavior Intervention for Trauma in Schools, Dialectical Behavior Therapy Skills Training for Emotional Problem Solving for Adolescents, and Promoting Alternative Thinking.

3. How to position and integrate SMH within multitiered systems of support for optimum school-wide implementation.

4. The common challenges educators can encounter in the field when attempting to integrate these SMH services.

This chapter focuses on the evolution of expanded school mental health (SMH) practices and policies in support of the overall well-being and educational success of students. Often, the language used among and between educators and mental health practitioners can be complicated and misunderstood. The content within this chapter shapes the concepts of mental health in schools—from a historical and prevalence-based perspective to current practices and advances to address the mental health needs of all students.

There is a significant national movement toward more comprehensive SMH services, which, when done well, help improve student social, emotional, and behavioral functioning and reduce and remove barriers to their learning. This chapter provides background on SMH, including a review of mental health needs of children and youth, limitations of traditional approaches, advantages of expanding services in schools, a brief history of the field, and a review of specific programs. It also reviews population-based approaches, with particular emphasis on multitiered systems of support (MTSS) and positive behavioral interventions and supports (PBIS). Efforts to interconnect SMH and PBIS are presented, reflecting a critical advancement in the field. Resources for building and expanding SMH programs, challenges to them, and ideas for overcoming challenges are also presented.

Mental Health Needs of Children and Youth and Services for Them

Improving and increasing mental health services for youth and families has been a national priority for many years, as reflected in reports by the U.S. Surgeon

General (U.S. Public Health Service, 2000; U.S. Surgeon General, 1999). A growing research base has documented many problems in the U.S. mental health system for children, youth, and families (President's New Freedom Commission, 2003; U.S. Public Health Service, 2000). For example, results from national epidemiological studies report that 20% (or 1 in 5) of children age 13 to 18 currently have, or in the past have had, a serious debilitating mental disorder (Merikangas et al., 2010). The prevalence estimate for younger children age 8 to 15 is about 13%. However, only 50.6% of children between 8 and 15 years old received treatment for mental health concerns in 2014 (National Institute of Mental Health, n.d.). Even more troubling, Latinx Americans and African Americans received treatment at one half the rate of White Americans (Substance Abuse and Mental Health Services Administration, 2015).

For children and youth, the quality and effectiveness of mental health services are affected by many factors. At the individual level, familial factors such as stress, stigma, demanding schedules, and limited knowledge of mental health conditions and treatment may be contributing factors to youth not receiving treatment (Weist, 1997). Systematic barriers such as waiting times and insurance requirements can also greatly reduce the opportunity for youth to receive adequate services (McKay, Lynn, & Bannon, 2005). A study conducted by Mojtabai et al. (2010) measured perceptions of people seeking mental health services. Results indicated that 44.8% of their participants with a mental disorder chose not to receive treatment, indicating they would work on the problem on their own, with concerns about the helpfulness of the mental health system.

Community-based mental health providers rely heavily on caregiver involvement since they are seen as the gatekeepers to their child or adolescent accessing services (Haine-Schlagel, Mechammil, & Brookman-Frazee, 2017). This factor—that is, whether families seek services for their children—is foundational to improvement in emotional–behavioral (EB) problems presented by children (Dowell & Ogles, 2010; Haine-Schlagel & Walsh, 2015). In addition, traditional sites for delivering mental health services, such as community mental health centers (CMHCs) struggle with other issues, such as poor connections to other youth-serving systems and bureaucratic barriers (e.g., overcoming hurdles to obtain fee-for-service reimbursement), that attenuate their effectiveness (Gopalan et al., 2010; Nock & Ferriter, 2005). These barriers also get in the way of mental health staff delivering evidence-based practices, which are associated with increased training and practice demands and the need for ongoing implementation support (Evans & Weist, 2004; Schaeffer et al., 2005).

Development of Expanded School Mental Health Services

Within this context of increasing recognition of problems associated with mental health services in traditional sites such as CMHCs, there has been a growing national movement toward expanding services to children and youth "where they are" (Weist & Ghuman, 2002), in settings that are almost universally encountered, such as schools (Burns et al., 1995; Weist, 1997). These expanded SMH programs involve partnerships between schools and community mental health agencies toward greater depth and quality in prevention, early intervention, and intervention efforts (Weist, 1997; Weist, Lever, Bradshaw, & Owens, 2014). The word *expanded* is used purposefully to convey that collaborating community clinicians augment services delivered by school-employed mental health staff such as psychologists, counselors, social workers, special educators, nurses, and others. In recent decades, SMH programs have grown substantially, thanks in part to the recognition that partnerships between community providers and school-based professionals can be mutually beneficial. These partnerships have been linked with enhanced treatment outcomes and satisfaction with services (Lever et al., 2009; Weist, Proescher, Prodente, Ambrose, & Waxman, 2001) and more efficient resource use (Anderson-Butcher & Ashton, 2004; Rappaport, Osher, Greenberg Garrison, Anderson-Ketchmark, & Dwyer, 2003).

Brief History

Beginning in 1995, the Maternal and Child Health Bureau's Office of Adolescent Health within the Health Resources and Services Administration began its Mental Health Services in Schools initiative. This initiative involved the establishment of two national centers for SMH, the Center for School Mental Health (CSMH) at the University of Maryland and the Center for Mental Health in Schools at the University of California, Los Angeles, along with infrastructure support to five states (Kentucky, Maine, Minnesota, New Mexico, and South Carolina) to build systems to support SMH (Adelman & Taylor, 1999). These states received funding for 3 years, and both national centers were funded until 2010. Since then, one national center, the CSMH, has been funded and remains very active in leading the field (see http://csmh.umaryland.edu). The CSMH has sponsored an annual conference on SMH since 1995 and continues to advance effective practices and to impact national, state, and local policies.

Community of Practice Emphasis

In 2004, a partnership began with the Individuals with Disabilities Education Act Partnership (IDEA Partnership) at the National Association of State Directors of Special Education and CSMH (Weist et al., 2017). From this effort began the National Community of Practice (CoP) on Collaborative School Behavioral Health, which included a wide range of stakeholders invested in the SMH agenda. This included diverse youth-serving systems such as education, mental health, child welfare, juvenile justice, disabilities, primary health care, family advocacy, and others, as well as the full range of disciplines involved in the work, such as teachers (in general and special education), school psychologists and counselors, school administrators, community mental health staff and leaders, leaders from other systems, and family/youth advocates and consumers of mental health services. The CoP also included multiple states, national organizations, and local leaders working together to advance the SMH agenda, recognizing that the systematic work of building the field rested on a platform of interdisciplinary and cross-system relationships and strong stakeholder involvement (Weist et al., 2017). There are a number of examples of successful interdisciplinary and cross-system approaches in SMH (Adelman & Taylor, 1999, 2008; Anderson-Butcher & Ashton, 2004; Anderson-Butcher et al., 2008, 2010; Weist, Grady Ambrose, & Lewis, 2006).

Specific School Mental Health Programs

Several mental health interventions have been developed to be implemented in the school setting. One such program, Cognitive Behavioral Intervention for Trauma in Schools (CBITS; Jaycox, 2004), was developed to be used with children who have been exposed to traumatic experiences and are displaying mild to moderately significant symptoms of posttraumatic stress, anxiety, and depression. It focuses on the delivery of psychoeducation regarding trauma, relaxation training, cognitive therapy, exposure, and problem solving. The CBITS protocol was developed with Spanish-speaking Latinx youth in mind and has been shown to be effective in reducing symptoms of trauma and depression (Allison & Ferreira, 2017; Kataoka et al., 2003), and has additionally shown success in reducing symptoms of posttraumatic stress disorder, depression, and psychosocial dysfunction in larger randomized controlled trials (Stein et al., 2003). Other examples of programs developed for use within the school system are the Dialectical Behavior Therapy Skills Training for Emotional Problem Solving for Adolescents (Mazza, Dexter-Mazza, Miller, Rathus & Murphy, 2016), which helps youth cope with emotional stress and improve decision making; the universal prevention program Promoting Alternative Thinking Strategies (Greenberg, Kusche, Cook, & Quamma, 1995), which attempts to help students develop self-control and enhance interpersonal problem-solving skills; and the Linking the Interests of Families and Teachers (Reid, Eddy, Fetrow, & Stoolmiller, 1999) program, which is intended to be used with children near high-crime areas in an effort to reduce their conduct problems.

SMH programs have shown success in meeting the needs of a variety of social, emotional, and behavioral needs of students. Historically, many of these programs have targeted EB concerns, depression, and conduct problems with various levels of effectiveness (for detailed reviews, see CSMH, 2013; Rones & Hoagwood, 2000). At the universal level of delivery, SMH programs have shown to be effective in reducing the reported rates of anxiety in children and adolescents (Collins, Woolfson, & Durkin, 2014; Skryabina, Taylor, & Stallard, 2016) and have shown improvements in anxious symptoms in children as young as ages 5 to 7 (Ruocco, Gordon, & McLean, 2016). Programs such as Surviving the Teens® Suicide Prevention and Depression

Awareness Program have been shown to be effective methods of increasing youth knowledge about both symptoms of depression and suicidality in youth ages 10 to 19, as well as improving their communication with others about serious EB issues they might be experiencing (Strunk, King, Vidourek, & Sorter, 2014). SMH programs have also shown to be effective in reducing the severity of hyperactivity, impulsivity, and oppositional behavior, as well as improving peer relationships and overall functioning (Owens et al., 2005). Successful SMH programs have been developed and adapted for a variety of specific demographic populations as well, such as Latinx youth (Jaycox, 2004), youth living in inner-city environments (Bruns, Walrath, Glass-Siegel, & Weist, 2004; Ginsburg, Becker, Kingery, & Nichols, 2008), and youth living in rural areas (Albright et al., 2013).

Making Connections to Population-Based Approaches and Positive Behavioral Interventions and Supports

Adopting population-based approaches, including periodic school-wide screening for EB problems to identify and monitor the needs of students (Dowdy, Ritchey, & Kamphaus, 2010) has been an important development for the SMH field (Doll & Cummings, 2008). These population-based approaches can help shift SMH services from a reactive, resource-intensive approach that focuses exclusively on treating selected individuals (e.g., those in special education) to a proactive continuum of services that incorporates prevention, early intervention, and treatment to promote the well-being and mental health of the entire school population.

Multitiered Systems of Support and Positive Behavioral Interventions and Supports

MTSS is one such framework for promoting the positive social, emotional, behavioral, and academic functioning of students (Sugai & Horner, 2009). Drawing from public health and prevention science frameworks (Mrazek & Haggerty, 1994; O'Connell, Boat, & Warner, 2009), MTSS approaches employ a three-tiered system to address student needs along a continuum of target populations and intervention intensity. This includes Tier 1 supports for all students that focus on universal promotion and prevention (e.g., social emotional learning curriculums, positive school climate), Tier 2 strategies for students at risk of or demonstrating early signs of issues that focus on early identification and targeted intervention (e.g., targeted mentoring programs, group social skills training), and Tier 3 interventions for students demonstrating more significant problems that focus on more intensive, individualized intervention or treatment (Horner, Sugai, & Anderson, 2010).

PBIS is one of the most widely used examples of an MTSS in education. Currently, around 26,000 schools are implementing PBIS, a framework emphasizing a focus on positive behavior, data-based decision making, implementing a range of evidence-based practices, and ensuring strong implementation support for these practices (Horner et al., 2010; Office of Special Education Programs, 2017). When effectively implemented, PBIS has been associated with improved teaching (McIntosh, Horner, Chard, Boland, & Good, 2006), improvements in student behavior (Anderson & Kincaid, 2005), and improvements in student academic performance (Kincaid, Knoster, Harrower, Shannon, & Bustamante, 2002).

Interconnected Systems Framework

Although PBIS offers a robust implementation structure, in practice, its strong emphasis on *behavior* and universal Tier 1 supports leaves a gap in the delivery of more intensive interventions for many students who may benefit from mental health services (Eber, Weist, & Barrett, 2013). Relatedly, traditional SMH efforts, while effective in improving access to care (Atkins et al., 2006) and associated with improved student outcomes (CSMH, 2013), have lacked an implementation structure for integrating their services within the full MTSS continuum. To capitalize on the complementary strengths of PBIS and SMH, the interconnected systems framework (ISF) was developed to promote the integrated, rather than parallel, delivery of these two approaches toward comprehensive services and depth and quality within all three tiers of the MTSS (Barrett, Eber, & Weist, 2013).

Challenges in School Mental Health Needing Enhanced Attention

While there has been a significant increase in the focus of schools on mental health issues, and the associated development of more comprehensive SMH programs and services, there are still many significant challenges being encountered in this work. Several of the more prominent challenges are reviewed here.

Wait-to-Fail Method

The wait-to-fail method, or basing the start of supportive intervention for students on evidence of them doing poorly or struggling, continues to be prevalent in many schools/school districts (Reid, Gonzalez, Nordness, Trout, & Epstein, 2004; Webster-Stratton, 2000). In some schools/districts, serving students with EB difficulties is largely based on a reactive approach that addresses a behavior problem *after* it has occurred, rather than proactively *preventing* the behavior problem (Cook & Wright, 2009). Common reactive approaches used by schools/districts include the use of office referrals, out-of-school suspensions, and even expulsions. Chronic use of suspensions and expulsions harms teacher–student relationships and exacerbates the risk for academic failure, delinquency, and school dropout (Elliot, Hamburg, & Williams, 1998; National Longitudinal Transition Study of Special Education Students, 2005; U.S. Department of Education, 2003).

SMH programs—especially when they are integrated with PBIS, as in the ISF—can work purposefully toward creating more proactive approaches to identify early signs of student risk factors or EB needs, which sets the stage for effective early intervention. For example, in a recent study, Splett et al. (2018) documented that implementing a universal screener to identify student social and EB concerns increased identification of these concerns by 180% over traditional methods such as office referrals for behavioral problems. A clear need for the field is adequate infrastructure, including resources, training, and implementation support for such screening efforts, and ensuring adequate follow-up in the form of evidence-based Tier 2 or 3 interventions for students presenting elevated needs (Lane, Oakes, Crocker, & Weist, 2017).

Limited Teacher Training and Support

Ironically, special education teachers serving students with significant social and EB problems have been found more likely to be uncertified and to have fewer years of teaching experience than other types of special education teachers (Billingsley, Fall, & Williams, 2006). Furthermore, a recent national survey of school-based practices revealed that only 9% of schools reported training all their teachers, both general education and special education teachers, to identify and recognize social and EB concerns in students (Romer & McIntosh, 2005).

Another concern is the high rates of stress and burnout among teachers and staff who work with students with social–emotional and behavioral difficulties (Lever, Mathis, & Mayworm, 2017). To counter burnout and turnover, school districts and administrators should pay increased attention to how to support school staff for effective teaching, but also how to effectively work with challenging behaviors students present in classrooms (Kern, George, & Weist, 2016). In addition, providing training, such as Youth Mental Health First Aid (https://www.mentalhealthfirstaid.org/), can provide a solid base for educators to further understand mental health conditions and help prevent escalation of issues. Ideally, schools will also consider strategies to directly support teachers—for example, through programs that focus on stress reduction and personal wellness enhancement (Lever et al., 2017).

Limited Use of Empirically Supported Practices

A notable report by Knitzer, Steinberg, and Fleisch (1990) drew national attention to the lack of empirically supported practices in most special education programs for addressing the needs of students with significant social and EB challenges. The authors reported that the purpose of most of these self-contained programs was to isolate and quarantine students from the general population. Many of these programs failed to even provide basic academic and social–emotional skills training to students who were known to lack such skills.

Recognizing the reality that ineffective practices in schools may perpetuate (Kern et al., 2016), an important strategy is to ensure ongoing quality assessment and improvement (QAI) efforts of teaching practices and efforts occurring within the MTSS to improve student social and EB functioning (Weist et al., 2005). Comprehensive and ongoing professional development and implementation support is foundational to these QAI efforts, including interdisciplinary training with educators; diverse staff involved in prevention and intervention within the MTSS, including school-employed mental health staff (e.g., school psychologists, counselors); and collaborating staff from community agencies (e.g., clinical social workers, psychologists, licensed professional counselors; Michael, Bernstein, Owens, Albright, & Anderson-Butcher, 2014; Weist et al., 2005). Improvement of QAI and professional development requires an honest assessment of limitations in current efforts (Morris & Hanley, 2001) and a paradigm shift toward a real commitment to ongoing professional development and QAI, along with sufficient resources and support for them (Michael et al., 2014). Within this context, a particular need is to strengthen MTSS teams, ensuring they have the right participants (e.g., school- and community-employed mental health staff, educators, administrators, school nurses, family members) and that meetings focus on active use of data and refining and improving empirically supported practices delivered at Tiers 1, 2, and 3 (Barrett et al., 2013; Splett et al., 2017).

Ensuring That Students With Emotional–Behavioral Needs Receive Appropriate Services

Schools, in large part, dramatically underidentify and underserve students with social and EB problems (Walker, Nishioka, Zeller, Severson, & Feil, 2000), with services falling far short of meeting the needs of more than one-fifth of students who present more significant problems (Merikangas et al., 2010). As indicated earlier, a clear need for the field is to increase systematic screening of student social and EB challenges (Lane et al., 2017). Ideally, screening data are collected broadly for the student body, and these will identify two-thirds or so of students with no real elevated social or EB needs but one-third or more with borderline or more significant needs (Splett et al., 2018). The challenge then is to implement a continuum of empirically supported practices for students presenting low-level Tier 2 needs (e.g., a student with moderately elevated anxiety but no other EB problems and positive adaptive and academic functioning) all the way up to students presenting severe needs (e.g., a range of "internalizing" and "externalizing" problems, low adaptive and academic functioning). Unfortunately, most schools and SMH programs are not adequately identifying this continuum of student social and EB needs, and are failing to implement a range of empirically supported practices across it.

Disproportionality and Problematic Policies

Racial and ethnic disproportionality is a significant and longstanding problem within special education (Skiba et al., 2008). For example, African American students may be overrepresented in the emotional disabilities category, while Latinx students may be underrepresented (Chinn & Hughes, 1987; Oswald & Coutinho, 2001; Zhang & Katsiyannis, 2002). In addition, problematic educational policies, such as the social maladjustment exclusion for youth to receive special education services (i.e., denied services related to "willful misconduct"), disproportionally affect youth of color and contribute to the "school to prison pipeline" for them (Becker et al., 2011; Bradshaw, Mitchell, O'Brennan, & Leaf, 2010; Osher et al., 2012). Further, there is increasing concern about special education–related decision making that can seem arbitrary at best—for example, in determining whether a behavioral problem indicating a disciplinary consequence was a "manifestation" of a student's disability, a judgment for which there are few appropriate empirical parameters (Walker & Brigham, 2017). As the movement toward more comprehensive SMH services gains momentum, these limitations and policy barriers related to special education warrant increased and ongoing attention in research, practice, and policy.

Conclusion

Expanded SMH programs and services have grown from limited practices and programs to seeing the benefits of enhanced education–mental health system partnerships. In recent years, the SMH field has been advanced through a community of practice approach, emphasizing building cross-system and interdisciplinary approaches. Within this approach, relationships among various partners are foundational to progress. Considerable momentum for the field is being realized through connections to MTSS and frameworks such as PBIS. As more comprehensive SMH connects systematically to the MTSS, progress is made toward greater depth and quality in Tier 1 (promotion/prevention), Tier 2 (early intervention), and Tier 3 (intervention programs and services) interventions, with a range of resources available to assist schools, school districts, and communities in doing this work. As the SMH field is developing, a number of challenges are being identified, including moving beyond passive, wait-to-fail approaches; improving training and support to teachers; increasing the likelihood of empirically supported practices; ensuring that services match various levels of student needs; and overcoming inequities and policy challenges. The growing field of SMH and each of the core themes reviewed in this chapter are highly relevant to the improvement of special education programs and services. We are grateful for the opportunity to present this brief review.

REFLECTING AND UNDERSTANDING

1. What is the prevalence of serious mental illness in children, and what percentage typically receive treatment?

2. What are the various components of multitiered systems of support?

3. What results can be associated with successfully implementing positive behavioral interventions and supports?

4. What are two specific school mental health interventions?

5. What are three challenges to advancing expanded school mental health services?

ONLINE RESOURCES

- CSMH at the University of Maryland at Baltimore: http://csmh.umaryland.edu/

- Office of Special Education Programs Technical Assistance Center on PBIS: http://www.pbis.org/

- Information on ISF can also be found on the PBIS website: http://www.pbis .org/school/school-mental-health/ interconnected-systems

RECOMMENDED READINGS

Books

Leschied, A. D., Saklofske, D., & Flett, G. (2018). *Handbook of school-based mental health promotion: An evidence informed framework for implementation*. New York, NY: Springer.

Weist, M. D., Lever, N. A., Bradshaw, C. P., & Owens, J. S. (Eds.). (2014). *Handbook of school mental health: Research, training, practice, and policy*. New York, NY: Springer Science & Business Media.

PROFESSIONAL ORGANIZATIONS

The American Psychological Association: http://www.apa.org/ed/schools/index.aspx

The National Association of School Psychologists: https://www.nasponline.org/ resources-and-publications

National Registry of Evidence-Based Programs and Practices provided by the Substance Abuse and Mental Health Services Administration: https://www.samhsa.gov/nrepp

REFERENCES

Adelman, H. S., & Taylor, L. (1999). Mental health in schools and system restructuring. *Clinical Psychology Review*, *19*(2), 137–163.

Adelman, H. S., & Taylor, L. (2008). School-wide approaches to addressing barriers to learning and teaching. In B. Doll & J. Cummings (Eds.), *Transforming school mental health services: Population-based approaches to promoting the competency and wellness of children* (pp. 277–306). Thousand Oaks, CA: Corwin Press in cooperation with the National Association of School Psychologists.

Albright, A., Michael, K., Massey, C., Sale, R., Kirk, A., & Egan, T. (2013). An evaluation of an interdisciplinary rural school mental health programme in Appalachia. *Advances in School Mental Health Promotion*, *6*(3), 189–202.

Allison, A. C., & Ferreira, R. J. (2017). Implementing cognitive behavioral intervention for trauma in schools (CBITS) with Latino youth. *Child & Adolescent Social Work Journal*, *34*(2), 181–189.

Anderson, C. M., & Kincaid, D. (2005). Applying behavior analysis to school violence and discipline problems: Schoolwide positive behavior support. *Behavior Analyst*, *28*(1), 49–63.

Anderson-Butcher, D., & Ashton, D. (2004). Innovative models of collaboration to serve children, youths, families, and communities. *Children & Schools*, *26*(1), 39–53.

Anderson-Butcher, D., Lawson, H. A., Bean, J., Flaspohler, P., Boone, B., & Kwiatkowski, A. (2008). Community collaboration to improve schools: Introducing a new model from Ohio. *Children & Schools*, *30*(3), 161–172.

Anderson-Butcher, D., Lawson, H. A., Iachini, A., Flaspohler, P., Bean, J., & Wade-Mdivanian, R. (2010). Emergent evidence in support of a community collaboration model for school improvement. *Children & Schools*, *32*(3), 160–171.

Atkins, M. S., Frazier, S. L., Birman, D., Adil, J. A., Jackson, M., Graczyk, P. A., & McKay, M. M. (2006). School-based mental health services for children living in high poverty urban communities. *Administration and Policy in Mental Health and Mental Health Services Research*, *33*(2), 146–159.

Barrett, S., Eber, L., & Weist, M. D. (2013). *Advancing education effectiveness: An interconnected systems framework for positive behavioral interventions and supports (PBIS) and school mental health.* Center for Positive Behavioral Interventions and Supports (funded by the Office of Special Education Programs, U.S. Department of Education). Eugene: University of Oregon Press.

Becker, S. P., Paternite, C. E., Evans, S. W., Andrews, C., Christensen, O. A., Kraan, E. M., & Weist, M. D. (2011). Eligibility, assessment and educational placement issues for students classified with emotional disturbance: Federal and state-level analyses. *School Mental Health*, *3*(1), 24–34.

Billingsley, B., Fall, A., & Williams, T. (2006). Who is teaching students with emotional and behavioral disorders? A profile and comparison to other special educators. *Behavioral Disorders*, *31*(3), 252–264.

Bradshaw, C. P., Mitchell, M. M., O'Brennan, L. M., & Leaf, P. J. (2010). Multilevel exploration of factors contributing to the overrepresentation of Black students in office disciplinary referrals. *Journal of Educational Psychology*, *102*(2), 508–520.

Bruns, E. J., Walrath, C., Glass-Siegel, M., & Weist, M. D. (2004). School-based mental health services in Baltimore: Association with school climate and special education referrals. *Behavior Modification*, *28*(4), 491–512.

Burns, B. J., Costello, E. J., Angold, A., Tweed, D., Stangl, D., Farmer, E. M., & Erkanli, A. (1995). Children's mental health service use across service sections. *Health Affairs*, *14*(3), 147–159.

Center for School Mental Health. (2013). *The impact of school mental health: Educational, social, emotional, and behavioral outcomes.* Baltimore: University of Maryland Baltimore.

Chinn, P. C., & Hughes, S. (1987). Representation of minority students in special classes. *Remedial and Special Education*, *8*, 41–46.

Collins, S., Woolfson, L. M., & Durkin, K. (2014). Effects on coping skills and anxiety of a universal school-based mental health intervention delivered in Scottish primary schools. *School Psychology International, 35*(1), 85–100.

Cook, C., & Wright, D. B. (2009). *RTI in restrictive setting: The TIERS Model for students with emotional/behavioral disorders.* Horsham, PA: LRP.

Doll, B., & Cummings, J. (2008). Why population-based services are essential for school mental health and how to make them happen in your school. In B. Doll & J. Cummings (Eds.), *Transforming school mental health services: Population-based approaches to promoting the competency and wellness of children* (pp. 1–20). Thousand Oaks, CA: Corwin Press in cooperation with the National Association of School Psychologists.

Dowdy, E., Ritchey, K., & Kamphaus, R. W. (2010). School-based screening: A population-based approach to inform and monitor children's mental health needs. *School Mental Health, 2*(4), 166–176.

Dowell, K. A., & Ogles, B. M. (2010). The effects of parent participation on child psychotherapy outcome: A meta-analytic review. *Journal of Clinical Child and Adolescent Psychology, 39*, 151–162. http://dx.doi.org/10.1080/15374410903532585

Eber, L., Weist, M., & Barrett, S. (2013). An introduction to the Interconnected Systems Framework. In S. Barrett, L. Eber, & M. Weist (Eds.), *Advancing education effectiveness: An interconnected systems framework for positive behavioral interventions and supports (PBIS) and school mental health* (pp. 3–17). Center for Positive Behavioral Interventions and Supports (funded by the Office of Special Education Programs, U.S. Department of Education). Eugene: University of Oregon Press.

Elliot, D., Hamburg, B., & Williams, K. (1998). *Violence in American schools: New perspectives and solutions.* New York, NY: Cambridge University Press.

Evans, S. W., & Weist, M. D. (2004). Implementing empirically supported treatments in schools: What are we asking? *Clinical Child and Family Psychology Review, 7*, 263–267.

Ginsburg, G. S., Becker, K. D., Kingery, J. N., & Nichols T. (2008). Transporting CBT for childhood anxiety disorders into inner-city school-based mental health clinics. *Cognitive and Behavioral Practice, 15*(2), 148–158.

Gopalan, G., Goldstein, L., Klingenstein, K., Sicher, C., Blake, C., & McKay, M. M. (2010). Engaging families into child mental health treatment: Updates and special considerations. *Journal of the Canadian Academy of Child and Adolescent Psychiatry, 19*(3), 182–196.

Greenberg, M., Kusche, C., Cook, E., & Quamma, J. (1995). Promoting emotional competence in school-aged children: The effects of the PATHS curriculum. *Development and Psychopathology, 7*, 117–136.

Haine-Schlagel, R., Mechammil, M., & Brookman-Frazee, L. (2017). Stakeholder perspectives on a toolkit to enhance caregiver participation in community-based child mental health services. *Psychological Services, 14*(3), 373–386. doi:10.1037/ser0000095

Haine-Schlagel, R., & Walsh, N. E. (2015). A Review of Parent participation engagement in youth and family mental health treatment. *Clinical Child and Family Psychology Review, 18*, 133–150. http://dx.doi.org/10.1007/s10567-015-0182-x

Horner, R. H., Sugai, G. M., & Anderson, C. M. (2010). Examining the evidence base for school-wide positive behavior support. *Focus on Exceptional Children, 42*(8), 1–14.

Jaycox, L. H. (2004). *CBITS: Cognitive behavioral intervention for trauma in schools.* Longmont, CO: RAND.

Kataoka, S. H., Stein, B. D., Jaycox, L. H., Wong, M., Escudero, P., Tu, W., Zaragoza, C., & Fink, A. (2003). A school-based mental health program for traumatized Latino immigrant children. *Journal of the American Academy of Child and Adolescent Psychiatry, 42*(3), 311–318.

Kern, L., George, M., & Weist, M. D. (2016). *Step by step support for students with emotional and behavioral problems: Prevention and intervention strategies.* Baltimore, MD: Brookes.

Kincaid, D., Knoster, T., Harrower, J. K., Shannon, P., & Bustamante, S. (2002). Measuring the impact of positive behavior support. *Journal of Positive Behavior Interventions, 4*(2), 109–117.

Knitzer, J., Steinberg, Z., & Fleisch, B. (1990). *At the schoolhouse door: An examination of programs and policies for children with behavioral and emotional problems.* New York, NY: Bank Street College of Education.

Lane, K., Oakes, W., Crocker, J., & Weist, M. D. (2017). Building strong partnerships: Education and mental health systems working together to advance behavioral health screening in schools. *Report on Emotional & Behavioral Disorders in Youth*, 17(4), 93–101.

Lever, N., Mathis, E., & Mayworm, A. (2017). School mental health is not just for students: Why teacher and school staff wellness matters. *Report on Emotional & Behavioral Disorders in Youth*, 17(1), 6–12.

Lever, N., Mulloy, M., Evangelista, N., Vulin-Reynolds, M., Bryant, Y., McCree-Huntley, S., & Jordan, P. (2009). *School mental health and foster care: A training curriculum for parents, school-based clinicians, educators, and child welfare staff*. Retrieved from http://somvweb.som.umaryland.edu/Fileshare/SchoolMentalHealth/Resources/FostCare/FINAL_Training_Curriculum_Manual10.29.09.pdf

Mazza, J. J., Dexter-Mazza, E. T., Miller, A. L., Rathus, J. H., & Murphy, H. E. (2016). *DBT skills in schools: Skills training for emotional problem solving for adolescents (DBT STEPS-A)*. New York, NY: Guilford Press.

McIntosh, K., Horner, R. H., Chard, D. J., Boland, J. B., & Good, R. I. (2006). The use of reading and behavior screening measures to predict nonresponse to school-wide positive behavior support: A longitudinal analysis. *School Psychology Review*, 35(2), 275–291.

McKay, M. M., Lynn, C. J., & Bannon, W. M. (2005). Understanding inner city child mental health need and trauma exposure: Implications for preparing urban service providers. *American Journal of Orthopsychiatry*, 75(2), 201–210.

Merikangas, K. R., He, J., Burstein, M., Swanson, S. A., Avenevoli, S., Cui, L., Benjet, C.... Swendsen, J. (2010). Lifetime prevalence of mental disorders in U.S. adolescents: Results from the National Comorbidity Study Adolescent Supplement (NCS-A). *Journal of the American Academy of Child & Adolescent Psychiatry*, 49(10), 980–989.

Michael, K. D., Bernstein, S., Owens, J. S., Albright, A., & Anderson-Butcher, D. (2014). Preparing school mental health professionals: Competencies in interdisciplinary and cross-system collaboration. In M. D. Weist, N. A. Lever, C. P. Bradshaw, & J. S. Owens (Eds.), *Handbook of school mental health: Research, training, practice, and policy* (pp. 31–43). Boston, MA: Springer. doi:10.1007/978-1-4614-7624-5_3

Mojtabai, R., Olfson, M., Sampson, A., Jin, R., Druss, B., Wang, P. S., Wells, K. B.... Kessler, R. C. (2010). Barriers to mental health treatment: Results from the National Comorbidity Survey Replication (NCS-R). HHS Public Access. doi:10.1017/S0033291710002291

Morris, J. A., & Hanley, J. H. (2001). Human resource development: A critical gap in child mental health reform. *Administration and Policy in Mental Health and Mental Health Services Research*, 28, 219–227.

Mrazek, P. J., & Haggerty, R. J. (1994). *Reducing risks for mental disorders: Frontiers for preventative intervention research*. Washington, DC: National Academy Press.

National Institute of Mental Health. (n.d.). Use of mental health services and treatment among children. Retrieved January 16, 2015, from http://www.nimh.nih.gov/health/statistics/prevalence/use-of-mental-health-services-and-treatment-among-children.shtml

National Longitudinal Transition Study of Special Education Students. (2005). Retrieved October 22, 2017, from http://www.nlts2.org/index.html

Nock, M. K., & Ferriter, C. (2005). Parent management of attendance and adherence in child and adolescent therapy: A conceptual and empirical review. *Clinical Child and Family Psychology Review*, 8(2), 149–166.

O'Connell, M. E., Boat, T., & Warner, K. E. (2009). *Preventing mental, emotional, and behavioral disorders among young people: Progress and possibilities*. Washington, DC: National Academies Press.

Office of Special Education Programs. (2017). Technical Assistance Center on Positive Behavioral Interventions and Supports. Retrieved from http://www.pbis.org

Osher, D., Coggshall, J., Colombi, G., Woodruff, D., Francois, S., & Osher, T. (2012). Building school and teacher capacity to eliminate the school-to-prison pipeline. *Teacher Education and Special Education: Journal of the Teacher Education Division of the Council for Exceptional Children*, 35(4), 284–295.

Oswald, D. P., & Coutinho, M. J. (2001). Trends in disproportionate representation in special education: Implications for multicultural education policies. In C. A. Utley & F. E. Obiakor (Eds.), *Special education, multicultural education, and school reform: Components of a quality education for students with mild disabilities* (pp. 54–73). Springfield, IL: Charles C. Thomas.

Owens, J. S., Richerson, L., Beilstein, E. A., Crane, A., Murphy, C. E., & Vancouver, J. B. (2005). School-based mental health programming for children with inattentive and disruptive behavior problems: First-year treatment outcome. *Journal of Attention Disorders*, 9(1), 261–274.

President's New Freedom Commission. (2003). *Achieving the promise: Transforming mental health care in America.* Washington, DC: President of the United States. Retrieved from http://govinfo.library.unt.edu/mentalhealthcommission/reports/reports.htm

Rappaport, N., Osher, D., Greenberg Garrison, E., Anderson-Ketchmark, C., & Dwyer, K. (2003). Enhancing collaboration within and across disciplines to advance mental health programs in schools. In M. D. Weist, S. Evans, & N. Lever (Eds.), *Handbook of school mental health: Advancing practice and research* (pp. 107–118). New York, NY: Kluwer Academic/Plenum.

Reid, J., Eddy, M., Fetrow, R., & Stoolmiller, M. (1999). Description and immediate impacts of a preventative intervention for conduct problems. *American Journal of Community Psychology*, 27, 483–517.

Reid, R., Gonzalez, J. E., Nordness, P. D., Trout, A., & Epstein, M. H. (2004). A meta-analysis of the academic status of students with emotional/behavioral disturbance. *Journal of Special Education*, 38, 130–143.

Romer, D., & McIntosh, M. (2005). The roles and perspectives of school mental health professionals in promoting adolescent mental health. In D. L. Evans, E. B. Foa, R. E. Gur, H. Hendin, C. P. O'Brien, M. E. P. Seligman, & B. T. Walsh (Eds.), *Treating and preventing adolescent mental health disorders: What we know and what we don't know, a research agenda for improving the mental health of our youth* (pp. 597–616). Oxford, UK: Oxford University Press.

Rones, M., & Hoagwood, K. (2000). School-based mental health services: A research review. *Clinical Child and Family Review*, 3(4), 223–241.

Ruocco, S., Gordon, J., & McLean, L. A. (2016). Effectiveness of a school-based early intervention CBT group programme for children with anxiety aged 5–7 years. *Advances in School Mental Health Promotion*, 9(1), 29–49.

Schaeffer, C. M., Bruns, E., Weist, M. D., Stephan, S. H., Goldstein, J., & Simpson, Y. (2005). Overcoming challenges to evidence-based interventions in schools. *Journal of Youth and Adolescence*, 34, 15–22.

Skiba, R. J., Simmons, A. B., Ritter, S., Gibb, A. C., Rausch, M. K., Cuadrado, J., & Chung, C. (2008). Achieving equity in special education: History, status, and current challenges. *Exceptional Children*, 74(3), 264–288.

Skryabina, E., Taylor, G., & Stallard, P. (2016). Effect of a universal anxiety prevention programme (FRIENDS) on children's academic performance: Results from a randomised controlled trial. *Journal of Child Psychology and Psychiatry*, 57(11), 1297–1307.

Splett, J. W., Perales, K., Halliday-Boykins, C. A., Gilchrest, C., Gibson, N., & Weist, M. D. (2017). Best practices for teaming and collaboration in the interconnected systems framework. *Journal of Applied School Psychology*, 33(4), 347–368.

Splett, J. W., Trainor, K., Raborn, A., Halliday-Boykins, C., Garzona, M., Dongo, M., & Weist, M. D. (2018). Comparison of universal mental health screening to students already receiving intervention in a multitiered system of support. *Behavioral Disorders*, 43(3), 344–356.

Stein, B. D., Jaycox, L. H., Kataoka, S. H., Wong, M., Tu, W., Elliott, M. N., & Fink, A. (2003). A mental health intervention for schoolchildren exposed to violence. *Journal of the American Medical Association*, 290(5), 603–611.

Strunk, C. M., King, K. A., Vidourek, R. A., & Sorter, M. T. (2014). Effectiveness of the Surviving the Teens® suicide prevention and depression awareness program: An impact evaluation utilizing a comparison group. *Health Education and Behavior*, 41(6), 605–613.

Substance Abuse and Mental Health Services Administration. (2015). *Racial/ethnic differences in mental health service use among adults* (HHS Publication No. SMA-15-4906). Rockville, MD: Author. Retrieved July 2017 from https://www.samhsa.gov/data/sites/default/files/MHServicesUseAmongAdults/MHServicesUseAmongAdults.pdf

Sugai, G., & Horner, R. H. (2009). Responsiveness-to-intervention and school-wide positive behavior supports: Integration of multi-tiered system approaches. *Exceptionality, 17*(4), 223–237.

U.S. Department of Education. (2003). *Special Education Elementary Longitudinal Study (SEELS)*. Washington, DC: Office of Special Education and Rehabilitative Services.

U.S. Public Health Service. (2000). *Report of the Surgeon General's conference on children's mental health: A national action agenda*. Washington, DC: Department of Health and Human Services.

U.S. Surgeon General. (1999). *Mental health: A report of the Surgeon General*. Washington, DC: Department of Health and Human Services.

Walker, H. M., Nishioka, V. M., Zeller, R., Severson, H. H., & Feil, E. G. (2000). Causal factors and potential solutions for the persistent under-identification of students having emotional or behavioral disorders in the context of schooling. *Assessment for Effective Instruction, 26*, 29–40.

Walker, J. D., & Brigham, F. J. (2017). Manifestation determination decisions and students with emotional/behavioral disorders. *Journal of Emotional and Behavioral Disorders, 25*(2), 107–118. doi:10.1177/1063426616628819

Webster-Stratton, C. (Ed.). (2000). *How to promote social and academic competence in young children*. London, UK: Sage.

Weist, M. D. (1997). Expanded school mental health services. In T. H. Ollendick & R. J. Prinz (Eds.), *Advances in clinical child psychology* (Vol. 19, pp. 319–352). Boston, MA: Springer.

Weist, M. D., Flaherty, L., Lever, N., Stephan, S., Van Eck, K., & Bode, A. (2017). The history and future of school mental health. In J. R. Harrison, B. K. Schultz, & S. W. Evans (Eds.), *School mental health services for adolescents* (pp. 3–23). New York, NY: Oxford University Press.

Weist, M. D., & Ghuman, H. S. (2002). Principles behind the proactive delivery of mental health services to youth where they are. In M. Weist, H. Ghuman, & R. Sarles (Eds.), *Providing mental health services to youth where they are: School- and community-based approaches* (pp. 1–14). New York, NY: Taylor Francis.

Weist, M. D., Grady Ambrose, M., & Lewis, C. P. (2006). Expanded school mental health: A collaborative community-school example. *Children & Schools, 28*(1), 45–50.

Weist, M. D., Lever, N. A., Bradshaw, C. P., & Owens, J. S. (Eds.). (2014). *Handbook of school mental health: Research, training, practice, and policy*. New York, NY: Springer Science & Business Media.

Weist, M. D., Proescher, E., Prodente, C., Ambrose, M. G., & Waxman, R. P. (2001). Mental health, health, and education staff working together in schools. *Child and Adolescent Psychiatric Clinics of North America, 10*(1), 33–43.

Weist, M. D., Sander, M. A., Walrath, C., Link, B., Nabors, L., Adelsheim, S., Moore, E.... Carrillo, K. (2005). Developing principles for best practice in expanded school mental health. *Journal of Youth and Adolescence, 34*, 7–13.

Zhang, D., & Katsiyannis, A. (2002). Minority representation in special education: A persistent challenge. *Remedial and Special Education, 23*, 180–187.

12

Current Trends in Preparing General Education Teachers to Work With Students With Disabilities

David F. Bateman and Jenifer Cline

This Chapter Will Cover:

1. The need for strong leaders of general education.
2. The need for general and special education teachers to work together.
3. The separate training programs that exist for general and special education.
4. The pressure that exists on general education teachers for students to make progress.
5. Integrated models for preparing and supporting both general and special education teachers.

Improved Outcomes for Students With Disabilities

When thinking about the education of students with disabilities, the focus is typically on the training and preparation of special education teachers and related service providers. There is significantly less scrutiny on the training, preparation, and needs of general education teachers related to their training and preparation in educating students with disabilities. This is a glaring issue since most students with disabilities spend the majority of their time in school in the general education classroom (Bateman & Cline, 2016). Additionally, the majority of students with disabilities start school not eligible for special education and related services, and it is the general education teachers and staff who notice that the student may require additional assistance to access the curriculum and be successful in the general education setting. This raises crucial questions about the training, skills, and support needed for general education teachers to effectively identify and instruct students with disabilities. The purpose of this chapter is to highlight key differences between special education and general education and then emphasize strategies that can be used to work with students in all classes.

Special Education Compared With General Education

Licensure Is Separate

When teachers become certified, they typically become certified in a content area or, at the elementary level, as "general education." For example, at the secondary level a teacher would become certified in science or social studies or math. The same is also true of special education teachers at the secondary level. They become certified as special education teachers in a specific content area but then work as general special education teachers. However, there is a significant need for more teachers to work at the secondary level as special education teachers. Getting certified in the content area as well as special education is creating some concerns in terms of having enough teachers to teach special education. The intent of the team process in the Individuals with Disabilities Education Act (IDEA) is that each team member is on the team because of his or her particular expertise. The general education teacher is there because of his or her expertise in the curriculum. The special education teacher is there because of his or her expertise and knowledge of how to work with students in special education and understanding of the special education process.

Under No Child Left Behind (NCLB), teachers were required to be "highly qualified," and, therefore, the licensure described above added more pressure on schools to hire teachers certified in a content area as well as in special education. It is difficult to argue there is not a need for "highly qualified" teachers, but state and teacher prep programs would also need to understand the intent of the team process for IDEA when determining what is needed to be highly qualified. The need for highly qualified staff requires both special education and general education teachers to have an understanding of special education and the curriculum. Teacher training programs also parallel this train of thought in that there are separate tracks for preparation for the different certification areas. Although the "highly qualified" standard was removed from the Every Student Succeeds Act (ESSA; the reauthorization of NCLB), teacher prep programs and districts need to weigh this previous standard when training and considering staff for hiring.

Training for General Education Teachers

There is a significant amount of content to cover for individuals seeking certification to work as general education teachers. In many states, students in their first semester of their undergraduate program start their major and get on a track of classes. They stay on that track with little to no electives or opportunities to step off the sequence of courses, or they will be delayed a semester. For students on these tracks, it is often very difficult to take additional courses related to students with disabilities (or elective courses in general). Added to this, the preparation programs for the training of general education teachers are often housed in separate departments from those faculties that work to train special education teachers.

For training purposes for general education teachers, most states require only one course related to the education of students with disabilities: the introduction to special education course. One state, Pennsylvania, requires three courses, typically an introduction to special education course, a course on adapting curriculum, and a course on assessment. The change in Pennsylvania is the result of a class-action lawsuit that alleged the state was not doing enough to foster the inclusion of students with disabilities in general education classrooms (Public Interest Law Center, 2017). This three-course requirement, however, is the exception among states.

Inclusion of students with disabilities in the general education programs is important not only because it is a core component of IDEA but also because it is good for both general education and special education students. Least restrictive environment is a component of IDEA requiring individualized education program (IEP) teams to work to educate students with their nondisabled peers to the greatest extent appropriate. The idea behind this is that they will then have access to the same educational opportunities as any other student. However, when thinking of the bigger picture, it is an important concept due to the fact that it will empower students with disabilities to interact and participate in their communities when they are out of school. General education students also benefit from seeing the learning and physical differences of others, and it allows them the opportunity to work to include others who have differences and also to work in teams drawing from the strengths and differences of others.

IDEA outlines the educational rights of students with disabilities. General education teachers need to be aware of these rights so they are able to work on IEP teams and be functional members. It is also important because many IEPs have a large portion of services that are carried out in the general education classroom.

Students receiving special education services or students who have a disability are considered to be "at risk." At risk is not a category for training in and of itself (Bateman & Cline, 2016), because students can flow in and out of the at-risk category, and this leads to great difficulty in defining the exact prevalence numbers. It could be defined so broadly as to be almost meaningless, but each and every student has issues that are important to him or her and need to be addressed. The needs of a student who is at risk because of homelessness are very different from the needs of a student who has health issues, or even those of a student who has seen or has had to deal with domestic violence. Each one of these is an individual need; however, each student is potentially considered at risk for school failure.

The needs of students who are at risk are important and should be addressed by every teacher and taken seriously. In most cases, being at risk is situational rather than innate (Gargiulo, 2015). With the exception of characteristics such as having a disability, a student's at-risk status is rarely related to his or her ability to learn or succeed academically and largely or entirely related to outside factors. A student attending a low-performing school could be considered at risk (Brendtro, Brokenleg, & Van Bockern, 2009). Underfunded schools could contribute to higher rates of course failures and problems with attrition (Brendtro et al., 2009). General education teachers work with numerous at-risk students each year. Their training must include skills to meet the needs of this population, which includes students with disabilities.

Recommendations for training:

1. Understanding conflict

2. Communication strategies

3. How to choose concepts in curriculum that are needed for the student to move on

4. Difference between accommodations, modification, and interventions

5. Use of an application model of education

6. Application to real-world situations (predictable and unpredictable)

Pressure on General Education Teachers

Under NCLB there was increasing pressure on states to demonstrate the performance of students. This manifested in the administration of annual statewide assessments. Students are expected to attain proficient standards and to demonstrate this on a yearly basis. Under NCLB there was also the expectation that schools achieve Adequate Yearly Progress (AYP). Although AYP was removed from the reauthorization of NCLB as ESSA, there is still an expectation that schools demonstrate progress on an annual basis.

In special education, leaders, administrators, and teachers have been working since 1975 to foster the inclusion of students with disabilities in the general education classroom and have made great strides in this area (Mastropieri & Scruggs, 2016). However, with the increase in demands for improvements in test scores and then judging teachers based on these, we have all but made general education teachers not want to work with (or have in their classes) students who might bring the scores down—such as students eligible for special education. There was also an expectation under NCLB that we would reduce the gap between the performance of general education students and the performance of those eligible for special education (Reese, 2005).

This pressure makes it difficult to talk with teachers about working with students with disabilities, because as it is currently formatted, the incentives are such that teachers are reinforced for having higher test scores and not reinforced for providing instruction to all students. There will be a need for strategies to work with students with disabilities (and at-risk students) that can help all general education teachers, but there also must be an awareness of the lack of incentives for working with students with disabilities, whose progress or growth may not be accurately measured using standardized test scores.

Recommendations for teachers:

1. Understand data and how to use data to make instructional decisions.

2. Understand your role in the development and implementation of functional behavior assessment and PBIS.

3. Work to understand your role in the special education process.

General Education Is a Place

The provision of education to students in general education has been a long-standing tradition in this country. Though there have been some changes (*Brown v. Board of Education of Topeka Kansas*, 1954, for example), on the whole education has been provided. General education is where the education of students who were considered nondisabled was provided.

Although it may not seem like it, individuals with disabilities are not new. There have always been children and young adults with disabilities, but educational services have not always been there to provide for them. In fact, as recently as the 1970s, it was legal to prevent students with disabilities from attending school (Johnson, 1986). One specific example allowed the exclusion of children who were physically or mentally incapacitated for schoolwork (Code of Virginia, 1973). The history of educational services for students with disabilities is filled with stories and examples of wholesale exclusion and legal denials. Often, the best a parent could hope for was some form of educational service in a state-run institution (Scheerenberger, 1983).

Special Education Is a Service

As noted above, special education is not a location, it is the specially designed instruction provided to students eligible for special education and related services. This service could be provided in a general education classroom, a special education classroom, a separate school, or even a hospital. Special education is the services a student needs to fill holes in knowledge and skills or to provide supports so he or she will be able to have access to, participate in, and make progress in the general curriculum. The general education classroom and curriculum is at the core of all special education programs developed for students with disabilities, and the goal of special education is to teach the students skills and provide supports so they no longer require special education.

Purpose of Special Education

As noted above, students with disabilities have been historically excluded from education services and, by definition, need something different than what is provided for all students to be successful. The focus of special education is no longer just to give these students access to education. The purpose of special education is to teach students the skills they need to be successful in the general education setting or develop as much independence as possible for adult life. Once a student is receiving special education services, the goal is to build the student's skill so he or she no longer requires the services. This is done with an individualized program designed to meet the student's needs in accordance with IDEA. The goal is to enable each student to use the potential he or she possesses to benefit from education. With this goal there are increased responsibilities for general education teachers. In fact, only a small proportion of students with disabilities currently receive more than 60% of their education outside the general education classroom (U.S. Department of Education, 2016).

IDEA (2004) defines special education as "specially designed instruction, at no cost to the parents, to meet the unique needs of a child with a disability." Still, what exactly is special education? Granted this is ambiguous, but special education broadly identifies the academic, physical, cognitive, and social–emotional instruction offered to children who are faced with one or more disabilities. Due to a specific disability, some student needs cannot be met within the traditional classroom environment. Special education programs and services adapt content, teaching methodology, and delivery instruction to meet the needs of each child.

Innovations in Special Education

Special education is responsible for large-scale implementation of a variety of reforms.

1. Special education has led the way in full-scale implementation of assessment data. It is imperative that districts take data on students with disabilities to determine if they are making progress. This is a requirement of special education services that has been adopted by general education.

2. Special education has led the way in individualized education. That is the heart of a student's IEP, and the personalization provided has been adopted by general educators for at-risk students.

3. Special education leads the way with a team approach to working with all students.

There are many current trends in education that special education has been doing for a long time. The following components of education have foundations of the process or the intent that has been included in special education for years.

Multitiered Systems of Support and Differentiated Instruction

Multitiered systems of support (MTSS), also known as response to intervention, is an every-education decision-making framework of evidence-based practices in instruction and assessment that addresses the needs of all students. Differentiated instruction is modified teaching that helps students with diverse academic needs work to master academic content. This can be used to address the needs of students with a variety of abilities in a classroom. Teachers can differentiate instruction with an individual student, within a small group, or with a whole class. It does not mean separate activities for a student. The activities should be related to teach the same content but changed to address the different ability levels of the students.

There are many ways that MTSS and differentiated instruction overlap and work together to help teachers provide access to the general education curriculum for students with disabilities.

What Is Differentiated Instruction?

When using differentiated instruction, instead of focusing your teaching on a few of the students (the ones thought to be in the middle) and hoping the students who are high achieving do not get bored and the ones who might be low achieving do not get lost, you will provide for all students in a class. Teachers using differentiated instruction match tasks, activities, and assessments with their students' interests and abilities.

With both MTSS and differentiated instruction there is a greater emphasis on explicit instruction provided by the teacher. Both of these frameworks focus on providing instruction and activities at the learning level of each individual student. MTSS sets more of a focus on the way a student responds to targeted interventions put in place, and the goal is to quickly increase the student's skills so he or she no longer requires the targeted interventions. However, differentiated instruction focuses more on the way the instruction is provided or the instructional strategies used.

Differentiated Instruction Versus Different Instruction

Many teachers think differentiating instruction means giving the students a different activity, book, or assignment to do instead of having them do the same or similar work as the others in the classroom. There may be some students who have disabilities so severe and profound that they will not be able to do the same assignment as others, but that is the exception. The important distinction between differentiated instruction and different instruction is to emphasize there are multiple ways to help students obtain the same information, at different levels of understanding, and demonstrate their knowledge to you.

Differentiated instruction must target and accommodate students' diverse needs and deficiencies in the learning process through careful changes in content, process, and products using the list below. It cannot just be activities that have no relation to the point of the material. Keep the end point in mind, and develop a variety of activities that help all students get to that point.

Differentiation Components

There are four main ways of providing differentiation for students: content, process, outcome, and environment. Each will be described in turn, with examples for elementary and secondary.

1. *Content differentiation.* This can be broadly defined as differentiation of what students need to learn and/or how the students will access

the information. Many times students at different levels of learning and understanding will have different expectations for the depth of their required knowledge on a particular concept.

2. *Process differentiation.* This is the way the teacher can modify the activities the student engages in to understand the content.

3. *Outcome differentiation.* Though all students are working toward the same goal, outcome differentiation allows the students different ways of presenting that they have learned the material.

4. *Environmental differentiation.* This is where the teacher changes the way the classroom looks and feels. You can move seats around, set up activities in different corners, and turn lights on or off. Use the classroom and the material within to change the learning environment. Teachers already do some of that when placing students in either rows or groups, and determining where students will spend their free time. This asks the teacher to consider the environment as a part of helping the students participate in the classroom experience with a greater focus on instruction.

Universal Design for Learning

One effective way of including all students in the classroom is to use the principles of universal design for learning (UDL). UDL works with all students, including those with disabilities and those who are at risk. The purpose is to create course materials and presentations accessible to all students, not just a few, or not just those in the middle. Under the principles of UDL, students are provided the information in multiple ways and, in turn, allowed multiple ways to express their comprehension. By providing different ways for the students to receive and present information, they will become more engaged in learning and what they know can be more adequately assessed.

The history of UDL is involved with changes to society as a result of the passage of the Americans with Disabilities Act of 1990. The goal after the passage of the act was to make society more physically accessible, in part to make it so doors, water fountains, walkways, and entrances were accessible to all, and so businesses would not have to spend a lot of time and money constantly retrofitting (U.S. Equal Employment Opportunity Commission, 2009). Examples of these changes and how they benefit others include the following:

1. *Sidewalk ramps:* Originally designed for people who use wheelchairs, walkers, crutches, or canes, but now also benefit parents with strollers and kids on skateboards.

2. *Closed captioning:* Originally designed for individuals who are deaf or hard of hearing, but now also used in gyms and libraries.

3. *Automatic doors at businesses:* Designed to help individuals who use wheelchairs, walkers, crutches, or canes, but now also benefit people carrying packages and make it easier to move items in and out of stores.

The goal of the above changes was to make buildings physically accessible. The goal of UDL is to make the classroom and learning accessible to all. UDL is not simply one teaching practice, as the needs of individuals who are deaf and hard of hearing are often different from the needs of those who are blind or visually impaired. UDL combines the best of teaching to make the classroom more accessible for all types of learners (Rose, Meyer, Strangman, & Rappolt, 2002). Keep that in mind when making decisions about modes of presentation and methods of assessment.

Students perceive information differently based not only on their disability but also on the experiences they bring to the classroom. Some students have traveled widely and seen and done activities others could only dream of, while other students may not have had much exposure to written material or have had a differing amount of language experiences after spending time with their parents. There are also students with sensory disabilities (students with low vision or blindness or a hearing impairment) or a learning disability who may require multiple or different modes of presentation of material. These students may be all sitting in the same class. No one presentation strategy is going to work for all of them.

Universal Design for Learning for Behavior

One goal of UDL is to keep the students engaged in the class and the lesson. Teaching and using methods that allow the students to participate and then learn from the lesson should dramatically help with attention and behavior problems. Students have problems when they cannot access the material or the information is presented in a manner unclear to them and they can no longer make contributions to the class or they feel others are doing significantly better than they are.

When thinking of UDL for behavior, there are three important components for all students that need to be addressed:

1. Safety

2. Predictability

3. Consistency

Students need to be able to come to school and know they are coming to a safe environment, one that is predictable, and one where there is a certain level of consistency. This allows them to focus on the other tasks in school, including learning and socialization. This means you will have to focus on providing a consistent and safe learning environment for the students and work to address any of their concerns. You need to make sure any threat or distraction to the students is minimized and they can focus on the tasks in front of them.

Good instruction is good instruction is good instruction, regardless of the content (Stipek, 2002). Teaching appropriate behavior skills in the classroom is no different. The skills and expectations for the classroom need to be taught as much as (if not more than) the academic components. If you do not have good behaviors in the classroom, it is very difficult to provide instruction to the students. The following are UDL examples of rules and strategies for teaching behavior management in the classroom:

1. Have three to five overarching behavior expectations.

2. Rules are agreed on.

3. Rules are defined for the specific setting and location.

4. Rules are clearly communicated and understood by all.

5. Rules are taught in different settings.

6. Rules are posted.

7. Rules are demonstrated by adults.

For more information on UDL, the reader is referred to the UDL Center, which has a nice PDF that can help explain the different levels and supports required to assist students with learning. It can be found at http://udlguidelines.cast.org/.

Conclusion

General education teachers are often the front line not only in identifying students with disabilities but also in the provision of services. There are differences between general education and special education teacher preparation, roles, and responsibilities, but they must work together as an educational team to meet the needs of students with disabilities. Teacher preparation programs and policymakers need to understand how general education and special education programs and teachers can and will work together to make the education for all students better. Special education is an exciting field with many challenges and many opportunities, but the services for students with disabilities are better (and can be easier) when we work together. This chapter highlighted some of the differences, and it is important to understand them. However, it is the similarities and the need to work with students on a day-to-day basis that should bring us together.

REFLECTING AND UNDERSTANDING

1. Why is general education important for special education service?

2. In what ways should general and special education work together?

3. In what ways should general and special education conduct preservice training together?

4. What pressure is on general education teachers for students to make progress?

5. What is universal design for learning?

6. What are multitiered systems of support?

ONLINE RESOURCES

- Center of Response to Intervention at American Institutes for Research: https://www.rti4success.org/

- Comprehensive, Integrated, Three-Tiered Models of Prevention: http://www.ci3t.org/

- LD Online: http://www.ldonline.org/educators

- National Association of School Psychologists: http://www.nasponline.org/

- National Center on Intensive Interventions: https://intensiveintervention.org/

- National Center for Learning Disabilities: https://www.ncld.org

- National Education Association: http://www.nea.org/home/17676.htm

- Teacher Vision: https://www.teachervision.com/teaching-strategies/special-needs

- U.S. Department of Education's What Works Clearinghouse: https://ies.ed.gov/ncee/wwc/

- What Special Ed Teachers Wish General Ed Teachers Knew: https://www.teachervision.com/blog/morning-announcements/what-special-ed-teachers-wish-general-ed-teachers-knew

RECOMMENDED READINGS

Books

Bateman, D. F., & Bateman, C. F. (2014). *A principal's guide to special education* (3rd ed.). Arlington, VA: Council for Exceptional Children. Co-published by the National Association of Elementary School Principals and the National Association of Secondary School Principals.

Bateman, D. F., & Cline, J. L. (2016). *A teacher's guide to special education*. Alexandria, VA: ASCD and the Council for Exceptional Children.

Bateman, D. F., & Cline, J. L. (2016). *Using data to improve student learning*. Port Chester, NY: National Professional Resources.

Brown-Chidsey, R., & Bickford, R. (2015). *Practical handbook of multi-tiered systems of support building academic and behavioral success in schools*. New York, NY: Guilford Press.

Articles

Collins, L. W., Sweigart, C. A., Landrum, T. J., & Cook, B. G. (2017). Navigating common challenges and pitfalls in the first years of special education: Solutions for success. *Teaching Exceptional Children, 49*, 213–222.

Cook, B. G., & Schirmer, B. R. (2003). What is special about special education? Overview and analysis. *Journal of Special Education, 37*, 200–205.

Sweigart, C. A., & Collins, L. W. (2017). Supporting the needs of beginning special education teachers and their students. *Teaching Exceptional Children, 49*(4), 209–212.

Yell, M. L., & Bateman, D. F. (2017). Endrew v. Douglas County Supreme Court Decision. *Teaching Exceptional Children, 50*(10), 7–15.

PROFESSIONAL ORGANIZATIONS

ASCD: https://www.ascd.org

Council for Exceptional Children: https://www.cec.sped.org/

REFERENCES

Bateman, D. F., & Cline, J. L. (2016). *A teacher's guide to special education.* Alexandria, VA: ASCD and the Council for Exceptional Children.

Brendtro, L. K., Brokenleg, M., & Van Bockern, S. (2009). *Reclaiming youth at risk: Our hope for the future.* Bloomington, IN: Solution Tree.

Brown v. Board of Education of Topeka Kansas, 347 U.S. 483 (1954).

Code of Virginia, Section 22.275.3 (1973).

Gargiulo, R. M. (2015). *Special education in contemporary society* (5th ed.). Los Angeles, CA: Sage.

Individuals with Disabilities Education Act, 20 U.S.C. § 1400 *et seq.*

Johnson, T. P. (1986). *The principal's guide to the educational rights of handicapped students.* Reston, VA: National Association of Secondary School Principals.

Mastropieri, M. A., & Scruggs, T. E. (2016). *The inclusive classroom: Strategies for effective differentiated instruction* (6th ed.). Upper Saddle River, NJ: Pearson.

Public Interest Law Center. (2017). *Gaskin v. Commonwealth.* Retrieved from https://www.pubintlaw.org/cases-and-projects/gaskin-v-commonwealth/

Reese, W. J. (2005). *America's public school: From the common school to No Child Left Behind.* Baltimore, MD: Johns Hopkins University Press.

Rose, D., Meyer, A., Strangman, N., & Rappolt, G. (2002). *Teaching every student in the digital age: Universal design for learning.* Alexandria, VA: ASCD.

Scheerenberger, R. C. (1983). *A history of mental retardation.* Baltimore, MD: Paul H. Brookes.

Stipek, D. (2002). *Motivation to learn: Integrating theory and practice* (4th ed.). Upper Saddle River, NJ: Pearson.

U.S. Department of Education. (2016). *2016 annual report to Congress on the Individuals with Disabilities Education Act.* Washington, DC: Author.

U.S. Equal Employment Opportunity Commission. (2009). *Annual report on the federal workforce.* Washington, DC: Author.

Prisons, jails, and juvenile justice facilities have in many places become the new "mental hospitals" and "homes for the retarded"[1] and they do not treat our children much better than the old institutions did.

—National Disability Rights Network (2015, p. 13)

---

[1] It is very important to note here that these phrases and their ilk should never be used in a current context, which is why they appear here in quotes. They represent and are bound tightly to a period in our history that has come to its end, and so has the language representing it. However, it is similarly important to remember that history and to honor with honesty the struggles of those in the disability rights movement who made the change possible. Therefore, in this report we will use these words when they are necessary to provide a historical context and only then.

13

The School-to-Prison Pipeline

Christine A. Christle, Joseph B. Ryan, and Michelle Dunn

This Chapter Will Cover:

1. The development of the school-to-prison pipeline (STPP).
2. The background regarding the increased use and roles of school resource officers in public schools.
3. The risk factors for the STPP and its impact on the lives of students with disabilities, public schools, and society.
4. The current issues and trends of the STPP.
5. Recommendations for school leaders, special educators, and schools to effectively use school resource officers and help prevent the STPP.

An alarming trend in this country has been the criminalization of our schoolchildren. While exact numbers are difficult to obtain, about 66,000 school-age youth are involved in the juvenile justice system (JJS). Some estimates suggest that about one-third of those are students identified with a disability under the Individuals with Disabilities Education Act (IDEA) (Redfield & Nance, 2018). In the 1970s, prior to the enactment of IDEA, most school personnel were ill-equipped to deal with students with disabilities who exhibited challenging behaviors. As a result, many of these students were denied access to conventional public schools. Nearly half a century later, children with special needs have since gained access to public schools, but unfortunately, many school personnel are still ill-equipped to deal with educating students with disabilities, particularly those who exhibit challenging behaviors. Thus, a great number of these students have been pushed out of public schools and become involved with the JJS (Rivkin, 2009/2010; Rocque & Snellings, 2018). During the 2015–2016 academic year, more than 291,100 students were referred or subjected to school-related arrest, 82,800 of whom were students with disabilities (U.S. Department of Education, Office for Civil Rights, 2018). This process in which youth are referred to law enforcement by schools is commonly referred to as the school-to-prison pipeline (STPP). The STPP is a construct used by advocates, policymakers, and researchers that describes certain public school policies and practices, particularly related to discipline, that increase the probability of student involvement in the JJS (Owens, 2017; Skiba, Arredondo, & Williams, 2014).

It appears that both the public school system and the JJS have simultaneously shifted their focus over the past generation from providing preventive,

Key Terms

- exclusionary discipline
- school-to-prison pipeline (STPP)
- school resource officer (SRO)

instructive, and rehabilitative services to more reactive and punitive measures (Mallett, 2016). Perhaps most disturbing is that the STPP has been disproportionately impacting many marginalized groups of students, including minorities and students with disabilities (Ryan, Katsiyannis, Counts, & Shelnut, 2018). Quinn and colleagues found that youth with learning disabilities and emotional disturbances are at an increased risk of placement in juvenile correctional facilities (Quinn, Rutherford, & Leone, 2001; Quinn, Rutherford, Leone, Osher, & Poirier, 2005). In this chapter we discuss the STPP by (a) exploring the development of the STPP; (b) describing the risk factors for this trajectory and its impact on the lives of students with disabilities, public schools, and society; (c) examining the current issues and trends of the STPP; and (d) offering recommendations for school leaders, special educators, and schools to help prevent the STPP.

Development of the School-to-Prison Pipeline

Zero Tolerance and School Exclusionary Discipline Policies

The term *zero tolerance* originated in the United States during the 1980s and referred to new "get tough" policies in response to the illegal drug trade. During this time, youth homicide rates were also on the rise, which likely kindled a fear of an epidemic in youth violence. School districts began responding to both drug and school violence issues by adopting zero tolerance policies that mandated predetermined consequences for school discipline policy infractions. For example, students in many schools were automatically expelled for possession of drugs and weapons, or for gang-related activities. In addition, out-of-school suspensions were mandated for certain less serious infractions such as fighting, disruption, and even dress-code violations (Leone et al., 2003; Mallett, 2016; Skiba & Losen, 2015/2016; Wald & Losen, 2003). Unfortunately, these reactive and punitive exclusionary discipline policies discouraged school administrators from making discretionary considerations based on student motivation or mitigating circumstances surrounding infractions.

As violent crime rates for youth continued to rise during the mid-'90s, federal laws were enacted to permit the transfer of juvenile offenders to adult courts and correctional facilities (Wald & Losen, 2003). This was permitted even though the majority of offenses committed by juveniles were non-violent crimes. At this same time, the presence of law enforcement within schools also began to increase significantly. While police were assigned to some schools as early as the 1950s, their presence has grown significantly in recent decades (Ryan et al., 2018). Law enforcement officers assigned to schools are referred to by a variety of names (e.g., school marshal, prevention resource officer, and school peace officer); however, they are most commonly referred to as school resource officers, or SROs. SROs are uniformed, armed police officers assigned to work directly in schools. Duties generally involve a combination of (a) law enforcement, (b) teaching, and (c) mentoring.

It is currently estimated that there are between 14,000 and 20,000 SROs assigned to about one-third of our nation's public schools, making it one of the fastest growing branches of policing in the United States (National Association of School Resource Officers, n.d.). This growth has been in response to numerous societal concerns, ranging from gun violence, drugs, and most recently school shootings (Ryan et al., 2018). The largest expansion of SROs has been made possible by federal funding, including legislative initiatives such as the Safe Schools Act of 1994, the 1998 amendment to the Omnibus Crime Control, and the Safe Streets Act of 1968.

One specific area of concern regarding the use of SROs has been their increased involvement in school disciplinary issues, which have historically been addressed by teachers and school administrators. As previously discussed, recent reports have shown an increase in schools' use of punitive/exclusionary disciplinary approaches, including suspension, seclusion, restraint, and even criminal charges (Bracey et al., 2013; Robers, Zhang, Truman, & Snyder, 2012). These trends highlight a consistent theme that many of today's teachers struggle with classroom management and dealing with challenging student behaviors (Oliver & Reschly, 2014; Onderi & Odera, 2012). Surveys report that 41% of educators claim student misbehavior interferes with their ability to teach (Robers, Zhang, Morgan, & Musu-Gillette, 2014). This is not surprising given about an almost equal percentage (43%) of schools report inadequate levels of teacher training in behavior management (NCES, 2014).

The increased use of punitive/exclusionary disciplinary approaches is concerning given these approaches are often ineffective in addressing problem behaviors because they (a) are reactive in nature and implemented only after the behavior occurs, (b) fail to teach appropriate alternative behaviors to students, (c) may inadvertently reinforce a problem behavior, and (d) all too often remove students from the educational learning environment (Ryan, Katsiyannis, Peterson, & Chmelar, 2007). For instance, despite the popularity of suspending students in schools nationwide, there is little evidence that it is effective in improving student behavior (Christle, Nelson, & Jolivette, 2004). In contrast, research shows that once students are suspended, they are more likely to receive additional suspensions (Atkins et al., 2002; Dupper, 1994). Hence, there is serious concern that involving SROs for behavior management issues will only increase the likelihood of student contact with the JJS, further promoting the STPP (Counts, Randall, Ryan, & Katsiyannis, 2018).

Risk Factors and Impact of the School-to-Prison Pipeline

Risk Factors

The risk factors for youth involvement in the JJS may be found in every life domain (individual, family, school, community, and peer group), and the more risk factors to which a youth is exposed, the greater the likelihood she or he will experience negative outcomes such as incarceration.

While the educational system can often be an antidote for individual, family, peer, and community risks, researchers have identified school-based policies and practices that exacerbate the risk for youth contact with the JJS (Christle, Jolivette, & Nelson, 2005; Leone et al., 2003; Skiba et al., 2014; Wald & Losen, 2003). These school policies and practices include high student–teacher ratios, lack of trained staff, few evidence-based instructional strategies used by teachers, lack of allowances for diversity and individual differences, weak and inconsistent leadership, and unclear school rules with reliance on exclusionary discipline (Christle & Yell, 2008).

Many students with disabilities (e.g., autism spectrum disorder, emotional disturbance, intellectual disability, specific learning disability, other health impairment, attention deficit hyperactivity disorder) experience individual risk factors due to cognitive processing characteristics that affect judgment and intent. These characteristics generally include impulsivity, poor problem-solving skills, poor reasoning skills, and poor social skills. In addition, many of these students have difficulty interpreting others' behaviors, organizing, and determining consequences for their actions. Furthermore, many students with disabilities experience mental health–related problems, especially students identified as having an emotional disturbance (Yell, Smith, Katsiyannis, & Losinski, 2018). Another risk factor is academic difficulties, particularly in reading (Drakeford, 2002; Leone, Krezmien, Mason, & Meisel, 2005; Malmgren & Leone, 2000). For example, in a review of the literature on the academic characteristics of incarcerated youth, Foley (2001) noted that the average reading levels of incarcerated youth were reported as 2 years below those of nondelinquent peers. It has been suggested that some states use third-grade literacy scores to predict the number of future prison beds needed. Although we found no evidence for this claim, there is a connection between literacy skills and incarceration rates.

When risk factors from other domains intersect with the school risk factors, a student's progression toward involvement in the JJS is accelerated. For example, a student with cognitive and academic deficits (individual factors) from a low socioeconomic background (family factor) may experience frustration when the academic demands in school are too difficult. This student may exhibit noncompliant or disruptive behaviors. In response, school personnel often react with disciplinary practices that remove the student from academic instruction (e.g., in-school or out-of-school suspension). This becomes a vicious cycle as the student's frustration increases, resulting in a display of even more challenging behaviors. In response, the school's use of exclusionary discipline also increases, and in many cases, students are referred to law enforcement. The U.S. Department of Education (2015) has even cautioned schools recently that SROs are more likely to criminalize minor school infractions and to push students unnecessarily into the STPP.

Impact

Incarcerating youth, especially those with disabilities, increases their risk for negative outcomes and does not make schools safer. According to the Office of Juvenile Justice and Delinquency Prevention (2015), 45,567 juvenile offenders were held in residential placement facilities in this nation on October 26, 2016. These juveniles are likely to experience devastating life outcomes in the forms of education failure, social isolation, limited postschool career options, and increased risk of continued involvement in the JJS and later the adult system (Mallett, 2016; Wald & Losen, 2003). For example, estimates indicate that more than one-fourth of students who return from the JJS will drop out of school within 6 months, and almost half of them will be reincarcerated within 3 years (Horowitz, Rawe, & Whittaker, 2017). While school personnel may hold false assumptions that their school climate is improved by deferring rule infractions to law enforcement officials and pushing out "problem" students, the opposite has proven to be true.

While the intent behind SROs has always been to create safer schools for students, an unintended effect has been the increased opportunities for negative interactions between youth and police. This has resulted in an increase in the number of youth being referred to the JJS (Sickmund & Puzzanchera, 2014; U.S. Department of Education, Office for Civil Rights, 2014). The Justice Policy Institute (2011) found that schools with SROs had 5 times as many arrests for disorderly conduct as schools without SROs. Besides hindering youth's successful transition to adulthood and negatively affecting schools, incarcerating school-age youth cost taxpayers billions of dollars per year. The Justice Policy Institute's recent report estimates the average annual cost to incarcerate one youth is $148,767, but the total collateral cost to society for incarcerating our youth (e.g., recidivism, lost tax revenue, and reliance on public assistance) is between $8 billion and $21 billion (Justice Policy Institute, 2011).

Current Issues and Trends Involving the School-to-Prison Pipeline

Although youth incarceration rates have been steadily declining since the mid-'90s, we continue to incarcerate more youth in the United States than in any other industrialized nation (Annie. E. Casey Foundation, 2013). Issues that continue to promote the STPP involve (a) individual factors such as mental health needs; (b) school policies and programming, specifically exclusionary discipline and use of SROs; and (c) societal factors such as the economics of fostering a prison-industrial complex (PIC).

Individual Factors

Many youth end up in the JJS because mental health services are either unavailable or inaccessible in the schools or community. In fact, some youth advocates consider the JJS to be the de facto system for youth needing mental health services, with an estimated two-thirds of incarcerated youth having a mental health and/or substance abuse disorder (Meservey & Skowyra, 2015). It is currently estimated that 20% of youth live with a mental health condition, but only one-third of these actually receive needed services (Eber, Weist, & Barrett, 2013). Legislative efforts have been unsuccessful for more than a decade to pass a bill that would provide funding to states to build more comprehensive school-based mental health services and supports. For instance, the Mental Health in Schools Act has been introduced a half dozen times between 2007 and 2017, but the bill has yet to pass (Civic Impulse, 2018). Although mental health services are limited and inconsistent in our schools and funding is sparse, there is a growing momentum to provide coordinated, quality services, such as the interconnected systems framework. This framework integrates components of school mental health with the tiered system of positive behavioral interventions and supports to improve both services to students and staff skill development (Eber et al., 2013).

School Policies and Programming

Exclusionary Discipline

Suspension and expulsion continue to be widely used in public schools despite the lack of research demonstrating their efficacy for improving school safety (Colombi & Osher, 2015; Skiba et al., 2014). For students with disabilities, Rivkin (2009/2010) describes three disciplinary exclusion strategies that are commonly used by schools: (a) refraining from identifying students with emotional disturbance, (b) expelling students from the regular school but providing services in an alternative setting, and (c) referring students to juvenile court for prosecution of a crime. One form of protection students with disabilities are afforded against these types of exclusionary practices comes from IDEA. IDEA 2004 mandates that if schools attempt to change the placement of a student with a disability due to a violation of the school's code of conduct, the individualized education program (IEP) team must first conduct a manifestation determination meeting within 10 school days. The objective of the manifestation determination is to determine if a student's behavior was the result of his or her disability or if the behavior in question was the direct result of the local educational agency's failure to implement the student's IEP (e.g., teacher did not modify classroom assignments as stated in the IEP). If the team determines that the behaviors were a manifestation of the child's disability, a functional behavior assessment (FBA) must be conducted to implement a behavior intervention plan (BIP) for the student. It is important to remember that IDEA expressly states that the statute does not prevent school officials from reporting any crime committed by a student. In the event a student does commit a serious offense (i.e., drugs, weapons, serious bodily injury), school officials may unilaterally place students with disabilities in an interim alternative setting (e.g., special day school) for up to 45 days (20 U.S.C. §1415[k][6], 2004).

School Resource Officers

The presence of SROs in schools has become increasingly commonplace. In just the past decade the percentage of schools with SROs has increased from 32% to 42% (Musu-Gillette, Zhang, Wang, Zhang, & Oudekerk, 2017). Despite this dramatic increase, there is no evidence to suggest that the presence of SROs has contributed to school safety. To date, findings merely show that the increased numbers of SROs have resulted in an increased number of nonviolent arrests at schools (Na & Gottfredson, 2013). Making matters worse, these arrests have disproportionately impacted those students who experience the most challenges in schools, including students with disabilities and minorities (Mallett, 2016; U.S. Department of Education, Office for Civil Rights, 2017). Another serious concern regarding the use of SROs is that in the absence of clear policies to provide guidance on their use in schools, their responsibilities have continuously evolved over time, resulting in mission creep (Ryan et al., 2018). While legislation and guidelines can help limit mission creep, research shows that currently only 32 states have legislation related to the topic of SROs, most of which provide minimum guidance (Counts et al., 2018).

Societal Factors

The Economics of Fostering a Prison-Industrial Complex

The United States has the highest incarceration rate of all Western industrialized countries, with a trend of changing prison management from federal and state to private, for-profit corporations (Meiners & Reyes, 2008). This shift reflects a troubling change in priorities from prevention and rehabilitation to increasing profitability and expanding the corrections industry. Considering the risk that involvement with the JJS poses for continued incarceration, the JJS can be a feeder institution for the PIC, and schools can enable the PIC by funneling students into the JJS. Paralleling this trend, spending for education in this country has been steadily decreasing over the past few decades, while spending on corrections has continued to increase (Mallett, 2016). Policymakers, practitioners in the JJS and schools, and taxpayers are likely unaware of how we may be unintentionally advancing the revenues for the PIC while at the same time ruining the lives of individuals, especially those with disabilities. According to the 2011–2012 National Inmate Survey, about 30% of state and federal inmates reported having a disability (Bronson, Maruschak, & Berzofsky, 2015). Youth and disability advocates can begin reversing this trend by making others aware of the PIC and supporting schools in adopting evidence-based prevention strategies, especially for students with disabilities, to keep them in school and out of the STPP.

Recommendations

People are constantly hoping to find single causes and/or fixes for diseases, disabilities, and other problems such as the STPP. The reality is that these are wicked problems with complex underlying causal factors, and they require multifaceted remedies. Schools are central to the lives of youth, and school personnel are well positioned to play a key role in preventing the STPP. Because educational attainment is a substantial deterrent to youth incarceration, school personnel can provide protective factors against existing risks for involvement with the JJS by providing systematic, empirically based prevention and intervention strategies and partnering with parents and community agencies. In this section, we provide specific recommendations for school leaders, special educators, and schools that use SROs to help them stem the flow of the STPP by providing appropriate educational services for students with disabilities.

Recommendations for School Leaders

School-Wide Positive Behavioral Interventions and Supports

Over the past several decades, researchers have pushed for schools to move away from using punitive approaches of behavior management and instead assess the school for a basis of change (Horner & Sugai, 2000; Walker, Ramsey, & Gresham, 2004). An effective evidence-based approach for doing this is through school-wide positive behavioral interventions and supports (SWPBIS). The SWPBIS process focuses on the design, implementation, and maintenance of primary (preventive), secondary (problematic), and tertiary (intensive) interventions to reduce problem behaviors and support desired behavior for all students within a school. A major advantage of SWPBIS over other intervention processes is the structure and support of the interventionists in monitoring student behavior. Researchers have long identified that the failure to collect and use data to guide interventions has been a downfall of many behavioral interventions (Mooney, Ryan, Denny, & Gunter, 2012). School leaders are a key factor in the successful implementation of SWPBIS by (a) providing training/support to school staff, (b) writing SWPBIS policy, (c) collecting and monitoring data to provide successful interventions, (d) regularly use data for decision making, and much, much more.

A critical component of any SWPBIS is ensuring that teachers are equipped with effective class-wide interventions. School leaders can support teachers through professional development and ongoing, data-driven coaching. The National Technical Assistance Center on Positive Behavioral Interventions and Supports offers resources for class-wide interventions, including (a) teaching expectations, (b) acknowledging expected behavior, (c) managing rule violations, and (d) adjusting strategies based on data. When class-wide and school-wide systems are linked, the effects of both are strengthened.

Functional Behavioral Assessments

While FBAs have long been an effective practice within applied behavior analysis, they have been required as an integral part of BIPs for children with special needs since the passage of IDEA in 1997. FBAs help determine the antecedents, consequences, and contextual/environmental variables associated with a child's maladaptive behavior. FBAs have decades of research support helping teachers gain a better understanding of conditions associated with the occurrence of children's challenging behaviors and enabling staff to develop interventions more likely to help prevent the behavior or respond to it by developing appropriate replacement behaviors (Mooney et al., 2012). School leaders can ensure that FBAs and BIPs are successful by ensuring they are implemented correctly and with fidelity.

Recommendations for Special Educators

Social–Emotional Learning

Special educators can create positive and safe classrooms by promoting social and emotional learning (SEL). The purpose of SEL school-based programming is to promote the development of competencies across contexts to facilitate positive relationships, academic success, and prosocial behavior (Elias, 2006). SEL programs and practices foster the development of five interrelated competencies: (a) self-awareness (the ability to identify and recognize one's emotions, strengths, areas of growth, and a general sense of confidence and efficacy), (b) self-management (the ability to control one's impulses, manage stress, set goals, persevere, and maintain motivation), (c) social awareness (an awareness of one's self in relation to another, the ability to feel empathy and respect for others, and the ability to take another's perspective), (d) relationship skills (the ability to cooperate, seek and provide help, and communicate effectively), and (e) responsible decision making (the ability to evaluate and reflect on decisions to be made, and to be aware of one's personal and ethical responsibilities; Schonert-Reichl, Kitil, & Hanson-Peterson, 2017). These five competencies are said to form the building blocks of healthy development. The conceptual SEL framework established by the Collaborative for Academic, Social, and Emotional Learning (CASEL) is grounded in prevention science and developmental research (Rimm-Kaufman & Hulleman, 2015; Zins, Bloodworth, Weissberg, & Walberg, 2004). Special educators can visit the CASEL website to learn more about SEL and access guides on selecting and implementing SEL programs in their schools (https://casel.org).

Effective Instruction

Special educators can maximize student learning by following principles from the teacher effectiveness research and using reputable sources to find appropriate evidence-based practices and programs for delivering individualized instruction based on each student's needs. Yell and Rozalski (2014) describe eight principles from the teacher effectiveness research: (a) *maximizing academic engaged time* by carefully planning lessons that actively engage students in relevant and meaningful content, as well as monitoring and reinforcing engagement; (b) *ensuring high rates of correct academic responding* by asking many questions, requiring choral or unison responding, and providing immediate feedback; (c) *maximizing the amount of content covered* by carefully planning lessons, using time-management strategies, and monitoring the progress of the content covered throughout the year; (d) *matching assignments to student ability* by first determining student's ability using curriculum-based assessments and then monitoring student's progress using curriculum-based measurement; (e) *teaching academic content explicitly* by providing an explanation or model of a skill or concept, guiding students through the application of the skill, and providing many opportunities for the students to practice independently, with corrective feedback to ensure mastery and generalization; (f) *scaffolding student instruction* by providing supports while students are learning skills or concepts, such as charts, concept maps, or graphic organizers; (g) *using direct instruction* by delivering lessons using rapid pacing, signaling, choral responding, individual responding, corrective feedback, reteaching, reinforcement, guided practice, and independent practice; and (h) *monitoring student progress* by frequently and systematically collecting data on student performance to determine if students are progressing and whether instructional changes are needed.

In addition to following effective teaching principles, special educators can maximize student outcomes by selecting and implementing appropriate evidence-based practices and programs. The IRIS Center, funded by the U.S. Department of Education's Office of Special Education Programs, offers resources on evidence-based instructional and intervention practices. Special educators can review the three IRIS Center modules on identifying and selecting evidence-based practices, implementing a practice or program with fidelity, and evaluating learner outcomes and fidelity (https://iris.peabody .vanderbilt.edu). IRIS also provides a list of organizations that are trustworthy sources for current evidence-based practices for students in grades K–12, and summaries of research on the effectiveness of various instructional strategies and interventions.

Recommendations for Schools Using School Resource Officers

Determine the Need and Effectiveness of School Resource Officers

First, SROs should be used only once there is an established need within a school, not because there is available funding. Legislatures at both the state and federal level historically have responded to horrific events such as school shootings with an overreactionary response, which ranges from arming teachers to increasing police presence on all school campuses. Such strategies are often inappropriate, ineffective, and based solely on emotion and fear, rather than causative connections (Mallett, 2016). Schools should conduct a needs assessment to properly assess their current safety needs and best determine if using SROs is an appropriate response. This assessment can continue to be used as a method for evaluating the effectiveness of safety efforts, including SRO use.

Establish Policies or Guidelines for School Resource Officers

Districts that use SROs should establish guidelines regarding their use. Unfortunately, a recent review of state SRO policies found that only 32 states currently have some form of legislation that provides either requirements or guidelines for schools regarding SROs (Counts et al., 2018). The majority of states that do have policies provide very limited guidance regarding SRO programs related to either requirements or training.

Develop a Memorandum of Understanding

Another recommendation is for districts that use SROs to develop a memorandum of understanding (MOU) or memorandum of agreement (MOA).

MOUs or MOAs clarify the roles and responsibilities between school districts, local law enforcement, and other critical stakeholders (e.g., community leaders, business partners). Unfortunately, only 13 states (CT, DE, FL, IN, MD, MO, NH, PA, RI, SC, TN, TX, UT) require either an MOU or MOA between education and law enforcement entities (Counts et al., 2018). Fortunately, there are numerous templates available from the U.S. Department of Justice, National Association of School Resource Officers, and other sources to help districts and states develop an effective MOU. These resources are provided at the end of this chapter.

Require Specialized Training

Another important recommendation is that SROs require specialized training in dealing with youth. This is critical given that police academies spend less than 1% of total training hours on juvenile justice issues (Strategies for Youth, 2013). National Association of School Resource Officers provides nationally recognized training for SROs, which includes 40 hours on topics relevant to youth and schools (e.g., understanding school law, students with special needs, school safety, crime prevention, and emergency operations plans). Specialized training courses can be found at http://nasro.org.

Conclusion

A quality education may be the most desirable and economical prevention and intervention strategy for students at risk of incarceration (Gable, Hendrickson, Tonelson, & Van Acker, 2002), as students are more likely to experience success and engage in appropriate and prosocial behaviors when teachers provide positive and safe learning environments and implement evidence-based, effective instructional practices (Christle et al., 2005; Gunter & Denny, 1998; Gunter, Denny, Kenton, & Venn, 2000). In this chapter we examined procedures used by many public schools, particularly those related to discipline, that increase the probability of student involvement in the JJS and entry into the STPP. We discussed the development, risk factors, impact, and current trends of the STPP. Finally, we offered recommendations for school leaders, special educators, and schools that use SROs to help them stem the flow of the STPP by providing appropriate educational services for students with disabilities.

REFLECTING AND UNDERSTANDING

1. Why do you believe there has been a recent increase in the use of school resource officers in public schools?

2. Explain several reasons for the concern over the increased numbers and use of school resource officers in schools.

3. Describe several risk factors that can make students especially vulnerable to the school-to-prison pipeline.

4. How can schools continue to maintain a safe climate while not placing students at risk for the school-to-prison pipeline?

5. What recommendations would you provide to a school administrator who is facing an increasing level of behavioral challenges within the school building?

6. What recommendations would you provide to a school administrator who will be hiring a school resource officer for the upcoming school year?

ONLINE RESOURCES

- American Civil Liberties Union (ACLU): https://www.aclu.org/issues/juvenile -justice/youth-incarceration

  o The ACLU is engaged in several state-based campaigns to reduce youth incarceration and redirect resources to community-based alternatives to jail and prison.

- Annie E. Casey Foundation: http://www.aecf.org/

  o Provides resources for helping children at risk of poor educational, economic, social, and health outcomes.

- Collaborative for Academic, Social, and Emotional Learning (CASEL): https://casel.org/

  o CASEL promotes integrated academic, social, and emotional learning for all children in preschool through high school.

- IRIS Center: https://iris.peabody.vanderbilt.edu/

  o Resources on evidence-based practices for preservice preparation and professional development programs.

- National Disability Rights Network: http://ndrn.org

  o Nonprofit membership organization for the protection and advocacy of individuals with disabilities.

- Office of Juvenile Justice and Delinquency Prevention: https://www.ojjdp.gov/index.html

  o Information and resources to support local and state efforts to prevent delinquency and improve the juvenile justice system

- Office of Special Education Programs National Technical Assistance Center on Positive Behavioral Interventions and Supports: http://www.pbis.org/

  o Technical assistance for improving social, emotional, and academic outcomes for all students, including students with disabilities and students from underrepresented groups.

RECOMMENDED READINGS

Memoranda of Understanding/ Agreement

Broward County, FL, MOU: http://www.ncjfcj.org/sites/default/files/Broward%20Co%20Collaborative%20Agreement%20on%20School%20Discipline%20-%20MOU.pdf

MOU Guidance Advancement Project: http://b.3cdn.net/advancement/cf357b9f96d8c55ff8_rdm6ib9js.pdf

National School Board Association Council of School Attorneys: http://www.aswdlaw.com/wp-content/uploads/2013/10/1013_InqAnalysis-FINAL.pdf

U.S. Department of Justice: http://www.cops.usdoj.gov/pdf/2013_MOU-FactSheet_v2_091613.pdf

REFERENCES

Annie E. Casey Foundation. (2013). *Reducing youth incarceration in the United States*. Baltimore, MD: Author. Retrieved from http://www.aecf.org/resources/reducing-youth-incarceration-in-the-united-states/

Atkins, M. S., McKay, M. M., Frazier, S. L., Jakobsons, L. J., Arvanitis, P., Cunningham, T., Brown, C., & Lambrecht, L. (2002). Suspensions and detentions in an urban, low-income school: Punishment or reward? *Journal of Abnormal Child Psychology*, 30(4), 361–371.

Bracey, J. R., Geib, C. F., Plant, R., O'Leary, J. R., Anderson, A., Herscovitz, L., O'Connell, M., & Vanderploeg, J. J. (2013). Connecticut's comprehensive approach to reducing in-school arrests: Changes in statewide policy, systems coordination and school practices. *Family Court Review*, 51(3), 427–434.

Bronson, J., Maruschak, L. M., & Berzofsky, M. (2015). *Disabilities among prison and jail inmates, 2011–12* (NCJ 249151). Retrieved from https://www.bjs.gov/content/pub/pdf/dpji1112.pdf

Christle, C. A., Jolivette, K., & Nelson, C. M. (2005). Breaking the school to prison pipeline: Identifying school risk and protective factors for youth delinquency. *Exceptionality*, 13(2), 69–88.

Christle, C. A., Nelson, C. M., & Jolivette, K. (2004). School characteristics related to the use of suspension. *Education and Treatment of Children*, 27(4), 509–526.

Christle, C. A., & Yell, M. L. (2008). Preventing youth incarceration through reading remediation: Issues and solutions. *Reading and Writing Quarterly*, 24, 148–176.

Civic Impulse. (2018). H.R. 2913, 115th Congress: Mental Health in Schools Act of 2017. Retrieved from https://www.govtrack.us/congress/bills/115/hr2913

Colombi, G., & Osher, D. (2015). *Advancing school discipline reform*. Arlington, VA: National Association of State Boards of Education. Retrieved from http://www.air.org/sites/default/files/downloads/report/Advancing-School-Discipline-Reform-Sept-2015.pdf

Counts, J., Randall, K. N., Ryan, J. B., & Katsiyannis, A. (2018). School resource officers in public schools: A national review. *Education and Treatment of Children*, 41(4), 405–430.

Drakeford, W. (2002). The impact of an intensive program to increase the literacy skills of youth confined to juvenile corrections. *Journal of Correctional Education*, 53, 139–144.

Dupper, D. R. (1994). Reducing out-of-school suspensions: A survey of attitudes and barriers. *Children & Schools*, 16(2), 115–123.

Eber, L., Weist, M. D., & Barrett, S. (2013). An introduction to the Interconnected Systems Framework. In S. Barrett, L. Eber, & M. Weist (Eds.), *Advancing education effectiveness: An interconnected systems framework for positive behavioral interventions and supports (PBIS) and school mental health* (pp. 3–17). Center for Positive Behavioral Interventions and

Supports (funded by the Office of Special Education Programs, U.S. Department of Education). Eugene: University of Oregon Press.

Elias, M. J. (2006). The connection between academic and social-emotional learning. In M. J. Elias & H. Arnold (Eds.), *The educator's guide to emotional intelligence and academic achievement* (pp. 4–14). Thousand Oaks, CA: Corwin Press.

Foley, R. M. (2001). Academic characteristics of incarcerated youth and correctional educational programs: A literature review. *Journal of Emotional and Behavioral Disorders, 9*(4), 248–259.

Gable, R. A., Hendrickson, J. M., Tonelson, S. W., & Van Acker, R. (2002). Integrating academic and non-academic instructions for students emotional/behavioral disorders. *Education & Treatment of Children, 25*, 459–475.

Gunter, P. L., & Denny, R. K. (1998). Trends and issues in research regarding academic instruction of students with emotional and behavioral disorders. *Behavioral Disorders, 24*(1), 44–50.

Gunter, P. L., Denny, R. K., Kenton, R., & Venn, M. L. (2000). Modifications of instructional materials and procedures for curricular success of students with emotional and behavioral disorders. *Preventing School Failure, 44*(3), 116–121.

Horner, R. H., & Sugai, G. (2000). School-wide behavior support: An emerging initiative. *Journal of Positive Behavior Interventions, 2*, 231–232.

Horowitz, S. H., Rawe, J., & Whittaker, M. C. (2017). *The state of learning disabilities: Understanding the 1 in 5.* New York, NY: National Center for Learning Disabilities. Retrieved from https://www.ncld.org/the-state-of-learning-disabilities-understanding-the-1-in-5

Justice Policy Institute. (2011). *Education under arrest: The case against police in schools.* Retrieved from http://www.justice-policy.org/research/3177

Leone, P. E., Christle, C. A., Nelson, C. M., Skiba, R., Frey, A., & Jolivette, K. (October, 2003). *School failure, race, and disability: Promoting positive outcomes, decreasing vulnerability for involvement with the juvenile delinquency system.* College Park, MD: National Center on Education, Disability, and Juvenile Justice. Retrieved from http://www.edjj.org/Publications/

Leone, P. E., Krezmien, M., Mason, L., & Meisel, S. M. (2005). Organizing and delivering empirically based literacy instruction to incarcerated youth. *Exceptionality, 13*(1), 89–102.

Mallett, C. A. (2016). The school-to-prison pipeline: A critical review of the punitive paradigm shift. *Child & Adolescent Social Work Journal, 33*, 15–24. doi:10.1007/s10560-015-0397-1

Malmgren, K., & Leone, P. E. (2000). Effects of a short-term auxiliary reading program on the reading skills of incarcerated youth. *Education and Treatment of Children, 23*, 239–247.

Meiners, E. R., & Reyes, K. B. (2008). Re-making the incarceration-nation: Naming the participation of schools in our prison industrial complex. *University of Pennsylvania Graduate School of Education's Online Urban Education Journal.* Retrieved from https://www.urbanedjournal.org/

Meservey, F., & Skowyra, K. R. (2015). *Caring for youth with mental health needs in the juvenile justice system: Improving knowledge and skills.* Retrieved from https://www.ncmhjj.com/resources/caring-youth-mental-health-needs-juvenile-justice-system-improving-knowledge-skills/

Mooney, P., Ryan, J. B., Denny, R. K., & Gunter, P. L. (2012). Behavior modification/traditional techniques for students with EBD. In J. P. Bakken, F. E. Obiakor, & A. F. Rotatori (Eds.), *Advances in special education: Behavioral disorders: Current perspectives and issues: Identification, assessment, and instruction of students with EBD* (pp. 173–202). Bingley, UK: Emerald Group.

Musu-Gillette, L., Zhang, A., Wang, K., Zhang, J., & Oudekerk, B. A. (2017). *Indicators of school crime and safety: 2016.* Washington, DC: National Center for Education Statistics, U.S. Department of Education, and Bureau of Justice Statistics, Office of Justice Programs, U.S. Department of Justice. Retrieved from https://nces.ed.gov/pubs2017/2017064.pdf

Na, C., & Gottfredson, D. C. (2013). Police officers in schools: Effects on school crime and the processing of offending behaviors. *Justice Quarterly, 30*, 619–650. doi:10.1080/07418825.2011.615754

National Association of School Resource Officers. (n.d.). *Frequently asked questions*. Retrieved from https://nasro.org/frequently-asked-questions/

National Disability Rights Network. (2015). *Orphanages, training schools, reform schools, and now this? Recommendations to prevent the disproportionate placement and inadequate treatment of children with disabilities in the juvenile justice system*. Washington, DC: Author. Retrieved from http://www.ndrn.org/images/Documents/Issues/Juvenile_Justice/NDRN_-_Juvenile_Justice_Report.pdf

Office of Juvenile Justice and Delinquency Prevention. (2015). *Statistical briefing book*. Washington, DC: U.S. Department of Justice, Office of Justice Programs. Retrieved from https://www.ojjdp.gov/ojstatbb/corrections/qa08201.asp?qaDate=2016

Oliver, R. M., & Reschly, D. J. (2014). Teacher preparation in classroom organization and behavior management. In P. Sindelar, E. McCray, M. Brownell, & B. Lignugaris (Eds.), *The handbook of research on special education teacher preparation* (pp. 288–301). New York, NY: Routledge, Taylor & Francis Lane Akers.

Onderi, H. L., & Odera, F. Y. (2012). Discipline as a tool for effective school management. *Educational Research*, *3*(9), 710–716

Owens, E. G. (2017). Testing the school-to-prison pipeline. *Journal of Policy Analysis and Management*, *36*(1), 11–37. doi:0.1002/pam.21954

Quinn, M. M., Rutherford, R. B., & Leone, P. E. (2001). Students with disabilities in correctional facilities. Arlington, VA: Council for Exceptional Children, ERIC Clearinghouse on Disabilities and Gifted Education.

Quinn, M. M., Rutherford, R. B., Leone, P. E., Osher, D. M., & Poirier, J. M. (2005). Youth with disabilities in juvenile corrections: A national survey. *Exceptional Children*, *71*(3), 339–345.

Redfield, S. E., & Nance, J. P. (2018). *School-to-prison pipeline*. American Bar Association Joint Task Force on Reversing the School-to-Prison Pipeline. Retrieved from https://www.americanbar.org/content/dam/aba/images/racial_ethnic_justice/Final%20School2PrisonPipeline-2nd-012618.pdf

Rimm-Kaufman, S. E., & Hulleman, C. S. (2015). Social emotional learning in elementary school settings: Identifying mechanisms that matter. In J. A. Durlak, C. E. Domitrovich, R. P. Weissberg, & Gullotta, T. P. (Eds.), *Handbook of social emotional learning* (pp. 151–166). New York, NY: Guilford Press.

Rivkin, D. H. (2009/2010). Decriminalizing students with disabilities. *New York Law School Law Review*, *54*, 909–952.

Robers, S., Zhang, A., Morgan, R. E., & Musu-Gillette, L. (2014). *Indicators of school crime and safety*. Washington, DC: U.S. Department of Education, Institute of Education Sciences, and National Center for Education Statistics. Retrieved from https://nces.ed.gov/pubs2015/2015072.pdf

Robers, S., Zhang, J., Truman, J., & Snyder, T. D. (2012). *Indicators of school crime safety: 2011*. Washington, DC: Bureau of Justice Statistics. Retrieved from https://www.bjs.gov/content/pub/pdf/iscs11.pdf

Rocque, M., & Snellings, Q. (2018). The new disciplinology: Research, theory, and remaining puzzles on the school-to-prison pipeline. *Journal of Criminal Justice*, *59*, 3–11. http://dx.doi.org/10.1016/j.jcrimjus.2017.05.002

Ryan, J. B., Katsiyannis, A., Counts, J., & Shelnut, J. C. (2018). The growing concerns regarding school resource officers. *Intervention in School and Clinic*, *53*(3), 188–192. doi:101177/1053451217702108

Ryan, J. B., Katsiyannis, A., Peterson, R., & Chmelar, B. (2007). IDEA 2004 and disciplining students with disabilities. *National Association of Secondary School Principals Bulletin*, *91*(2), 130–140.

Schonert-Reichl, K. A., Kitil, M. J., & Hanson-Peterson, J. (2017). To reach the students, teach the teachers: A national scan of teacher preparation and social and emotional learning. A report prepared for the Collaborative for Academic, Social, and Emotional Learning (CASEL). Vancouver: University of British Columbia. Retrieved from http://www.casel.org/wp-content/uploads/2017/02/SEL-TEd-Full-Report-for-CASEL-2017-02-14-R1.pdf

Sickmund, M., & Puzzanchera, C. (2014). *Juvenile offenders and victims: 2014 national report*. Pittsburgh, PA: National Center for Juvenile Justice. Retrieved from https://www.ojjdp.gov/ojstatbb/nr2014/downloads/NR2014.pdf

Skiba, R. J., Arredondo, M. I., & Williams, N. T. (2014). More than a metaphor: The contribution of exclusionary discipline to a school-to-prison pipeline. *Equity & Excellence in Education, 47*(4), 546–564.

Skiba, R. J., & Losen, D. L. (2015/2016). From reaction to prevention: Turning the page on school discipline. *American Educator, 39*(4), 4–44.

Strategies for Youth. (2013). *If not now, when? A survey of juvenile justice training in America's police academies.* Retrieved from http://strategiesforyouth.org/sfysite/wp-content/uploads/2013/03/SFYReport_02-2013_rev.pdf

U.S. Department of Education. (2015). *Compendium of school discipline laws and regulations for the 50 states, District of Columbia and the U.S. territories.* Retrieved from https://safesupportivelearning.ed.gov/resources/school-discipline-guidance-package-compendium-school-discipline-laws-and-regulations

U.S. Department of Education, Office for Civil Rights. (2014, March). *Civil rights data collection data snapshot: School discipline* (Issue Brief No. 1). Washington DC: Author

U.S. Department of Education, Office for Civil Rights. (2017). *Data and research: Civil rights data collection (CRDC).* Retrieved from https://www2.ed.gov/about/offices/list/ocr/data.html

U.S. Department of Education, Office for Civil Rights. (2018, April). *2015–16 civil rights data collection: School climate and safety.* Retrieved from https://www2.ed.gov/about/offices/list/ocr/docs/school-climate-and-safety.pdf

Wald, J., & Losen, D. F. (2003). Defining and redirecting a school-to-prison pipeline. *New Directions for Youth Development, 99,* 9–15.

Walker, H. M., Ramsey, E., & Gresham, F. M. (2004). *Antisocial behavior in school: Evidence based practices* (2nd ed.). Belmont, CA: Wadsworth/Thomson Learning.

Yell, M. L., & Rozalski, M. E. (2014). Teaching students with EBD I: Effective teaching. In M. L. Yell, N. Meadows, E. Drasgow, & J. Shriner (Eds.), *Evidenced-based practices for educating students with emotional and behavioral disorders* (2nd ed.). Upper Saddle River, NJ: Pearson/Merrill Education.

Yell, M., Smith, C., Katsiyannis, A., & Losinski, M. (2018). Mental health services, free appropriate public education, and students with disabilities: Legal considerations in identifying, evaluating, and providing services. *Journal of Positive Behavior Interventions. 20*(2), 67–77.

Zins, J. E., Bloodworth, M. R., Weissberg, R. P., & Walberg, H. J. (2004). The scientific base linking social and emotional learning to school success. In J. E. Zins, R. P. Weissberg, M. C. Wang, & H. J. Walberg (Eds.), *Building academic success on social and emotional learning: What does the research say* (pp. 3–22). New York, NY: Teachers College Press.

Teacher Shortages and Teacher Attrition in Special Education

Issues and Trends

Timothy J. Landrum, Lauren W. Collins, and Chris A. Sweigart

This Chapter Will Cover:

1. The various reasons why teachers in special education face shortages and how it is symptomatic of a longstanding set of complex problems.

2. How the recent decrease in demand for special education teachers can be traced to philosophical shifts toward more inclusive educational approaches and placements.

3. The link between the production of new teachers and attrition among currently-practicing teachers, and how they both cause shortages.

4. How to battle teacher attrition and increase teacher retention through mentoring and induction programs that aim to support teachers through their unique challenges.

Since at least the beginnings of the special education era marked by the passage of P.L. 94-142, the Education for All Handicapped Children Act of 1975 (now known as the Individuals with Disabilities Education Act, or IDEA), policymakers, scholars, and administrators have grappled with the challenges of maintaining a teacher workforce that is sufficient in number, and sufficiently qualified, to meet the needs of students with identified disabilities in America's public schools (e.g., Dewey et al., 2017). The importance of this distinction—between a sufficient number of teachers and a sufficient number who are specifically qualified to teach certain students—has been a source of particular debate and concern. Indeed, untangling the problems of teacher shortages with respect to students with disabilities is exceedingly difficult. For example, in the earliest days of special education in the 94-142 era, an overarching concern was the training and hiring of qualified special education teachers, who taught largely in resource rooms, self-contained classrooms, or other more restrictive settings. As schools moved toward more inclusive education at the end of the 20th century, a simultaneous emphasis on standards-driven accountability meant that teachers not only would be held to higher standards in teaching content but would do so with a broader diversity of learners in their classrooms, including students with identified disabilities. Further, the role of the special education teacher evolved, from one who taught largely in isolation, or taught only students with disabilities, to one who often followed students with disabilities into

Key Terms

- mentoring
- teacher attrition
- teacher induction
- teacher retention
- teacher shortage

general education environments and served in co-teaching settings or in other collaborative roles.

Already faced with shortages of teachers in general, and special education teachers in particular, the demands that schools provide fully inclusive education to all students and that content instruction be delivered by highly qualified teachers meant that school districts were faced with extraordinary, and in some ways competing, challenges. In this shifting context, it is not surprising that states have hired thousands of teachers on emergency or temporary licenses to fill critical teaching vacancies (e.g., Sutcher, Darling-Hammond, & Carver-Thomas, 2016); the vast majority of these teachers are not fully qualified in a content area, or qualified to teach students with disabilities. In his analysis of long-term trends in supply and demand of special education teachers, Boe (2006) noted that teacher shortages historically are both an overall numbers problem (i.e., too few individuals to fill a given number of teaching positions) and a qualification problem (i.e., too few individuals with a specific teaching certification to fill specific jobs). Darling-Hammond and Sykes (2003) went so far as to suggest that, at least at the time of their writing, there was not in fact an overall shortage of teachers in the United States but, rather, a distribution problem. Specifically, they noted, "The hiring of unqualified teachers is generally a result of distributional inequities, rather than overall shortages of qualified individuals. Contrary to what some believe, the United States does not face an overall shortage of qualified teachers" (p. 3). Darling-Hammond and Sykes did allow that in certain fields, notably including special education, real shortages of qualified teachers have generally been persistent.

It is true that there has been some fluctuation in the degree of overall demand for special education teachers over time, a point we return to later in this chapter, but despite this, states have also consistently reported a number of chronic concerns (Sutcher et al., 2016). First, regardless of how shortages are measured, special education has consistently remained among the highest areas of need for teachers in the entirety of the United States, along with STEM teachers and teachers of students who are English language learners (ELL). Second, states report that higher-poverty districts and schools are characterized by higher teacher shortages, higher levels of teacher attrition, and a lower percentage of nationally board-certified teachers (e.g., Kentucky Legislative Research Commission, 2012). Moreover, this problem is widespread; Sutcher et al. (2016) reported that across the United States, "teachers working on emergency credentials (the least qualified of the underprepared teachers), were three times more likely to serve in a high-poverty, high-minority school than in a low-poverty, low-minority school" (p. 13). Finally, attrition and turnover appear to be especially challenging problems among special education teachers (e.g., Billingsley, 2004).

There are two logical means to address the problem of a teacher shortage: train more teachers initially and retain more of the teachers already working the field. Between these two options, Darling-Hammond and Sykes (2003) argued that retention is the far greater problem. To solve teacher shortages, they argued, "the chief problem will not be producing more new teachers, as many seem to believe. The main problem is an exodus of new teachers from the profession, with more than 30% leaving within five years" (p. 3).

In this chapter we focus primarily on this latter concern: examining and improving teacher retention, which we argue is a particular challenge with regard to special education teachers. Toward this end, we focus specifically on the ideas undergirding induction, a process of enculturating new teachers into the profession in ways that help them thrive and persist in the profession. To provide context for this discussion, we first briefly describe the nature and extent of teacher shortages in special education, and highlight a number of forces that have impacted, and likely will continue to impact, demand. Next, we consider teacher attrition and factors that predict whether teachers persist in the profession. Finally, we describe current and emerging research on concepts around teacher induction, or the process by which teachers are oriented and socialized into the teaching profession. It is this latter set of concepts that scholars suggest may offer the most promise in ameliorating the persistent shortage of special education teachers that has been observed in the United States for decades.

Teacher Shortages in Special Education

An overall shortage of qualified special education teachers in the United States has been documented in the literature since at least 1985; noting that 98% of school districts in the nation were reporting special education teacher shortages, McLeskey, Tyler, and Saunders Flippin (2004) referred to these shortages as both severe and chronic. Because the shortage of special education teachers is related to and impacted by many broader factors, we consider in this section (a) national shortages of teachers generally, (b) shortages in special education compared with teachers overall, and (c) shifts in both demographics and policy that may impact demand for special education teachers.

National Teacher Shortages

A temporary leveling off of demand for teachers was observed in the first decade of the 21st century when supply caught up to and even exceeded demand by most estimates. As might be expected, this was attributed to two convergent forces. First, the school-age population in the United States leveled off, resulting in stagnant growth in the demand for new teachers. Second, despite lessening demand during this time, the production of new teachers continued at essentially the same rate. Following this temporary respite, there is now compelling evidence that demand has reemerged. As Dewey et al. (2017) noted, "teacher shortages are back in the news" (p. 315). In mapping historical and projected teacher supply (the production of new teachers) and demand nationally for teachers of all types for the 20-year period from 2005 through 2025, Sutcher et al. (2016) suggested that the annual demand for teachers surpassed supply around 2013. They further projected that the deficit in supply versus demand would exceed 100,000 teachers nationally by 2018 and that the trend of demand exceeding supply would continue through 2025.

Again, the reasons for this reversal are not surprising. Sutcher et al. (2016) reported that enrollments in teacher education programs—the pipeline to the teaching profession—dropped by 35% from 2009 to 2014, a drop of roughly 240,000 potential teachers. At the same time, the school population has shown evidence of new growth. According to the National Center for Education Statistics (NCES; see Hussar & Bailey, 2013), the number of children attending school in the United States, relatively flat from about 2006 to 2013, showed evidence of increasing again about 2013 and is projected to increase by as many as 3 million students in the subsequent decade (Sutcher et al., 2016). Sutcher et al. offered yet another potential reason for increased demand for teachers. They speculated that schools cut certain programs and increased pupil–teacher ratios (from about 15.3 to 1 to about 16 to 1) during the worst of the economic recession in the United States, and following a period of general economic recovery, districts are now moving to restore programs and reduce pupil–teacher ratios once again.

In terms of sheer numbers, according to the NCES, about 3.2 million teachers were employed by public schools in the fall of 2017, but as we have noted, shortages of qualified teachers to fill vacancies were estimated to be approaching 100,000 and to exceed this figure by 2018 and beyond (Sutcher et al., 2016). In addition to supply and demand based on production of new teachers and population growth, efforts to understand teacher shortages must take into account *attrition*. Historical trends suggest that about 8% of teachers (about 256,000 teachers among the 3.2 million teaching in 2017) leave teaching in a given year (Sutcher et al., 2016). A number of terms have been used to describe the movement of teachers within and, more important, out of the profession. The broadest term used to describe schools' need to hire new teachers is *turnover*, which refers to the number of teachers who leave a particular teaching assignment each year. Perhaps the most important element of this turnover is true *attrition*, which refers to those teachers who leave the profession altogether (referred to somewhat more informally as "leavers"). A further distinction here is between those who leave teaching due to retirement and those who voluntarily leave teaching prior to retirement. According to data provided by Sutcher et al. (2016), the largest contributor to annual attrition is what scholars refer to as pre-retirement attrition—when teachers voluntarily leave the teaching profession for reasons other than retirement. This form of attrition accounts for more than half (53%) of all "leavers" from teaching; in other words, more teachers quit the teaching profession each year than retire from teaching. Second and most germane to this chapter is that voluntary pre-retirement attrition has consistently been documented to be about twice as high among special education teachers as among other groups of teachers.

Shortages of Special Education Teachers

A number of studies and various state-level and national reports bear out the particular impact on special education of this continuing teacher-shortage phenomenon. For example, the National Coalition on Personnel Shortages in Special Education and Related Services (n.d.) reported that 49 states reported shortages of special education teachers or related services personnel for the 2013–2014 school year. Sutcher et al. (2016) reported that 48 states plus the District of Columbia reported shortages of special education teachers for 2015–2016. As we have noted, despite some ebb and flow in the degree of shortage and the distribution problem Darling-Hammond and others have observed, the problem of teacher shortages in special education shows no signs of slowing and, indeed, by many accounts is projected to worsen in the coming decade (Sutcher et al., 2016).

It is important to note that while most national reports and indicators suggest that the chronic shortage of teachers abated somewhat around 2005, real shortages have persisted in most high-need areas, including special education, ELL, and STEM fields. In 2008 the Bureau of Labor Statistics predicted the demand for special education teachers would increase by 15% from 2006 to 2016 (Bureau of Labor Statistics, U.S. Department of Labor, 2008). The American Association for Employment in Education (AAEE) conducts an annual survey of colleges, universities, and school districts to assess demand for educators across 59 fields of teaching. For the 2016–2017 school year, this survey indicated "considerable shortages" (the highest rating category indicating demand in their survey) for each of the 10 areas of special education certification assessed (e.g., mild/moderate disabilities, severe/profound disabilities, emotional and behavioral disorders, hearing impairment). Moreover, this highest level of demand was consistent across every geographical region in the United States (AAEE, 2017). In sum, data suggest that real teacher shortages—not merely distribution or qualification problems—persist in special education, are evident across geographic regions of the United States, and transcend categorical areas within special education. Moreover, even if demand eases, actual shortages are projected to continue into the foreseeable future. In the next section, we consider factors that have historically impacted the demand for special education teachers and must be taken into account in any analyses or policy initiatives aimed at addressing teacher shortages and attrition in special education.

Issues That Impact Demand

Overall Demand for Special Education Teachers

The demand for special education teachers is, of course, driven directly by both the number of students schools identify as having disabilities and how schools serve those so identified. According to Yell (2019), the original passage of 94-142 had two immediate impacts on schools. First, in the mid-1970s many students with disabilities were probably attending school, but a large percentage of them were most likely not being served in ways that met their needs appropriately. Second, prior to 94-142, a significant number of students with disabilities had been excluded from school altogether. For essentially three decades following the passage of IDEA, the number of students with disabilities identified by schools rose steadily, driving a collateral increase in the demand for special education teachers. In 2005, however, the increase in the number of students with disabilities identified in schools actually leveled off for the first time, and the demand for special education teachers, while it was still not fully met, also declined (Boe et al., 2013). The reasons for this decline in the number of students identified with disabilities in school are complex and, indeed, not entirely clear. However, a number of factors have been identified as possible contributors. Boe et al. (2013) described four such factors: (a) the overall number of students with disabilities, (b) service delivery models used to serve students with disabilities, (c) special education funding, and (d) attrition among special education teachers. For example, it has been suggested that the evolution and growth of certain early intervention (e.g., Reading First) or tiered support practices (e.g., response to intervention [RTI]) may have slowed identification in some disability areas (e.g., Dewey et al., 2017). Dewey at al. suggested specifically that RTI and Reading First initiatives might have contributed directly to lowered identification rates for specific learning disabilities, a category that had accounted for essentially half of all students with disabilities during the last decades of the 20th century. In addition to a potential reduction in the overall number of students formally identified with disabilities, demand for teachers has also been impacted by changes in the ways students with disabilities receive specialized instruction. These changes have been largely driven by a general move toward more inclusive education for students with disabilities.

Philosophical Shifts in Service Delivery

Historically, specialized instruction was delivered primarily in settings outside of the general education classroom. Although the passage of P.L. 94-142 in 1975 focused specific attention on educating students with disabilities in the least restrictive environment (LRE) in which their needs could be met, much of special education throughout the 1970s and 1980s consisted of instruction delivered in resource rooms or self-contained classrooms. Such arrangements were especially common models for serving students with high-incidence disabilities. Almost as soon as P.L. 94-142 became law, however, debate began about the very concept of LRE. In the most literal sense, the general education classroom is of course the least restrictive setting along the continuum of alternative placements that 94-142 required. Conceptually, however, it has been argued that restrictiveness involves more than points along a single dimension (e.g., Crockett, 2014). The notion that LRE refers to the least restrictive environment *in which a student's needs can be met* implies that for some students a spot along the continuum of placements that appears less restrictive in a linear sense (e.g., the regular classroom) may in fact be more restrictive in that the student's individual needs cannot be addressed appropriately (e.g., for a student who requires intensive doses of highly individualized instruction). Although debate continues even today about LRE and its interpretation (e.g., Crockett & Kauffman, 2013), an overt effort began in the late 1980s and 1990s toward more inclusive placements. At that time, these arguments were driven largely by ethical, moral, or philosophical beliefs that students with disabilities should fully participate in all aspects of schooling, including academics, alongside their peers without disabilities (e.g., Gartner & Lipsky, 1987; Stainback & Stainback, 1984).

More recently, standards-based reforms have placed even greater emphasis on educating students with disabilities in general education classrooms. In 2001, the No Child Left Behind Act (NCLB) established the first legislative requirement that students with disabilities were to be held to the same academic standards as their typically developing peers. This emphasis on general education standards created even greater support for the movement toward full inclusion for students with disabilities, as placement in general education environments typically provides the opportunity for easier physical access to the general education curriculum.

Shifts in policy and practice that increase access to the general curriculum for students with disabilities also led to the burgeoning use of specific service delivery models that support inclusion, such as co-teaching. As a result, districts may have concluded that they simply did not need as many special education teachers to support students with disabilities, who are spending a greater percentage of their time in general education settings (e.g., Boe et al., 2013). Toward this point, Dewey et al. (2017) also speculated that schools may be inclined to hire more paraprofessionals rather than special education teachers to support students with disabilities, as these students receive their primary instruction in general education environments. Although it has been difficult to identify the precise number or percentage of students with disabilities served through co-teaching specifically (e.g., Cook, Landrum, Oshita, & Cook, 2017), the trend toward more inclusive service delivery models has continued, and there is consensus on these two broad points: (a) co-teaching has grown rapidly as a service delivery model, and (b) in general, co-teaching and other inclusive arrangements mean that fewer special education teachers overall may be needed to serve students with disabilities.

Although philosophical and legislative shifts initially shaped the ways students with disabilities were served, the economic benefits of these shifts have likely created unique influences that may drive how special education services are delivered. Such shifts in service arrangements (e.g., toward inclusion and co-teaching) may have reduced pressure on districts in terms of the number of special education teachers needed to adequately teach an increasing number of students with disabilities in the general education classroom. Despite these shifts in policy and practice over time, it remains important to note that never in the post–94-142 era has the demand for special education teachers been fully met.

Attrition, Turnover, and Induction

Even when the demand for special education teachers lessens, or the shortage of special education teachers is reduced, there is reason for concern about high rates of teacher attrition and turnover in special education. The idea that new special education teachers are less likely to stay in the field than their peers has been identified as a key area of focus in addressing chronic teacher shortages in special education (Billingsley, Griffin, Smith, Kamman, & Israel, 2009). We have provided a brief overview of data supporting the ideas that (a) historical rates of teacher attrition—leaving the profession short of retirement—average 8% annually; (b) rates of attrition in special education are even higher; and (c) targeting attrition has been identified as a key area of focus in addressing chronic teacher shortages in special education. In this section we elaborate on issues of attrition and turnover, and discuss the role of new teacher induction as a possible way of ameliorating the high rates of burnout and attrition that appear to directly contribute to the persistent shortage of special education teachers.

Attrition and Turnover

McLeskey and Billingsley (2008) reported that on average 6.74% of all special education teachers leave teaching each year, while 8.27% transfer to general education and 7.85% transfer to a different school. Note that this equates to a turnover rate of nearly 23% for special education teachers in a given year and an actual loss of roughly 15% of all special education teachers annually. This attrition rate is especially high among new and uncertified teachers, and beginning special education teachers are about 2.5 times more likely to leave teaching than are other beginning teachers (McLeskey & Billingsley, 2008).

In part to provide a framework for analyzing the problems of burnout and attrition, Billingsley and colleagues (2009) provided a comprehensive and cogent synthesis of the concerns expressed by new and beginning special education teachers. Specifically, they conducted a review of single-case, survey, and qualitative research published from 1990 through 2008 related to new special education teachers' concerns during their initial years of teaching. The results of this literature summary indicated that new special educators struggle as they enter the profession with complex challenges that might be categorized into three broad areas: (a) inclusion and collaboration, (b) pedagogy, and (c) managing roles. We note that while many of these concerns are those that any new teacher or employee would experience (e.g., working under the supervision of an administrator), many are specific to special education teachers or are routine concerns that are complicated by the demands of educating students with disabilities in a changing educational landscape. Under each broad category used by Billingsley et al. to frame the challenges new special education teachers experience, a number of specific concerns were delineated.

Under *inclusion and collaboration*, Billingsley et al. (2009) included broad concerns associated with "interactions with adults" (p. 8), which involves working with parents, collaborating with other professionals in both general and special education, managing and supervising the work of assistants or paraprofessionals, and even working with administrators. The importance of this category of concerns seems particularly compelling given that many of the studies summarized by Billingsley et al. predated major initiatives and policy shifts (e.g., NCLB). Further, it would seem that new and beginning special education teachers in particular may be less prepared for and thus potentially more stressed by the pressures associated with the continued movement in education toward greater access to the general curriculum for all students with disabilities. Note that this includes not merely access but increased accountability for progress toward standards dictated by the general curriculum, as well as relatively new and evolving models of service delivery that demand explicit, prescribed forms of collaboration (i.e., co-teaching).

In addition to navigating interactions with other adults, Billingsley et al. (2009) noted specific challenges that special educators encounter regarding *pedagogy*. A traditional view of special education might hold that special education teachers' training is focused largely on the design and delivery of specialized instruction, and the adaptation or modification of curricula. In contrast, general education teachers may be thought of as prepared with a high level of specific content-area expertise. To the extent this is true, a number of unique pedagogical challenges may emerge for both. For special educators, one of the most fundamental challenges may be the demand that they plan and deliver specific instruction and supports for students across multiple content areas, including challenging content at the secondary level (e.g., mathematics, science, social studies; Billingsley et al., 2009). This challenge is obviously exacerbated when caseloads are large, or when service delivery models are varied or logistically cumbersome.

Finally, under *managing roles*, the more common and persistent concerns of beginning special educators included time and scheduling, caseloads, paperwork and logistics, and role confusion. The first of these are surely interrelated. Faced with a large number of students with varying needs who require services that may vary tremendously in type and intensity, and who most likely receive those services in multiple settings, the management logistics alone are daunting. The latter concern, role confusion, undoubtedly exacerbates these challenges. For example, students with disabilities—indeed, any student with or without an identified disability who may be struggling with particular content—may need doses of highly specialized instruction, scaffolding or other supports, and more frequent and more detailed review and reteaching, to name only a few instructional modifications or adaptations. Who is responsible for delivering these additional supports? Moreover, is there a clear and shared understanding of where the responsibility lies for anticipating needs for these supports, planning and delivering them based on formative assessment, and making sure through summative assessments that all students have met specific curricular goals and standards?

New Teacher Induction and Mentoring

There is no question that special education teachers face significant and unique challenges during the first several years of teaching. Like all new teachers, they must adapt to their new professional role as they assume for the first time complete responsibility for their own classroom and for the learning of each of their assigned pupils. Similarly, like all new teachers they must adapt to new schedules and routines, new physical surroundings, and new colleagues and supervisors. We believe it can be argued that the unique learning challenges of students with identified disabilities create an induction period that can be especially stressful, challenging, and potentially overwhelming. Indeed, as we have noted, teachers who do not have the necessary supports during induction appear to be less likely to remain in the field (Billingsley et al., 2009). Many schools and districts have formal mentoring or induction programs designed to support new teachers, but even in cases where such structures are not overt or formalized, there appear to be several key elements of induction that may be associated with greater persistence in the profession. It may be important to distinguish between the two interrelated terms *mentoring* and *induction*. Ingersoll and Strong (2011) noted that while the terms are often used interchangeably in the literature, induction typically refers to a time period, or the process that occurs during the time period associated with the first few years of an individual's enculturation into a new job role.

The National Association of State Boards of Education (Sun, 2012) provided a comprehensive definition of induction and, indeed, used the term *comprehensive induction* to guide their discussion of these constructs. Noting that mentoring is but one element of induction, they defined comprehensive induction as including (a) a minimum of 2 years of support for new teachers; (b) high-quality mentoring during this time, provided by mentors who were carefully selected and specifically prepared for their mentor roles; (c) the consistent provision of common planning time for new teachers with other teachers; (d) access to continuing professional development; and (e) evaluation of new teachers according to clear standards throughout the induction period (p. 5). They further estimated that less than 1% of new teachers in the United States could be considered to have received this level of comprehensive induction.

Mentoring specifically captures at least two layers of induction that may be critical to teachers' success and thus their likelihood of staying in the field. We think of mentors as necessary both for socialization reasons and for professional reasons related to being an effective teacher of students with disabilities. On a personal or social level, a mentor can provide a touchstone for the brand-new special education teacher as the new teacher adjusts to the many professional and personal demands associated with a new job—new surroundings, new colleagues, and new administrators and bosses. Mentors can help new teachers sort out questions large and small about their day-to-day work, including matters ranging from supplies, materials, budgets, technology, photocopying, schedules, and routines to more substantive matters around things such as school discipline policies and practices, and teacher performance evaluation and review. Whereas mentoring is needed for various reasons over the course of a career, literature seems to support the idea that effective mentoring of special education teachers during this induction period may be an especially critical component of efforts to reduce the disproportionate attrition that continues to characterize new and beginning special education teachers (Billingsley et al., 2009).

There is extensive literature on mentoring and induction programs for all new teachers (e.g., Strong, 2009), guided by evidence or at least beliefs that such programs not only keep teachers in the field longer but also make them better teachers (Ingersoll & Strong, 2011). For example, Ingersoll and Strong reviewed 15 studies of new-teacher induction programs and found that new teachers' participation in formal induction programs resulted in positive impacts across several domains. Teachers participating in induction programs showed improved attitudes and retention. In addition, induction seemed to result in improved teaching practice, including fostering better student engagement; developing, implementing, and adjusting instruction; and managing classroom behavior. Finally, and importantly, the students of teachers who participated in induction showed positive achievement outcomes compared with those of teachers who did not participate in induction. Despite these promising findings, Ingersoll and Strong suggested that methodological limitations in the induction literature base leave a number of questions in demand of further exploration. For example, we do not fully understand the specific content of induction activities or the nature of induction activities (e.g., time, intensity, duration) that may be associated with differential outcomes for teachers and students. Related to this, especially for administrators in times of budget limitations and teacher shortages, is the need for specific analyses of the costs and benefits of induction. Finally, Ingersoll and Strong suggest that context may matter, and it is not clear whether and how induction should vary across schools or districts that may differ in important ways (e.g., socioeconomic status, urban vs. suburban vs. rural settings) or across levels (elementary, middle, and high school) or contexts (general vs. special education teachers).

Unique Induction Issues in Special Education

In addition to simply learning a new job, adapting to a new environment and colleagues, and learning the ropes in that new environment—things all new employees must do—there may be some fundamental stressors associated with teaching students with disabilities. Specifically, students with disabilities have some of the greatest learning and behavioral challenges teachers will see. Further, these students often demand supports that go beyond instruction or behavior management (e.g., personal care, medical or health services, physical supports). Beginning on the first day of their new teaching job, special education teachers are expected to respond to a highly diverse set of extremely demanding needs across myriad contexts (Sweigart & Collins, 2017).

In an effort to support the competing demands that new special education teachers encounter, induction and mentoring programs should be designed to support new teachers in areas that have been identified as being the most challenging during the first few years of teaching (see Billingsley et al., 2009). Specifically, mentors should be prepared to support novice teachers in managing their workload, collaborating with other professionals, using assessment to inform instruction, managing student behavior, adequately planning and addressing curricular demands within various time constraints, and understanding legal mandates and implications.

A potential avenue for better supporting teacher induction, and potentially reducing teacher attrition, involves more explicit and deeper partnerships between teacher preparation programs and local schools. Criticisms of teacher preparation programs (e.g., Holmes Group, 1995) have often centered on perceptions that there was a disconnect between the theory-heavy training preservice teachers were presumed to receive and the practical teaching demands newly certified teachers face, especially when they enter the profession in challenging schools (e.g., high-poverty schools). Professional development schools (PDS) and residency models (e.g., DeMonte, 2015,

2016) are two mechanisms through which educator preparation programs might partner with local schools to make training more authentic, deeper, and more consistent with the teaching demands teachers will face once hired. By their very nature, such models promote active collaboration between university faculty and local school administration and teachers, and typically increase the presence of both university faculty and teacher candidates in schools. Most important for our purposes, there is some evidence that such efforts can positively impact teachers' persistence in the field. Latham and Vogt (2007), for example, conducted a longitudinal comparison between teachers who were trained in a traditional model and teachers who were trained in a model that included strong school partnerships, including PDS. Compared with teachers who completed traditional preparation programs, teachers who participated in teacher preparation through a PDS model were more likely to enter and remain in the field.

Residency models of teacher preparation are receiving similar attention and emphasis. DeMonte (2016) described the potential benefits and burgeoning examples of such models, which require teacher candidates to be embedded in partner schools for longer periods (typically at least a full school year) than traditional practica and student teaching experiences might provide. Examples included a recent investment of $34 million from the Bill and Melinda Gates Foundation that went toward grants focused on transforming teacher preparation programs. As described by DeMonte, while these grants varied in specifics, all were intentionally targeted toward the improvement of the clinical training teachers receive. Continued research is needed to assess whether and how such models impact teacher performance in the classroom and, ultimately, their persistence in the field through and beyond their induction years.

Supporting New Special Educators

Although many districts and individual schools have adopted formal mentoring programs to support special education teachers during the induction years, these supports are not universal. In some cases, special educators will need to identify their own areas of need and find supports in lieu of a formal mentoring program. One way for special education teachers to identify their own needs is through the use of self-assessment (Collins, Sweigart, Landrum, & Cook, 2017; Ross & Bruce, 2007).

Self-Assessment

Based on the areas identified by Billingsley and colleagues (2009), Collins et al. (2017) suggested that new special education teachers should complete a self-assessment that targets the areas of collaboration, instruction, responsibilities, and relationships. While all of these have been identified as important for the development and retention of new special education teachers, the critical importance of effective instruction cannot be ignored (Kauffman & Badar, 2014), especially when considering teaching students with disabilities. Although the use of evidence-based practices is the most effective approach to positively impacting student outcomes (Cook & Schirmer, 2003), there is evidence that special education teachers implement ineffective practices as often as, if not more frequently than, those that are evidence-based (e.g., Burns & Ysseldyke, 2009). Logic would suggest that special educators' increased use of evidence-based practices may positively influence the likelihood that they remain in the field. That is, if teachers are (a) managing the behavior of their students effectively and (b) employing instructional strategies that yield positive academic outcomes, it is possible that the reinforcing nature of these outcomes might mitigate or interrupt traditional pathways toward burnout and ultimately attrition. We acknowledge that more research is needed to validate these hypotheses regarding actual teacher outcomes, but efforts toward thwarting the development of factors known to be associated with burnout certainly offer the possibility of improved student outcomes at a minimum. Consequently, self-assessment should specifically target instructional goals and include a component for supporting teachers as they move toward those goals.

Beyond Self-Assessment

Even though self-assessment offers a logical starting place, new special educators will certainly benefit from additional resources and supports to help them implement effective instructional practices. As noted by Ross and Bruce (2007), the use of self-assessment is "constructive but insufficient" (p. 155), and providing teachers with self-assessment tools without offering other supports (e.g., coaching) may actually have the opposite effect on professional growth. As part of the self-assessment framework suggested by Collins et al. (2017), new special education teachers are encouraged to locate specific resources and professional development opportunities that would help them meet the goals identified through self-assessment. When considering ways to meet these goals, new special education teachers should (a) use reliable, web-based resources to supplement materials and trainings that are provided by their district or school (see Landrum & Collins, in press) and (b) engage in the use of performance feedback to develop fluency in selected evidence-based practices (Collins et al., 2017).

Although new special education teachers may have access to professional development opportunities, it is well-known that the one-shot nature of professional development falls short of meeting special education teachers' needs. Indeed, special educators report that ongoing and continuous support is critical to their effective use of evidence-based practices (Jones, 2009). Therefore, new special education teachers need resources to support them in between professional development trainings.

The Internet provides a vast resource that offers limitless information and materials that can be helpful to special educators during their induction years, but teachers must of course use extraordinary care and caution when identifying and selecting web-based resources. Given the proliferation of Internet-based resources and the ready access the Internet provides, Landrum and Collins (in press) offered general guidelines for educators seeking reliable information regarding evidence-based practices. They suggested that when selecting web-based resources, teachers should understand and pay close attention to (a) websites' domains (e.g., .gov, .com, .org, .edu); (b) the affiliation of the website or material (e.g., research centers, professional organizations); (c) references provided on the website or within a specific resource (e.g., websites that cite empirical evidence); and (d) "red flags" that may indicate some likelihood of inaccurate or unsupported information (i.e., websites that promote pseudoscience). Even after identifying reliable web-based information that provides guidance on both identifying and implementing appropriate evidence-based practices, new special education teachers undoubtedly need continued support in the form of coaching and feedback (e.g., Briere, Simonsen, Sugai, & Myers, 2015; Rathel, Drasgow, Brown, & Marshall, 2014) as they begin to build their fluency in a particular practice.

There is evidence to suggest that the use of performance feedback provides new special education teachers with an effective approach in increasing their use of specific evidence-based practices (Cornelius & Nagro, 2014; Fallon, Collier-Meek, Maggin, Sanetti, & Johnson, 2015; Sweigart, Collins, Evanovich & Cook, 2016). During performance feedback, a trained observer collects data on a teacher's implementation of a selected practice. Following the observation, the teacher receives immediate feedback (i.e., data) through a personal conversation, delivery of progress-monitoring documents, or electronic correspondence. Although the observation is intended to monitor a teacher's use of a practice, performance feedback can also include information about student outcomes as a result of a teacher's fidelity of implementation of a given practice (Fallon et al., 2015). In some cases, feedback has been delivered during the observation session through wireless, bug-in-ear technology (e.g., Scheeler, McAfee, Ruhl, & Lee, 2006). More research is needed to define the essential characteristics of effective performance feedback, but it is evident that feedback is most effective when it is delivered immediately (Scheeler, Ruhl, & McAfee, 2004) and includes a specific review of the data (Fallon et al., 2015). Similar to feedback that is beneficial for students, performance feedback for teachers is most effective when it includes positive statements that offer specific suggestions for teachers to make corrections (Scheeler et al., 2004).

Given the empirical support for the use of performance feedback in improving the implementation fidelity of evidence-based practices, it would seem that the use of performance feedback could be an important part of an induction program designed to influence the likelihood that a special educator will remain in the field. If new special education teachers are supported in ways that (a) immediately reinforce or improve their pedagogy and (b) directly connect their teaching behaviors to student outcomes, it seems likely that they will feel more successful and empowered. Cultivating successful teaching experiences that may be reinforcing to special education teachers and encouraging new special educators to continually adopt the use of evidence-based practices would seem to be critical elements of induction. Such activities are undoubtedly critical to successfully teaching students with disabilities. We would argue further, though specific research is still needed, that such activities may also offer promise in ameliorating special education teacher burnout and attrition.

Conclusion

Although there are discrepancies in the ways teacher shortages are measured, and thus reports vary as to the precise nature and extent of teacher shortages in special education, there is broad consensus that such shortages of special education teachers exist, that the shortages have been chronic, and that shortages show no signs of abating (Darling-Hammond, Furger, Shields, & Sutcher, 2016; McLeskey et al., 2004). Most scholars also agree that the shortages can be categorized as severe and that virtually all states, geographic regions, and districts in the United States are impacted. Moreover, there is strong evidence that (a) attrition and turnover are particular problems for special education compared with teachers generally and (b) attrition and turnover are worse in high-poverty districts. To address shortages, scholars have examined both initial supply or pipeline issues (i.e., how teachers are drawn into and prepared for the profession) and retention issues. With regard to retention, estimates reliably suggest that special education teachers leave at a rate about twice that of their general education colleagues. Darling-Hammond and others have argued that retention is the far greater problem in reducing teacher shortages, given how many teachers leave the profession early in their careers. Mentoring and induction programs appear to be a necessary support for new special education teachers and a viable approach to increasing retention rates, especially when such programs include opportunities for teachers to identify specific instructional needs, and establishing systems or mechanisms for obtaining regular feedback designed to help them improve their performance. Although research supports mentoring and induction practices that help teachers implement evidence-based practices with fidelity, and such practices show promise in promoting positive student outcomes, more research is needed to determine whether, how, and to what extent such efforts truly impact beginning special education teacher retention and persistence in the profession.

REFLECTING AND UNDERSTANDING

1. How do shortages of special education teachers compare with shortages of teachers in general?

2. What factors contribute to shortages of special education teachers specifically?

3. There is some evidence that the demand for special education teachers may be decreasing. What are some reasons for this?

4. What unique challenges do special education teachers face in their first years of teaching?

5. What are some characteristics of mentoring or induction programs that show promise for retaining special education teachers in the profession?

ONLINE RESOURCES

- "Critical Shortages in Special Education Teachers. Sound Familiar?" (American Institutes for Research, 2016): https://www.air.org/resource/critical-shortages-special-education-teachers-sound-familiar

- "Teacher Shortage Areas" (U.S. Department of Education, 2017): https://www2.ed.gov/about/offices/list/ope/pol/tsa.html

- "Teacher Shortages: What We Know" (Aragon, 2016), Education Commission of the States: https://www.ecs.org/wp-content/uploads/Teacher-Shortages-What-We-Know.pdf

RECOMMENDED READINGS

Journals

Bettini, E. A., Cheyney, K., Wang, J., & Leko, C. (2015). Job design: An administrator's guide to supporting and retaining special educators. *Intervention in School and Clinic, 50,* 221–225.

Dewey, J., Sindelar, P. T., Bettini, E., Boe, E. E., Rosenberg, M. S., & Leko, C. (2017). Explaining the decline in special education teacher employment from 2005 to 2012. *Exceptional Children, 83,* 315–329.

Rock, M. L., Spooner, F., Nagro, S., Vasquez, E., Dunn, C., Leko, M., Luckner, J.... & Jones, J. L. (2016). 21st century change drivers: Considerations for constructing transformative models of special education teacher development. *Teacher Education and Special Education, 39*(2), 98–120.

Articles

Brownell, M. T., & Sindelar, P. T. (2016). Preparing and retaining effective special education teachers: Systemic solutions for addressing teacher shortages. *Council for Exceptional Children Policy Insider.* Retrieved from http://edprepmatters.net/2016/03/preparing-and-retaining-effective-special-education-teachers-systemic-solutions-for-addressing-teacher-shortages/

Sutcher, L., Darling-Hammond, L., & Carver-Thomas, D. (2016). *A coming crisis in teaching? Teacher supply, demand, and shortages in the US.* Learning Policy Institute. Retrieved from https://learningpolicyinstitute.org/product/coming-crisis-teaching

REFERENCES

American Association for Employment in Education. (2017). *Educator supply and demand report: Executive summary.* Retrieved from http://www.aaee.org/resources/Documents/AAEE%20Supply%20_%20Demand%20Report%20 2017%20Ex%20Summary_fnl.pdf

Billingsley, B. S. (2004). Special education teacher retention and attrition: A critical analysis of the research literature. *Journal of Special Education, 38*(1), 39–55.

Billingsley, B. S., Griffin, C. C., Smith, S. J., Kamman, M., & Israel, M. (2009). *A review of teacher induction in special education: Research, practice, and technology solutions* (NCIPP Doc. No. RS-1). Gainesville: University of Florida, National Center to Inform Policy and Practice in Special Education Professional Development.

Boe, E. E. (2006). Long-term trends in the national demand, supply, and shortage of special education teachers. *Journal of Special Education, 40*, 138–150.

Boe, E. E., deBettencourt, L. U., Dewey, J., Rosenberg, M., Sindelar, P., & Leko, C. (2013). Variability in demand for special education teachers: Indicators, explanations, and impacts. *Exceptionality, 21*(2), 103–125.

Briere, D. E., Simonsen, B., Sugai, G., & Myers, D. (2015). Increasing new teachers' specific praise using a within-school consultation intervention. *Journal of Positive Behavior Interventions, 17*(1), 50–60.

Bureau of Labor Statistics, U.S. Department of Labor. (2008). *Occupational outlook handbook 2009.* New York, NY: Skyhorse.

Burns, M. K., & Ysseldyke, J. E. (2009). Reported prevalence of evidence-based instructional practices in special education. *Journal of Special Education, 43*, 3–11.

Collins, L. W., Sweigart, C. A., Landrum, T. J., & Cook, B. G. (2017). Navigating common challenges and pitfalls in the first years of special education: Solutions for success. *Teaching Exceptional Children, 49*, 213–222.

Cook, B. G., & Schirmer, B. R. (2003). What is special about special education? Overview and analysis. *Journal of Special Education, 37*, 200–205.

Cook, S. E. C., Landrum, K. A., Oshita, L. M. Y. O., & Cook, B. (2017). Co-teaching and students with disabilities: A critical analysis of the empirical literature. In D. P. Hallahan & J. M. Kauffman (Eds.), *The handbook of special education* (pp. 147–159). New York, NY: Routledge.

Cornelius, K. E., & Nagro, S. A. (2014). Evaluating the evidence base of performance feedback in preservice special education teacher training. *Teacher Education and Special Education, 37*, 133–146.

Crockett, J. (2014). Reflections on the concept of the least restrictive environment in special education. In B. G. Cook, M. Tankersley, & T. Landrum (Eds.), *Advances in learning and behavioral disabilities. Vol. 27: Special education past, present, and future* (pp. 39–62). Bingley, UK: Emerald.

Crockett, J. B., & Kauffman, J. M. (2013). *The least restrictive environment: Its origins and interpretations in special education.* New York, NY: Routledge.

Darling-Hammond, L., Furger, R., Shields, P. M., & Sutcher, L. (2016). *Addressing California's emerging teacher shortage: An analysis of sources and solutions.* Palo Alto, CA: Learning Policy Institute.

Darling-Hammond, L., & Sykes, G. (2003). Wanted, a national teacher supply policy for education: The right way to meet the "highly qualified teacher" challenge. *Education Policy Analysis Archives, 11*(33), 1–55.

DeMonte, J. (2015). *A million new teachers are coming: Will they be ready to teach?* Washington, DC: American Institutes for Research.

DeMonte, J. (2016). Toward better teacher prep. *Educational Leadership, 73*(8), 66–71.

Dewey, J., Sindelar, P. T., Bettini, E., Boe, E. E., Rosenberg, M. S., & Leko, C. (2017). Explaining the decline in special education teacher employment from 2005 to 2012. *Exceptional Children, 83*, 315–329.

Fallon, L. M., Collier-Meek, M. A., Maggin, D. M., Sanetti, L. M., & Johnson, A. H. (2015). Is performance feedback for educators an evidence-based practice? A systematic review and evaluation based on single-case research. *Exceptional Children, 81*, 227–246.

Gartner, A., & Lipsky, D. K. (1987). Beyond special education: Toward a quality system for all students. *Harvard Educational Review, 57*, 367–396.

Holmes Group. (1995). *Tomorrow's schools of education: A report of the Holmes Group.* East Lansing, MI: Author.

Hussar, W. J., & Bailey, T. M. (2013). *Projections of education statistics to 2022* (NCES 2014-051). U.S. Department of Education, National Center for Education Statistics. Washington, DC: U.S. Government Printing Office.

Ingersoll, R. M., & Strong, M. (2011). The impact of induction and mentoring programs for beginning teachers: A critical review of the research. *Review of Educational Research, 81*, 201–233.

Jones, M. L. (2009). A study of novice special educators' views of evidence-based practices. *Teacher Education and Special Education, 32*, 101–120.

Kauffman, J. M., & Badar, J. (2014). Instruction, not inclusion, should be the central issue in special education: An alternative view from the USA. *Journal of International Special Needs Education, 17*(1), 13–20.

Kentucky Legislative Research Commission. (2012). *Tracking teacher shortages: Trends and continuing questions* (Research Report 395). Retrieved from http://www.lrc.ky.gov/lrcpubs/RR395.pdf

Landrum, T. J., & Collins, L. W. (in press). Sources of evidence-based practice in EBD: Issues and challenges. In B. Cook, M. Tankersley, & T. Landrum (Eds.), *Advances in learning and behavioral disabilities* (Vol. 30). Bingley, UK: Emerald.

Latham, N. I., & Vogt, P. (2007). Do professional development schools reduce teacher attrition: Evidence from a longitudinal study of 1,000 graduates. *Journal of Teacher Education, 58*, 153–167.

McLeskey, J., & Billingsley, B. S. (2008). How does the quality and stability of the teaching force influence the research to practice gap? A perspective on the teacher shortage in special education. *Redial and Special Education, 29*(5), 293–305.

McLeskey, J., Tyler, N. C., & Saunders Flippin, S. (2004). The supply of and demand for special education teachers: A review of research regarding the chronic shortage of special education teachers. *Journal of Special Education, 38*, 5–21.

National Coalition on Personnel Shortages in Special Education and Related Services. (n.d.). *Special education personnel shortages factsheet.* Retrieved from https://specialedshortages.org/resources/

Rathel, J. M., Drasgow, E., Brown, W. H., & Marshall, K. J. (2014). Increasing induction-level teachers' positive-to-negative communication ratio and use of behavior-specific praise through e-mailed performance feedback and its effect on students' task engagement. *Journal of Positive Behavior Interventions, 16*, 219–233.

Ross, J. A., & Bruce, C. D. (2007). Teacher self-assessment: A mechanism for facilitating professional growth. *Teaching and Teacher Education, 23*, 146–159.

Scheeler, M. C., McAfee, J. K., Ruhl, K. L., & Lee, D. L. (2006). Effects of corrective feedback delivered via wireless technology on preservice teacher performance and student behavior. *Teacher Education and Special Education, 29*, 12–25.

Scheeler, M. C., Ruhl, K. L., & McAfee, J. K. (2004). Providing performance feedback to teachers: A review. *Teacher Education and Special Education, 27*, 396–407.

Stainback, W., & Stainback, S. (1984). A rationale for the merger of special and regular education. *Exceptional Children, 51*, 102–111.

Strong, M. (2009). *Effective teacher induction and mentoring: Assessing the evidence.* New York, NY: Teachers College Press.

Sun, C. (2012). *Teacher induction: Improving state systems for supporting new teachers* (National Association of State Boards of Education Discussion Guide). Arlington, VA: NASBE.

Sutcher, L., Darling-Hammond, L., & Carver-Thomas, D. (2016). *A coming crisis in teaching? Teacher supply, demand, and shortages in the U.S.* Palo Alto, CA: Learning Policy Institute.

Sweigart, C. A., & Collins, L. W. (2017). Supporting the needs of beginning special education teachers and their students. *Teaching Exceptional Children*, *49*(4), 209–212.

Sweigart, C. A., Collins, L. W., Evanovich, L. L., & Cook, S. C. (2016). An evaluation of the evidence base for performance feedback to improve teacher praise using CEC's quality indicators. *Education and Treatment of Children*, *39*, 419–444.

Yell, M. L. (2019). *The law and special education* (5th ed.). Upper Saddle River, NJ: Pearson.

Preparing Future Leaders and Administrators of Special Education

Mary Lynn Boscardin

This Chapter Will Cover:

1. The need for strong leaders of special education.
2. Special education leadership positions, roles, and responsibilities.
3. Professional standards as an anchor for professional identities and a guide for special education leadership preparation and professional development.
4. The importance of special education leadership preparation for meeting the vision, mission, and goals of special education.
5. Integrated models for preparing and supporting leaders of special education.

Several researchers over the years have considered best ways to prepare administrators of special education. History has shown that early research in special education leadership was limited to rudimentary sources of knowledge and understanding of special education administration roles and responsibilities held by local directors of special education (Arick & Krug, 1993; Brabandt, 1969; Finkbinder, 1981; Forgnone & Collings, 1975; Kern & Mayer, 1970; Marro & Kohl, 1972; Prillaman & Richardson, 1985; Stile, Abernathy, & Pettibone, 1985; Stile & Pettibone, 1980; Valesky & Hirth, 1992; Whitworth & Hatley, 1979). More recent scholarship examines special and general education leadership within the context of broad standards and domains intended to specifically advance the field of special education leadership and administration (Boscardin, 2011, 2017; Boscardin, McCarthy, & Delgado, 2009; Crockett, 2011, 2012, 2017; Crockett, Becker, & Quinn, 2009; Murphy, 2002; O'Brien, 2006).

Boscardin (2007) questioned what is special about special education administration and the type of preparation required of special education leaders. Distinct preparation of leaders for special education at the building and district levels, in addition to state and federal levels, has been recognized in recent scholarship (Boscardin, 2017; Council of Chief State School Officers [CCSSO], 2017). In this chapter, we will explore the need for leaders of special education; who fulfills special education leadership roles; the value of professional standards to special education leadership preparation; leadership preparation for meeting the vision, mission, and goals of special education; and integrated models for preparing leaders of special education.

Key Terms

- special education administration and leadership
- special education administration standards
- special education leadership preparation

Is There a Need for Special Education Leaders?

Leadership roles and responsibilities have become more complex due to the ever expanding umbrella of inclusiveness and programming for students with disabilities. The U.S. Department of Education (2006) reported that more than 20,000 administrators hold the primary responsibility for overseeing the provision of special education and related services in school districts and state agencies across the United States. Periodic studies of special education leaders provide a reasonable, if not completely up-to-date, picture of the current situation. The Office of Special Education Programs (OSEP), in the past, provided annual data regarding hiring data of administrators of special education at the state and district levels. Unfortunately, this 2006 census on local and state special education supervisors and directors is the last national count conducted by OSEP in the U.S. Department of Education (Boscardin & Lashley, 2019). The last time these data were collected by OSEP, it was found that the need for special education administrators and supervisors in local school systems and agencies nationwide increased by 25%, from 14,604 in 1999 to 18,241 in 2006 (U.S. Department of Education, 2006).

Local districts employ about 18,000 local administrators; most notably, though, in 2006 a steady 5% (900) of in-service special education administrators did not meet their state's minimum certification requirements for each year of the census (U.S. Department of Education, 2006). According to the 2006 data, the need for state education agency special education administrative personnel increased by 9%, from 1,080 in 1999 to 1,178 in 2006 (U.S. Department of Education, 2006). The advent of retiring baby boomers suggests the imperative to produce "qualified and effective" administrators of special education at the local, state, and federal levels who have the passion and drive to set direction and promote a vision that extends well beyond compliance. Estimates of annual demand show losses are unsustainable. The demand for new administrators varies by state from 15% (2,700) to 32% (5,760), while shortages have been documented at 10% (1,800) per year.

Since 2006, there are examples of states, such as Kansas and Washington, no longer offering licensure for administrators of special education and offering only general education administrative licenses (Boscardin, Weir, & Kusek, 2010). An example from one state without a required administrator of special education (ASE) credential illustrates the result of decisions to discontinue ASE credentialing: The Washington Professional Educator Standards Board found in 2012 that only 50% of currently serving ASEs in the state at the district level held initial certification as special education teachers or related-services providers. Massachusetts, a state that does require an ASE license/credential, relies on generic leadership standards for licensing by the Department of Elementary and Secondary Education, while institutions of higher education are required to meet the Council for the Accreditation of Educator Preparation (CAEP) unit standards, and those that seek specialized professional associations recognition are reviewed based on the Council for Exceptional Children (CEC) Administrator of Special

Education Specialty set knowledge and skills as recognized by CAEP. The practice of states offering only general education administration licensure might be attributed to the education of students with disabilities becoming a shared responsibility with building principals and other educational leaders in the nation's 14,000 school districts and more than 100,000 elementary and secondary schools (Crockett, 2017). This practice, however, allows for uncredentialed administrators who are not well-versed in special education programming and policy to hold special education leadership positions, potentially compromising the ability to effectively advocate for students with disabilities.

Most special education administrators lead from a central office requiring a district-wide vision and mission. Historically, Brabandt (1969) found that none of the 98 veteran administrators of special education in his study met the standards established by the CEC or the requirements of doctoral programs offered by institutions of higher education. Most respondents had training as general educators or school psychologists but were not specifically trained as administrators of special education. Of the 12 states represented by the participants in Brabandt's study, only two had certification requirements for administrators of special education, four had certification requirements for supervisors of special education, and one required the CEC standards for administrators of special education be met. All 12 states required a general administrative credentialing. Interestingly, 41 years later, Boscardin and colleagues (2010) found growth but not the type of growth one might expect. Of the 50 states, 27 states have separate special education administrative credentialing that included five states requiring endorsements, 12 requiring certificates, seven requiring licenses, and three requiring a hybrid license that combines general education administrator licenses with ASE endorsements. These trends do not bode well for the supply of well-qualified, highly effective leaders of special education.

In addition to the ASE being critical to guiding and supporting special education, the principal is pivotal to ensuring that school buildings are places for inclusive and effective student learning and engagement. Some principals have opted for dual licensure/certification/endorsement. Effective principal leadership for students with disabilities, while similar to and derivative of special education leadership, remains specialized to the degree they provide oversight of students with disabilities within the buildings they serve. Principals who acquire additional special education leadership skills to provide for the unique needs and circumstances of students with disabilities are able to expand learning opportunities and services required for success (Billingsley, McLeskey, & Crockett, 2014).

Billingsley (2007) argues that teachers also play critical roles in the leadership of special education. According to Billingsley, preparation of special education teacher leaders is important to developing and supporting special and general education teachers. Teacher leaders availing themselves of the opportunity to earn National Board Certification was one of the most valuable professional experiences special education teacher leaders could have, and many of these board-certified teachers have gone on to serve as mentors for others (National Boards for Professional Teaching Standards, 2016).

The Importance of Professional Standards to Special Education Leadership Preparation

Three organizations, the National Council for Accreditation of Teacher Education (NCATE), Teacher Education Accreditation Council, and the Interstate New Teacher Assessment and Support Consortium, generated professional preparation standards. Recently, these organizations have merged to become what is now known as the Council for the Accreditation of Educator Preparation (CAEP). CAEP is the primary arbiter of standards for educator preparation. The CAEP professional standards offer benchmarks from which to ascertain whether candidates possess the necessary knowledge, skills, and dispositions to fulfill the demands of the position. The standards form a solid foundation for candidates, regardless of credentialing routes.

The leadership behaviors, functions, and values in national standards and advanced specialty sets emanate from professional organizations, such as the CEC and the National Educational Leadership Preparation (NELP) Board, with input from federal education agencies, university researchers, and allied stakeholders. The knowledge, skills, and dispositions are embedded in all aspects of professional preparation and development (Boscardin, 2016). Each set of leadership professional standards has been validated and offers a uniform set of knowledge, skills, and dispositions that provide leaders with the behaviors, functions, and values necessary to fulfill leadership responsibilities. In this section, we will consider the influence of the standards on the preparation of leaders of special education.

The Evolution of Special Education Administration Advanced Specialty Sets

Special education leadership knowledge-based competencies began to emerge in concert with discrete coursework and field-based requirements in the mid-1960s. In an early study, Rude and Sasso (1988) asked leaders of special education to rank Colorado special education administration standards. They found that management and supervision, legislative and legal issues, and leadership and decision making were rated highest, while computer literacy, research skills, and collective bargaining expertise were rated lowest. Since the Rude and Sasso study, national standards emerged and have evolved, with each iteration reflecting changes in priorities for administrators of special education.

Professional knowledge and skills for administrators of special education were first developed by the CEC with the sponsorship of the Council of Administrators of Special Education in 1999 as part of a specialized professional association for recognition by the NCATE. The CEC advanced specialty set for administrators of special education has undergone three validations, with the last occurring in 2009. A realignment occurred in 2012 to conform with the CAEP requirement that specialty sets include seven domains. The CEC advanced specialty set domain areas include (a) assessment and evaluation; (b) curricular content knowledge; (c) programs, services, and outcomes; (d) research and inquiry; (e) leadership and policy; (f) professional and ethical practice; and (g) collaboration. As the CEC (2015) indicates, the domains are not specific to administrators of special education. The domains are also applied to other professionals falling under the advanced specialty areas, such as diagnostic specialists, technology specialists, transition specialists, early childhood specialists, early intervention specialists, and deaf and hard of hearing specialists. The CEC relies on each profession to develop knowledge and skill statements that align with professional identities within each domain, resulting in an imperfect alignment (Boscardin et al., 2009).

Knowledge and skills of practicing professionals are believed to continue to grow over the course of a career, increasing the range and repertoire as leaders further their development (Avery, Tonidaniel, Griffith, & Quinones, 2003; Barbuto, Fritz, Matkin, & Marx, 2007; Cox, 2006; Darling-Hammond, LaPointe, Meyerson, Orr, & Cohen, 2007; Hersey, Blanchard, & Johnson 2012; Mumford, Marks, Connelly, Zaccaro, & Reiter-Palmon, 2000). Research has shown that leadership skill development is a dynamic process that follows a developmental continuum and is not limited to a specific role or position (Garand, 2014; Mosley, Boscardin, & Wells, 2014; Tudryn, Boscardin, & Wells, 2016). With the introduction of each educational reform policy, there appears to be a tacit assumption that the completion of a certain set of pre-specified requirements indicates that candidates have acquired the capacity to implement the new policies. A developmental continuum implies the need for continued professional development that is anchored by the standards.

The integration of multiple experiences buttressed by coursework eases the transition of leaders of special education from the preservice phase to the induction phase. Evidence-based leadership practices offer a foundation for leaders to support improved instructional practices by teachers and educational achievement of students (Boscardin, 2004, 2007; Leithwood, Louis, Anderson, & Wahlstrom, 2004). Underscored is the importance of pairing experiences with research-based knowledge and skill acquisition that continue to inform practice.

Leadership Standards

To thoroughly understand the role of leadership standards, we begin with an examination of the CEC Advanced Specialty Set for Administrators of Special Education, followed by a discussion of the general education Professional Standards for Educational Leaders (PSEL; National Policy Board for Educational Administration, 2018) and the NELP standards. The National Policy Board for Education Administration (NPBEA) and the CCSSO unanimously voted to adopt on November 2, 2015, the PSEL (National Policy Board for Educational Administration, 2018). In 2016, the NPBEA officially acquired the PSEL, solidifying its role in the education community as the leading voice for and steward of effective general education leadership practice.

Much can be learned from the PSEL even though it defines educational leadership broadly (National Policy Board for Educational Administration, 2018). The PSEL articulates the knowledge and skills expected of school-building leaders and simultaneously emphasizes the improved learning, achievement, development, and well-being of *each* student—an important change in language to special educators, whose focus is on the individual student. Growing out of a theory of school improvement, values of leadership are embedded within three related clusters thought to propel each student to academic and personal success: (a) curriculum, instruction and assessment, and community of care and support for students; (b) professional capacity of school personnel, professional community for teachers and staff, meaningful engagement of families and community, and operations and management; and (c) mission, vision and core values, ethics and professional norms, and equity and cultural responsiveness. Leadership behavioral or attitudinal dispositions or convictions complete the knowledge and skill paradigm for building level leaders. The PSEL (National Policy Board for Educational Administration, 2018) dispositions, demonstrated through both verbal and nonverbal behaviors, include being growth-oriented, collaborative, innovative, analytical, ethical, perseverant, reflective, and equity-minded. While it is essential that educational organizations be led by those who possess beliefs and attitudes supportive of those they lead, the goals for novice leaders include acquiring appropriate dispositions and achieving basic mastery of leadership competencies.

Following the adoption of the PSEL, the National Policy Board for Educational Administration convened a committee in December 2015 to develop the NELP standards, replacing the PSEL standards. The NELP standards (2018) provide greater specificity around performance expectations for novice building-level and district-level leaders and define high-quality educational leadership preparation. Like the Educational Leadership Constituent Council standards that preceded them, two sets of NELP standards were developed specifically for the principalship (building leadership) and the superintendency (district leadership) to be used to review educational leadership programs through the CAEP advanced program review process. The NELP standards are intended to guide preparation program design, accreditation review, and state program approval. These standards specify expected preservice leader knowledge and skill acquisition and assist with the induction of novice leaders.

There are eight NELP standards for building-level leadership: (1) mission, vision, and core values; (2) ethics and professional norms; (3) equity and cultural leadership; (4) instructional leadership; (5) community and external leadership; (6) operations and management; (7) human resource leadership; and (8) internship and clinical practice. For the district-level standards, Standards 1 through 5 and 8 remain unchanged, but Standards 6 and 7 reflect the broader mission of the role of the superintendency. The two new district-level standards include management of people, data, and processes, and policy, governance, and advocacy. The distinctive feature of these two sets of standards is that the internship and clinical experiences are included as a standard rather than a stand-alone expectation. Professional development, internships, and peer coaching extend formal preparation.

Unfortunately, disability is only addressed broadly and treated as a bias in each of the NELP sets of standards under Element 3.4. While critical issues of bias, marginalization, deficit-based schooling, and low expectations are covered under Element 3.3, equally important to success are organizational and system supports that elevate outcomes for students with disabilities and their families.

Leadership Preparation for Meeting the Vision, Mission, and Goals of Special Education

The development of accomplished educational leaders of special education targets leadership practices that foster learning (Hitt & Tucker, 2016). Early models for preparation of special education leaders and administrators were more basic and designed as a one-size-fits-all approach. Studies introduced the idea that prior teaching (Brabandt, 1969; Milazzo & Blessing, 1964; Prillaman & Richardson, 1985; Stile et al., 1985; Stile & Pettibone, 1980; Valesky & Hirth, 1992); courses of study that include educational foundations and educational administration, with electives in psychology, guidance, and research methods, and practicum experiences (Brabandt, 1969; Kern & Mayer, 1970; Milazzo & Blessing, 1964); and internships/practica (Brabandt, 1969; Finkbinder, 1981; Marro & Kohl, 1972; Milazzo & Blessing, 1964; Prillaman & Richardson, 1985; Stile et al., 1985; Stile & Pettibone, 1980; Valesky & Hirth, 1992) are important to developing effective administrators of special education. Additionally, admissions requirements included a master's degree in special education and certification as a teacher in some area of special education (Brabandt, 1969; Prillaman & Richardson, 1985). As the field of special education administration advanced, closer attention was given to core administrative courses and field experiences (Finkbinder, 1981; Kern & Mayer, 1970). University faculty identified the following content:

> (a) knowledge of federal, state, and local functions and responsibilities in special education; (b) supervisory and/or administrative experience; (c) an understanding of preservice and inservice educational activity; (d) community public relations experiences related to special education; and (e) involvement in direct services to one or more types of exceptional children. (Milazzo & Blessing, 1964, p. 133)

Researchers early on identified the need for extending training through professional development and continuing education programs for in-service administrators of special education (Forgnone & Collings, 1975; Kern & Mayer, 1970; Prillaman & Richardson, 1985; Stile et al., 1985; Stile & Pettibone, 1980; Valesky & Hirth, 1992). Affiliation with local, state, and national professional organizations related to special education was also an important aspect to being an ASE (Milazzo & Blessing, 1964). Continuing education, a recent addition to credentialing requirements for administrators of special education since the passage of the Every Student Succeeds Act (ESSA, 2015), was used to build and maintain professional leadership knowledge and skill capacity.

Most leaders of special education work for district, intermediate, or state education agencies. Regardless of education agencies served, administrators of special education are responsible for ensuring that all students with disabilities are taught using evidence-based instructional practices, have access to and achieve in the general education curriculum, and are provided adequate resources to support teaching and learning (Boscardin,

2004; DiPaola & Walther-Thomas, 2003). Some also work for federal education agencies. Over time, special education administrative leadership roles have changed in response to cultural, political, and pedagogical shifts in the field. Some leadership preparation programs today can be characterized as having become homogenized, as some states have merged administrative credentialing under a single umbrella, only differing at the practicum level. Outside of credentialing, what is agreed on as curricula for leadership for special education is varied; some curricula are targeted at the local district director, while others are more broadly focused, with the idea that leaders of special education can be building, district, intermediate, or state based, requiring different levels of preparation.

The Individuals with Disabilities Education Act (IDEA, 2004) calls for high-quality professional development for all leaders serving students with disabilities, including training in the following areas:

(a) Instructional leadership; (b) behavioral supports in the school and classroom; (c) paperwork reduction; (d) promoting improved collaboration between special education and general education teachers; (e) assessment and accountability; (f) ensuring effective learning environments; and (g) fostering positive relationships with parents. (IDEA, 20 U.S.C. §1462[a][7])

Effective leaders "who understand what teachers need to teach and *why* they need it, are more apt to provide resources to meet the instructional needs of the students" (Wakeman, Browder, Flowers, & Ahlgrim-Delzell, 2006, p. 167; emphasis in original).

Contemporary courses of study highlight special education policy and law; disability and social policy; special education organization and management; and program planning, implementation, and evaluation (Boscardin & Messing, 2016). Because of the emphasis on accountability and stakeholder involvement, making sense of large data sets has been added to curricula (Boscardin & Messing, 2016). General education curriculum mainstays remain: general education school law; school finance with a focus on resources and equity; personnel management; politics in education; foundations of educational leadership that cover the multiple approaches to leadership; and practica/internships in special education leadership at the local, state, and federal levels. Crockett (2017) also identified content and dispositions specifically related to leading and administering special education that include (a) advocating for individually meaningful educational attainment, (b) ensuring evidence-based instructional practices and progress-monitoring systems for students with disabilities, (c) providing appropriate opportunities for the professional learning and evaluation of special education personnel, (d) providing special education personnel with supportive working conditions and resources, and (e) encouraging collaboration that supports the delivery of specially designed instruction.

Unfortunately, there is a dearth of literature about the preparation of state directors of special education, leaving a heavy reliance on translating literature in a way that makes sense for preparation for this position. State directors of special education rely on the same standards and advanced specialty set for administrators of special education even though responsibilities can vary from local and intermediate directors of special education. The State Systemic Improvement Plans (SSIP) allude to what is expected of state directors. There are three phases to SSIP reporting, and within each phase are specific components:

> Phase I components: (1) data analysis, (2) analysis of infrastructure to support improvement and build capacity, (3) state-identified measurable result for students with disabilities, (4) selection of coherent improvement strategies, and (5) theory of action

> Phase II components: (1) infrastructure development, (2) support for local education agencies (LEAs) implementation of evidence-based practices, and (3) evaluation (Phase II builds on the five components developed in Phase I.)

> Phase III components: continued focus on evaluation of the above components

In analyzing the SSIP components, the following three broad areas of importance for state directors of special education emerge: (1) governance, policy, and laws (compliance); (2) personnel preparation, educational programming, and evaluation (accountability); and (3) stakeholder involvement and engagement.

In addition to the SSIPs, the *PSEL 2015 and Promoting Principal Leadership for the Success of Students with Disabilities* (CCSSO, 2017) and existing literature indirectly suggest an extensive list of knowledge and skills expected of state directors: (a) understanding the interface between federal, state, and local policies and laws governing the education of students with disabilities; (b) setting state goals and expectations for the education of students with disabilities; (c) engaging diverse groups of statewide stakeholders; (d) possessing mediation and conflict management skills; (e) having a deep understanding of state government systems and bureaucracies; (f) adopting and extending professional practice standards for all leaders throughout the state responsible for students with disabilities; (g) developing a philosophy, vision, mission, and principles for effective leadership and instructional practice for special education; (h) improving credentialing for leaders of special education; (i) improving leader preparation through program accreditation and approval processes; (j) providing incentives and resources for special education program improvement and innovation; and (k) promoting meaningful professional development and evaluation of all leaders of special education. A deeper understanding of how state directors of special education apply these topics would benefit future preparation.

Effective principal leadership for students with disabilities, while similar to and derivative of effective leadership for all students, remains specialized to the degree there is legislated oversight of compliance and student learning outcomes. ESSA defines effective principals as follows:

> SEC. 2243 (3) developing or implementing programs for recruiting, developing, and placing school leaders to improve schools implementing comprehensive support and improvement activities and targeted support and improvement activities under section 1111(d), including through

cohort-based activities that build effective instructional and school leadership teams and develop a school culture, design, instructional program, and professional development program focused on improving student learning.

Principals who adopt additional skills are better able to provide for the unique needs and circumstances of students with disabilities and to provide the learning opportunities and services required for their success. Specific practices that are tailored and adjusted to specific environments and populations can better meet the learning needs of students with disabilities (CCSSO, 2017).

Professional development for teacher leaders of special education is equally important. Content might include team teaching, observation, coaching, and mentoring to solve problems of practice. Another option for advancing teacher leadership opportunities includes the creation of collegial professional learning communities (PLCs), where ongoing learning and teacher leadership are part of the school culture. The PLCs are "connected to and derived from teachers' work with their students" (Darling-Hammond & McLaughlin, 1995, p. 598). Additionally, using a combination of the aforementioned techniques that are based on and linked to student instruction with in-service teachers outside the academy helps promote improved pedagogy that advances positive learning outcomes.

The key to creating effective leadership preparation programs is to develop a model that not only anticipates the growing needs of future leaders but is nimble, flexible, and agile enough to respond over time to the ever changing demands of the field. Integrating leadership standards and specialty sets with evidence-based leadership practices offers a way to rethink and reculture schools to change the status quo (Murphy, 2002; York-Barr & Duke, 2004).

Integrated Models for Preparing Leaders of Special Education

Bellamy and Iwaszuk (2017) noted that the pipeline has almost run dry in terms of producing sufficient numbers of administrators of special education. Increasing the pipeline of effective leaders of special education depends on a symbiotic relationship between curricula exemplars and program delivery options. It is possible to develop curricula exemplars, but ineffective program delivery options for those aspiring to be leaders of special education render the information inaccessible and disrupt the pipeline. Preparation for special education leadership and administration for the purpose of this discussion is divided into two parts: curricular content considerations and delivery options.

Curricular Content Considerations

An integrated model is proposed that combines the complexity of the demands on leaders of special education and shared visions within the leadership domains discussed earlier in this chapter. The driving force behind this model is the belief that it is possible to prepare effective leaders of special education who are able to address problems of policy and practice regardless of position. The overarching goal of the integrated model for preparing leaders of special education results in successful learners, improved instruction, positive educational outcomes, and advocacy. Validated special education leadership preparation requirements and professional practices follow a proficiency continuum, much like the leadership continuum that empowers leaders to develop in a direction that maximizes the educational well-being of students with disabilities (Garand, Boscardin, & Wells, in preparation; Mosley et al., 2014; Provost, Boscardin, & Wells, 2010; Schulze & Boscardin, 2018; Tudryn et al., 2016).

When we combine the CEC advanced specialty set for administrators of special education (2015), the NELP standards (2018), the most recent thinking of Bellamy and Iwaszuk (2017) as part of their Washington State Expanding Capacity for Special Education Leadership project, and the results of feedback from 74 of the Council of Administrators of Special Education Board of Directors from the fall 2017 meeting, a fuller picture of the roles and responsibilities of leaders and administrators of special education emerges (see Table 15.1).

Table 15.1 Administrator of Special Education Leadership Domains	
Leadership and Administration for Special Education Domains	**Knowledge and Skills Related to Leadership and Administration for Special Education**
Mission, vision, core values, and direction setting	• Engage transformational leadership principles • Apply foundations of leadership • Set strategic goals to support effective leadership • Develop an annual plan • Seek representation of key stakeholders
Organizational leadership and management	• Develop multiple strategies and approaches to leadership • Create an awareness of the effects of gender, race, culture, age, disability, and socioeconomic status on leadership • Execute policies and procedures • Build capacity • Effect systems change • Coordinate related services • Design comprehensive and effective systems
Program oversight and improvement and instructional leadership	• Identify indicators • Provide oversight • Develop improvement plans • Employ multiple forms of evaluation • Oversee student assessment and evaluation and personnel professional development • Implement curriculum frameworks • Design multitiered systems of support • Implement instructional improvement and services • Provide educational adaptations and modifications • Collect and review student learning data • Review student transition plans • Provide student access and opportunities to technology

(Continued)

Table 15.1 (Continued)	
Leadership and Administration for Special Education Domains	**Knowledge and Skills Related to Leadership and Administration for Special Education**
Human and resource management	• Create and oversee budgets • Manage data processes • Participate in facilities management • Oversee personnel recruitment and selection • Supervise and evaluate personnel performance • Implement professional development programs • Engage in research and inquiry • Build staffing models • Recruit and retain racially, ethnically, linguistically, socioeconomically, and gendered diverse personnel
Collaboration and communication	• Engage collaborative and distributed leadership principles • Build relationships that involve families and community partners • Develop interagency relationships and agreements • Provide multiple dispute resolution options • Engage conflict resolution strategies
Policy implementation and legal and ethical practice	• Encourage advocacy • Create compassionate, caring, respectful, humane policies and culture • Comply with organizational governance and bylaws • Apply federal and state legislation and regulations • Implement dispute resolution using mediation and due process
Equity and cultural responsiveness	• Examine data for over- and underrepresentation, racial, ethnic, linguistic, socioeconomic status, and gender diversity, and philosophical and political diversity • Fairly and equitably respond to all needs • Engage in unbiased practices

Some of the domains directly apply to preservice and newly inducted leaders of special education, while other domains apply to the effects leaders of special education accomplish through systems change. The domains are clearly interdependent versus independent. Independent domains suggest compartmentalized leadership where interdependency is integrative. How leaders apply the discrete behaviors and functions within and across domains depends as much on their cultural backgrounds and affinities for particular approaches to leadership as on their formal preparation. For example, organizational leadership and management focuses on leaders' self-awareness of their own affinity for particular leadership behaviors in relation to their own cultural backgrounds. Research has shown that age (Vecchio & Boatwright, 2002), gender (Johnson, Busch, & Slate, 2008; Kawatra & Krishnan, 2004; Slater, 2004; Weir, 2017), and cultural and ethnic backgrounds (Ayman & Korabik, 2010) influence approaches to leadership. Types and longevity of work experience also play a role (Goldring & Taie, 2014; Papa & Baxter, 2005; Tekleselassie & Villarreal, 2011). Improved self-awareness may help leaders rethink special education leadership approaches and strategies.

There is evidence that many leaders are not born; rather, most leaders who grow in expertise with experience become transformational leaders (Darling-Hammond et al., 2007; Hersey, Blanchard, & Johnson, 2012). Transformational leaders understand the importance of forming relationships and using inspiration to move an organization forward rather than focusing on goals alone (Hallinger, 2003; Leithwood, 2004; Leithwood & Jantzi, 2000; Tudryn et al., 2016). The following represent domains that advance the organization of special education: (a) mission, vision, core values, and direction setting; (b) policy implementation and legal and ethical practice; and (c) equity and cultural responsiveness. These domains represent the overall ethos supporting the early foundational tenets of special education: a free appropriate public education and an individualized special education program. In addition to engaging transformational leadership to move the organization forward, distributed leadership broadens the umbrella of expertise by using the range of knowledge and skills others bring to the table within the organization (Elmore, 2000; Gronn, 2008; Hulpia, Devos, & Van Keer, 2011; Lee & Hallinger, 2012; Mosley et al., 2014; Sheppard, Hurley, & Dibbon, 2010; Spillane, Halverson, & Diamond, 2004; Spillane & Harris, 2008; Tudryn et al., 2016).

Accomplishing goals and objectives and related instructional leadership, human and resource management, collaboration and communication, and program oversight and improvement relies on transactional leadership practices (Barnett & McCormick, 2004; Heck & Marcoulides, 1993; Leithwood & Jantzi, 2000; Mosley et al., 2014; Sadler, 2003). As leadership becomes more closely tied to evidence-based instructional practices and student outcomes, Pont, Nusche, and Moorman (2008) suggest that it is almost impossible for leaders to redirect attention away from transactional metrics, such as test scores, to other equally important areas requiring other forms of leadership as long as leadership duties and responsibilities are nested in measures of accountability. Instructional and collaborative leadership share a codependency with transactional leadership. Instructional leaders seek to change the outcomes for students by altering pedagogy and instructional techniques in schools (Ashton & Duncan, 2012; Hallinger, 2003, 2005; Leithwood, 2001; Tudryn et al., 2016). Collaborative leadership relies on (a) common goals (Friend & Cook, 2010; Welch & Sheridan, 1995), (b) joint work (Gray, 1995; Little, 1990; Welch & Sheridan, 1995), (c) parity (Cole & Knowles, 1993; Friend & Cook, 2010; Welch & Sheridan, 1995), and (d) voluntary participation (Friend & Cook, 2010; Slater, 2004) to improve instruction and learning.

There is no place for passive, noninvolved laissez-faire leadership (Heck & Marcoulides, 1993; Lewin, Lippitt, & White, 1939; Mosley et al., 2014; Webb, 2007) if the intent is to continue to transform special education programs and services. Through preparation, leaders of special education come to understand the opportunities to engage strategic leadership and reculture organizations. Preparation programs set the foundation for continued growth through developing lifelong learners over the course of a leadership career, increasing range and repertoire (Hersey et al., 2012). Research has shown that leadership knowledge and skill development is a dynamic continuous process that follows a developmental continuum and is not limited to a specific role/position (Garand, 2014; Mosley et al., 2014;

Tudryn et al., 2016). The complex work of special education demands multifaceted leaders who are able to combine standards, the advanced specialty set, and dimensions of special education leadership with approaches and strategies for transforming organizations (Coleman, 2011; Pepper, 2010).

Delivery Options

Nationally accredited university preparation programs in special education administration and policy have demonstrated they are grounded in evidence-based practices and offer research to practice experiences. History shows that special education leadership preparation was present in institutions of higher education before and after the passage of the Education for All Handicapped Children Act in 1975, directed by leaders that included Robert Henderson at the University of Illinois, Philip R. Jones at Virginia Tech, Daniel Sage at Syracuse University, and Leo Connor at Teachers College–Columbia University. During the academic year 1965–1966, federal grants funded postgraduate training in special education administration at four universities; by 1971, more than 20 university programs were funded (Jones & Wilkerson, 1975). Additional impetus for innovation was provided in 1970, when another special education administrator, Edwin W. Martin, director of the U.S. Office of Education's Bureau of Education for the Handicapped, awarded a planning grant to the University Council for Educational Administration to promote the integration of leadership preparation through the General–Special Education Administration Consortium (Pazey & Yates, 2019).

As noted earlier, Bellamy and Iwaszuk (2017) have argued that the pipeline for supplying administrators of special education has been rendered ineffective. It is not that existing university programs are ineffective but that university programs have not been able to maintain the legacies established by their founders due to retirements or resignations, followed by reallocation of resources to other units and the changing needs of those seeking credentialing. Changes in higher education have disrupted messaging connecting strong leaders of special education with higher special education teacher retention rates. Marketplace forces, such as the offering of alternate routes to credentialing by state departments of education and professional organizations, have also dictated changes to how leaders are prepared. Future administrators of special education are typically older, have families, are employed, and are no longer willing to travel beyond their home radius to institutions of higher education as they might have in the past to seek credentialing. Further driving future leaders to seek programs that better meet their needs is the dissolution of tuition reimbursement programs offered by school districts and agencies to their employees serving students with disabilities.

As a result, these colliding forces have caused a rethinking of special education leadership preparation delivery options. Some institutions of higher education have retained course offerings, while others have moved away from offering on-campus programming, shifting to off-site face-to-face programs, online asynchronous programs, and hybrid programs that combine face-to-face or synchronous programming with online learning and are aligned with modules or tasks.

The University of Wisconsin–Madison developed a cooperative all-course-plus-practicum course of study with the University of Wisconsin–Whitewater to make the program more accessible to aspiring leaders in the central regions of Wisconsin. All required coursework, with the exception of the Director of Special Education and Pupil Services certification, is offered on the Whitewater campus. The Director of Special Education and Pupil Services certification requires completion of two classes in Madison not offered on the Whitewater campus. As an example of a program that has moved away from an all-coursework model, Washington State has developed a 2-year cohort model that commences with a 3-day institute and then combines field-based internships with weekend face-to-face sessions and online support for performance tasks that are used in the place of courses (Bellamy & Iwaszuk, 2017).

The definition for state-approved programs has expanded beyond programs sponsored by higher education institutions to professional associations, LEAs, intermediate education agencies (IEAs), and other organizations. State-approved programs are designed to meet the requirements for a specific administrator credential. Candidates seeking preparation through LEAs, IEAs, or other organizations most often are responsible for finding a school district and administrator within the state where the credential is being sought who holds a valid professional credential in the same role and level, has been rated as proficient in his or her most recent summative evaluation, has been trained as a mentor, and is willing to supervise the candidate. The organization must also provide appropriate seminars or workshops to assist the candidate in adequately addressing professional standards.

The panel review as a route to licensure with state departments of education offers candidates the opportunity to use a combination of their education (formal schooling and coursework) and their professional experience as a means to demonstrate that they hold the qualifications necessary for credentialing as an ASE. Most panel review routes are only available for administrator credentialing candidates who have the specific prerequisite experiences. The process can include (1) compilation of requisite materials by the candidate and (2) an interview with a panel of experienced administrators and educators.

As a cautionary tale, not all alternate preparation routes offer depth and breadth of preparation; nor are they all nationally recognized. Rather, these routes often represent fast tracks to credentialing. The one constant for those preparing to be leaders of special education administration may be demonstrating that professional standards have been minimally met. Exemplary models of special education leadership development continue to guide professional development and encourage lifelong learning.

Conclusion

In this chapter, we took a comprehensive approach to examining factors that contribute to the preparation of administrators of special education. Some options are rigorous and high-quality, while others are not. The intent of this chapter was not to pass judgment but simply to provide a framework for those interested in creating first-rate preparation and professional development opportunities for preservice and in-service leaders of special education. When reflecting on this comprehensive review, it seems prudent to be circumspect about the state of preparation of special education leaders and administrators. Is the field of special education administration on the cusp of a cataclysmic shift as federal policy continues to swing toward a preference for entrepreneurial educational enterprises? Will recent federal policy shifts diminish the role core standards have served as the basis for professional identities and as the foundation for special education leadership programs? There will always be one constant when providing special education services and programs: There will continue to be students with disabilities in our schools who deserve effective special education leadership, and offering anything less than exemplary preparation and continued professional development to our future leaders overseeing special education programs and services is not an option.

REFLECTING AND UNDERSTANDING

1. Why is there a need for strong leaders and administrators of special education? Who benefits from well-prepared leaders of special education?

2. How do special education leadership roles and responsibilities affect the provision of special education programs and services at the local, state, and federal levels?

3. How do professional standards anchor professional identities and guide special education leadership preparation and professional development?

4. Identify key components related to preparing leaders of special education to meet the vision, mission, and goals of special education.

5. If you were to develop an integrated model for preparing leaders of special education, how would you interface key components?

ONLINE RESOURCES

- Advanced specialty set for administrators of special education: https://www.cec.sped.org/Standards/Special-Educator-Professional-Preparation-Standards/CEC-Initial-and-Advanced-Specialty-Sets

- National Policy Board for Educational Administration: http://npbea.org/

RECOMMENDED READINGS

Books

Boscardin, M. L. (2011). Using professional standards to inform leadership in special education. In J. M. Kauffman & D. P. Hallahan (Eds.), *Handbook of special education* (pp. 378–390). New York, NY: Taylor & Francis.

Boscardin, M. L. (2017). Transforming leadership in special education: Converging policies, professional standards, and scholarship (pp. 489–500). In J. M. Kauffman, D. P. Hallahan, & P. C. Pullen (Eds.), *Handbook of special education* (2nd ed.). New York, NY: Taylor & Francis.

Boscardin, M. L., & Lashley, C. L. (2019). Expanding the leadership framework: An alternate view of professional standards through a social justice lens. In J. Crockett, B. Billingsley, & M. L. Boscardin (Eds.), *The handbook of leadership and administration for special education* (2nd ed., pp. 39–59). New York, NY: Routledge.

Council for Exceptional Children. (2015). *What every special educator must know: Professional ethics and standards* (7th ed.). Arlington, VA: Author.

Crockett, J. B. (2011). Conceptual models for leading and administrating special education. In J. M. Kauffman & D. P. Hallahan (Eds.), *Handbook of special education* (pp. 351–362). New York, NY: Taylor & Francis.

Crockett, J., Billingsley, B., & Boscardin, M. L. (Eds.). (2019). *The handbook of leadership and administration for special education* (2nd ed.). New York, NY: Routledge.

Articles

Billingsley, B. S., McLeskey, J., & Crockett, J. B. (2014). *Principal leadership: Moving towards inclusive and high-achieving schools for students with disabilities.* Retrieved from http://www.smcoe.org/assets/files/about-smcoe/superintendents-office/statewide-special-education-task-force/Principal-Leadership-Moving-Toward-Inclusive-and-High-Achieving-Schools-for-Students-With-Disabilities%20copy.pdf

Boscardin, M. L. (2004). Transforming administration to support science in the schoolhouse for students with disabilities. *Journal of Learning Disabilities, 37,* 262–269.

Boscardin, M. L. (2007). What is special about special education administration? Considerations for school leadership. *Exceptionality, 15,* 189–200.

Boscardin, M. L., Schulze, R., Tudryn, P., & Rude, H. (2018). Do leaders of special education share similar perceptions of standards guiding the leadership and administration of special education? *Journal of Special Education Leadership, 31,* 61–85.

Boscardin, M. L., Weir, K., & Kusek, C. (2010). A national study of credentialing requirements for administrators of special education. *Journal of Special Education Leadership, 23,* 61–75.

Hitt, D. H., & Tucker, P. D. (2016). Systematic review of key leader practices found to influence student achievement: A unified framework. *Review of Educational Research, 86,* 531–569.

Lashley, C. L., & Boscardin, M. L. (2003). Special education administration at a crossroads. *Journal of Special Education Leadership, 16,* 63–75.

Schulze, R., & Boscardin, M. L. (2018). Leadership perceptions of principals with and without special education backgrounds. *Journal of School Leadership, 28,* 4–30.

Tudryn, P., Boscardin, M. L., & Wells, C. W. (2016). Distributed leadership through the lens of special education leaders. *Journal of Special Education Leadership, 29,* 3–22.

Briefs, Practice Guides, and Reports

Bellamy, G. T., Crockett, J. B., & Nordengren, C. (2014). *Preparing school leaders for every student's learning* (Document No. LS-2). Retrieved from http://www.smcoe.org/assets/files/about-smcoe/superintendents-office/statewide-special-education-task-force/Preparing-School-Leaders-for-Every-Student-s-Learning%20copy.pdf

Bellamy, G. T., & Iwaszuk, W. (2017). *Responding to the need for new local special education administrators: A case study.* Unpublished manuscript. Bothel: University of Washington.

Louis, K., Leithwood, K., Wahlstrom, K., & Anderson, S. (2016). *Investigating the links to improved student learning: Final report of research findings.* Minneapolis: University of Minnesota.

PROFESSIONAL ORGANIZATIONS

Council for Administrators of Special Education: http://www.casecec.org

Council for Exceptional Children: https://www.cec.sped.org/

Higher Education Council for Special Education: http://hecse.net/

National Policy Board for Educational Administration: http://npbea.org/

University Council for Educational Administration: http://www.ucea.org/

REFERENCES

Arick, J. R., & Krug, D. A. (1993). Special education administrators in the United States: Perceptions on policy and personnel issues. *Journal of Special Education, 27*(3), 348–364.

Ashton, B., & Duncan, H. (2012). A beginning rural principal's toolkit: A guide for success. *Rural Educator, 34,* 19–31.

Avery, D., Tonidaniel, S., Griffith, K., & Quinones, M. (2003). The impact of multiple measures of leader experience on leader effectiveness. *Journal of Business Research, 56,* 673–679.

Ayman, R., & Korabik, K. (2010). Leadership: Why gender and culture matter. *American Psychologist, 65,* 157–170. doi:10.1037/a0018806

Barbuto, J. E., Jr., Fritz, S., Matkin, G. S., & Marx, D. B. (2007). *Effects of gender, education, and age upon leaders' use of influence tactics and full range leadership behaviors* (Faculty Publications: Agricultural Leadership, Education & Communication Department, Paper 40). Retrieved from http://digitalcommons.unl.edu/aglecfacpub/40

Barnett, K., & McCormick, J. (2004). Leadership and individual: Principal–teacher relationships in schools. *Educational Administration Quarterly, 40*, 406–434.

Bellamy, G. T., & Iwaszuk, W. (2017). *Responding to the need for new local special education administrators: A case study.* Unpublished manuscript. Bothel: University of Washington.

Billingsley, B. S. (2007). Recognizing and supporting the critical roles of teachers in special education leadership. *Exceptionality, 15*(3), 163–176.

Billingsley, B. S., McLeskey, J., & Crockett, J. B. (2014). *Principal leadership: Moving towards inclusive and high-achieving schools for students with disabilities.* Retrieved from http://www.smcoe.org/assets/files/about-smcoe/superintendents -office/statewide-special-education-task-force/Principal-Leadership-Moving-Toward-Inclusive-and-High-Achieving -Schools-for-Students-With-Disabilities%20copy.pdf

Boscardin, M. L. (2004). Transforming administration to support science in the schoolhouse for students with disabilities. *Journal of Learning Disabilities, 37*, 262–269.

Boscardin, M. L. (2007). What is special about special education administration? Considerations for school leadership. *Exceptionality, 15*, 189–200.

Boscardin, M. L. (2011). Using professional standards to inform leadership in special education. In J. M. Kauffman & D. P. Hallahan (Eds.), *Handbook of special education* (pp. 378–390). New York, NY: Taylor & Francis.

Boscardin, M. L. (2016). Transforming educational leadership to support personalized learning. *Australian Educational Leader, 38*(1), 8–16.

Boscardin, M. L. (2017). Transforming leadership in special education: Converging policies, professional standards, and scholarship (pp. 489–500). In J. M. Kauffman, D. P. Hallahan, & P. C. Pullen (Eds.), *Handbook of special education* (2nd ed.). New York, NY: Taylor & Francis.

Boscardin, M. L., & Lashley, C. L. (2019). Expanding the leadership framework: An alternate view of professional standards through a social justice lens. In J. Crockett, B. Billingsley, & M. L. Boscardin (Eds.), *The handbook of leadership & administration for special education* (2nd ed., pp. 39–59). New York, NY: Routledge.

Boscardin, M. L., McCarthy, E., & Delgado, R. (2009). An integrated research-based approach to creating standards for special education leadership. *Journal of Special Education Leadership, 22*, 68–84.

Boscardin, M. L., & Messing, D. (2016, August). *Pathways to leadership for administrators of special education.* Presented at the U.S. Department of Education, Office of Special Education Programs, Project Director's Conference, Washington, D.C.

Boscardin, M. L., Weir, K., & Kusek, C. (2010). A national study of state credentialing requirements for administrators of special education. *Journal of Special Education Leadership, 23*, 61–75.

Brabandt, E. W., Jr., (1969). *A comparative analysis of actual professional training, state credential requirements, and professional training requirements recommended by the Council for Exceptional Children for administrators of special education* (Doctoral dissertation, Colorado State College). Ann Arbor: University Microfilms, 1969, No. 69-15.

Cole, A. L., & Knowles, J. G. (1993). Teacher development partnership research: A focus on methods and issues. *American Educational Research Journal, 30*, 473–495.

Coleman, A. (2011). Towards a blended model of leadership for school-based collaborations. *Educational Management Administration and Leadership, 39*, 296–316.

Council for Exceptional Children. (2015). *What every special educator must know: Professional ethics and standards* (7th ed.). Arlington, VA: Author.

Council of Chief State School Officers. (2017). *PSEL 2015 and promoting principal leadership for the success of students with disabilities.* Retrieved from https://www.ccsso.org/sites/default/files/2017-10/PSELforSWDs01252017_0.pdf

Cox, B. (2006). What personality inventories and leadership assessments say about aspiring principals. *ERS Spectrum, 24*, 13–20.

Crockett, J. B. (2011). Conceptual models for leading and administrating special education. In J. M. Kauffman & D. P. Hallahan (Eds.), *Handbook of special education* (pp. 351–362). New York, NY: Taylor & Francis.

Crockett, J. B. (2012). Developing educational leaders for the realities of special education in the 21st century. In J. B. Crockett, B. S. Billingsley, & M. L. Boscardin (Eds.), *Handbook of leadership and administration for special education* (pp. 52–66). New York, NY: Taylor & Francis.

Crockett, J. B. (2017). Conceptual models for leading and administrating special education. In J. M. Kauffman & D. P. Hallahan (Eds.), *Handbook of special education* (2nd ed., pp. 461–473). New York, NY: Routledge.

Crockett, J. B., Becker, M. K., & Quinn, D. (2009). Reviewing the knowledge base of special education leadership and administration. *Journal of Special Education Leadership, 22*, 55–67.

Darling-Hammond, L., LaPointe, M., Meyerson, D., Orr, M. T., & Cohen, C. (2007). *Preparing school leaders for a changing world: Lessons from exemplary leadership development programs.* Stanford, CA: Stanford University, Stanford Educational Leadership Institute.

Darling-Hammond, L., & McLaughlin, M. W. (1995). Policies that support professional development in an era of reform. *Phi Delta Kappan, 76*(8), 597–604.

DiPaola, M. F., & Walther-Thomas, C. (2003). *Principals and special education: The critical role of school leaders* (COPSSE Document No. IB-7). Gainesville: University of Florida, Center on Personnel Studies in Special Education.

Education for All Handicapped Children Act, 20 U.S.C. §1400 *et seq.* (1975).

Elmore, R. F. (2000). *Building a new structure for school leadership.* Washington, DC: Albert Shanker Institute.

Every Student Succeeds Act. 20 U.S.C. 6301 *et seq.* (2015).

Finkbinder, R. L. (1981). Special education administration and supervision: The state of the art. *Journal of Special Education, 15*, 485–495.

Forgnone, C., & Collings, G. D. (1975). State certification endorsement in special education administration. *Journal of Special Education, 9*, 5–9.

Friend, M., & Cook, L. (2010). *Interactions: Collaboration skills for school professionals* (6th ed.). Columbus, OH: Merrill.

Garand, A. C. (2014). *Perceptions of leadership through the lens of special education administrators and principals.* Unpublished doctoral dissertation, University of Massachusetts at Amherst.

Garand, A., Boscardin, M. L., & Wells, C. W. (in preparation). *Perceptions of leadership through the lens of special education administrators and principals.*

Goldring, R., & Taie, S. (2014). Principal attrition and mobility: Results from the 2012–13 principal follow-up survey. *First Look* (NCES 2014-064). Washington, DC: National Center for Education Statistics.

Gray, B. (1995). Obstacles to success in educational collaboration. In L. C. Rigsby, M. C. Reynolds, & M. C. Wang (Eds.), *School-community connections exploring issues/or research and practice* (pp. 71–100). San Francisco, CA: Jossey-Bass.

Gronn, P. (2008). The future of distributed leadership. *Journal of Educational Administration, 26*(2), 141–158.

Hallinger, P. (2003). Leading educational change: Reflections on the practice of instructional and transformational leadership. *Cambridge Journal of Education, 33*, 329–351.

Hallinger, P. (2005). Instructional leadership and the school principal: A passing fancy that refuses to fade away. *Leadership and Policy in Schools, 4*, 1–20.

Heck, R. H., & Marcoulides, G. A. (1993). Principal leadership behaviors and school achievement. *NASSP Bulletin, 77*, 20–28.

Hersey, P., Blanchard, K. H., & Johnson, D. E. (2012). *Management of organizational behavior: Utilizing human resources* (10th ed.). Englewood Cliffs, NJ: Prentice Hall.

Hitt, D. H., & Tucker, P. D. (2016). Systematic review of key leader practices found to influence student achievement: A unified framework. *Review of Educational Research, 86,* 531–569.

Hulpia, H., Devos, G., & Van Keer, H. (2011). The relation between school leadership from a distributed perspective and teachers' organizational commitment: Examining the source of the leadership function. *Educational Administration Quarterly, 47*(5), 728–771.

Individuals with Disabilities Education Act, 20 U.S.C. §1400 *et seq.* (1997).

Individuals with Disabilities Education Act, 20 U.S.C. § 1400 *et seq.* (2004).

Johnson, S., Busch, S., & Slate, J. R. (2008). *Leadership behaviors of school administrators: Do men and women differ.* Paper presented at the National Council of Professional Administration.

Jones, P. R., & Wilkerson, W. R. (1975). Preparing special education administrators. *Theory Into Practice, 14,* 105–109.

Kawatra, S., & Krishnan, V. R. (2004). Impact of gender and transformational leadership on organizational culture. *NMIMS Management Review, 16,* 1–6.

Kern, W. H., & Mayer, J. F. (1970). Certification of directors of special education programs: The results of a national survey. *Contemporary Education, 42,* 126–128.

Lee, M. S., & Hallinger, P. (2012). Exploring the impact of national context on principals' time use: Economic development, societal culture, and educational system. *School Effectiveness and School Improvement, 23*(4), 461–482.

Leithwood, K. (2001). School leadership in the context of accountability policies. *International Journal of Leadership in Education, 4,* 217–235.

Leithwood, K. (2004). *Educational leadership: A review of the research.* Philadelphia, PA: Laboratory for Student Success, Mid-Atlantic Regional Educational Laboratory, U.S. Department of Education.

Leithwood, K., & Jantzi, D. (2000). The effects of transformational leadership on organizational conditions and student engagement with school. *Journal of Educational Administration, 38,* 12–129.

Leithwood, K., Louis, K. S., Anderson, S., & Wahlstrom, K. (2004). *How leadership influences student learning* (executive summary). University of Minnesota and University of Toronto, commissioned by the Wallace Foundation (downloadable at http://www.wallacefoundation.org).

Lewin, K., Lippitt, R., & White, R. (1939). Patterns of aggressive behavior in experimentally created "social climates." *Journal of School Psychology, 10,* 271–299.

Little, J. W. (1990). Teachers as colleagues. In A. Lieberman (Ed.), *Schools as collaborative cultures* (pp. 165–193). New York, NY: Falmer Press.

Marro, T. D., & Kohl, J. S. (1972). Normative study of the administrative position in special education. *Exceptional Children, 39*(1), 5–14.

Milazzo, T. C., & Blessing, K. R. (1964). The training of directors and supervisors of special education programs. *Exceptional Children, 31,* 129–141.

Mosley, J. I., Boscardin, M. L., & Wells, C. W. (2014). Perceptions of principal leadership behaviors in an era of accountability. *Journal of School Leadership, 24,* 1038–1072.

Mumford, M., Marks, M., Connelly, M., Zaccaro, S., & Reiter-Palmon, R. (2000). Development of leadership skills: Experience and timing. *Leadership Quarterly, 11,* 87–114.

Murphy, J. (Ed.). (2002). *The educational leadership challenge: Redefining leadership for the 21st century.* Chicago, IL: University of Chicago Press.

National Boards for Professional Teaching Standards. (2016). *What teachers should know and be able to do.* Arlington, VA: Author.

National Policy Board for Educational Administration. (2018). *National educational leadership preparation (NELP) standards.* Reston, VA: Author. Retrieved from http://www.npbea.org

O'Brien, P. (2006). *"They know who I am": Leadership capabilities in special education.* New South Wales, Australia: Premiers Special Education Scholarship sponsored by the Anika Foundation.

Papa, F. J., & Baxter, I. A. (2005). Dispelling the myths and confirming the truths of the imminent shortage of principals: The case of New York State. *Planning and Changing, 36*(3–4), 217–234.

Pazey, B. L., & Yates, J. R. (2019). Conceptual and historical foundations of special education administration. In J. Crockett, B. Billingsley, & M. L. Boscardin (Eds.), *Handbook of leadership in special education* (2nd ed., pp. 18–38). London, UK: Routledge.

Pepper, K. (2010). Effective principals skillfully balance leadership styles to facilitate student success: A focus for the reauthorization of ESEA. *Changing and Planning, 41,* 42–56.

Pont, B., Nusche, D., & Moorman, H. (2008). Improving school leadership. *Volume 1: Policy and practice.* Retrieved March 13, 2016, from http://dx.doi.org/10.1787/9789264044715-en

Prillaman, D., & Richardson, R. (1985). State certification-endorsement requirements for special education administrators. *Journal of Special Education, 19*(2), 231–236.

Provost. J., Boscardin, M. L., & Wells, C. W. (2010). Perceptions of principal leadership behaviors in Massachusetts in the era of education reform. *Journal of School Leadership, 20,* 532–560.

Rude, H., & Sasso, G. (1988). Colorado special education administrative competencies. *Teacher Education and Special Education, 11,* 139–143.

Sadler, P. (2003). *Leadership.* London, UK: Kogan Page.

Schulze, R., & Boscardin, M. L. (2018). Leadership perceptions of principals with and without special education backgrounds. *Journal of School Leadership, 28,* 4–30.

Sheppard, B., Hurley, D., & Dibbon, D. (2010). *Distributed leadership, teacher morale, and teacher enthusiasm: Unraveling the leadership pathways to school success.* Paper presented at the American Educational Research Association.

Slater, L. (2004). Collaboration: A framework for school improvement. *International Electronic Journal for Leadership in Learning, 8,* 1206–9620.

Spillane, J., Halverson, R., & Diamond, J. (2004). Towards a theory of leadership practice: A distributed perspective. *Journal of Curriculum Studies, 36*(1), 3–34.

Spillane, J. P., & Harris, A. (2008). Distributed leadership through the looking glass. *British Educational Leadership, Management & Administration Society, 22,* 31–34.

Stile, S., Abernathy, S., & Pettibone. T. (1985). Training and certification of special education administrators: A 5-year follow-up study. *Exceptional Children, 53,* 209–212.

Stile, S. W., & Pettibone, T. J. (1980). Training and certification of administrators in special education. *Exceptional Children, 46*(7), 530–533.

Tekleselassie, A. A., & Villarreal, P. I. (2011). Career mobility and departure intentions among school principals in the United States: Incentives and disincentives. *Leadership and Policy in Schools, 10,* 251–293.

Tudryn, P., Boscardin, M. L., & Wells, C. W. (2016). Distributed leadership through the lens of special education leaders. *Journal of Special Education Leadership, 29,* 3–22.

U.S. Department of Education. (2006). *Twenty-sixth annual report to Congress on the implementation of Individuals with Disabilities Education Act.* Washington, DC: U.S. Government Printing Office.

Valesky, T. C., & Hirth, M. A. (1992). Survey of the states: Special education knowledge requirements for school administrators. *Exceptional Children, 58*(5), 399–406.

Vecchio, R., & Boatwright, K. (2002). Preferences for idealized styles of supervision. *Leadership Quarterly, 13,* 327–342.

Wakeman, S., Browder, D., Flowers, C., & Ahlgrim-Delzell, L. (2006). Principals' knowledge of fundamental and current issues in special education. *NASSP Bulletin, 90,* 153–174.

Webb, K. (2007). Motivating peak performance: Leadership behaviors that stimulate employee motivation and performance. *Christian Higher Education, 6,* 53–71.

Weir, K. E. (2017). *The leadership experiences of female special education administrators.* Unpublished doctoral dissertation, University of Massachusetts, Amherst.

Welch, M., & Sheridan, S. (1995). *Educational partnership: Serving students at risk.* Fort Worth, TX: Harcourt Brace.

Whitworth, J. E., & Hatley, R. V. (1979). Certification and special education leadership personnel: An analysis of state standards. *Journal of Special Education, 13,* 297–305.

York-Barr, J., & Duke, K. (2004). What do we know about teacher leadership? Findings from two decades of scholarship. *Review of Educational Research, 74,* 255–316.

Index

Figures and tables are indicated by f or t following the page number.

LRE (least restrictive environment), 11–12, 16, 193, 226–227
Lucio, Eddie, Jr., 98
Luckasson, R., 157

Macrosystems, 156
MacSuga-Gage, A. S., 113
Manifestation determination review (MDR), 95–96, 210
Martin, C., 128
Massachusetts, 242
Maternal and Child Health Bureau, 177
Math instruction, 114
Maupin, A. N., 142
Mazzotti, V. L., 113
McKenna, J. W., 113–114
McKown, L., 114
McLaughlin, M. W., 250
MDR (manifestation determination review), 95–96, 210
Memorandum of understanding (MOU), 214–215
Mental Health in Schools Act (proposed), 210
Mental health needs. *See* School mental health (SMH) services
Mental Health Services in Schools initiative, 177
Mentoring, 230–231
Mesosystems, 156
Meta-analyses, 118
Methodological disputes, 9–11
Microsystems, 156
Milazzo, T. C., 247
MOU (memorandum of understanding), 214–215
Multitiered systems of support (MTSS)
  Ci3T model and, 27
  differentiated instruction and, 196–200
  discipline and, 101
  family-school partnerships and, 59–61, 60f
  inclusion and, 84
  mental health needs and, 179
  See also Positive Behavioral Interventions and Supports (PBIS)

Narrative literature reviews, 118
National Academies of Sciences, Engineering, and Medicine (NASEM), 160
National Autism Center, 118
National Community of Practice (CoP) on Collaborative School Behavioral Health, 177–178
National Disability Rights Network, 98
National Educational Leadership Preparation (NELP) Board, 246
National Policy Board for Education Administration (NPBEA), 245, 246
National Professional Development Center, 118
National Technical Assistance Center on Positive Behavioral Interventions and Supports, 212
National Technical Assistance Center on Transition (NTACT), 74–75, 84, 118

No Child Left Behind (NCLB), 128, 192, 194, 227
Northwest Colorado Board of Cooperative Educational Services (2014), 81

Observations, 234
Odom, S. L., 140
Office for Civil Rights (OCR), 5
Office of Special Education and Rehabilitative Services (OSERS), 3, 5
Office of Special Education Programs (OSEP), 5, 80, 130, 242
Outcome differentiation, 198

Parent training, 58–59
Parent Training and Information Centers (PTIs), 58–59
Parental involvement
  free appropriate public education and, 39, 48
  language differences and early childhood, 145
  mental health treatment seeking and, 176
  overview, 53–54
  teachers lacking skills about, 56–57, 63t
  training for parents and, 58–59
  transition planning and services, 83
  See also Family-school partnerships
Park, K. L., 112
PATHS (Promoting Alternative Thinking Strategies), 143t, 178
PBIS. *See* Positive Behavioral Interventions and Supports (PBIS)
PDS (professional development schools), 231–232
Pedagogy, 229
Peer-reviewed research, 10–11
Pennington, R. C., 114
Pennsylvania, 193
Performance deficits, 104
Performance feedback, 234
Person-family interdependent planning, 61
Physical abuse, 98–99
PIC (prison-industrial complex), 211
P.L. 94-142. *See* Individuals with Disabilities Education Act (IDEA)
Placement issues, 11–12, 94–95, 210
PLCs (professional learning communities), 250
Plotner, A. J., 113
Police in schools, 206–207, 208, 210–211, 214–215
Positive Behavioral Interventions and Supports (PBIS)
  ADHD and, 5
  bullying and, 160–167, 165–166t
  discipline and, 101–104, 102–103t
  in IEPs, 6–7
  mental health needs and, 179–180
  school-to-prison pipeline and, 212
Positive Parenting Program (Triple P), 144t
Poverty, 144, 145
Power differentials, 55–56, 63t, 147
Practice Guides, 118
Practice-based evidence, 119

A SAGE Publishing Company

CORWIN HAS ONE MISSION: to enhance education through intentional professional learning. We build long-term relationships with our authors, educators, clients, and associations who partner with us to develop and continuously improve the best evidence-based practices that establish and support lifelong learning.

Solutions YOU WANT | Experts YOU TRUST | Results YOU NEED

 EVENTS

>>> **INSTITUTES**

Corwin Institutes provide large regional events where educators collaborate with peers and learn from industry experts. Prepare to be recharged and motivated!

corwin.com/institutes

 ON-SITE PD

>>> **ON-SITE PROFESSIONAL LEARNING**

Corwin on-site PD is delivered through high-energy keynotes, practical workshops, and custom coaching services designed to support knowledge development and implementation.

corwin.com/pd

>>> **PROFESSIONAL DEVELOPMENT RESOURCE CENTER**

The PD Resource Center provides school and district PD facilitators with the tools and resources needed to deliver effective PD.

corwin.com/pdrc

 ONLINE

>>> **ADVANCE**

Designed for K–12 teachers, Advance offers a range of online learning options that can qualify for graduate-level credit and apply toward license renewal.

corwin.com/advance

Contact a PD Advisor at (800) 831-6640 or
visit www.corwin.com for more information